Russian
FOR
DUMMIES®
2ND EDITION

by Andrew Kaufman, PhD, and Serafima Gettys, PhD

WILEY

John Wiley & Sons, Inc.

Russian For Dummies®, 2nd Edition

Published by
John Wiley & Sons, Inc.
111 River St.
Hoboken, NJ 07030-5774
www.wiley.com

WILEY

About the Authors

Andrew Kaufman, PhD, is a Russian literature and culture scholar who has spent the last 15 years bringing alive the Russian classics to Americans young and old. An innovative, award-winning teacher of Russian language, literature, and culture, Dr. Kaufman holds a PhD in Slavic Languages and Literatures from Stanford University and currently lectures at the University of Virginia.

Author of *Understanding Tolstoy,* Dr. Kaufman has discussed Russian literature and culture on national and international TV and radio programs. Known as a passionate, down-to-earth, and inspirational speaker and workshop facilitator, he was a featured Tolstoy expert for Oprah's Book Club in 2004 and cowrote the Reader's Guide to Tolstoy's *The Death of Ivan Ilyich* for the National Endowment for the Arts' "Big Read" program. He is currently at work on *Give* War and Peace *a Chance*, to be published by Free Press.

Fluent in Russian, Dr. Kaufman has lectured at the Gorky Institute of World Literature of the Russian Academy of Sciences and at the Leo Tolstoy Museum and Estate at Yasnaya Polyana. Having lived and studied extensively in Russia, he has also worked as an interpreter, translator, and management consultant.

Dr. Kaufman also trained and worked as a professional actor for close to a decade. He helps people appreciate the rich tradition of Russian literature and draws on his acting skills to create captivating and enlightening talks, as well as inspirational readings from the Russian classics. He is currently a Lecturer and an ACE Faculty Fellow at the University of Virginia, where he created and teaches a community-based literature course, "Books Behind Bars: Life, Literature, and Community Leadership," in which students lead discussions about Russian literature with incarcerated youth at juvenile correctional and treatment centers in Virginia.

Serafima Gettys, PhD, earned her doctorate degree in Foreign Language Education from A.I. Hertzen State Pedagogical University, Leningrad, USSR. Before coming to the U.S. in 1990, Dr. Gettys taught English, American Studies, and Methodology of Teaching Foreign Language at A.I. Hertzen University of Education. In the U.S., she taught Russian at Stanford University and the University of California at Berkeley. She is currently a Director of the Foreign Language Program at Lewis University, where she also teaches Russian. Dr. Gettys is also a member of a number of professional language associations. She is the author of more than 30 publications in the area of foreign language education.

The second edition of *Russian For Dummies* was prepared by Dr. Gettys.

Authors' Acknowledgments

Andrew Kaufman: I would like to thank my colleague, former Stanford professor, and coauthor, Serafima Gettys, one of the most original and inspired Russian language teachers I know. Her grace, infectious love of Russian, and professionalism were instrumental in making this book happen — and a joy to write.

A hearty thanks to Georgette Beatty at Wiley for her expert guidance and her encouragement throughout the writing process, and to Tracy Boggier at Wiley for her supervision and coordination, and for making this book possible. I'd also like to thank Christy Pingleton, the copy editor, and Carol Apollonio and Natalia Rekhter, the technical reviewers, for helping to make sure that every sentence in the book is both accurate and readable.

A heartfelt thanks to my agent, Margot Maley-Hutchison of Waterside Productions, for her expert representation and skillful problem resolution throughout.

Thanks to all my colleagues and students at the University of Virginia for helping to create a supportive and stimulating environment in which to share our common passion for Russian literature and culture.

I am grateful to my former professors at Stanford University and Amherst College for their mentorship and for helping me to discover the fascinating world of Russian language, literature, and culture.

Finally, and most importantly, I thank my wife, Corinne, whose love, generosity, and encouragement are the greatest gifts a writer could ever hope for.

Serafima Gettys: Many thanks to Andy Kaufman for bringing this project to my attention and for taking on the responsibility of organizing and managing the project.

Many thanks go to Stanford University for bringing Andy and me together at an earlier point in our lives, first as teacher and student, later as colleagues, and now finally as coauthors. Warm thanks also to my past and current students of Russian at various schools, both in Russia and the United States, who constantly challenge and inspire me and without whom this book would not have been written.

A loving thanks also to my family, husband Steve and daughter Anna. Their love has been an inspiration throughout.

Publisher's Acknowledgments

We're proud of this book; please send us your comments at http://dummies.custhelp.com. For other comments, please contact our Customer Care Department within the U.S. at 877-762-2974, outside the U.S. at 317-572-3993, or fax 317-572-4002.

Some of the people who helped bring this book to market include the following:

Acquisitions, Editorial, and Vertical Websites

Senior Project Editor: Georgette Beatty
(*Previous Edition: Georgette Beatty*)

Acquisitions Editor: Tracy Boggier

Copy Editor: Christine Pingleton
(*Previous Edition: Sarah Faulkner*)

Assistant Editor: David Lutton

Editorial Program Coordinator: Joe Niesen

Technical Editors: Carol Apollonio,
Natalia Rekhter

Vertical Websites: Rich Graves,
Marilyn Hummel

CD Producer: Her Voice Unlimited, LLC

Editorial Manager: Michelle Hacker

Editorial Assistant: Alexa Koschier

Art Coordinator: Alicia B. South

Cover Photo: ©iStockphoto.com/
Alexander Bryljaev

Cartoons: Rich Tennant
(www.the5thwave.com)

Composition Services

Project Coordinator: Patrick Redmond

Layout and Graphics: Claudia Bell, Carl Byers

Proofreader: Mildred Rosenzweig

Indexer: Potomac Indexing, LLC

Illustrator: Elizabeth Kurtzman

Publishing and Editorial for Consumer Dummies

 Kathleen Nebenhaus, Vice President and Executive Publisher

 Kristin Ferguson-Wagstaffe, Product Development Director

 Ensley Eikenburg, Associate Publisher, Travel

 Kelly Regan, Editorial Director, Travel

Publishing for Technology Dummies

 Andy Cummings, Vice President and Publisher

Composition Services

 Debbie Stailey, Director of Composition Services

Contents at a Glance

Table of Contents

Introduction

. . . .

Speaking more than one language is like living more than one life, one of the ancient philosophers said. And it's true — traveling in a foreign country such as Russia suddenly becomes a lot more exciting when you can engage in elegant small talk with a hotel receptionist, compliment your tour guide's dress, or actually read the menu and order the food that you really want. Being able to ask for things instead of pointing at them and getting directions from the locals instead of staring at a map are some of the little things that make you feel at home.

You don't even need to cross the ocean to immerse yourself in Russian culture; you can find little Russian neighborhoods (or even pretty big ones!) in many American cities. Whether your colleagues, your neighbors, or your friends speak Russian, the best way to win their hearts is to speak their language to them.

Now, *Russian For Dummies,* 2nd Edition, won't make you a fluent reader of the original works of Dostoevsky (most Russians themselves need some preparation for that). It will, however, equip you with phrases necessary to function in many life situations, from shopping to visiting the theater. And little gems of cultural wisdom offered throughout the book help you not only translate the language, but also understand Russians so much better. So, buckle up, and good luck on your journey! Or, as the Russians like to say, **Желаем вам удачи!** (zhi-*lah*-eem vahm ooh-*dah*-chee!) (*We wish you good luck!*)

About This Book

The best thing about *Russian For Dummies,* 2nd Edition, is that you don't have to read all the way through it to get the information you need. You can open the table of contents, find the section that interests you at the moment, and start talking! You don't have to read the previous chapters to understand any sections of this book. And if you decide that you want more information about something, a convenient system of cross-references takes you to just the right place.

Another thing you don't need to do is memorize long vocabulary lists or grammar rules. We give you ready-made phrases; you just need to read them to start using them right away to impress your Russian friends!

Conventions Used in This Book

Here are some conventions that allow you to navigate through this book with maximum ease:

- ✔ We present Russian in Russian, or what is also known as the Cyrillic alphabet. You can see the Cyrillic alphabet in Chapter 2. Russian terms are easily found in the text because they're set in **boldface**.

- ✔ Each Russian word or sentence is followed by its pronunciation shown in English letters, and its English translation, respectively, in parentheses. In each pronunciation, the stressed syllable is in *italics;* translations are also in italics.

  Here's a little example to give you an idea of what we mean: The phrase for "I love you" in Russian is **Я тебя люблю** (ya tee-*bya* lyooh-*blyooh*) (*I love you*).

- ✔ Verb conjugations (lists that show you the forms of a verb) are given in tables in this order:

      The *I* form

      The *you* (informal singular) form

      The *he/she/it* form

      The *we* form

      The *you* (formal singular or plural) form

      The *they* form

  Pronunciations follow in the second column.

The meaning of a phrase doesn't always equal the sum of the individual words the phrase consists of. In this case, we talk about a literal meaning (the meaning of the individual words) and an idiomatic meaning (the actual meaning of the phrase in conversation). If the literal translation of a phrase differs from its idiomatic meaning, we give you both the idiomatic and the literal meanings in parentheses. For instance: **Как дела?** (kahk dee-*lah*?) (*How are you?* Literally: *How is business?*)

In each chapter, look for the following elements:

- ✔ **Talkin' the Talk:** These real-life dialogues illustrate how native speakers use words and phrases in a particular section of the book. These informal dialogues are the actual conversations you may hear in similar situations. You can also play an audio version of these dialogues to help you grasp them even faster!

✔ **Words to Know:** This element follows every Talkin' the Talk and provides pronunciation and transcription of key words and expressions you encounter in the dialogue.

✔ **Fun & Games:** Find this section at the end of each chapter. These fun activities allow you to use the new words and phrases you encounter in each chapter to answer questions and solve puzzles.

What You're Not to Read

We like to think that you'll read every word in this book, but we also know that you're eager to start speaking Russian. So feel free to skip the sidebars (the gray-shaded boxes sprinkled throughout the book); they contain interesting information but aren't essential to your study of Russian.

Foolish Assumptions

When we started writing this book, we tried to imagine what our future reader was going to be like. In the end, we came up with a list of foolish assumptions about who we think wants to read this book. Do you recognize yourself in these descriptions?

✔ You know no Russian — or if you took Russian in high school, you don't remember a word of it.

✔ You're not looking for a book that will make you fluent in Russian; you just want to know some words, phrases, and sentence constructions so that you can communicate basic information in Russian.

✔ You don't want to have to memorize long lists of vocabulary words or a bunch of boring grammar rules.

✔ You want to have fun and learn a little bit of Russian at the same time.

How This Book Is Organized

Russian For Dummies, 2nd Edition, consists of five parts. Each part of the book offers something different.

Part 1: Getting Started

In this part, you find the essentials of the Russian language. Chapter 1 gives you an overview of what you discover in this book. Chapter 2 introduces the Russian alphabet, Chapter 3 gives you a crash course on Russian grammar, and Chapter 4 gets you started with some basic Russian expressions. Chapter 5 is the right place to turn to if you want to talk about numbers, times, and measurements in Russian. And finally, Chapter 6 encourages you to start speaking Russian in the comfort of your home.

Part II: Russian in Action

Part II prepares you for most social situations that you need to handle in Russian. Chapter 7 shows you how to make small talk; Chapter 8 is all about asking for directions in a strange city. Chapters 9 and 10 prepare you to talk about food and shopping. Chapter 11 equips you with words and phrases you can use while going out on the town. Chapter 12 takes you on a tour of your office and equips you with the necessary phrases to make phone calls and use a computer. In Chapter 13, you find out how to talk about fun things, such as sports, reading, and other hobbies.

Part III: Russian on the Go

This part covers all the aspects of traveling, such as planning your trip (Chapter 14), settling your financial matters (Chapter 15), discussing transportation (Chapter 16), and arranging for a place to stay (Chapter 17). Chapter 18 prepares you for handling emergencies.

Part IV: The Part of Tens

The Part of Tens is an unusual part of this book; it gives you lists of fun things to know, such as ten ways to pick up Russian quickly and ten things never to say in Russian. This part is also the place to find ten favorite Russian expressions and to pick up ten phrases that make you sound authentically Russian.

Part V: Appendixes

Russian For Dummies, 2nd Edition, also includes four appendixes, which bring together some useful information. In Appendix A, you find two mini-dictionaries (both Russian-to-English and English-to-Russian) for quick reference. Appendix B contains verb tables that show you how to conjugate regular and irregular verbs. Appendix C contains descriptions of all the audio dialogues and tells you in which chapter you can find the text of each dialogue. And Appendix D offers the answer keys to the Fun & Games sections of each chapter.

Icons Used in This Book

For your convenience, we marked some information in this book with special icons. Check out this guide to the icons, and the next time you see one of them, you'll know what to expect!

From famous Russian writers to a polite way to decline an invitation, this icon marks a wide variety of curious and useful facts about Russian culture.

If you're curious about how the Russian language works or if you want to expand your command of Russian to the extent of making up your own phrases, these bits of grammatical information may be of interest to you.

This icon indicates those Talkin' the Talk dialogues that are featured on audio tracks, allowing you not only to read but also to hear real, conversational Russian.

This icon points out some important information about Russian that's worth remembering.

This icon signals a useful bit of information that can make life easier for you, whether it's a handy way to remember a useful word or an insider's advice on how to better handle a certain situation.

This icon attracts your attention to something you need to know to avoid a common mistake.

Where to Go from Here

Now that you're familiar with the anatomy of *Russian For Dummies,* 2nd Edition, you can embark on your journey. You can start anywhere, and you don't have to go in a specific order. Just choose a topic that seems appealing, find the corresponding chapter in the table of contents, and start speaking Russian!

If you're at a loss about where to start, please take our advice and begin with Chapter 2: It provides you with a very powerful tool — the ability to read Russian. Chapter 3 is a good place to get a grasp on the essentials of Russian grammar. After that, you can go straight to the sections that deal with information you need urgently. Wherever you decide to start, you can find plenty of useful phrases to get you speaking Russian and exploring the benefits that your language skill brings. And now we wish you **Счастливого пути!** (sh'ees-*lee*-vah-vah pooh-*tee*!) (*Bon voyage!*)

Part I
Getting Started

In this part . . .

Part I is the beginning of your exciting journey with
Russian. Here you get the essential information you
need to take you through the rest of this book. First, we
put you at ease with the Russian alphabet and give you
the basics of Russian grammar. We also provide some
handy expressions you can start using right away and
help you get your numbers, times, and measurements
straight. Finally, we encourage you to start speaking
Russian at home.

Chapter 1

Russian in a Nutshell

Russian has a reputation for being a difficult language. Is it? We would say *different* is a better word to describe the experience of studying Russian. Russian actually is a distant cousin of English: They both belong to a huge Indo-European family of languages — unlike, say, Arabic, Chinese, or Japanese, which belong to completely different language family clans.

This chapter provides you with a taste of Russian; get ready to study this fascinating language!

Discovering How Easy the Russian Alphabet Really Is

If you were to ask people on the street what they think the most difficult thing about learning Russian is, most of them (slightly taken aback by your question) would likely say "The alphabet!"

But we're here to tell you that nothing could be farther from the truth: The Russian alphabet is perhaps the easiest part of learning Russian. In fact, you may be surprised to hear that most people are able to start reading Russian in several hours! That's how easy the Russian alphabet is!

Don't believe us? Consider this: The Russian alphabet, often called the *Cyrillic* alphabet, was named after a 9th century Byzantine monk named Cyril, who developed it with the help of his brother, Methodius. (Please don't ask us why Methodius's name wasn't added to the name of the alphabet: Life isn't fair.) Cyril and Methodius wanted to translate the Bible into one of the Slavic languages spoken by the Eastern European pagan tribes, because the brothers were planning to convert those tribes to Christianity. These languages had never been written down before. When the brothers were creating their alphabet, they borrowed quite a few letters from the Latin alphabet to indicate the sounds produced by the tribes. Luckily for those tribes (and for anyone studying Russian), a lot of the borrowed letters sound the same in Russian as they do in any Latin-based alphabet (like English).

Are you ready to jump in and start reading Russian? Chapter 2 shows you how to sound out the letters of the Russian alphabet.

Tackling Basic Grammar

In addition to the alphabet, grammar is responsible for earning Russian its reputation for being a difficult language. Don't worry, though! Chapter 3 makes your transition from English grammar to Russian grammar as smooth as possible. We give you the scoop on Russian nouns, pronouns, adjectives, verbs, adverbs, and sentence construction.

One benefit of Russian: Compared to English, which enforces the strictest order of words on its speakers, Russian allows a completely free, almost anarchic order of words. For example, in the sentence "The dog chased the boy," the Russian words for *boy* and *dog* can switch places and the sentence will still mean "The dog chased the boy."

But to fully enjoy this freedom of word order, Russians had to pay a dear price: six grammatical cases (nominative, genitive, accusative, dative, instrumental, and prepositional), which anybody who speaks Russian has to constantly juggle in order to create sentences that make sense. Don't let this fact, however, intimidate you. With the guidelines we provide in Chapter 3, you'll have a handle on cases in no time.

Easing into Common Expressions

In Chapter 4, we present numerous basic Russian expressions that enable you to start speaking Russian immediately (and politely). Here are just a few of the easiest, shortest ones:

- Привет! (pree-*vyeht*!) (*Hi!*)

- Как дела? (kahk dee-*lah*?) (*How are you?*)

- Пока! (pah-*kah*!) (*Bye!*)

- Спасибо! (spuh-*see*-bah!) (*Thank you!*)

- Понятно! (pah-*nyat*-nah!) (*I see!*)

- Да. (dah.) (*Yes.*)

- Да-да-да! (dah-dah-dah!) (*Yes-yes-yes!*) The repetition makes your *yes* stronger.

- Нет. (nyeht.) (*No.*)

- Нет-нет-нет! (nyeht-nyeht-nyeht!) (*No-no-no!*) You guessed it —this expression makes your *no* stronger.

- Простите! (prahs-*tee*-tee!) or Извините! (eez-vee-*nee*-tee!) (*Sorry!*) This word is a bit longer than its English counterpart, but it comes in handy for acknowledging the blunders you may make as a beginning Russian speaker.

- Ой! (ohy!) (*Oh!*) This term serves to express a wide range of emotions, such as fear, surprise, delight, anger, and many more.

- Ай! (ahy!) (*Ah!*) Use this expression in place of Ой if you prefer, or just for the sake of variety.

Counting on Numbers, Times, and Measurements

Even if you were bad at math in high school, don't underestimate the importance of numbers, times, and measurements while learning a new language (including Russian). Just think about the activities you can then perform: using currency, calculating prices, exchanging phone numbers, setting meeting times, making sense of addresses and zip codes, and a lot more. So, don't even think about missing Chapter 5 — it brings you up to speed on all these topics.

In the meantime, you can start using Russian numbers by counting on both hands:

- один (ah-*deen*) (*one*)

- два (dvah) (*two*)

- ✔ **три** (tree) (*three*)
- ✔ **четыре** (chee-*ti*-ree) (*four*)
- ✔ **пять** (pyat') (*five*)
- ✔ **шесть** (shehst') (*six*)
- ✔ **семь** (syehm') (*seven*)
- ✔ **восемь** (*voh*-seem') (*eight*)
- ✔ **девять** (*dyeh*-veet') (*nine*)
- ✔ **десять** (*dyeh*-seet') (*ten*)

Speaking Russian around the House

A great way to practice Russian is to wander around your home! Each time you enter a room, recall its name in Russian:

- ✔ **кухня** (*koohkh*-nyeh) (*kitchen*)
- ✔ **столовая** (stah-*loh*-vuh-yeh) (*dining room*)
- ✔ **гостиная** (gahs-*tee*-nuh-yeh) (*living room*)
- ✔ **спальня** (*spahl'*-nyeh) (*bedroom*)
- ✔ **туалет** (tooh-uh-*lyeht*) (*bathroom*)
- ✔ **гараж** (guh-*rahsh*) (*garage*)

Chapter 6 introduces you to Russian words for common rooms, household items, and regular everyday activities, such as eating, drinking, sleeping, and doing chores.

Using Russian in Social Scenarios

After practicing Russian at home, you can take it outside. Part II comes in handy in a lot of life scenarios: making small talk with new acquaintances, asking for directions, eating out and shopping, going out on the town, communicating and handling routine tasks at work, and enjoying hobbies. The following sections give you a sense of what to expect.

Starting conversations

If you want to learn a new language, making small talk is a valuable skill to have. Chapter 7 helps you initiate conversations with folks in Russian. You find out how to state where you're from, talk about your nationality and ethnicity, give your age, and discuss your family.

You'll also be armed with a battery of questions that are great ice-breakers, such as the following:

> **Откуда вы?** (aht-*kooh*-duh vi?) (*Where are you from?*)
>
> **Сколько вам лет?** (*skohl'*-kah vahm lyeht?) (*How old are you?*)
>
> **У вас большая семья?** (ooh vahs bahl'-*shah*-yeh seem'-*ya*?) (*Do you have a big family?*)
>
> **Кто вы по-профессии?** (ktoh vi pah-prah-*fyeh*-see-ee?) (*What do you do?*)

Finding your way around

Asking for directions is what tourists in all countries of the world do. If you're in Russia (or traveling in any new place where Russian is the main language), it doesn't hurt to carry a map with you at all times, just in case. That way if you ask passers-by for directions, they can explain which way to go by just pointing it out to you on the map. But first you need to attract a passer-by's attention. The best way to do this is to say the following: **Извините, где. . . ?** (eez-vee-*nee*-tee, gdyeh. . . ?) (*Excuse me, where is. . . ?*) plus the place you're looking for in the nominative case. For full details on asking for (and understanding) directions, see Chapter 8.

Eating out and buying food

A fun (and satisfying!) activity for practicing your Russian is going out to eat. At a Russian restaurant or café, you may discover that the names of dishes on the menu are translated into English followed by very flowery explanations; the wait staff usually understands English, as long as it covers the menu. When placing an order, you can just point to the item you want. You can also add the following phrase, just to show off your Russian: **Я буду . . .** (ya *booh*-dooh . . .) (*I will have . . .*) followed by the name of the item in the accusative case.

You can discover more Russian to use while eating out and buying food at a market in Chapter 9.

Going shopping

To indicate that they want to buy an item, Russians use a language structure that, in a way, reflects the shortages in merchandise they experienced in Soviet times: **У вас есть. . . ?** (ooh vahs *yehst'*. . . ?) (*Do you have. . . ?*) plus the name of the item in the nominative case.

A couple of Russian phrases are especially useful when you go shopping. To ask how much something costs, use the phrase **Сколько стоит . . . ?** (*skohl'*-kah *stoh*-eet. . . ?) (*How much does . . . cost?*), inserting the name of the item in the nominative case, if you're buying one thing. If you're buying more than one thing, ask **Сколько стоят. . . ?** (*skohl'*-kah *stoh*-eet. . . ?) (*How much do . . . cost?*), using the word for the items in the nominative plural form.

Chapter 10 features a lot more shopping vocabulary and phrases for getting help, trying on clothes, asking for specific colors, and paying for the merchandise you buy.

Exploring entertainment opportunities

Exploring new places and meeting new people are always fun. When you head out on the town, you may choose from a variety of activities; for instance, you may decide to check out a museum, a movie, or a play.

Seeing a classical Russian ballet, either in the newly renovated Bolshoy Theater in Moscow or the Mariinsky Theater in St. Petersburg, is a must for any self-respecting tourist in Russia.

Going out on the town often involves making plans, buying tickets, and finding the correct seating. Chapter 11 helps you navigate all these tasks in Russian.

Doing business and communicating

If you're planning a business trip to Russia or need to speak to Russian colleagues in your home office, you should definitely go over Chapter 12. There you find common words and phrases used in an office setting. In addition, you find guidance to help you master the art of telephone conversations in Russian — and don't forget about using computers and sending correspondence!

Enjoying sports, hobbies, recreation, and more

Hobbies can take many forms, and you may want to share information about yours with friends and acquaintances in Russian. For example:

- ✔ If you're a sports fan, you better know how to talk about your favorite sports in Russian. (Also, prepare to be converted into a soccer or hockey fan — these are Russians' two most favorite games.)

- ✔ Russians are avid readers and, for the most part, very well-read individuals. So if you're speaking Russian, be prepared to say at least something about books and literature genres you like or dislike.

    Beware: Saying "I don't read much" can earn you a tarnished reputation.

- ✔ If you happen to be in Russia in summer, late spring, or early autumn, don't miss the experience of going to a country house on a weekend. You'll never forget it.

Flip to Chapter 13 for more about hobbies and the great outdoors.

Getting a Handle on Travel Topics

After you've had time to practice Russian at home, you may consider traveling to Russia. Be sure to acquaint yourself with the following tasks in Russian:

- ✔ **Preparing for a trip:** Planning a trip is an enjoyable part of the travel process, and we let you enjoy it to the fullest with phrases and words you need to decide where you want to go, book your trip, and pack. All this info and more is in Chapter 14.

- ✔ **Making sense of money:** Financial matters can be very confusing when you travel to a different country. That's because you deal with foreign currency while performing such everyday transactions as getting money out of an ATM, using your credit card, and paying with cash. Chapter 15 provides plenty of guidance on how to manage your money and perform financial transactions.

- ✔ **Getting around with local transportation:** Clearly, expertise in using various types of public transportation is an important skill a traveler should have. Dealing with public transportation isn't as easy as it may seem if you're speaking a new language! Don't panic, though; just turn to Chapter 16 for help.

✔ **Securing a place to stay:** Hotels, as you know, can be good, bad, or ugly. To avoid the latter, we provide you with essential questions you may want to ask before buying into a deal. Chapter 17 provides Russian vocabulary that helps you make hotel reservations, check in, resolve issues, and pay your bill.

✔ **Taking action during emergencies:** We hope you won't need any of the expressions we provide in Chapter 18 during your trip. But it's always a good idea to plan for emergencies. Here's one word that lets others know you need help: **Помогите!** (pah-mah-*gee*-tee!) (*Help!*) — don't forget it!

Chapter 2

Checking Out the Russian Alphabet

In This Chapter

▶ Deciphering the letters of the Russian alphabet

▶ Properly pronouncing Russian letters

Suppose you're walking in the Russian district of an American city and are suddenly in the mood for food. You'll be glad you can read Russian when you see a building with the sign **РЕСТОРАН** (ree-stah-*rahn*) on it, because you'll know that the building is exactly what you're looking for — a *restaurant!*

Knowing how to read Russian is a great stepping stone to speaking Russian properly. As you read this chapter, trust your eyes, ears, and intuition, and you'll quickly discover that reading Russian isn't that hard after all. In this chapter you discover how to recognize all the letters of the Russian alphabet, and we introduce you to the basic rules of Russian pronunciation.

Recognizing Russian Letters (It's Easier Than You Think)

When people talk about studying a foreign language, they often mention the alphabet to measure their success (or lack thereof) in mastering the language. You may often hear comments like "I just know the alphabet" or "I don't even know the alphabet!" In other words, the alphabet is seen as the first, unavoidable step in learning a language.

Knowing the alphabet — or rather, the sounds that the letters of the new language correspond to — is indeed very important. This is especially true of languages like Russian, in which nearly every letter corresponds to only one sound. What a relief from English, where one letter often represents several different sounds, depending on the word it's used in. In fact, for those poor souls studying English, knowing the English alphabet isn't so much a help as an obstacle.

Not so in Russian! When you study Russian, the Russian alphabet (also known as the *Cyrillic* alphabet) is your ticket to reading Russian, and knowing how to read Russian is very important in mastering spoken Russian. That's because an average Russian word is much longer than an average English word.

If you're like most English speakers, you probably think that the Russian alphabet is the most challenging aspect of picking up the language. But not to worry. The Russian alphabet isn't as hard as you think. In fact, the alphabet is a piece of cake. In the following sections, we show you how to recognize all the letters of the Russian alphabet.

Introducing the entire alphabet

The Russian alphabet is based on the Cyrillic alphabet, which was named after the ninth-century Byzantine monk, Cyril (see the sidebar "Who was this Cyril guy, anyway?" later in this chapter). Over a period of centuries, many attempts were made to shorten Cyril's original alphabet from its original 43 letters. Today, the alphabet is still pretty lengthy — 33 letters in all, compared to 26 letters in the English alphabet. But don't panic. Throughout this book, every Russian word or phrase is accompanied by its phonetic *transcription* so you can see how to pronounce it (we convert the Russian letters into familiar Latin symbols, which are the same symbols the English alphabet uses).

This isn't to say, however, that English and Russian sounds are completely the same; they absolutely aren't (see the later section "Sounding Like a Real Russian with Proper Pronunciation" for details). But because your chances of learning to sound like a real Russian just by reading this book are rather slim, we use what phoneticians call *approximation* and consider most English sounds and their Russian counterparts to be the same, as long as native speakers of Russian have no difficulty recognizing them. Yes, Russians will discern your accent as not being authentic, but they'll be able to understand you!

Table 2-1 has the details on Cyrillic letters. In the first column, you see the uppercase and lowercase versions of the letter, respectively. The second column shows how the Russian letters are pronounced using familiar English letters and example words. The third column of the table indicates whether the letter is a vowel or a consonant:

✔ You may remember from your English classes that vowels are the sounds that are usually said with an open mouth, without stopping the flow of air coming from the lungs. The English letters *A, E, I, O* and *U* are vowels.

✔ Letters like *B, K, L, M, N, P,* and *T* are consonants: They're all pronounced with some sort of obstruction that gets in the way of the air coming out of your lungs.

You may wonder why you need this information, another burden for your poor memory. Believe it or not, knowing whether the sound is a vowel or a consonant comes in handy in helping you understand some very important grammatical rules as you delve deeper into the language.

Play Track 1 to hear the pronunciation of the Russian alphabet.

Table 2-1	The Russian Alphabet	
Russian Letter	*Pronunciation*	*Vowel or Consonant*
Аа	*ah* in a stressed syllable, as the *a* in *father*; *uh* in an unstressed syllable, as the *u* in *upstage*	Vowel
Бб	*b* as in *book*; *p* at the end of a word	Consonant
Вв	*v* as in *valve*; *f* at the end of a word	Consonant
Гг	*g* as in *grotto*; *k* at the end of a word	Consonant
Дд	*d* as in *dad*; *t* at the end of a word	Consonant
Ее	*yeh* in a stressed syllable, as the *ye* in *yes* or *yesterday*; *ee* in an unstressed syllable, as in *beet* or *birdseed*	Vowel
Ёё	*yoh* as the *yo* in *yoke*	Vowel
Жж	*zh* as the *s* in *pleasure*; *sh* at the end of a word	Consonant
Зз	*z* as in *zoo*; *s* at the end of a word	Consonant
Ии	*ee* as in *beet*	Vowel
Йй	very short *y* as in *York*	Vowel or consonant
Кк	*k* as in *key*	Consonant
Лл	*l* as in *lamp*	Consonant

(continued)

Table 2-1 *(continued)*

Russian Letter	Pronunciation	Vowel or Consonant
Мм	*m* as in *mom*	Consonant
Нн	*n* as in *no*	Consonant
Оо	*oh* in a stressed syllable, as the *o* in *opus*; *ah* in an unstressed syllable, as the *a* in *father*	Vowel
Пп	*p* as in *parrot*	Consonant
Рр	*r* as in *red*	Consonant
Сс	*s* as in *so*	Consonant
Тт	*t* as in *tea*	Consonant
Уу	*ooh* as the *oo* in *shoot*	Vowel
Фф	*f* as in *flag*	Consonant
Хх	*kh* like you're clearing your throat or like the *ch* in Scottish *loch*	Consonant
Цц	*ts* as in *tsetse* fly	Consonant
Чч	*ch* as in *chair*	Consonant
Шш	*sh* as in *woosh*	Consonant
Щщ	soft *sh* as in *sheep* or *sherbet*	Consonant
ъ	A "hard sign," transcribed as ″ but not pronounced, so for the purposes of this book, we just ignore it!	Neither
Ы	*i* as in *bit*	Vowel
ь	A "soft sign" that makes the preceding consonant soft; we show it as '	Neither
Ээ	*eh* as the *e* in *end*	Vowel
Юю	*yooh* as the *Yu* in *Yukon*	Vowel
Яя	*ya* as in *yahoo* if stressed; *ee* if unstressed and not in the final syllable of a word; *yeh* if unstressed and in the final syllable of a word	Vowel

Note the letter **Йй** in Table 2-1. Scholars don't agree on this one: Some believe it's a consonant; others think it's a vowel. We don't want to take sides in this matter, so we list it as both a consonant and a vowel.

Who was this Cyril guy, anyway?

Picture this: The year is sometime around A.D. 863. Two Byzantine monks and brothers, Cyril and Methodius, were commissioned by their emperor to Christianize the East European pagan tribes. To carry out the emperor's order, the two brothers had to transcribe the Bible into Slavic. This task was very daunting because the Slavs didn't have any written language at the time, and the Slavic dialect they were working with contained a lot of bizarre sounds not found in any other language.

One of the brothers, Cyril, came up with an ingenious idea: Create a Slavic alphabet from a mishmash of Greek, Hebrew, and old Latin words and sounds. That was a clever solution, because by drawing on different languages, Cyril's alphabet contained practically every sound necessary for the correct pronunciation of Russian.

In honor of Cyril's clever idea, the alphabet became known as the Cyrillic alphabet. The Cyrillic script is now used by more than 70 languages, ranging from Eastern Europe's Slavic languages (Russian, Ukrainian, Belarusian, Bulgarian, Serbian, and Macedonian) to Central Asia's Altaic languages (Turkmen, Uzbek, Kazakh, and Kirghiz).

Our advice for you is to go over the alphabet as many times as needed to memorize letter-sound correspondences while you listen to Track 1. (We provide extra help in the later section "Sounding Like a Real Russian with Proper Pronunciation.") Test yourself a couple of times: Cover the pronunciation column in Table 2-1 and say out loud the sound that corresponds to each Russian letter. If you forget a sound, you can peek at the corresponding English letter. Keep at it until you can say each letter. And keep the table handy for future reference!

I know you! Familiar-looking, same-sounding letters

You may notice that some of the letters in the Russian alphabet in Table 2-1 look a lot like English letters: For example, check out **Аа, Вв, Ее, Кк, Мм, Нн, Оо, Рр, Сс,** and **Хх.** Guess what? Some (but not all!) of them even sound like English letters. The letters that look like English and are pronounced like English letters are

   ✔ **Аа** pronounced as *ah* or *uh* depending on the stress: *ah* in a stressed syllable and *uh* in an unstressed syllable

> ✔ **Кк** pronounced as *k*

> ✔ **Мм** pronounced as *m*

> ✔ **Оо** pronounced as *oh* or *ah* depending on the stress: *oh* in a stressed syllable and *ah* in an unstressed syllable

> ✔ **Тт** pronounced as *t*

Playing tricks: Familiar-looking, different-sounding letters

Some Russian letters look like English letters but are pronounced differently. You want to watch out for these:

> ✔ **Вв:** The capital letter in this pair looks exactly like the English *B,* but don't trust appearances: The letter is pronounced like the English letter *v,* as in *victor* or *vase.*

> ✔ **Ее:** English speakers very often feel an irresistible urge to say it like *ee,* as in the English word *geese* — but that sound in Russian is made by the letter **И**. In fact, it should be pronounced as *ye* in **yesterday**. Be aware, though, that the letter **Ее** *is* sometimes pronounced as *ee,* but only in an unstressed position in a word.

> ✔ **Ёё:** Note the two cute little dots and don't confuse this one with the English letter *E* — Ее and Ёё are two different letters! Ёё is pronounced like the *yo* in **yoke**.

> ✔ **Нн:** This letter looks like the English *H,* but actually it's pronounced like *n,* as in *Nick.*

> ✔ **Pp:** In Russian, this letter is pronounced like an *r,* not like the English letter *P,* as in *Peter.*

> ✔ **Сс:** This letter is always pronounced like the *s* in **sun** and never like the *k* in *cake.*

> ✔ **Уу:** This letter is pronounced like the *oo* in **shoot**, never like the *y* in **yes**.

> ✔ **Хх:** Never pronounce this letter *z* or *ks,* like the first and last *x,* respectively, in the word **Xerox**. In Russian, the sound it represents is a coarse-sounding, guttural *kh,* similar to the German *ch.* (See "Surveying sticky sounds," later in this chapter, for info on pronouncing this sound.)

How bizarre: Weird-looking letters

As you've probably noticed, quite a few Russian letters don't look like English letters at all:

- ✔ Бб
- ✔ Гг
- ✔ Дд
- ✔ Жж
- ✔ Зз
- ✔ Ии
- ✔ Йй
- ✔ Лл
- ✔ Пп
- ✔ Фф

- ✔ Цц
- ✔ Чч
- ✔ Шш
- ✔ Щщ
- ✔ ъ
- ✔ Ыы
- ✔ ь
- ✔ Ээ
- ✔ Юю
- ✔ Яя

Don't panic over these letters. They look weird but are easy to pronounce. Mastering them is just a matter of memorizing their proper pronunciations. (Refer to Table 2-1 for details on how to say each letter.)

You may recognize several of these weird letters, such as **Ф**, **Г**, and **П**, from learning the Greek alphabet during your fraternity or sorority days.

Talkin' the Talk

Anna Ivanovna (**Анна Ивановна**) is teaching her little daughter, Katya (**Катя**), to read while they're passing by a sign that says **Банк** (*bahnk*) (*bank*).

Анна Ивановна: **Катя, прочитай это слово.**
kah-tya, prah-chee-*tahy eh*-tah *sloh*-vah.
Katya, read this word.

Катя: **Я не могу!**
ya nee mah-*gooh!*
I can't!

Анна Ивановна:	**Нет, ты можешь! Какая первая буква?** nyeht, ti *moh*-zhish'! kuh-*kah*-yeh *pyehr*-vuh-yeh *boohk*-vuh? *No, you can! What is the first letter?*
Катя:	**В?** v? *V?*
Анна Ивановна:	**Нет.** nyeht. *No.*
Катя:	**Б?** b? *B?*
Анна Ивановна:	**Верно! А вторая буква?** *vyehr*-nah! ah ftah-*rah*-yeh *boohk*-vuh? *Correct! And the second letter?*
Катя:	**Вторая буква А!** ftah-*rah*-yeh *boohk*-vuh ah! *The second letter is A!*
Анна Ивановна:	**Молодец! А что после А?** mah-lah-*dyehts!* uh shtoh *pohs*-lee ah? *Way to go! And what is after A?*
Катя:	**Н! Банк!** n. bahnk! *N. Bank!*
Анна Ивановна:	**Очень хорошо!** *oh*-cheen' khah-rah-*shoh*! *Very good!*

Words to Know

слово	<u>sloh</u>-vah	word
Я не могу	ya nee mah-<u>gooh</u>	I can't
нет	nyeht	no
буква	<u>boohk</u>-vuh	letter
верно	<u>vyehr</u>-nah	correct
Молодец!	mah-lah-<u>dyehts</u>!	Way to go!
очень хорошо	<u>oh</u>-cheen' khah-rah-<u>shoh</u>	very good

Sounding Like a Real Russian with Proper Pronunciation

Compared to English pronunciation, which often has more exceptions than rules, Russian rules of pronunciation are fairly clear and consistent. In this section, you discover some of the basic rules and patterns of Russian pronunciation. In addition, we show you how to say some of the more difficult letters.

Understanding the one-letter-one-sound principle

For the most part, one Russian letter corresponds to one sound. For example, the letter **K** is always pronounced *k*, and the letter **M** is always pronounced *m*. This pattern is different from English, where a letter can be pronounced in different ways depending on the word it's in. For instance, consider the two different pronunciations for the letter *c* in the words *cat* and *race*.

Such drastic differences never happen in Russian, but to be quite honest, you may note occasions when a letter in Russian sounds *slightly* different depending on its position in a word. Take, for example, the Russian word жук (zhoohk) (*beetle*) where the first letter ж is pronounced *zh,* like the *s* in *pleasure*. In the word гараж (guh-*rahsh*) (*garage*), however, the ж is pronounced *sh* rather than *zh*. Why? Because when it appears at the end of a word, ж (zh) is pronounced as ш (sh). (For more information, flip to the later sections "Vowels misbehavin': Understanding when vowels change sounds" and "Cat got your tongue? Consonants losing their voice.")

Giving voice to vowels

Vowels are the musical building blocks of every Russian word. If you flub a consonant or two, you'll probably still be understood. (To avoid such flubs, though, check out "Enunciating consonants correctly," later in this chapter.) But if you don't pronounce your vowels correctly, there's a good chance you won't be understood at all. So it's a good idea to get down the basic principles of saying Russian vowels, which we cover in the following sections.

That's stretching it: Lengthening out vowels

If you want to sound more Russian, don't shorten your vowels like English speakers often do. When you say **Aa, Oo,** or **Уy,** open your mouth really wide, like a Russian opera singer. Also, be sure not to round your mouth after **Oo** or **Уy,** and purposefully stretch out the sounds to make them a little bit longer. Imagine, for example, that you're in your room on the second floor, and your mom is downstairs in the kitchen. You call her by saying "Mo-o-o-m!" That's the way Russians say their vowels (except for the shouting part!).

Some stress is good: Accenting the right vowels and getting used to shifting accents

Stress is an important concept in Russian. Putting a stress in the wrong place isn't just a formal mistake. It can hinder communication, because the meaning of a word can change based on where the stress is. For example, the word замок (*zah*-mahk) means *castle*. However, if you shift the stress from the first syllable to the last, the word замок (zuh-*mohk*) now means *lock*.

Unfortunately, no hard and fast rules about stress exist. Stress in Russian is unpredictable and erratic, though you begin to recognize some patterns as you learn more. The harsh truth, however, is that each word has its own stress pattern. What happens if you stress the vowel in the wrong place? Certainly, nothing terrible: The earth will continue to rotate around its axis. What may happen, however, is that the person you're talking to may have a hard time understanding you and take longer to grasp what you really mean.

Before learning a new Russian word, find out which vowel to stress. Look in any Russian-English dictionary, which usually marks stress by putting the sign ´ over the stressed syllable. In a dictionary, замок (*zah*-mahk) (*castle*) is written за́мок, and замок (zuh-*mohk*) (*lock*) is written замо́к.

Vowels misbehavin': Understanding when vowels change sounds

Some Russian letters change their behavior depending on whether they're in a stressed or an unstressed syllable. The vowels **Аа, Оо, Ее,** and **Яя,** for example, sound like *ah, oh, yeh,* and *ya* when they're in a stressed syllable, but when they're in an unstressed position, they sound like *uh, ah, ee,* and *yeh,* respectively.

Here are some examples of how one letter is pronounced differently in different positions:

- ✓ You write **Колорадо** (*Colorado*) but say kah-lah-*rah*-dah. Notice how all the *o*'s in this word are pronounced *ah* rather than *oh*. None of them are pronounced *oh* because they all appear in unstressed syllables.

- ✓ You write **хорошо** (*good, well*) but say khah-rah-*shoh*. Here we have three *o*'s. Notice how the first and the second *o*'s are pronounced *ah,* whereas the last one, in the stressed syllable, is pronounced *oh.*

- ✓ You write **направо** (*to the right*) but say nuh-*prah*-vah. Notice that the first *a* is pronounced *uh* because it's not in the stressed syllable, the second *a* is pronounced *ah* because it's in the stressed syllable, and the final *o* is pronounced *ah* because it's not stressed.

- ✓ You write **Петербург** (*Petersburg*) but say pee-teer-*boohrk*. Notice how the *e* is pronounced as *ee* in each case because it's not stressed.

Hear that hiss: Saying sibilants with vowels

The letters **ж, ц, ч, ш,** and **щ** are called *sibilants,* because they emit a hissing sound. When certain vowels appear after these letters, those vowels are pronounced slightly differently than normal.

- ✓ After a sibilant, **e** is pronounced *eh* (as in *end*) and **ё** is pronounced *oh* (as in *opus*). Examples are the words **центр** (tsehntr) (*center*) and **шёл** (shohl) (*went by foot;* masculine).

- ✓ The sound *ee* always becomes *i* after one of these sibilants, regardless of whether the *ee* sound comes from the letter **и** or from an unstressed **e.** Take, for example, the words **машина** (muh-*shi*-nuh) (*car*) and **больше** (*bohl'*-shi) (*bigger*).

Enunciating consonants correctly

Like Russian vowels (see the preceding section), Russian consonants follow certain patterns and rules of pronunciation. If you want to sound like a real Russian, you need to keep the basics in the following sections in mind.

Say it, don't spray it! Relaxing with consonants

When pronouncing the letters **Пп, Тт,** or **Кк,** English speakers are used to straining their tongue and lips. This strain results in what linguists call *aspiration* — a burst of air that comes out of your mouth as you say these sounds. To see what we're talking about, put your hand in front of your mouth and say the word "top." You should feel air against your hand as you pronounce the word.

In Russian, however, consonants are pronounced without aspiration. In other words, say it, don't spray it! In fact, you should totally relax your tongue and lips before saying the Russian **Пп, Тт,** or **Кк.** For example, imagine a woman who has just had a stroke. She isn't able to put too much effort into her consonants. Believe it or not, that's almost the way you should say your Russian consonants. Relax your lips as much as possible, and you'll say them correctly. To practice saying consonants without unnecessary aspiration, again, put your hand in front of your mouth and say the following Russian *cognates* (words that Russian borrowed from English): **парк** (pahrk) (*park*), **лампа** (*lahm*-puh) (*lamp*), and **танк** (tahnk) (*tank*). Practice until you don't produce a puff of air with these words!

Cat got your tongue? Consonants losing their voice

Some consonants (namely **Бб, Вв, Гг, Дд, Жж,** and **Зз**) are called *voiced consonants* (because they're pronounced with the voice), but they become devoiced when they appear at the end of a word; in other words, they kind of lose their voice.

So, at the end of a word:

- ✔ **Бб** is pronounced *p*.
- ✔ **Вв** is pronounced *f*.
- ✔ **Гг** is pronounced *k*.
- ✔ **Дд** is pronounced *t*.
- ✔ **Жж** is pronounced *sh*.
- ✔ **Зз** is pronounced *s*.

For example, in the word **Волков,** should the final letter **в** be pronounced *v* or *f*? In this case, you pronounce it *f* (vahl-*kohf*) because a **в** at the end of a word is pronounced *f*.

Nutty clusters: Pronouncing consonant combinations

To those who don't know Russian, Russian speech often sounds like an endless flow of consonant clusters. Combinations of two, three, and even four consonants are quite common. Take, for example, the common word for *hello* in Russian — **здравствуйте** (*zdrah*-stvoohy-tee), which has two difficult consonant combinations (**здр** and **ств**). Even Russians have a hard time saying all the sounds in this long word; in fast, colloquial speech, Russians replace it with **здрасте** (*zdrahs*-tee). Or take the word for *opinion* in Russian — **взгляд** (vzglyat). The word contains four consonants in a row: **взгл.**

How in the world do Russians say these words without choking? They come naturally to Russians because Russian is their native language. You, on the other hand, simply need to practice. Here are some words that contain consonant clusters you may want to repeat at leisure:

- ✔ **обстоятельство** (ahp-stah-*ya*-teel'-stvah) (*circumstance*)
- ✔ **поздравлять** (pah-zdruhv-*lyat'*) (*to congratulate*)
- ✔ **преступление** (pree-stoohp-*lyeh*-nee-ee) (*crime*)
- ✔ **рождество** (razh-dees-*tvoh*) (*Christmas*)
- ✔ **вздор** (vzdohr) (*nonsense*)
- ✔ **взглянуть** (vzglya-*nooht'*) (*to look/glance*)

Surveying sticky sounds

Some Russian letters and sounds are difficult for speakers of English. Take a look at the following sections to find out how to pronounce some of them.

The bug sound zh

The *zh* sound corresponds to the letter **Жж.** It looks kind of like a bug, doesn't it? It sounds like a bug, too! In pronouncing it, try to imitate the noise produced by a bug flying over your ear — *zh-zh-zh.* . . . The sound is similar to the sound of the *s* in the words *plea**s**ure* and *mea**s**ure.*

The very short i sound

The short *i* sound corresponds to the letter **Йй.** This letter's name is **и краткое** (ee *kraht*-kahee), which literally means *a very short i,* but it actually sounds like the very short English *y*. This sound is what you hear when you say the word *York*. You should notice your tongue touching the roof of your mouth when you say this sound.

The guttural sound kh

The Russian letter that corresponds to the *kh* sound is **Xx**. To say it, imagine that you're eating and a piece of food gets stuck in your throat. What's the first reflex your body responds with? Correct! You try to cough it up. Remember the sound your throat produces? The Russian *kh* makes this sound. It's similar to the German *ch*.

The revolting sound i

To say the *y* sound correctly, imagine that you're watching something really revolting, like an episode from a reality competition show where the participants are gorging on a plate of swarming bugs. Now recall the sound you make in response to this. This sound is pronounced something like *i*, the short vowel sound of the English *i*, and that's how you pronounce the Russian **ы**. Because this letter appears in some commonly used words, including **ты** (ti) (*you*; informal singular), **вы** (vi) (*you*; formal singular or plural), and **мы** (mi) (*we*), it's important to say it as best you can.

The soft sign

The soft sign is the letter **ь**. We transcribe it using the symbol ', and it doesn't have a sound. Its only mission in life is to make the preceding consonant soft. This sound is very important in Russian because it can change the meaning of a word. For example, without the soft sign, the word **мать** (maht') (*mother*) becomes **мат,** which means *obscene language*. And when you add a soft sign at the end of the word **вон** (vohn) (*over there*), it becomes **вонь** (vohn') and means *stench*. See how important the soft sign is?

So, here's how you can make consonants soft:

1. **Say the consonant — for example, Лл, Тт, or Дд — and note where your tongue is.**

   You should feel that the tip of your tongue is touching the ridge of your upper teeth, and the rest of the tongue is hanging in the mouth like a hammock in a garden on a nice summer day.

2. **While you're still pronouncing the consonant, raise the body of your tongue and press it against the hard palate.**

   The process is exactly the same as preparing a piece of bubble gum for blowing a bubble by flattening the gum on the roof of your mouth. Bingo: You're ready to pronounce your soft consonant. Can you hear how the quality of the consonant changes? It sounds much "softer" now, doesn't it?

The hard sign

The hard sign is represented by the letter **ъ.** Whereas the soft sign makes the preceding consonant sound soft (see the preceding section), the hard sign makes it — yes, you guessed it — hard. The good news is that this letter (which is transcribed as ") is rarely ever used in contemporary Russian. And even when it is, it virtually doesn't change the pronunciation of the word. So, why does Russian have this sign? For two purposes:

- ✔ To harden the preceding consonant
- ✔ To retain the hardness of the consonant before the vowels **Ее, Ёё, Юю,** and **Яя**

Without the hard sign, these consonants would normally soften. When a hard sign (**ъ**) separates a consonant and one of these vowels, the consonant is pronounced without softening, as in the word **подъезд** (pahd-*yehzd*) (*porch*), for example.

Don't worry too much about this one if your native language is English. Native speakers of English rarely tend to soften their Russian consonants the way Russians do it. In other words, if you're a native English speaker and you come across the situation described here, you'll probably make your consonant hard, pronouncing it correctly by default!

Fun & Games

Match the Russian letters in the first column with the sounds they correspond to in the second column. You can find the answers in Appendix D.

1. **Н**   a. r
2. **Р**   b. n
3. **Г**   c. ee
4. **Я**   d. ya
5. **И**   e. g

Chapter 3

Warming Up with Russian Grammar Basics

*I*n any language, grammar is the glue that ties together all the words in a sentence. Russian involves more grammar than English does, but fortunately it's all very structured, and you can easily master it if you put forth a little effort.

You may be surprised to find out that English and Russian are distant relatives. Both belong to the same family of Indo-European languages. Although they're distantly related, they have one big difference: Unlike English, Russian is a *flectional language,* which is a fancy way of saying that it has lots of different word endings. A single word may acquire a multitude of different endings depending on the role it plays in a sentence.

In this chapter, you discover how and why Russian words drop and acquire new endings. You find out how to change Russian nouns for different grammatical cases and how to spice up your speech with pronouns, adjectives, verbs, and adverbs. You also find out how to form complete sentences that make you sound like a real Russian.

Beginning with Nouns and Pronouns

The best way to start getting a feel for Russian grammar is to understand nouns' grammatical gender (not to be confused with biological gender!). After that, you can easily make a singular noun plural and replace all types of nouns with pronouns. We give you the information you need in the following sections.

Defining a noun's gender

Unlike English nouns, all Russian nouns, even those indicating inanimate objects, have a gender: masculine, feminine, or neuter. Determining a noun's gender is surprisingly easy (a lot easier than determining, say, the gender of a kitten): You just need to look at the noun's ending. Here's how:

✔ If a noun ends in a consonant or **й**, the noun is masculine.

✔ If a noun ends in **а** or **я**, the noun is feminine.

✔ If a noun ends in **е**, **ё**, or **о**, the noun is neuter.

✔ If a noun ends in **ь** (the soft sign) it may be either feminine or masculine. To figure it out, look up the word in a Russian dictionary (either a hard-copy version or online): All Russian nouns in the dictionary have a gender notation.

For example, the noun **стол** (stohl) (*table*) is masculine, because it ends in the consonant **л**. The word **лампа** (*lahm*-puh) (*lamp*) ends in **а**, and is, therefore, feminine. The word **море** (*moh*-ree) (*sea*) is neuter because it ends in **е**. It's that simple!

In the majority of cases, the grammatical gender of words denoting living beings coincides with their biological gender. For example, the word **мальчик** (*mahl'*-cheek) (*boy*) is a masculine noun and the word **девушка** (*dyeh*-voohsh-kuh) (*young woman*) is a feminine noun, just as you'd expect.

When it comes to inanimate objects, gender is completely unpredictable and illogical — it doesn't seem to have any relationship to the meaning of the word. Why, for example, is the word **дверь** (dvyehr') (*door*) feminine? Or why are **пол** (pohl) (*floor*), **окно** (ahk-*noh*) (*window*), and **занавеска** (zuh-nuh-*vyehs*-kuh) (*curtain*) masculine, neuter, and feminine, respectively? Nobody can answer these questions for you. Sorry!

Of course, there are exceptions; grammar wouldn't be grammar without exceptions! Here are a few common words indicating (biologically at least) masculine beings that look like feminine nouns in Russian:

✔ **дедушка** (*dyeh*-doohsh-kuh) (*grandfather*)

✔ **дядя** (*dya*-dyeh) (*uncle*)

✔ **папа** (*pah*-puh) (*dad*)

Note: Wondering why you need to know this stuff about genders? The gender of a noun determines how the noun changes for Russian grammatical cases. We tell you about cases a little later in this chapter.

Making a noun plural

In English, nouns are usually made plural by adding an "s." Russian uses a different set of suffixes. To make a Russian noun plural, follow the simple steps in Table 3-1.

Table 3-1	How to Make a Noun Plural
If a noun in its dictionary form ends in	*To form its plural form*
A consonant	Add -ы: стол → столы (stah-*li*) (*tables*)
-й	Replace it with -и: герой → герои (gee-*roh*-ee) (*heroes*)
-а	Replace it with -ы: лампа → лампы (*lahm*-pi) (*lamps*)
	If the stem ends in **г, к, х, ц, ч, ш,** or **щ,** replace with -и rather than ы
-я	Replace it with -и: няня → няни (*nya*-nee) (*nannies*)
-е	Replace it with -я: море → моря (mah-*rya*) (*seas*)
-о	Replace it with -а: окно → окна (*ohk*-nuh) (*windows*)
-ь	Replace it with -и: лошадь → лошади (*loh*-shuh-dee) (*horses*)

The rules in Table 3-1 have a few important exceptions. Some consonants, namely ж (zh), ш (sh), щ (sh'), г (g), к (k), and х (kh), are very touchy. They just don't tolerate the letter ы (i) after them, preferring и (ee) instead. Take, for example, the word книга (*knee*-guh) (*book*). According to Table 3-1, you should replace the final -а with -ы to form its plural. But the touchy г doesn't tolerate the -ы ending. It takes an -и ending instead. So the plural of книга is книги (*knee*-gee) (*books*).

Replacing nouns with pronouns

From your grammar lessons in school, you probably remember that a *pronoun* is a word used instead of a noun. Words like *I, you, he, she, it, we,* and *they* are all called pronouns or, to be more specific, personal pronouns. One of the reasons why we need pronouns is to avoid needless repetitions of one and the same noun: you can always replace *John* with *he, Mary* with *she, car* with *it,* and so on. Table 3-2 shows Russian pronouns and their English equivalents. (Flip to Chapter 4 for details on informal versus formal versions of "you.")

Table 3-2	Russian Personal Pronouns		
Singular Russian Pronouns	*Singular English Pronouns*	*Plural Russian Pronouns*	*Plural English Pronouns*
Я (ya)	*I*	**мы** (mi)	*we*
ты (informal) (ti)	*you*	**вы** (vi)	*you*
вы (formal) (vi)	*you*	**они** (ah-*nee*)	*they*
он (ohn)	*he*		
она (ah-*nah*)	*she*		
он, она, оно (ohn, ah-*nah*, ah-*noh*)	*it*		

As Table 3-2 indicates, the word *it* may be translated into Russian by three different words. The choice of the Russian pronoun here depends on . . . yes, you guessed it, the gender of the noun *it* replaces. Use **он** to replace a masculine noun, **она** to replace a feminine noun, and **оно** for a neuter noun.

Because Russian nouns indicating inanimate objects have genders, their pronoun replacements may literally translate to *he* or *she* in English. Consider these examples:

✔ The word **машина** (muh-*shi*-nuh) (*car*) is replaced by **она** (ah-*nah*) in Russian, which literally means *she* in English.

✔ The word **дом** (dohm) (*house*) is replaced by **он** (ohn) in Russian, which literally means *he* in English.

The Case of Russian Cases: What Are They For?

One very nice feature of English is that words don't change their form, no matter where they are in a sentence. Take, for example, the word *table*. You may say *The table is round*, or *There is a book on the table*, or *There is no table in the room*. No matter where in a sentence you use the word *table*, a table is a table is a table.

Not so in Russian . . . the Russian word for *table* in each of the preceding sentences has a different ending in each instance — **стол** (stohl), **столе** (stah-*lyeh*), and **стола** (stah-*lah*) — because of the different role the word **стол** plays in each sentence. These roles are indicated in Russian by grammatical case and case endings.

What's a case? In simple terms, *cases* are sets of endings that words take to indicate their function and relationship to other words in the sentence. If you've studied languages such as Latin or German, you know that different languages have different numbers of cases. Russian has 6 cases, which isn't that bad compared to Finnish, which has 15! English speakers, on the other hand, never have to bother with cases.

In the following sections, you discover the six different cases in Russian and how to use them. (Later in this chapter, we explain the specific endings that nouns, pronouns, and adjectives take in each case.)

The nominative case

Nouns, pronouns, and adjectives always appear in the nominative case in an English-Russian dictionary. The main function of the nominative case is to indicate the subject of the sentence. All the Russian words we use in the earlier section "Beginning with Nouns and Pronouns" are in the nominative case. The nominative case requires no changes in ending.

As a rule, the subject behaves the same way in Russian as it does in English. It answers the question "Who or what is performing the action?" For example, in the sentence **Девочка изучает русский язык** (*dyeh-*vahch-kuh ee-zooh-*chah-*eet *roohs-*keey ee-*zik*) (*A girl studies Russian*), the word **девочка,** indicating a girl who studies Russian, is the subject of the sentence and consequently is used in the nominative case.

The genitive case

One of the important functions of the genitive case is to indicate possession. It answers the question "Whose?" In the phrase **книга девочки** (*knee-*guh *dyeh-*vahch-kee) (*the girl's book*), the word **девочка** takes the genitive case (**девочки**) because she's the book's owner.

The genitive case also is used to indicate an absence of somebody or something when you combine it with the word **нет** (nyeht) (*no/not*), as in **Здесь нет книги** (zdees' neet *knee-*gee) (*There's no book here*). **Книги** (*knee-*gee) (*book*) is in the genitive case because the book's absence is at issue.

In addition, Russian uses the genitive case after many common prepositions, including the following:

- ✔ **без** (byehs) (*without*)
- ✔ **вместо** (*vmyehs-*tah) (*instead of*)

✔ **из** (ees) (*out of*)

✔ **мимо** (*mee*-mah) (*past*)

✔ **около** (*oh*-kah-lah) (*near*)

✔ **у** (ooh) (*by, by the side of*)

The accusative case

The accusative case is very often used to indicate a direct object, which is the object of the action of the verb in a sentence. For example, in the sentence **Я люблю литературу** (ya lyooh-*blyooh* lee-tee-ruh-*tooh*-rooh) (*I love literature*), the word *literature* is in the accusative case because it's the direct object of the verb. That's why the form of the word is no longer **литература** (lee-tee-ruh-*tooh*-ruh; the nominative case) but rather **литературу** (lee-tee-ruh-*tooh*-rooh).

Verbs like **читать** (chee-*taht'*) (*to read*), **видеть** (*vee*-deet') (*to see*), **слушать** (*slooh*-shuht') (*to hear*), and **изучать** (ee-zooh-*chaht'*) (*to study*) take the accusative case. As in English, these verbs in Russian are *transitive verbs* (verbs that require a direct object).

The accusative case is also required in sentences containing verbs of motion, which indicate destination of movement. For instance, if you want to announce to your family that you're going to **Россия** (rah-*see*-yeh) (*Russia*), **Россия** takes the form of the accusative case, which is **Россию** (rah-*see*-yooh).

You also use the accusative case after certain prepositions, such as **про** (proh) (*about*) and **через** (*chyeh*-rees) (*through*).

The dative case

Use the dative case to indicate an indirect object, which is the person (or thing) for whom (or which) the action in a sentence is performed. Consider this example sentence:

> **Я дал учителю сочинение.** (ya dahl ooh-*chee*-tee-lyooh sah-chee-*nyeh*-nee-ee.) (*I gave the teacher my essay.*)

The word **учителю** (ooh-*chee*-tee-lyooh) (*teacher*) is, in fact, the dative form of the word **учитель** (ooh-*chee*-tyehl'). The original dictionary form of the word changes because in this sentence *teacher* functions as an indirect object. (*My essay* acts as the direct object, which we cover in the preceding section.)

You also use the dative case after certain prepositions, such as **к** (k) (*toward*) and **по** (poh) (*along*).

Some frequently used verbs, such as **помогать** (puh-mah-*gaht'*) (*to help*) and **позвонить** (puh-zvah-*neet'*) (*to call*), force the nouns that come after them into the dative case. The implication with these verbs in Russian is that you're giving help or making a call *to somebody,* which suggests an indirect receiver of the action of the verb.

The instrumental case

As the name suggests, the instrumental case is often used to indicate the instrument that assists in carrying out an action. So, when you say that you're writing a letter with a pen, you have to put **ручка** (*roohch*-kuh) (*pen*) in the instrumental case, which is **ручкой** (*roohch*-kahy).

You also use the instrumental case after certain prepositions, such as the following:

- **между** (*myezh*-dooh) (*between*)
- **над** (naht) (*over*)
- **перед** (*pyeh*-reet) (*in front of*)
- **под** (poht) (*below*)
- **с** (s) (*with*)

The prepositional case

The prepositional case is so named because it's used only after certain prepositions. Older Russian textbooks frequently refer to it as the locative case, because it often indicates the location where an action takes place. No wonder it's used with the prepositions **в** (v) (*in*) and **на** (nah) (*on*).

The prepositional case is also used after the prepositions **о** (oh) and **об** (ohb), two Russian words that mean *about.* So when you say to that special someone, *I am constantly thinking about you,* make sure to put **ты** (ti) (*you;* informal singular) in the prepositional case, which is **тебе** (tee-*byeh*): **Я постоянно думаю о тебе** (ya pahs-tah-*ya*-nuh *dooh*-muh-yooh uh tee-*byeh*).

By the way, you may wonder why the English preposition *about* has two different Russian equivalents: **o** and **ob.** For your information, you use **o** if the following word begins with a consonant. You use **ob** if the following word begins with a vowel.

Putting Nouns and Pronouns in the Correct Cases

Nouns and pronouns are the building blocks of any sentence, but they need to be in the proper case (as you find out earlier in this chapter). In the following sections, you discover how to change the endings of nouns and pronouns depending on their function in a sentence.

Checking out cases for singular nouns

As you see earlier (in the section "The Case of Russian Cases: What Are They For?"), in Russian you can't just use a singular noun in its dictionary form all the time; you need to very carefully put it in a certain grammatical case. Use the information in the following sections to find out exactly what you need to do to put the dictionary form of a singular noun (also known as the nominative case) into another desired case form.

Switching to the genitive case

Table 3-3 explains how to transform a singular noun in the nominative case into the genitive case, which you use to indicate possession.

Table 3-3	How to Put a Singular Noun into the Genitive Case
If a singular noun in the nominative case ends in	**To put the noun in the genitive case**
A consonant	Add -**а**: **дом** (dohm) (*house*) → **дома** (*doh*-muh)
-**й**, -**е**, or -**ь** and is masculine	Replace -**й**, -**е**, or -**ь** with -**я**: **море** (*moh*-ree) (*sea*) → **моря** (*moh*-rya)
-**а**	Replace -**а** with -**ы**: **мама** (*mah*-muh) (*mother*) → **мамы** (*mah*-mi)
-**я** or -**ь** and is feminine	Replace -**я** or -**ь** with -**и**: **няня** (*nya*-nyeh) (*nanny*) → **няни** (*nya*-nee)
-**о**	Replace -**о** with -**а**: **окно** (ahk-*noh*) (*window*) → **окна** (ahk-*nah*)

Switching to the accusative case

Table 3-4 explains how to put a singular noun in the nominative case into the accusative case, which you use to indicate a direct object.

Table 3-4   How to Put a Singular Noun into the Accusative Case

If a singular noun in the nominative case ends in	To put the noun in the accusative case
A consonant, and the noun is for a living person or thing	Add -**а**: **студент** (stooh-*dyehnt*) (*student*) → **студента** (stooh-*dyehn*-tuh)
A consonant, and the noun is for an inanimate object	Don't do anything
-**й** or -**ь** and is masculine	Replace -**ь** with -**я**: **преподаватель** (pree-pah-duh-*vah*-teel') (*professor*) → **преподавателя** (pree-pah-duh-*vah*-tee-lyeh)
-**а**	Replace -**а** with -**у**: **мама** (*mah*-muh) (*mother*) → **маму** (*mah*-mooh)
-**я**	Replace -**я** with -**ю**: **няня** (*nya*-nyeh) (*nanny*) → **няню** (*nya*-nyooh)
-**е** or -**о**; or -**ь** and is feminine	Don't do anything

Switching to the dative case

Table 3-5 explains how to transform a singular noun in the nominative case into the dative case, which you use to indicate an indirect object.

Table 3-5   How to Put a Singular Noun into the Dative Case

If a singular noun in the nominative case ends in	To put the noun in the dative case
A consonant	Add -**у**: **дом** (dohm) (*house*) → **дому** (*doh*-mooh)
-**й**, -**е**, or -**ь** and is masculine	Replace -**й**, -**е**, or -**ь** with -**ю**: **море** (*moh*-ree) (*sea*) → **морю** (*moh*-ryooh)
-**а** or -**я**	Replace -**а** or -**я** with -**е**: **мама** (*mah*-muh) (*mother*) → **маме** (*mah*-mee)
-**о**	Replace -**о** with -**у**: **окно** (ahk-*noh*) (*window*) → **окну** (ahk-*nooh*)
-**ь** and is feminine	Replace -**ь** with -**и**: **лошадь** (*loh*-shuhd') (*horse*) → **лошади** (*loh*-shuh-dee)
-**ие** or -**ия**	Replace -**е** or -**я** with -**и**: **Калифорния** (kuh-lee-*fohr*-nee-yeh) (*California*) → **Калифорнии** (kuh-lee-*fohr*-nee-ee)

Switching to the instrumental case

Table 3-6 explains how to put a singular noun in the nominative case into the instrumental case, which you use to indicate the instrument that helps carry out an action.

Table 3-6　How to Put a Singular Noun into the Instrumental Case

If a singular noun in the nominative case ends in	To put the noun in the instrumental case
A consonant	Add **-ом**: **студент** (stooh-*dyehnt*) (*student*) → **студентом** (stooh-*dyehn*-tahm)
-й or **-ь** and is masculine	Replace **-й** or **-ь** with **-ем**: **преподаватель** (pree-pah-dah-*vah*-teel') (*professor*) → **преподавателем** (pree-pah-dah-*vah*-tee-leem)
-а	Replace **-а** with **-ой**: **мама** (*mah*-muh) (*mother*) → **мамой** (*mah*-mahy)
-я	Replace **-я** with **-ей**: **няня** (*nya*-nyeh) (*nanny*) → **няней** (*nya*-nyehy)
-е or **-о**	Add **-м**: **окно** (ahk-*noh*) (*window*) → **окном** (ohk-*nohm*)
-ь and is feminine	Add **-ю**: **лошадь** (*loh*-shuhd') (*horse*) → **лошадью** (*loh*-shuhd'-yooh)

Switching to the prepositional case

Table 3-7 explains how to change a singular noun from the nominative case into the prepositional case, which you use only after certain prepositions.

Table 3-7　How to Put a Singular Noun into the Prepositional Case

If a singular noun in the nominative case ends in	To put the noun in the prepositional case
A consonant	Add **-е**: **студент** (stooh-*dyehnt*) (*student*) → **студенте** (stooh-*dyehn*-tee)
-й, -а, -я, or **-о**	Replace these letters with **-е**: **мама** (*mah*-muh) (*mother*) → **маме** (*mah*-mee)
-е	Don't do anything
-ь and is masculine	Replace **-ь** with **-е**: **преподаватель** (pree-pah-dah-*vah*-teel') (*professor*) → **преподавателе** (pree-pah-dah-*vah*-tee-lee)

If a singular noun in the nominative case ends in	To put the noun in the prepositional case
-ь and is feminine	Replace **-ь** with **-и**: **лошадь** (*loh*-shud′) (*horse*) → **лошади** (*loh*-shuh-dee)
-ия or **-ие**	Replace **-я** or **-е** with **-и**: **Калифорния** (kuh-lee-*fohr*-nee-yeh) (*California*) → **Калифорнии** (kuh-lee-*fohr*-nee-ee)

Trying your hand at changing the case of a singular noun

All the tables in the preceding sections may look kind of scary at first, but they're actually easy to use.

Imagine you want to brag to your Russian friends about your new car by saying *I bought a car.* The first part of the sentence is **Я купил** (ya kooh-*peel*) (*I bought*). But what do you do with the noun *car*? In this sentence, **машина** (muh-*shi*-nuh) (*car*) is a direct object of the action expressed by the verb **купил**. The accusative case is for nouns that serve as direct objects, so you have to change **машина** from the nominative case to the accusative case.

The next step is to find the appropriate table (Table 3-4, by the way). It tells you exactly what to do to put your noun in the accusative case. Ask yourself: What letter does the word **машина** end in? The last letter in the word **машина** is **-a**. Table 3-4 indicates that when a word ends in **-a**, you replace the **-a** with **-y**. This little operation creates the word **машину** (muh-*shi*-nooh) (*car*).

So here's your complete sentence:

> **Я купил машину.** (ya koo-*peel* muh-*shi*-nooh.) (*I bought a car.*)

Congratulations! You just created your first Russian sentence!

Putting plurals into proper cases

Russian plural nouns, like singular nouns, take different endings depending on the case they're in. In the following sections, you find out how to obtain the plural forms of nouns in different cases. Because we cover what plural nouns look like in the nominative case in Table 3-1, we begin with the genitive case. ***Note:*** You start each transformation with the singular noun in the nominative case.

Plurals in the genitive case

Of all cases, the genitive plural case is perhaps the most unpleasant one, because it has so many exceptions that you just need to memorize. These exceptions, however, are usually listed in any Russian dictionary. You can find all the endings for this case in Table 3-8; keep in mind that you use them to indicate possession.

Table 3-8 How to Put a Noun into the Genitive Plural Case

If a singular noun in the nominative case ends in	To form the genitive plural
A consonant other than -ж, -ц, -ч, -ш, or -щ	Add -ов: **студент** (stooh-*dyehnt*) (*student*) → **студентов** (stooh-*dyehn*-tuhf)
-ж, -ч, -ш, or -щ	Add -ей: **ключ** (klyoohch) (*key*) → **ключей** (klyooh-*chyehy*)
-ц	Add -ев: **месяц** (*myeh*-seets) (*month*) → **месяцев** (*myeh*-see-tsehf)
-й	Replace -й with -ев: **герой** (gee-*rohy*) (*hero*) → **героев** (gee-*roh*-eef)
-a	Drop the -a: **мама** (*mah*-muh) (*mother*) → **мам** (mahm)
-я	Replace -я with -ь: **баня** (*bah*-nya) (*sauna*) → **бань** (bahn')
-e or -ь	Replace -e or -ь with -ей: **море** (*moh*-ree) (*sea*) → **морей** (mah-*ryehy*)
-o	Drop the -o: **окно** (ahk-*noh*) (*window*) → **окон** (*oh*-kuhn)
-ие or -ия	Replace -e or -я with -й: **здание** (*zdah*-nee-yeh) (*building*) → **зданий** (*zdah*-neey)

Plurals in the accusative case

Table 3-9 explains how to transform a singular noun in the nominative case into the accusative plural case, which indicates a direct object.

Table 3-9 How to Put a Noun into the Accusative Plural Case

If a singular noun in the nominative case	To form the accusative plural
Indicates a living being and ends in a consonant or in -й, -a, -я, or -ь	Refer to the corresponding endings in Table 3-8, because in these instances, the accusative plural is the same as the genitive plural.
Indicates an inanimate object and ends in a consonant or in -й, -a, -я, -e, -ё, -o, or -ь	Make no change. It looks exactly like the nominative plural (see Table 3-1).

You may wonder: What if a singular noun indicates a living being and ends in -e, -ё, or -o? In Russian, nouns indicating living beings do not end in these letters.

Plurals in the dative case

Table 3-10 explains how to change a singular noun in the nominative case into the dative plural case, which indicates an indirect object.

Table 3-10	How to Put a Noun into the Dative Plural Case
If a singular noun in the nominative case ends in	_To form the dative plural_
A consonant	Add -**ам**: **студент** (stooh-_dyehnt_) (_student_) → **студентам** (stooh-_dyehn_-tuhm)
-**й**, -**я**, -**е**, or -**ь**	Replace -**й**, -**я**, -**е**, or -**ь** with -**ям**: **герой** (gee-_rohy_) (_hero_) → **героям** (gee-_roh_-yehm)
-**а** or -**о**	Replace -**а** or -**о** with -**ам**: **мама** (_mah_-muh) (_mother_) → **мамам** (_mah_-muhm)

Plurals in the instrumental case

Table 3-11 explains how to put a singular noun in the nominative case into the instrumental plural case, which indicates an instrument that helps carry out an action.

Table 3-11	How to Put a Noun into the Instrumental Plural Case
If a singular noun in the nominative case ends in	_To form the instrumental plural_
A consonant	Add -**ами**: **студент** (stooh-_dyehnt_) (_student_) → **студентами** (stooh-_dyehn_-tuh-mee)
-**й**, -**я**, -**е**, or -**ь**	Replace -**й**, -**я**, -**е**, or -**ь** with -**ями**: **герой** (gee-_rohy_) (_hero_) → **героями** (gee-_roh_-ee-mee)
-**а** or -**о**	Replace -**а** or -**о** with -**ами**: **мама** (_mah_-muh) (_mother_) → **мамами** (_mah_-muh-mee)

Plurals in the prepositional case

Table 3-12 explains how to transform a singular noun in the nominative case into the prepositional plural case, which is used only after certain prepositions.

Table 3-12 How to Put a Noun into the Prepositional Plural Case

If a singular noun in the nominative case ends in	To form the prepositional plural
A consonant	Add -**ах**: **студент** (stooh-*dyehnt*) (*student*) → **студентах** (stooh-*dyehn*-tuhkh)
-**й**, -**я**, -**е**, or -**ь**	Replace -**й**, -**я**, -**е**, or -**ь** with -**ях**: **герой** (gee-*rohy*) (*hero*) → **героях** (gee-*roh*-yehkh)
-**а** or -**о**	Replace -**а** or -**о** with -**ах**: **мама** (*mah*-muh) (*mother*) → **мамах** (*mah*-muhkh)

Trying your hand at putting nouns into plural cases

To get comfortable with putting plural nouns into the correct case, apply the tables in the preceding sections to a real-life situation. Imagine that your friend asks you whether you have a pencil:

> **У тебя есть карандаш?** (ooh tee-*bya* yest' kuh-ruhn-*dahsh*?) (*Do you have a pencil?*)

You, being by nature a very generous person, say that you have a lot of pencils, meaning that your friend is free to use all of them. It may come as a surprise to you, but when you make this statement, the word **много** (*mnoh*-gah) (*many/a lot of*) requires the noun used with it to take the genitive plural form. Thus, in your sentence, the word **карандаши** (kuh-ruhn-duh-*shi*) (*pencils*) takes the genitive plural case.

What does Table 3-8 say about words that end in -**ш**? Yep, you need to add the ending -**ей** to the singular noun in the nominative case. You say

> **У меня много карандашей.** (ooh mee-*nya mnoh*-gah kuh-ruhn-duh-*shyehy*.) (*I have many pencils.*)

We admit that the genitive plural case is a tough one, so here's an example using the dative plural case. Imagine that you ask your friend, a Russian professor, whether he has a book that you want to borrow. It appears he does, but, unfortunately, he can't give it to you because he has already given it to his students. He says

> **Я дал книгу студентам.** (ya dahl *knee*-gooh stooh-*dyehn*-tuhm.) (*I gave the book to the students.*)

Your friend uses the form **студентам** because it's the dative plural form of the word **студенты** (stooh-*dyen*-ti) (*students*), which is the indirect object of the sentence. The singular nominative form of this word is **студент** (stooh-*dyehnt*), and he just added **-ам**, as shown in Table 3-10.

Perusing the correct cases of pronouns

Like singular and plural nouns, Russian pronouns have different forms for all the cases. The following sections show how pronouns change for cases. Compare them with their dictionary (nominative case) form (refer to Table 3-2).

Pronouns in the genitive and accusative cases

Table 3-13 shows all Russian pronouns in the genitive case, which indicates possession. The forms for the accusative case, which indicates a direct object, are the same as those for the genitive case.

Table 3-13 Russian Pronouns in the Genitive and Accusative Cases

Singular Pronoun in the Nominative Case	Singular Pronoun in the Genitive and Accusative Cases	Plural Pronoun in the Nominative Case	Plural Pronoun in the Genitive and Accusative Cases
я	**меня** (mee-*nya*) (*me*)	мы	**нас** (nahs) (*us*)
ты	**тебя** (tee-*bya*) (*you*, informal)	вы	**вас** (vahs) (*you*)
вы	**вас** (vahs) (*you*, formal)	они	**их** (eekh) (*them*)
он, оно	**его** (ee-*voh*) (*him, it*)		
она	**её** (ee-*yoh*) (*her*)		

Pronouns in the dative case

Table 3-14 shows all Russian pronouns in the dative case, which indicates an indirect object.

Table 3-14	Russian Pronouns in the Dative Case		
Singular Pronoun in the Nominative Case	Singular Pronoun in the Dative Case	Plural Pronoun in the Nominative Case	Plural Pronoun in the Dative Case
я	мне (mnyeh) (me)	мы	нам (nahm) (us)
ты	тебе (tee-byeh) (you, informal)	вы	вам (vahm) (you)
вы	вам (vahm) (you, formal)	они	им (eem) (them)
он, оно	ему (ee-moo) (him, it)		
она	ей (yehy) (her)		

Pronouns in the instrumental case

Table 3-15 shows all Russian pronouns in the instrumental case, which indicates an instrument used to help carry out an action.

Table 3-15	Russian Pronouns in the Instrumental Case		
Singular Pronoun in the Nominative Case	Singular Pronoun in the Instrumental Case	Plural Pronoun in the Nominative Case	Plural Pronoun in the Instrumental Case
я	мной (mnohy) (me)	мы	нами (nah-mee) (us)
ты	тобой (tah-bohy) (you, informal)	вы	вами (vah-mee) (you)
вы	вами (vah-mee) (you, formal)	они	ними/ими (nee-mee/ee-mee) (them)
он, оно	ним /им (neem/eem) (him, it)		
она	ней/ей (nyehy/yehy) (her)		

Pronouns in the prepositional case

Table 3-16 shows all Russian pronouns in the prepositional case, which is used only after certain prepositions.

Table 3-16	Russian Pronouns in the Prepositional Case		
Singular Pronoun in the Nominative Case	**Singular Pronoun in the Prepositional Case**	**Plural Pronoun in the Nominative Case**	**Plural Pronoun in the Prepositional Case**
я	**мне** (mnyeh) (*me*)	мы	**нас** (nahs) (*us*)
ты	**тебе** (tee-*byeh*) (*you*, informal)	вы	**вас** (vahs) (*you*)
вы	**вас** (vahs) (*you*, formal)	они	**них** (neekh) (*them*)
он, оно	**нём** (nyohm) (*him, it*)		
она	**ней** (nyehy) (*her*)		

Trying your hand at using a pronoun in a different case

So, how do you use all the tables in the preceding sections? Here's an example: Imagine that somebody asks you whether you saw Nina today:

Ты видел Нину? (ti *vee*-deel *nee*-nooh?) (*Did you see Nina?*)

You didn't. In preparing to answer this question, you may decide not to use the word "Nina" again but to replace it with the pronoun *her*. Because *Nina* is a direct object, you have to use the accusative case in translating the word *her*. Using Table 3-13, you discover that the accusative case of **она** (ah-*nah*) (*she*) is **её** (ee-*yoh*) (*her*). You respond

Я не видел её. (ya nee *vee*-deel ee-*yoh*.) (*I didn't see her.*)

Decorating Your Speech with Adjectives

Adjectives spice up your speech. An adjective is a word that describes, or *modifies*, a noun or a pronoun, like *good, nice, difficult,* or *funny*. In the following sections, you discover how to use adjectives and how to change their endings for different cases.

The English words *the, a,* and *an* are called articles, and they're technically adjectives because they modify nouns. You use articles all the time in English, but these words don't exist in Russian, so you don't need to worry about how to say them. When you want to say *the, a,* or *an,* all you have to do is say the noun you mean. For example, *the store* and *a store* in Russian are simply **магазин** (muh-guh-*zeen*). *The girl* and *a girl* are simply **девушка** (*dyeh*-voohsh-kuh).

Making sure that adjectives and nouns agree

A Russian adjective is like a jealous lover. It can't live without the noun or the pronoun it describes. In English, an adjective never changes its form no matter what word it modifies or where it's used in a sentence, but a Russian adjective always agrees with the noun or pronoun it modifies in gender, number, and case. (In this section, we cover gender and number; see the next section for more about adjectives and cases.)

Russian dictionaries list adjectives in their singular masculine form in the nominative case (the first column in Table 3-17). Singular masculine adjectives end in only three ways: **-ий, -ой,** and **-ый.** The trick is to correctly select the ending for an adjective's feminine, neuter, and plural forms; dictionaries don't provide these forms because dictionary compilers assume that you know how to do it. So it's time to figure it out! Table 3-17 shows how to change an adjective's ending so that it agrees with its noun in gender and number in the nominative case.

Table 3-17	Changing an Adjective to Agree with a Noun in the Nominative Case		
If an adjective in its dictionary (singular masculine) form ends in	*To put it in a singular feminine form*	*To put it in a singular neuter form*	*To put it in a plural form*
-ий: последний (pahs-*lyehd*-neey) (*the last*)	Replace **-ий** with **-яя: последний → последняя**	Replace **-ий** with **- ее: последний → последнее**	Replace **-ий** with **-ие: последний → последние**
-ой or **-ый: новый** (*noh*-viy) (*new*)	Replace **–ой** or **-ый** with **-ая: новый → новая**	Replace **ой** or **-ый** with **-ое: новый → новое**	Replace **ой** or **-ый** with **-ые: новый → новые**

Now put the rules in Table 3-17 to work. Take the word **последний** (pahs-*lyehd*-neey) (*last*). As you see, in its dictionary (singular and masculine) form, the adjective has the ending **-ий.** How do you change the ending of this adjective to say *the last word* in Russian?

Figure out the gender of the noun the adjective modifies, *word.* Its Russian equivalent is **слово** (*sloh*-vah). The ending in this word is **-о,** and the ending **-о** in a noun indicates neuter gender (refer to the earlier section "Defining a noun's gender"). What ending does **последний** take when it's used with a singular neuter noun? Looking back at Table 3-17, you see that the ending is **-ее.** So *the last word* in Russian is **последнее слово** (pahs-*lyehd*-nee-ee *sloh*-vah).

Putting adjectives into other cases

Unfortunately, the preceding section doesn't tell you the whole story because adjectives change not only in terms of gender and number, but also for cases. Table 3-18 explains how to do it. You make changes to the singular masculine form of the adjective, as shown in Table 3-18. The feminine endings for adjectives are the same for all cases except the accusative. The plural genitive and plural prepositional endings for adjectives are the same; so are the plural dative and the plural instrumental endings.

Take a look at this example of how to use Table 3-18 in a real-life conversation. Imagine that you ask your friend to tell you about his new house. Your request in English is *Tell me about your new house,* and it contains the adjective *new* in combination with the word *house.* Both should be used in the prepositional case because they're preceded by the preposition **о,** which requires the prepositional case. Note the gender of the Russian word for *house* — **дом** (dohm). It's masculine. That means that your adjective for *new* — **новый** — has to drop its original ending and take the prepositional case ending **-ом.** Here's your request in Russian:

> **Расскажи о твоём новом доме!** (ruhs-kuh-*zhi* uh tvah-*yohm noh*-vuhm *doh*-mee!) (*Tell me about your new house!*)

Table 3-18   How to Put Adjectives in the Genitive, Accusative, Dative, Instrumental, and Prepositional Cases

If the adjective modifies	To form the genitive case	To form the accusative case	To form the dative case	To form the instrumental case	To form the prepositional case
A masculine or neuter noun	Replace the original ending with -ого/его.	Replace the original ending with -ого/его if the noun that the adjective modifies is animate; otherwise, it's the same as the nominative case (refer to Table 3-17).	Replace the original ending with -ому/ему.	Replace the original ending with -ым/им.	Replace the original ending with -ом/ем.
A feminine noun	Replace the original ending with -ой/ей.	Replace the original ending with -ую/юю.	Replace the original ending with -ой/ей.	Replace the original ending with -ой/ей.	Replace the original ending with -ой/ей.
A plural noun	Replace the original ending with -ых/их.	Replace the original ending with -ых/их if the noun that the adjective modifies is animate; otherwise, it's the same as the nominative case (refer to Table 3-17).	Replace the original ending with -ым/им.	Replace the original ending with -ыми/ими.	Replace the original ending with -ых/их.

Surveying possessive pronouns

Possessive pronouns indicate ownership or possession. Words such as *my, mine, your, yours, his, her, hers, our, ours, their,* and *theirs* are English possessive pronouns. In Russian, a possessive pronoun must always agree in number, gender, and case with the noun it refers to. Table 3-19 shows you how to use possessive pronouns to modify nouns of different genders and number in the nominative case (which is by far the case you'll use most).

Table 3-19 Forming Possessive Pronouns in the Nominative Case

English Possessive Pronoun	If It Modifies a Masculine Noun	If It Modifies a Feminine Noun	If It Modifies a Neuter Noun	If It Modifies a Plural Noun
my/mine	**мой** (mohy)	**моя** (mah-*ya*)	**моё** (mah-*yoh*)	**мои** (mah-*ee*)
your/yours (informal singular)	**твой/ваш** (tvohy/ vahsh)	**твоя/ ваша** (tvah-*ya/* *vah*-shuh)	**твоё/вашо** (tvah-*yoh/* *vah*-shee)	**твои/ ваши** (tvah-*ee/* *vah*-shee)
his	**его** (ee-*voh*)	**его** (ee-*voh*)	**его** (ee-*voh*)	**его** (ee-*voh*)
her/hers	**её** (ee-*yoh*)	**её** (ee-*yoh*)	**её** (ee-*yoh*)	**её** (ee-*yoh*)
our/ours	**наш** (nahsh)	**наша** (*nah*-shuh)	**наше** (*nah*-sheh)	**наши** (*nah*-shi)
your/yours (formal singular or plural)	**ваш** (vahsh)	**ваша** (*vah*-shuh)	**ваше** (*vah*-sheh)	**ваши** (*vah*-shi)
their/theirs	**их** (eekh)	**их** (eekh)	**их** (eekh)	**их** (eekh)

Say you're getting ready to go out on the town and you notice you've lost your favorite shirt. You want to say, *Where's my shirt?* Because **рубашка** (rooh-*bahsh*-kuh) (*shirt*) ends in **-a**, it's a feminine noun. (For more information, see "Defining a noun's gender" earlier in this chapter.) Because *my* modifies the feminine noun **рубашка**, it's written **моя** (mah-*ya*) (*my*) according to Table 3-19. The phrase you want is this:

Где моя рубашка? (gdyeh mah-*ya* rooh-*bahsh*-kuh?) (*Where's my shirt?*)

Talkin' the Talk

Anton (**Антон**) and Vladimir (**Владимир**) work at the same company. They have just finished work and are walking toward the parking lot so Anton can show his new car to Vladimir. (Track 2)

Владимир: **Это твоя машина?**
eh-tah tvah-*ya* muh-*shi*-nuh?
Is this your car?

Антон: **Да, это моя машина.**
dah, *eh*-tah mah-*ya* muh-*shi*-nuh.
Yes, it is my car.

Владимир: **Это новая машина?**
eh-tah *noh*-vuh-yeh muh-*shi*-nuh?
Is this a new car?

Антон: **Да, новая.**
dah, *noh*-vuh-yeh.
Yes, it's new.

Владимир: **Красивая машина!**
kruh-see-vuh-*ya* mah-*shi*-nuh!
Beautiful car!

Антон: **Спасибо. Да, мне нравится эта машина. Цвет хороший. Практичная. Ну, Мне пора. Пока!**
spuh-*see*-bah. dah, mnyeh *nrah*-veet-syeh *eh*-tuh mah-*shi*-nuh. tsvyeht khah-*roh*-shiy. prahk-*teech*-nuh-yeh. nooh, mnyeh pah-*rah*. pah-*kah*!
Thank you. Yes, I like this car. The color is nice. It is practical. Well, I need to go. Bye!

Владимир: **До завтра!**
dah *zahf*-truh!
See you tomorrow!

Words to Know

Это...?	<u>Eh</u>-tah...?	Is this...?
машина	muh-<u>shi</u>-nuh	car
Спасибо	spuh-<u>see</u>-bah	Thank you
пока	pah-<u>kah</u>	bye
Мне пора	mnyeh pah-<u>rah</u>	I need to go!
До завтра!	dah <u>zahf</u>-truh!	See you tomorrow!

Adding Action with Verbs

If nouns and pronouns are the building blocks and adjectives are the flavoring in a Russian sentence, then the verb is the engine. Without the verb, you can't express a complete thought. A Russian verb carries loads of important information. It can reveal whether an action was completed or resulted in something and whether the action occurs on a regular basis or is a one-time event. Russian verbs also reveal the number (and, in the past tense, the gender) of the person or thing performing the action.

In the following sections, we show you how to spot the infinitive of a verb and how to form verbs in the past, present, and future tenses. We also tell you about some basic but unusual verbs often used in Russian.

Spotting infinitives

Spotting Russian infinitives is easy, because they usually end in **-ть**, as in **читать** (chee-*taht'*) (*to read*), **говорить** (gah-vah-*reet'*) (*to speak*), and **видеть** (*vee*-deet') (*to see*).

Some Russian verbs (which are usually irregular) take the infinitive endings **-ти**, as in **идти** (eet-*tee*) (*to walk*), and **-чь'**, as in **мочь** (mohch') (*to be able to*). For a list of common irregular verbs, see Appendix B.

In a Russian dictionary, as in any language dictionary, verbs are always listed in their infinitive form, but the truth is that every Russian verb has *two* infinitive forms: imperfective and perfective. For example, the verb *to read* is translated by two Russian infinitives: **читать** (chee-*taht'*) and **прочитать** (pruh-chee-*taht'*). The first translation is an imperfective infinitive, and the second one is a perfective infinitive. This seemingly useless information comes in handy when you decide to talk about the past and future, as we discuss later in this chapter. So, bear with us!

Living in the present tense

Russian verbs have only one present tense. Like English verbs, Russian verbs *conjugate* (change their form) so that they always agree in person and number with the subject of the sentence. To conjugate most Russian verbs in the present tense, you drop the infinitive ending **-ть** and replace it with one of the six endings in Table 3-20. The verb we use in this table is **работать** (ruh-*boh*-tuht') (*to work*).

Table 3-20	Forming the Present Tense of Verbs	
If the subject of the sentence is	*Drop the infinitive verb ending (-Ть) and replace it with*	*Example*
Я (ya) (*I*)	**-ю**	**Я работаю.** (ya ruh-*boh*-tuh-yooh.) (*I work.*)
Ты (ti) (*you,* informal singular)	**-ешь**	**Ты работаешь.** (ti ruh-*boh*-tuh-eesh'.) (*You work.*)
он/она/оно (ohn/ah-*nah*/ah-*noh*) (*he/she/it*)	**-ет**	**Он/Она/Оно работает.** (ohn/ah-*nah*/ah-*noh* ruh-*boh*-tuh-eet.) (*He/She/It works.*)
Мы (mi) (*we*)	**-ем**	**Мы работаем.** (mi ruh-*boh*-tuh-eem.) (*We work.*)
Вы (vi) (*you,* formal singular or plural)	**-ете**	**Вы работаете.** (vi ruh-*boh*-tuh-ee-tee.) (*You work.*)
они (ah-*nee*) (*they*)	**-ют**	**Они работают.** (ah-*nee* ruh-*boh*-tuh-yooht.) (*They work.*)

The present tense in Russian corresponds to both the present simple and present continuous tenses in English. In other words, it denotes both the general action in the present tense (such as *I work*) and the action taking place at the moment of speaking (such as *I am working*).

Verbs that conjugate as **-ю, -ешь, -ет, -ем, -ете,** and **-ют** are called first-conjugation verbs. Second-conjugation verbs have the following endings: **-ю, -ишь, -ит, -им, -ите,** and **-ят.** So how do you know whether a verb uses the first or second conjugation? Easy: Dictionaries always indicate this situation. In addition, a lot of verbs conjugate — how should we put it? — any way they want to (in other words, in a completely unpredictable fashion!). How do you deal with such verbs? Always check the dictionary; dictionaries always indicate something peculiar in verb conjugations. However, they list only three forms — usually the **я** (*I*), **ты** (*you*; informal singular), and **они** (*they*) forms — with the hope that you can figure out the rest of the forms. ***Note:*** We alert you to regular verbs that follow the second-conjugation pattern and irregular verbs with conjugation peculiarities throughout this book.

Talking about the past tense

In the following sections, we show you how to form the past tense of Russian verbs and explain the differences between imperfective and perfective verbs.

Keeping it simple: Forming the past tense

To form the past tense of a Russian verb, all you need to do is drop the infinitive ending **-ть** and replace it with one of the four endings shown in Table 3-21. The verb we use in this table is **работать** (ruh-*boh*-tuht') (*to work*).

Table 3-21	**Forming the Past Tense of Verbs**	
If the subject of the sentence is	*Drop the infinitive ending -Tь and replace it with*	*Example*
masculine singular	**-л**	**Он работал.** (ohn ruh-*boh*-tuhl.) (*He worked.*)
feminine singular	**-ла**	**Она работала.** (ah-*nah* ruh-*boh*-tuh-luh.) (*She worked.*)
neuter singular	**-ло**	**Оно работало.** (ah-*noh* ruh-*boh*-tuh-lah.) (*It worked.*)
plural	**-ли**	**Они работали.** (ah-*nee* ruh-*boh*-tuh-lee.) (*They worked.*)

Imperfective or perfective? That is the question

English expresses past events either through the past simple tense (*I ate yesterday*) or the present perfect tense (*I have eaten already*). While *I ate yesterday* simply states a fact, *I have eaten already* emphasizes the completion of the action. Russian verbs do something similar by using what's called *verbal aspect:* When constructing a sentence in the past tense, you simply have to decide which of the two infinitives — perfective or imperfective — you're going to use:

> **Я ел вчера.** (ya yehl fchee-*rah*.) (*I ate yesterday.*)

> **Я уже поел.** (ya ooh-*zheh* pah-*yehl*.) (*I have eaten already.*)

The formation of the perfective infinitive is as unpredictable as the rest of Russian grammar. Our advice: When you memorize a new Russian verb, memorize both its perfective and imperfective aspects.

So when do you use the imperfective aspect and the perfective aspect?

- ✔ **The perfective aspect:** This form of the verb emphasizes the result or completion of an action. You also use the perfective aspect of a verb to emphasize a single, momentary event that took place in the past, such as breaking a plate. For example, to say you finished writing your resume, you use the perfective form of the verb **писать** (pee-*saht'*) (*to write*), because your emphasis is on the completion of the action. The perfective aspect of this verb is **написать** (nuh-pee-*saht'*), so you say

    > **Я написал резюме.** (ya nuh-pee-*sahl* ree-zyooh-*myeh*.) (*I have written my resume.*)

- ✔ **The imperfective aspect:** This form of the verb emphasizes the fact of an action in the past or expresses habitual or repeated action in the past. For example, to say that you were writing your resume all day, you use the imperfective form of the verb **писать** (pee-*saht'*) (*to write*), because your emphasis is on the fact of writing, not on the completion of the task. The imperfective aspect of this verb is **писать** (pee-*saht'*) (*to write*), so you say

    > **Я писал резюме целый день.** (ya pee-*sahl* ree-zyooh-*myeh tsyeh*-liy dyen'.) (*I was writing my resume all day.*)

Knowing which of the two aspects to select is important only when you speak about the past or the future (see the next section). Russian doesn't have aspects in the present tense. In other words, in describing present tense events, you use only the imperfective form of the verb.

Planning for the future tense

To describe an action that will take place in the future, Russian uses the future tense. While English has many different ways to talk about the future, Russian has only two: the future imperfective and the future perfective.

You use the *future imperfective* when you want to emphasize the fact that something will happen or be happening in the future, but you don't necessarily want to emphasize the result or completion of an action. You use the future perfective to emphasize result or completion of an action.

To form the future imperfective, you use the future tense form of the verb **быть** (bit') (*to be*) plus the imperfective infinitive. This combination translates into *will/will be*. Table 3-22 shows the conjugation of the verb **быть** in the future tense. (Find out more about this interesting verb in the next section.)

Table 3-22	The Verb быть in the Future Tense
Pronoun	*Correct Form*
я (*I*)	**буду** (*booh*-dooh)
ты (*you;* informal singular)	**будешь** (*booh*-deesh')
он/она/оно (*he/she/it*)	**будет** (*booh*-deet)
мы (*we*)	**будем** (*booh*-deem)
вы (*you;* formal singular or plural)	**будете** (*booh*-dee-tee)
они (*they*)	**будут** (*booh*-doot)

If you want to say *I will read* (but not necessarily finish reading) *the article*, you use the **я** (*I*) form of the verb **быть** plus the imperfective infinitive **читать** (chee-*taht'*) (*to read*): **Я буду читать статью** (ya *booh*-dooh chee-*taht'* staht'-*yooh*).

To form the future perfective, you simply conjugate the perfective form of the verb. For example, the perfective form of the verb *to read* is **прочитать** (pruh-chee-*taht'*); if you want to say *I'll read/finish reading the article today*, you say **Я прочитаю статью сегодня** (ya prah-chee-*tah*-yooh stuht'-*yooh* see-*gohd*-nyeh). In other words, you use the ending -**ю** for **я** (*I*) as you do in the present tense (refer to Table 3-20).

Using the unusual verb "to be"

Russian has no present tense of the verb **быть** (*to be*). To say *I'm happy*, you just say **Я счастлив** (ya sh'*as*-leef) (Literally: *I happy*). To say *That's John*, you just say **Это Джон** (*eh*-tuh dzhohn) (Literally: *That John*). The being verbs *am, are,* and *is* are implicitly understood in the present tense.

To express the verb *to be* in the past tense, you need to use the proper past tense form of the verb **быть**:

✔ **был** (bil) (*was*) if the subject is a masculine singular noun

✔ **была** (*bi*-lah) (*was*) if the subject is a feminine singular noun

✔ **было** (*bi*-lah) (*was*) if the subject is a neuter singular noun

✔ **были** (*bi*-lee) (*was*) if the subject is a plural noun or if the subject is **вы** (vi) (*you*; formal singular)

To express the verb *to be* in the future tense, you have to use the correct form of the verb **быть** in the future tense. (For conjugation, refer to Table 3-22.) To say *I will be happy*, you say **Я буду счастлив** (ya *booh*-dooh *sh'as*-leef), and for *I will be there*, you say **Я буду там** (ya *booh*-dooh tahm).

Talkin' the Talk

Natasha (**Наташа**) and Katya (**Катя**) are friends. A week ago Katya borrowed a book from Natasha but has not returned it yet. At school, Natasha asks Katya if she has finished reading the book. (Track 3)

Наташа: **Катя, ты прочитала книгу?**
kah-tya, ti prah-chee-*tah*-luh *knee*-gooh?
Katya, have you finished reading the book?

Катя: **Книгу? А-а, нет ещё не прочитала. Я медленно читаю.**
knee-gooh? ah, nyet ee-*shyoh* nee prah-chee-*tah*-luh.
ya *myehd*-lee-nah chee-*tah*-yooh.
The book? Ah, no, I have not finished reading it yet.
I am a slow reader.

Наташа: **Ну, когда ты её прочитаешь?**
nooh, kahg-*dah* ti ee-*yoh* prah-chee-*tah*-eesh'?
Well, when will you finish reading it?

Катя: **Я не знаю когда я её прочитаю. Скоро! Я сегодня вечером буду её читать.**
ya nee *znah*-yooh kahg-*dah* ya ee-*yoh* prah-chee-*tah*-yooh. *skoh*-rah! ya see-*vohd*-nyeh *vyeh*-chee-ruhm *booh*-dooh ee-*yoh* chee-*taht'*.
I don't know when I will finish reading it. Soon! I will read it tonight.

Words to Know

ты прочитала	ti prah-chee-<u>tah</u>-luh	you have finished reading
нет ещё	nyet ee-<u>shyoh</u>	not yet
медленно читаю	<u>myehd</u>-lee-nah chee-<u>tah</u>-yooh	slow reader
когда	kahg-<u>dah</u>	when
ты прочитаешь	ti prah-chee-<u>tah</u>-eesh'	you will finish reading
Не знаю	nee <u>znah</u>-yooh	I don't know
скоро	<u>skoh</u>-rah	soon

Expressing possession with a special phrase

У меня есть (ooh mee-*nya* yehst') means *I have* and is a very important phrase in everyday life. It's also very easy to use. Imagine that you're a married man, and you're talking to a young, attractive woman who seems to be flirting with you. To avert any further misunderstanding, you may want to insert this statement early on in the conversation:

> **У меня есть жена.** (ooh mee-*nya* yest' zhi-*nah*.) (*I have a wife.*)

Note that in this expression, the thing that's "possessed" doesn't need to change for any case and stays in its dictionary (nominative case) form.

Helping yourself with modal verbs

Modal verbs are verbs that not only indicate an action but also impart such meanings as necessity, possibility, ability, or obligation. English modal verbs are *can, must, could, might, should, ought to, have to,* and so forth. Compared to this list, Russian has a very modest number of modal verbs.

Tables 3-23 and 3-24 show the conjugations of the two most commonly used Russian modal verbs: **мочь** (mohch') (*can*) and **должен** (*dohl*-zhin) (*must*).

Table 3-23	The Verb мочь
Pronoun	*Conjugation*
я (*I*)	могу (mah-*gooh*)
ты (*you,* informal singular)	можешь (*moh*-zhish)
он/она/оно (*he/she/it*)	может (*moh*-zhit)
мы (*we*)	можем (*moh*-zhim)
вы (*you,* formal singular or plural)	можете (*moh*-zhi-tee)
они (*they*)	могут (*moh*-gooht)

Table 3-24	The Verb должен
Pronoun	*Conjugation*
я (masculine), он, ты (*I, he, you* [informal singular])	должен (*dohl*-zhin)
я (feminine), она, ты (*I, she, you* [informal singular])	должна (dahl-*zhnah*)
оно (*it*)	должно (dahl-*zhnoh*)
мы, вы, они (*we, you* [formal singular or plural], *they*)	должны (dahl-*zhni*)

Imagine you're making a mental promise to yourself to do something today: *I must do it today!* If you're a man, use the form должен. If you're a woman, go with должна followed by the perfective infinitive for the verb *to do*: Я должен/должна это сделать (ya *dohl*-zhin/dahl-*zhnah eh*-tah *sdyeh*-luht').

Providing Extra Details with Adverbs

Adverbs are words like *very, quickly,* and *beautifully.* They add information to a verb, an adjective, or even another adverb. Russian adverbs are one of the most uncomplicated parts of speech. Unlike nouns, verbs, and adjectives (which we discuss earlier in this chapter), adverbs never change their form. In the following sections, you discover the main categories of Russian adverbs: adverbs of manner and adverbs of time.

Describing how

You use some adverbs to describe *how* an action is performed. These adverbs are called *adverbs of manner,* and they're easy to spot because they usually end in **-o.** In fact, you can consider the ending **-o** as a kind of equivalent of the ending *-ly* in English adverbs.

Following are some adverbs of manner you're likely to hear and use a lot:

- **быстро** (*bis*-truh) (*quickly*)
- **легко** (leek-*koh*) (*easily*)
- **медленно** (*myehd*-lee-nuh) (*slowly*)
- **неправильно** (nee-*prah*-veel'-nuh) (*incorrectly*)
- **плохо** (*ploh*-khah) (*poorly*)
- **правильно** (*prah*-veel'-nah) (*correctly*)
- **просто** (*proh*-stuh) (*simply*)
- **хорошо** (khah-rah-*shoh*) (*well*)

Describing when and how often

To describe when and how often an action takes place, Russian uses *time adverbs*. Like adverbs of manner, time adverbs are recognizable because they usually end in **-o** (although sometimes in **-a**).

Following are some of the most common time adverbs:

- **иногда** (ee-nahg-*dah*) (*sometimes*)
- **никогда** (nee-kahg-*dah*) (*never*)
- **обычно** (ah-*bich*-nuh) (*usually*)
- **поздно** (*pohz*-nuh) (*late*)
- **рано** (*rah*-nuh) (*early*)
- **редко** (*ryehd*-kah) (*rarely*)
- **скоро** (*skoh*-ruh) (*soon*)
- **всегда** (fseeg-*dah*) (*always*)
- **часто** (*chahs*-tah) (*often*)

Constructing Sentences Like a Pro

The whole point of understanding Russian grammar is to make it possible to actually create Russian-sounding sentences. In the following sections, you discover how to do just that. You have a lot of freedom in terms of word order when you create Russian sentences. You get tips on putting together the parts of a sentence, and you see how to connect different parts of a sentence with conjunctions. You also find out how to form questions in Russian.

Enjoying the freedom of word order

One of the biggest differences between English and Russian is that English tends to have a fixed order of words, whereas Russian enjoys a free order of words.

In English, word order can often determine the meaning of a sentence. For example, in English you say *The doctor operated on a patient*, but you never say *A patient operated on the doctor*. It just doesn't make sense. But in Russian, the sentence *The doctor operated on a patient* can be said in four different ways:

- ✔ **Доктор оперировал больного.** (*dohk*-tahr ah-pee-*ree*-rah-vuhl bahl'-*noh*-vah.) (Literally, *The doctor operated on a patient.*)
- ✔ **Больного оперировал доктор.** (Literally, *On a patient operated the doctor.*)
- ✔ **Оперировал больного доктор.** (Literally, *Operated on a patient the doctor.*)
- ✔ **Оперировал доктор больного.** (Literally, *Operated the doctor on a patient.*)

The meaning, however, is the same: The doctor operated on a patient.

Russians owe their freedom of word order to the Russian case system; this system tells you exactly what role each word plays in the sentence. (For additional information on cases, see the earlier section "The Case of Russian Cases: What Are They For?").

Creating a Russian sentence step by step

The easiest way to construct a sentence in Russian is to break it down into pieces. Follow these steps:

1. **Translate the subject.**

   For example, imagine that you want to say *I'm reading an interesting article.* In this sentence, *I* is the subject. The subject of the sentence in most situations is expressed by the nominative case. It means you just use the dictionary translation for *I*, which is **Я** (ya).

2. **Translate the verb.**

   In this case, you want to translate *am reading. To read* is **читать** (chee-*taht'*) in Russian. You use the imperfective verb because you need the present tense. You drop the infinitive ending and are now left with the stem **чита-**. Next, you need to add to this stem the ending of the present tense form that agrees with the subject; in this case, the subject is **Я,** so the ending you need is **-ю** (refer to Table 3-20). You now have the Russian translation for *I am reading*: **Я читаю** (ya chee-*tah*-yooh).

3. **Put together the rest of the sentence, which may involve direct objects, indirect objects, adjectives, and so on.**

   In this example, you have a noun (*article*) modified by an adjective (*interesting*). *Interesting article* in Russian is **интересная статья** (een-tee-*ryehs*-nuh-yeh stuh-*t'ya*), but this is only its nominative case form. You have to change it into another case because in your sentence this phrase is a direct object of the verb *am reading*. Thus, both the noun and the adjective need to be put in the accusative case. The word **статья** turns into **статью** (stuh-*t'yooh*); refer to Table 3-4. Because an adjective has to agree with the noun it modifies in gender and number, the word **интересная** becomes **интересную** (een-tee-*ryehs*-nooh-yooh); refer to Table 3-17.

So, here's your finished sentence:

> **Я читаю интересную статью.** (ya chee-*tah*-yooh een-tee-*ryehs*-nooh-yooh stuh-*t'yooh*.) (*I am reading an interesting article.*)

You've created a complete Russian sentence!

Connecting with conjunctions

Sometimes you may want to connect words or phrases in a sentence with conjunctions, which are words like *and*, *but*, and *however*. Check out their Russian equivalents:

- **а** (ah) (*but*)
- **и** (ee) (*and*)
- **но** (noh) (*but, however*)

Following are a couple examples:

> **Сегодня хорошо и тепло.** (see-*vohd*-nyeh khah-rah-*shoh* ee teep-*loh*.) (*It is nice and warm today.*)

> **Сегодня солнечно, но холодно.** (see-*vohd*-nyeh *sohl*-neech-nuh, noh *khoh*-luhd-nah.) (*It is sunny but cold today.*)

Forming questions

Forming questions in Russian is easy. You simply begin your sentence with a question word, such as

- где (gdyeh) (*where*)
- как (kahk) (*how*)
- когда (kahg-*dah*) (*when*)
- кто (ktoh) (*who*)
- почему (pah-chee-*mooh*) (*why*)
- что (shtoh) (*what*)

Then you form your sentence as if you were making a statement (see the earlier section "Creating a Russian sentence step by step").

For example, say a man you know makes an exciting statement:

Я сегодня не завтракал. (ya see-*vohd*-nyeh nee *zahv*-truh-kuhl.) (*I didn't have breakfast today.*)

Being a polite person, you need to somehow respond to this news. To demonstrate that you listened carefully to what he had to say, you may ask your interlocutor why he didn't have breakfast:

Почему ты сегодня не завтракал? (pah-chee-*mooh* ti see-*vohd*-nyeh nee *zahv*-truh-kuhl?) (*Why didn't you have breakfast today?*)

It's as simple as that! No auxiliary verbs; no changing the verb back to its infinitive form as you have to do in English! You don't even have to invert the subject and the verb. Asking questions is so much easier in Russian than in English, isn't it?

A special type of question involves the word *whose*. Say that you find something that was probably lost by somebody. As a good Samaritan, you want to find the person to whom this thing belongs. The Russian words for *whose* are чей (chyehy), чья (ch'ya), чьё (ch'yoh), and чьи (ch'ee). And, yes, you were correct in your premonition — the form indeed depends on the gender or number of the noun indicating the lost object:

- **You use чей with masculine nouns.** For example: **Чей это зонтик?** (chyehy *eh*-tah *zohn*-teek?) (*Whose umbrella is it?*)

- **You use чья with feminine nouns.** For example: **Чья это книга?** (ch'ya *eh*-tah *knee*-guh?) (*Whose book is it?*)

- **You use чьё with neuter nouns.** For example: **Чьё это пальто?** (ch'yoh *eh*-tah pahl'-*toh*?) (*Whose coat is it?*)

- **You use чьи with plural nouns.** For example: **Чьи это книги?** (ch'ee *eh*-tah *knee*-gee?) (*Whose books are these?*)

Fun & Games

Here is a list of all the singular case forms the word **мама** (*mah*-muh) (*mama*) can take: **мама, мамы, маме, маму, мамой, маме.** Match each form on the left to the grammatical case it corresponds to on the right by writing the number of the case on the line next to the corresponding word form. Check your answers in Appendix D.

мамы _____	1. Nominative
мамой _____	2. Genitive
маме _____	3. Accusative
маму _____	4. Dative
мама _____	5. Instrumental
маме _____	6. Prepositional

Chapter 4

Getting Started with Basic Expressions

. . . .

In This Chapter

▶ Using informal and formal versions of "you"

▶ Knowing how to say hello and goodbye

▶ Making sense of Russian names

▶ Introducing yourself and others

▶ Trying out some popular expressions

. . . .

*J*ust as in English, greetings and introductions in Russian allow you to establish contact with other people and make a good first impression. In this chapter, we cover the formal and informal versions of "you," saying hello and goodbye, understanding Russian names, and introducing yourself and other folks. We also provide you with some handy everyday phrases that will help you win the hearts of Russians.

To Whom Am I Speaking? Being Informal or Formal

When you want to say hello in Russian, you need to consider who you're talking to first. Unlike in English (but similar to some languages, like French, German, and Spanish), Russian uses two different words for the word *you* — the informal **ты** (ti) and the formal **вы** (vi). (In English, no matter whom you're talking to — your close friend, your boss, the President of the United States, or your dog — you use the word *you*.)

Here's how to know when to use which form of *you*:

✔ **Informal:** Use the informal **ты** *only* when you're speaking to your parents, grandparents, siblings, children, and close friends. Use it only when you're speaking to an individual, not to a group of people.

✔ **Formal:** Use the formal **вы** when you talk to your boss, acquaintances, older people, or people you don't know very well, and anytime you're speaking to more than one person.

If you're a young person, you can safely use **ты** when addressing people your age, such as your classmates. However, don't dare to use **ты** when talking to your teacher, no matter how young she is! Using **ты** to address an elderly woman or your teacher may be taken as extreme rudeness, unless people make allowances for the fact that you're not a native Russian speaker.

As a rule, you should use the formal **вы** when addressing somebody you've never met before, an official, a superior, or someone who is older than you. As you get to know a person better, you may switch to the informal **ты**. You even have a way of asking that person whether he's ready to switch to **ты**:

Можно на ты? (*Mohzh-nah nuh ti?*) (*May I call you informal "you"?*)

If you're at all unsure about whether to use **вы** or **ты**, use **вы** until the person you're addressing asks you to use **ты** or addresses you with **ты**.

Comings and Goings: Saying Hello and Goodbye

Being able to use greetings and goodbyes in a culturally appropriate manner is essential no matter where you are. In the following sections, we show you how to say hello in a variety of ways, give you a few greetings to use throughout the day, tell you how to ask and answer the perennial "How are you?" and wrap up a conversation with goodbyes.

Saying hello to different people

To greet one person with whom you're on informal **ты** (ti) terms, use the word **здравствуй** (*zdrah*-stvoohy) (*hello*). To greet a person with whom you're on formal **вы** (vi) terms, use the longer word **здравствуйте** (*zdrah*-stvoohy-tee) (*hello*). (We cover **ты** and **вы** in the previous section.)

Note that the first letter **в** in **здравствуй** and **здравствуйте** is silent. Otherwise, those words would be hard for even Russians to pronounce!

Здравствуйте is also used to address more than one person. Use it when addressing two or more people, even if they're children, members of your family, or close friends (people with whom you're usually informal).

An even more informal way of saying *hello* in Russian is **привет** (pree-*vyeht*). It's similar to the English *hi*. You should be on pretty familiar terms with a person before you use this greeting.

Greeting folks at any time of day

You have ways to greet people in Russian other than the bulky **здравствуй** or **здравствуйте**, but how you use these greetings depends on what time of day it is:

- **Доброе утро** (*dohb*-rah-ee *ooht*-rah) (*Good morning*)
- **Добрый день** (*dohb*-riy dyehn') (*Good afternoon*)
- **Добрый вечер** (*dohb*-riy *vyeh*-cheer) (*Good evening*)

Note that Russians use these expressions only as greetings, not at leave-taking. (See the later section "Taking your leave" for details on goodbyes.) You can also use these expressions without giving any thought to whether the person you greet should be addressed with **ты** or **вы**. No matter whom you greet, you can safely use any of these phrases.

Handling "How are you?"

The easiest and most popular way to ask *How are you?* is **Как дела?** (kahk dee-*lah*?). It literally means *How are things [going]?* Pretty simple, right?

A word of caution: In the English-speaking world, "How are you?" is just a standard phrase often used in place of a greeting. The person asking this formulaic question doesn't expect to get a full account of how you're actually doing. But in Russia it's different. Russians want to know everything! When they ask you how you're doing, they are, in fact, genuinely interested in how you're doing and expect you to give them a more or less accurate account of the most recent events in your life.

How should you reply to **Как дела?** Although optimistic Americans don't hesitate to say "terrific" or "wonderful," Russians usually respond with a more reserved **хорошо** (khah-rah-*shoh*) (*good*) or **нормально** (nahr-*mahl'*-nah) (*normal* or *okay*), or even a very neutral **ничего** (nee-chee-*voh*) (*so-so*; Literally: *nothing*) or **неплохо** (nee-*ploh*-khah) (*not bad*).

If you're truly feeling great, go ahead and answer **прекрасно** (pree-*krahs*-nah) (*wonderful*) or **великолепно** (vee-lee-kah-*lyehp*-nah) (*terrific*). But beware that by saying *terrific* or *wonderful*, you're putting your Russian friend on guard: Russians know all too well that life is not a picnic. To a Russian, wonderful and terrific events are the exception, not the rule. To be on the safe side, just say either **ничего** or **неплохо**.

And don't stop there! Be sure to ask the person how she's doing. You simply say **А у вас?** (ah ooh vahs?) (*And you?* [formal]). If you want to be less formal, say **А у тебя?** (ah ooh tee-*bya*?) (*And you?*)

Taking your leave

The usual way to say *goodbye* in almost any situation is **До свидания!** (dah svee-*dah*-nee-yeh!), which literally means *Till [the next] meeting.* If you're on informal terms with somebody, you may also say **Пока** (pah-*kah*) (*Bye* or *See you later*).

The phrase you use when leaving in the evening or just before bed is **Спокойной ночи** (spah-*kohy*-nahy *noh*-chee) (*Good night*). The phrase works for both formal and informal situations.

Talkin' the Talk

Sasha (**Саша**) bumps into her classmate Oleg (**Олег**) on the subway. Sasha is just about to get off. (Track 4)

Олег:	**Саша, привет!**
	sah-shuh, pree-*vyeht!*
	Sasha, hi!

Саша:	**Ой, Олег! Привет! Как дела?**
	ohy, ah-*lyehk!* pree-*vyeht!* kahk dee-*lah?*
	Oh, Oleg! Hi! How are you?

Олег:	**Ничего. А у тебя?**
	nee-chee-*voh.* ah ooh tee-*bya?*
	Okay. And you?

Саша:	**Неплохо. Ой, это моя станция. До свидания, Олег.**
	nee-*ploh*-khah. ohy, *eh*-tah mah-*ya stahn*-tsi-yeh. dah svee-*dah*-nee-yeh, ah-*lyehk.*
	Not bad. Oh, this is my station. Goodbye, Oleg.

Олег:	**Пока!**
	pah-*kah!*
	Bye!

Words to Know

привет	pree-_vyeht_	hi
Как дела?	kahk _dee-lah?_	How are you?
ничего	nee-chee-_voh_	okay
А у тебя?	ah ooh tee-_bya?_	And you?
неплохо	nee-_ploh_-khah	not bad
до свидания	dah svee-_dah_-nee-yeh	goodbye
пока	pah-_kah_	bye

The Name Game: Deciphering Russian Names

The Russian word for _name_ is **имя** (_ee_-myeh), but you may not hear this word when people ask about your name. That's because what they actually ask is not "What is your name?" but literally, "How do people/they call you?" — **как вас зовут?** (kahk vahs zah-_vooht?_) in formal situations or **как тебя зовут?** (kahk tee-_bya_ zah-_vooht?_) in informal situations. Consequently, when you answer the question, you say how people, in fact, call you — for example, if your name is John, you say

> **Меня зовут Джон.** (mee-_nya_ zah-_vooht_ dzhohn.) (_My name is John;_ Literally: _They call me John._)

Saying names in Russian is a bit more complicated than in English. The reason is that in introducing themselves, especially in formal situations, Russians use the _patronymic_ (father's first name) right after the first name. The patronymic usually has the ending **-вич** (veech), meaning _son of,_ or **-овна/-евна** (_ohv_-nuh/ _yehv_-nuh), meaning _daughter of._ For example, a man named **Борис** (Boris) whose father's name is **Иван** (Ivan) would be known as **Борис Иванович** (**Иванович,** pronounced ee-_vah_-nah-veech, is the patronymic). A woman named **Анна** (Anna) whose father's name is **Иван** (Ivan) would be known as **Анна Ивановна** (**Ивановна,** pronounced ee-_vah_-nahv-nuh, is the patronymic). A Russian almost never formally addresses a person named **Михаил** (Mikhail) as just **Михаил** but rather as **Михаил** plus his patronymic with the suffix **-ович/-евич** (_oh_-veech/_yeh_-veech) (for instance, **Михаил Николаевич** for Mikhail Nikolayevich or **Михаил Борисович** for Mikhail Borisovich).

You may say that Russians have three names. The first name is a baptismal name; the second name is his or her father's first name with the ending **-ович/-евич** for men or **-овна/-евна** for women; and the third is the last name, or the family name.

Men's last names and women's last names have different endings. That's because Russian last names have genders. Although many Russian male last names have the ending **-ов** (ohf), female names take the ending **-ова** (*oh*-vuh). Imagine that your new acquaintance, **Анна Ивановна Иванова**, is a married woman. Her husband's last name isn't **Иванова** (ee-vuh-*noh*-vuh), but **Иванов** (ee-vuh-*nohf*). (Yes, your friend Anna has a father and a husband with the same name: Ivan.)

No matter what your relation is to another person (either informal or formal), you can still address that person by his or her first name and patronymic. So if you're unsure whether you're on informal **ты** or formal **вы** terms with someone, go ahead and address the person by the first name and patronymic, just to be safe. When you're clearly on friendly terms with the person, you can switch to using the first name only.

Breaking the Ice: Making Introductions

Making a good first impression is important for the beginning of any relationship. Russians tend to be more formal than Americans in how they approach a person they've just met. In the following sections, we show you the best ways to introduce yourself to somebody you've just met. We also show you phrases to use when getting acquainted with someone, and the best way to introduce your friends, family, and colleagues to new people.

Getting acquainted

In English, introducing yourself is the best way to start a conversation with somebody you don't know. Not so in Russian. When introducing themselves, Russians are a little more ceremonial. Russians like to suggest getting acquainted first, by saying "Let's get acquainted!" They have two ways to say this, depending on whether they're on formal **вы** (vi) or informal **ты** (ti) terms with the person (see "To Whom Am I Speaking? Being Informal or Formal" earlier in this chapter for info on these terms) as well as how many people they're addressing:

✔ **Addressing a person formally or addressing two or more people:**

Давайте познакомимся! (duh-*vahy*-tee pah-znuh-*koh*-meem-syeh!) (*Let's get acquainted!*)

✔ **Addressing a person informally:**

Давай познакомимся! (duh-*vahy* pah-znuh-*koh*-meem-syeh!) (*Let's get acquainted!*)

If somebody says one of these phrases to you, you should politely accept the suggestion. To respond, you can just use the first word of the question you were asked, which makes your task much easier:

✔ **If you were addressed formally or are in a group of people:**

Давайте (duh-*vahy*-tee) (*Okay*; Literally: *Let's*)

✔ **If you were addressed informally:**

Давай (duh-*vahy*) (*Okay*; Literally: *Let's*)

Introducing yourself

To introduce yourself in Russian, just say **Меня зовут** (Mee-*nya* zah-*vooht*) plus your name. (See "The Name Game: Deciphering Russian Names," earlier in this chapter, for how to ask others for their names.)

When you're introducing yourself, formality doesn't matter. **Меня зовут** and the other Russian phrases in this section are appropriate in both formal and informal situations.

After you're introduced to someone, you may want to say *Nice to meet you*. In Russian, you say **очень приятно** (*oh*-cheen' pree-*yat*-nah) (Literally: *very pleasant*). The person you've been introduced to may then reply **мне тоже** (mnyeh *toh*-zheh) (*same here*).

Introducing your friends, family, and colleagues

Everyday, common introductions are easy in Russian. When you want to introduce your friends, all you need to say is **Это . . .** (*eh*-tah . . .) (*This is . . .*). Then you simply add the name of the person (see "The Name Game: Deciphering Russian Names" earlier in this chapter for more info about names).

As in English, the same construction (**Это** + the person you're introducing) applies to a broad circle of people, including your family members. For example, to introduce your mother, you say

Это моя мама. (*eh*-tuh mah-*ya mah*-muh.) (*This is my mother.*)

To introduce your brother, you just say

> **Это мой брат.** (*eh*-tah mohy braht.) (*This is my brother.*)

To introduce other members of your family, see Chapter 7, where we provide words indicating other family members.

You can use the same simple method to introduce anybody. For example, when introducing your co-worker, you may want to say

> **Это мой коллега, Антон Александрович.** (*eh*-tah mohy kah-*lyeh*-guh, un-*tohn* uh-leek-*sahn*-drah-veech.) (*This is my colleague, Anton Aleksandrovich.*)

Talkin' the Talk

Anna (**Анна**) is approached by her friend, Viktor (**Виктор**), and his acquaintance, Boris Alekseevich (**Борис Алексеевич**). (Track 5)

Виктор:	**Ой, привет, Анна!** ohy, pree-*vyeht*, *ah*-nuh! *Oh, hi Anna!*
Анна:	**Привет Виктор! Как дела?** pree-*vyeht veek*-tahr! kahk dee-*lah?* *Hi, Viktor! How are you?*
Виктор:	**Ничего. А у тебя?** nee-chee-*voh*. ah ooh tee-*bya?* *Okay. And you?*
Анна:	**Неплохо.** nee-*ploh*-khah. *Not bad.*
Виктор:	**А это Борис Алексеевич.** ah *eh*-tah bah-*rees* uh-leek-*syeh*-ee-veech. *And this is Boris Alekseevich.*
Анна:	**Здравствуйте! Давайте познакомимся!** zdrah-stvoohy-tee! duh-*vahy*-tee pah-znuh-*koh*-meem-syeh! *Hello! Let's get acquainted!*
Борис Алексеевич:	**Давайте! Меня зовут Борис.** duh-*vahy*-tee! mee-*nya* zah-*vooht* bah-*rees*. *Let's! My name is Boris.*

Анна:	**Очень приятно!**
	oh-cheen' pree-*yat*-nah!
	Nice to meet you!

Борис Алексеевич:	**Мне тоже.**
	mnyeh *toh*-zheh.
	Nice to meet you, too.
	(Literally: *Same here.*)

Words to Know

Это	<u>eh</u>-tah	This is
Давайте познакомимся!	duh-<u>vahy</u>-tee pah-znuh-<u>koh</u>-meem-syeh!	Let's get acquainted!
Меня зовут	mee-<u>nya</u> zah-voo<u>ht</u>	My name is
Очень приятно!	*oh*-cheen' pree-<u>yat</u>-nah!	Nice to meet you!
мне тоже	mnyeh <u>toh</u>-zheh	likewise

You Can Say That Again: Using Popular Expressions

Using popular expressions is one way to make a great first impression when speaking Russian. We recommend that you memorize the phrases in the following sections, because they can come in handy in almost any situation.

Speaking courteously

Don't forget the manners your mother taught you when you're with a Russian speaker. Try out these simple phrases:

- ✔ пожалуйста (pah-*zhahl*-stuh) (*please* or *you're welcome* in response to *thank you*)

- ✔ Да, пожалуйста. (dah, pah-*zhahl*-stuh.) (*Yes, please.*)

- **Спасибо**. (spuh-*see*-bah.) (*Thank you.*)

- **Нет, спасибо.** (nyeht, spuh-*see*-bah.) (*No, thank you.*)

- **Спасибо большое.** (spuh-*see*-bah bahl'-*shoh*-ee.) (*Thank you very much.*)

You often use the word **пожалуйста** just after the verb when making a polite request, as in the following sentences:

> **Повторите, пожалуйста.** (pahf-tah-*ree*-tee, pah-*zhahl*-stuh.) (*Please repeat what you said.*)

> **Говорите, пожалуйста, медленнее.** (gah-vah-*ree*-tee, pah-*zhahl*-stuh, *myehd*-lee-nee-ee.) (*Please speak a little more slowly.*)

Excusing yourself

In English you say *sorry* to apologize for something you've done wrong and *excuse me* when you want to attract somebody's attention or make an interjection. Russian uses two words to express either meaning: **извините** (eez-vee-*nee*-tee) or **извините** (eez-vee-*nee*-tee) (*sorry* or *excuse me*).

To be even more polite when you excuse yourself in Russian, you can add the word **пожалуйста** (pah-*zhahl*-stuh) (*please*), as in the following sentences:

> **Извините, пожалуйста, мне пора.** (eez-vee-*nee*-tee, pah-*zhahl*-stuh, mnyeh pah-*rah*.) (*Excuse me, it's time for me to go.*)

> **Извините, пожалуйста, я не понимаю.** (eez-vee-*nee*-tee, pah-*zhahl*-stuh, ya nee pah-nee-*mah*-yooh.) (*Excuse me, I don't understand.*)

Arming yourself with other handy phrases

Someone new to speaking Russian (in Russia or anywhere else in the world) may want to know these common phrases:

- **Добро пожаловать!** (dahb-*roh* pah-*zhah*-lah-vuht'!) (*Welcome!*)

- **Поздравляю!** (pahz-druhv-*lya*-yooh!) (*Congratulations!*)

- **Желаю удачи!** (zhi-*lah*-yooh ooh-*dah*-chee!) (*Good luck!*)

- **Всего хорошего!** (vsee-*voh* khah-*roh*-shi-vah!) (*All the best!*)

- **Приятного аппетита!** (pree-*yat*-nah-vah uh-pee-*tee*-tuh!) (*Bon appetit!*)

✔ **Жалко!** (*zhahl*-kah!) (*Too bad!*)

✔ **Можно задать вам вопрос?** (*mohzh*-nah zuh-*daht'* vahm vah-*prohs*?)
(*Can I ask you a question?*)

In addition to the preceding phrases, Russians often use the following words
to express a wide range of emotions, such as fear, surprise, delight, anger,
and more (the expressions are interchangeable):

✔ **Ой!** (ohy!) (*Oh!*)

✔ **Ай!** (ahy!) (*Ah!*)

Talking about Talking: The Verb "To Speak"

If you've checked out all the expressions we provide earlier in this chapter,
you may be wondering how to say *to speak* in Russian. That's easy; it's **говорить** (gah-vah-*reet'*) (*to speak*). It's one of those second-conjugation verbs we
mention in Chapter 3. This is how it conjugates in the present tense:

Conjugation	Pronunciation
Я говорю	ya gah-vah-*ryooh*
Ты говоришь	ti gah-vah-*reesh'*
Он/она говорит	ohn/ah-*nah* gah-vah-*reet*
Мы говорим	mi gah-vah-*reem*
Вы говорите	vi gah-vah-*ree*-tee
Они говорят	ah-*nee* gah-vah-*ryat*

To find out whether your Russian conversation partner speaks English, you
may simply ask

> **Вы говорите по-английски?** (vi gah-vah-*ree*-tee pah-uhn-*gleey*-skee?) (*Do
> you speak English?*)

Keep in mind that you should use the formal version of *you* in this question!

Practice saying hello in Russian to the following people. Should you use **Здравствуйте** (*Zdrah*-stvoohy-tee) or **Здравствуй** (*Zdrah*-stvoohy)? Circle the correct choice in each of the following instances. Find the answers in Appendix D.

1. Your close friend   **Здравствуйте**   **Здравствуй**

2. Your boss   **Здравствуйте**   **Здравствуй**

3. Your teacher   **Здравствуйте**   **Здравствуй**

4. Your doctor   **Здравствуйте**   **Здравствуй**

5. Your pet   **Здравствуйте**   **Здравствуй**

6. A group of friends   **Здравствуйте**   **Здравствуй**

7. Several children   **Здравствуйте**   **Здравствуй**

Chapter 5

Getting Your Numbers, Times, and Measurements Straight

*W*hen you dive into the basics of any foreign language, a few tasks are especially important; you need to find out how to count, tell time, talk about dates, and measure things. This chapter has you covered on how to handle these fundamentals in Russian.

One by One: Counting in Russian

You probably don't need to know much about numbers beyond talking about how many siblings you have, telling time, or counting your money. But just in case, knowing the numbers in the following sections should help you with any other possible counting needs that may crop up.

The harsh truth is that each Russian **числительное** (chee-*slee*-teel'-nah-ee) (*number*) changes its form for all six cases! But unless you plan to spend a lot of time at mathematics or accounting conferences conducted in Russian, you won't find yourself in many practical situations in which you need to know all the different forms. That said, you definitely need to know numbers. So in the following sections, we give you all the numbers you need to know in the nominative case, with a few special changes to remember when you're using numbers with nouns. (Flip to Chapter 3 for an introduction to cases.)

From zero to ten

You're likely to use the numbers from zero to ten most often:

- ✔ **ноль** (nohl') (*zero*)
- ✔ **один** (ah-*deen*) (*one*)
- ✔ **два** (dvah) (*two*)
- ✔ **три** (tree) (*three*)
- ✔ **четыре** (chee-*ti*-ree) (*four*)
- ✔ **пять** (pyat') (*five*)
- ✔ **шесть** (shehst') (*six*)
- ✔ **семь** (syehm') (*seven*)
- ✔ **восемь** (*voh*-seem') (*eight*)
- ✔ **девять** (*dyeh*-vyeht') (*nine*)
- ✔ **десять** (*dyeh*-syeht') (*ten*)

From 11 to 19

Next in line are the numbers from 11 through 19. Here they are:

- ✔ **одиннадцать** (ah-*dee*-nuht-tsuht') (*11*)
- ✔ **двенадцать** (dvee-*naht*-tsuht') (*12*)
- ✔ **тринадцать** (tree-*naht*-tsuht') (*13*)
- ✔ **четырнадцать** (chee-*tir*-nuht-tsuht') (*14*)
- ✔ **пятнадцать** (peet-*naht*-tsuht') (*15*)
- ✔ **шестнадцать** (shis-*naht*-tsuht') (*16*)
- ✔ **семнадцать** (seem-*naht*-tsuht') (*17*)
- ✔ **восемнадцать** (vah-seem-*naht*-tsuht') (*18*)
- ✔ **девятнадцать** (dee-veet-*naht*-tsuht') (*19*)

Starting with the numeral 11, Russian numerals up through 19 follow a recognizable pattern of adding -**надцать** (*naht*-tsuht') to the numerals 1 through 9 (see the preceding section). You can, however, find a few slight deviations to this rule:

✔ двенадцать (dvee-*naht*-tsuht') (*12*) uses две (dvyeh) (*two*) rather than два (dvah) (*two*).

✔ четырнадцать (chee-*tir*-nuht-tsuht') (*14*) loses the final е in четыре (chee-*ti*-ree) (*four*).

✔ The numerals 15–19 all lose the final soft signs contained in 5–9. (For example, *15* is пятнадцать and not пятьнадцать).

From 20 to 99

After you master the first ten numerals, learning to say 21, 22, 32, 41, 52, and so on is as easy as saying one, two, three (sorry, no pun intended). The following list shows you the Russian words for multiples of ten:

✔ двадцать (*dvaht*-tsuht') (*20*)

✔ тридцать (*treet*-tsuht') (*30*)

✔ сорок (*soh*-rahk) (*40*)

✔ пятьдесять (pee-dee-*syat'*) (*50*)

✔ шестьдесять (shis-dee-*syat'*) (*60*)

✔ семьдесять (*syehm'*-dee-syeht') (*70*)

✔ восемьдесять (*voh*-seem'-dee-syeht') (*80*)

✔ девяносто (dee-vee-*nohs*-tah) (*90*)

You may notice that the numbers from 50 to 80 are created in a way that's similar to that of the numbers from 11 to 19, in this case, by adding десять to a singular numeral, which literally means *five of tens*, *six of tens*, and so on.

Although the word *dozen* — дюжина (*dyooh*-zhi-nuh) — exists in Russian, Russians are accustomed to counting by tens rather than by dozens. The price of eggs in a Russian grocery store, for example, is based on the purchase of ten eggs, not a dozen. Whereas in English you may say "dozens of people," Russians literally say "tens of people."

To say 21, 22, 31, 32, 41, 42, and so on, all you need to do is add the numerals 1 through 9 (which we list earlier in this chapter) to the numerals 20, 30, 40, and so on. For example, you form the numbers 21 and 22 like this:

✔ двадцать один (*dvaht*-tsuht' ah-*deen*) (*21*)

✔ двадцать два (*dvaht*-tsuht' dvah) (*22*)

From 100 to 999

You form each of the following numerals (except 100 and 200) by adding either **-ста** (stuh) or **–сот** (soht) to the numerals 3–10:

- ✔ **сто** (stoh) (*100*)
- ✔ **двести** (*dvyehs*-tee) (*200*)
- ✔ **триста** (*tree*-stuh) (*300*)
- ✔ **четыреста** (chee-*ti*-rees-tuh) (*400*)
- ✔ **пятьсот** (peet'-*soht*) (*500*)
- ✔ **шестьсот** (shi-*soht*) (*600*)
- ✔ **семьсот** (seem'-*soht*) (*700*)
- ✔ **восемьсот** (vah-seem'-*soht*) (*800*)
- ✔ **девятьсот** (dee-veet'-*soht*) (*900*)

Creating composite numbers in Russian is easy. Say you need to say 155 in Russian. Translate 100 into **сто**. Fifty in Russian is **пятьдесят**. Five is **пять**. And there you have it: The number 155 is **сто пятьдесят пять** (stoh pee-dee-*syat* pyat'). This process also applies to numbers larger than 1,000 (see the next section).

From 1,000 to beyond

In the following list, note how the word **тысяча** (*ti*-see-chuh) (*thousand*) changes form: In 1,000, Russian uses the noun in the nominative form; in 2,000, 3,000, and 4,000, the case is genitive singular; and from 5,000 to 9,000 the case again changes, this time to genitive plural! Also, note that when you say 1,000, you can skip the word for "one."

- ✔ **тысяча** (*ti*-see-chuh) (*1,000*)
- ✔ **две тысячи** (dvyeh *ti*-see-chee) (*2,000*)
- ✔ **три тысячи** (tree *ti*-see-chee) (*3,000*)
- ✔ **четыре тысячи** (chee-*ti*-ree *ti*-see-chee) (*4,000*)
- ✔ **пять тысяч** (pyat' *ti*-syehch) (*5,000*)
- ✔ **шесть тысяч** (shehst' *ti*-syehch) (*6,000*)
- ✔ **семь тысяч** (syehm' *ti*-syehch) (*7,000*)
- ✔ **восемь тысяч** (*voh*-seem' *ti*- syehch) (*8,000*)
- ✔ **девять тысяч** (*dyeh*-vyeht' *ti*-syehch) (*9,000*)

Тысячи is the genitive singular form and **тысяч** is the genitive plural form of **тысяча**. Notice how 2,000–4,000 require the genitive singular form, and 5,000–9,000 require the genitive plural form.

To say 10,000, use the number **десять** (*dyeh*-seet') (*10*) followed by the genitive plural form **тысяч**. This rule also applies to numbers beyond 10,000. Here are a few examples:

- ✔ **десять тысяч** (*dyeh*-seet' *ti*-seech) (*10,000*)

- ✔ **пятьдесят тысяч** (pee-dee-*syat ti*-seech) (*50,000*)

- ✔ **сто тысяч** (stoh *ti*-seech) (*100,000*)

And one really big number is quite simple: *1,000,000* is **миллион** (mee-lee-*ohn*).

Special rules for counting things and people

In Russian, counting just for the sake of counting — to while away time, perhaps — is one thing, but counting things or people — for example, money or members of your family — is something different. Not only does the numeral change sometimes, but the word indicating what you're counting changes as well. We provide some special rules to keep in mind in the following sections.

The number 1 followed by a noun

Don't assume that *one* will always remain **один** (ah-*deen*). Contrary to your expectations, it won't. Only if the noun you're referring to is masculine do you say **один** followed by the noun, as in **один человек** (ah-*deen* chee-lah-*vyehk*) (*one man*). If the noun is feminine, you say **одна**, as in **одна девушка** (ahd-*nah* dyeh-voohsh-kuh) (*one young woman*). And if the noun is neuter, you say **одно**, as in **одно окно** (ahd-*noh* ahk-*noh*) (*one window*). (See Chapter 3 for details on the gender of nouns.)

The number 2 followed by a noun

If you're talking about nouns that are masculine or neuter, you say **два** (dvah) for the number *two*; if the noun is feminine, use **две** (dvyeh) instead. The noun used with *two* needs to be put into the genitive singular case, as in **два человека** (dvah chee-lah-*vyeh*-kuh) (*two men*) or **два окна** (dvah ahk-*nah*) (*two windows*). (For rules on forming the genitive case for singular nouns, see Chapter 3.)

The numbers 3 and 4 followed by a noun

Like the numeral **два** (dvah) (*two*), **три** (tree) (*three*) and **четыре** (chee-*ti*-ree) (*four*) also require the noun used after them to be put into the genitive singular case. Fortunately, these numbers don't care about the gender of the noun they refer to. In other words, whether you say *four women* or *four men*, *four* is **четыре** in both phrases, even though the gender of the following nouns is obviously different.

The numbers 5 through 9 followed by a noun

Any noun you use after the numerals 5–9 must be put into the genitive plural case, as in the phrases **пять девушек** (pyat' *dyeh*-vooh-shik) (*five young women*) and **семь мальчиков** (syehm' *mahl*-chee-kahf) (*seven boys*). (See Chapter 3 for more on cases.) Unlike **один** (*one*) and **два** (*two*), these numbers don't change their form depending on the gender of the noun they're used with.

Ordinal numbers

Ordinal numbers are numbers that indicate order, such as first, second, and third. We list the first 20 here:

✔ **первый** (*pyehr*-viy) (*first*)

✔ **второй** (ftah-*rohy*) (*second*)

✔ **третий** (*tryeh*-teey) (*third*)

✔ **четвёртый** (cheet-*vyohr*-tiy) (*fourth*)

✔ **пятый** (*pya*-tiy) (*fifth*)

✔ **шестой** (shis-*tohy*) (*sixth*)

✔ **седьмой** (seed'-*mohy*) (*seventh*)

✔ **восьмой** (vahs'-*mohy*) (*eighth*)

✔ **девятый** (dee-*vya*-tiy) (*ninth*)

✔ **десятый** (dee-*sya*-tiy) (*tenth*)

✔ **одиннадцатый** (ah-*dee*-nuht-suh-tiy) (*11th*)

✔ **двенадцатый** (dvee-*naht*-suh-tiy) (*12th*)

✔ **тринадцатый** (tree-*naht*-suh-tiy) (*13th*)

✔ **четырнадцатый** (chee-*tir*-nuht-suh-tiy) (*14th*)

✔ **пятнадцатый** (peet-*naht*-suh-tiy) (*15th*)

✔ **шестнадцатый** (shis-*naht*-suh-tiy) (*16th*)

✔ **семнадцатый** (seem-*naht*-suh-tiy) (*17th*)

✔ **восемнадцатый** (vah-seem-*naht*-suh-tiy) (*18th*)

✔ **девятнадцатый** (dee-veet-*naht*-suh-tiy) (*19th*)

✔ **двадцатый** (dvuht-*sah*-tiy) (*20th*)

Russian uses a principle similar to one in English with ordinal numbers higher than 20. You say the first numeral (or numerals) normally (as you would a cardinal number), and put only the final numeral into ordinal form: for example, **двадцать первый** (*dvaht-*suht' *pyehr-*viy) *(21st)* or **сорок шестой** (*soh-*ruhk shis-*tohy*) *(46th).*

In Russian, ordinal numbers behave just like adjectives, which means they always agree in case, number, and gender with the nouns they precede. For more on this subject, see Chapter 3.

The Clock's Ticking: Telling (And Asking About) Time

Time is precious, especially when you travel: Some days, you never have enough of it! In this section, you find out how to state the **время** (*vryeh-*myeh) *(time)*, use terms for different times of the day and night, and inquire about the time.

Counting the hours

To indicate time, Russian uses the word **час** (chahs) *(hour)*. In other words, when stating that it's 2 o'clock, for example, Russians literally say "two hours." The noun **час** takes different cases depending on the numeral being used (see Chapter 3 for details on cases):

- After 1, you use the nominative case.
- After 2, 3, and 4, you use the genitive singular case, which is **часа** (chuh-*sah*).
- After 5 to 12, you use the genitive plural case, which is **часов** (chuh-*sohf*).

Adding the word **сейчас** (seey-*chahs*) *(now)* at the beginning of the statement indicating time is also customary. Here are a couple examples:

Сейчас час. (seey-*chahs* chahs.) *(It's 1 o'clock now.)*

Сейчас пять часов. (seey-*chahs* pyat' chuh-*sohf*.) *(It's 5 o'clock now.)*

Marking the minutes

In their fast-paced lives, most people plan their days not only down to the hour but also down to the **минута** (mee-*nooh*-tuh) *(minute)* or even the **секунда** (see-*koohn*-duh) *(second)*.

To indicate minutes when telling the time, use the simplest method: Just add the word **пятнадцать** (peet-*naht*-tsuht') (*15*), **тридцать** (*treet*-tsuht') (*30*), or **сорок пять** (*soh*-rahk pyat') (*45*) to the word indicating the hour. If, for example, it's 2:30 now, you can simply say **Сейчас два тридцать** (seey-*chahs* dvah *treet*-tsuht') (*It is 2:30 now*). If it's 2:13, say **Сейчас два тринадцать** (seey-*chahs* dvah tree-*nah*-tsuht'). Note that you don't need to use the word for "hour" when the time includes minutes.

However, if you happen to ask a Russian speaker about time (as we show you later in this chapter), prepare to hear something like the following:

> **Сейчас половина первого.** (seey-*chahs* pah-lah-*vee*-nuh *pyehr*-vah-vah.)
> (*It is half past twelve.*)

> **Сейчас половина десятого.** (seey-*chahs* pah-lah-*vee*-nuh dee-*sya*-tah-vah.)
> (*It is half past nine.*)

What Russians say in the preceding phrases roughly corresponds to the English phrase "Now is half of the [second/third/fourth and so on] hour," which seems to be somewhat logical, doesn't it? Note that in these expressions, the hour is indicated by the ordinal number in the genitive case (see Chapter 3). You may also hear **Сейчас четверть пятого** (seey-*chahs* chyeht-veert' *pya*-tah-vah) (*It's a quarter after four*) or **Сейчас без четверти семь** (seey-*chahs* byehs *chyeht*-veer-tee syehm') (*It's a quarter to seven*).

In all honesty, however, we don't believe that a Russian whom you ask about time will subject you to the torture of comprehending these complicated time phrases. After all, Russians have a reputation for being very compassionate people. That's why, most likely, if you do ask a passerby **Сколько сейчас времени?** (*skohl'*-kah see-*chahs* *vryeh*-mee-nee?) (*What time is it?*) and he recognizes you as a foreigner, he'll simply roll up his sleeve and show you the face of his own watch, so you can see the time for yourself.

Distinguishing day and night

Here are the words indicating the times of the day (the word *day*, by the way, is **день,** pronounced dyehn'):

- **утро** (*ooht*-rah) (*morning*)
- **день** (dyehn') (*afternoon*)
- **вечер** (*vyeh*-cheer) (*evening*)
- **ночь** (nohch') (*night*)

Be careful when you use these words following phrases that indicate the time, such as "2 o'clock in the afternoon." In situations like this, the words **утро, день, вечер,** and **ночь** take their genitive singular form, becoming **утра** (ooht-*rah*), **вечера** (*vyeh*-chee-ruh), **дня** (dnya), and **ночи** (*noh*-chee). For example, you say **два часа дня** (dvah chuh-*sah* dnya) (*two o'clock in the afternoon*).

Note, too, that Russians have their own way of dividing the 24-hour period into morning, afternoon, evening, and night:

- ✔ **утро** (*ooht*-rah) (*morning*): From 4 a.m. to noon or 1 p.m.

- ✔ **день** (dyehn') (*afternoon*): From noon or 1 p.m. to 5 or 6 p.m.

- ✔ **вечер** (*vyeh*-cheer) (*evening*): From 5 or 6 p.m. to 11 p.m. or midnight

- ✔ **ночь** (nohch) (*night*): From midnight to 4 a.m.

The Russian word for *noon* is **полдень** (*pohl*-deen'), and the word for *midnight* is **полночь** (*pohl*-nahch).

Understanding the 24-hour clock

Although Russians tend to use the 12-hour clock in everyday life, Russia, like other European countries, uses the 24-hour clock as the official time for schedules, timetables, meetings, and so forth.

The rules of stating time in a European (24-hour) way are the same as we state earlier: Just use the word **часов** after the numeral indicating an hour. So, in an e-mail message to employees, the boss may announce a 2 p.m. meeting like this:

> **Собрание начнётся в 14 часов.** (sahb-*rah*-nee-yeh nuhch-*nyoht*-syeh v chee-*tir*-nuht-tsuht' chuh-*sohf.*) (*The meeting will begin at 14 hours.*)

Note that the ending time of the meeting isn't even mentioned — expect the meeting to be very long.

Listen carefully for these numbers when you're at a Russian airport or train station! At these places, you may hear something like this:

Вылет самолёта на Москву в 20 часов 13 минут. (*vi*-leet suh-mah-*lyoh*-tuh nuh Mahs-*kvooh* v *dvaht*-tsuht' chuh-*sohf* tree-*naht*-tsuht' mee-*noot.*) (*The flight to Moscow is scheduled to depart at 20:13.*)

Asking for the time

With Russia still being the largest country in the world with nine time zones, keeping track of time there is especially important. A single flight from one Russian city to another may bring you to a completely different time zone. So if you don't have an expensive watch that shows the time on all the continents, you may want to arm yourself with this question ahead of time (sorry, no pun intended):

Сколько сейчас времени? (*skohl'*-kah seey-*chahs vryeh*-mee-nee?) (*What time is it?*)

The best way to attract a stranger's attention is to add **Извините** (eez-vee-*nee*-tee) (*Excuse me*) to the beginning of your question about time. You may even slightly touch the person to attract her attention. Russians don't seem to worry too much about "personal space" the way people in English-speaking countries do, and touching is okay.

Talkin' the Talk

John (**Джон**) is late to meet a friend in Moscow; he stops and asks a **прохожий** (prah-*khoh*-zhiy) (*passerby*) on the street to tell him the time. (Track 6)

Джон:	**Извините!** eez-vee-*nee*-tee! *Excuse me!*
Прохожий:	**Да?** dah? *Yes?*
Джон:	**Сколько сейчас времени?** *skohl'*-kah seey-*chahs vryeh*-mee-nee? *What time is it?*
Прохожий:	**Сейчас? Сейчас половина первого.** seey-*chahs*? seey-*chahs* pah-lah-*vee*-nuh *pyehr*-vah-vah. *Now? It is half past 12.*
Джон:	**А, спасибо.** ah, spuh-*see*-bah. *Ah, thank you.*

Words to Know

извините	*eez-vee-<u>nee</u>-tee*	*excuse me*
Сколько сейчас времени?	*<u>skohl</u>'-kah see-<u>chahs</u> <u>vryeh</u>-mee-nee?*	*What time is it?*
сейчас	*seey-<u>chahs</u>*	*now*
половина первого	*puh-luh-<u>vee</u>-nuh <u>pyehr</u>-vah-vah*	*half past 12*
спасибо	*spuh-<u>see</u>-bah*	*thank you*

It's a Date! Checking Out the Calendar

After you're comfortable with numbers and times in Russian, it only makes sense to put them together and talk about the calendar. In the following sections, we explain how to name days, months, years, seasons, and dates; we also show you how to talk about time relative to the present.

Naming the days of the week

Here are the days of the week in Russian. Note that in Russian, you don't capitalize the first letter:

- **понедельник** (pah-nee-*dyehl'*-neek) (*Monday*)
- **вторник** (*ftohr*-neek) (*Tuesday*)
- **среда** (sree-*dah*) (*Wednesday*)
- **четверг** (cheet-*vyehrk*) (*Thursday*)
- **пятница** (*pyat*-nee-tsuh) (*Friday*)
- **суббота** (sooh-*boh*-tuh) (*Saturday*)
- **воскресенье** (vahs-kree-*syehn'*-ee) (*Sunday*)

You may have noticed that the list begins not with Sunday but with Monday. That's because Russians believe that Monday, rather than Sunday, is the first day of the week. And, as a matter of fact, the word itself indicates that this is the case because the word **неделя** (nee-*dyeh*-lyeh) is *week* in English. In other words, **понедельник** means *the day beginning the week*. Discovering the story behind the origin of other days of the week is also fascinating:

- **вторник** has the same root as the word **второй** (vtah-*rohy*) (*second*).

- **среда** comes from the word **середина** (see-ree-*dee*-nuh) (*middle*).

- **четверг** sounds somewhat similar to **четвёртый** (cheet-*vyohr*-tiy) (*fourth*).

- **пятница** comes from **пятый** (*pya*-tiy) (*fifth*).

- The origin of the word **суббота** is "Sabbath."

- The Russian word for *resurrection* is **воскресенье**. (Recall that Jesus Christ rose up to heaven on Sunday.)

Things become a little more complicated when you indicate on what day something happened, especially if that day happens to be a Wednesday, Friday, or Saturday. The words indicating days of the week have to take the accusative case. The good news, however, is that only the Russian words for Wednesday, Friday, and Saturday have different endings (because they're feminine nouns); the endings of the other days, being masculine or neuter nouns, don't have to change (they retain their nominative case form). The Wednesday/Friday/Saturday changes look like this:

- **в среду** (f *sryeh*-dooh) (*on Wednesday*) (note the stress shift here)

- **в пятницу** (f *pyat*-nee-tsooh) (*on Friday*)

- **в субботу** (f sooh-*boh*-tooh) (*on Saturday*)

Talking about time relative to the present

Just as in English, Russian has lots of phrases to talk about a certain time in the past or future that relates to the present moment. Some time-related words that you may hear or say often in Russian are

- **сегодня** (see-*vohd*-nyeh) (*today*)

- **сегодня вечером** (see-*vohd*-nyeh *vyeh*-chee-rahm) (*tonight*)

- **сейчас** (see-*chahs*) (*now*)

- **скоро** (*skoh*-rah) (*soon*)

- **поздно** (*pohz*-nah) (*late*)

- **позже** (*pohz*-zheh) (*later*)

- **рано** (*rah*-nah) (*early*)

- **раньше** (*rahn'*-shi) (*earlier*)

- **вчера** (fchee-*rah*) (*yesterday*)

✔ **позавчера** (pah-zuh-fchee-*rah*) (*the day before yesterday*)

✔ **завтра** (*zahf*-truh) (*tomorrow*)

✔ **завтра вечером** (*zahf*-truh *vyeh*-chee-rahm) (*tomorrow night*)

Mentioning months and seasons

Both the English and Russian names for the months come from Latin (the word for *month* in Russian is **месяц**, pronounced *myeh*-seets). You can easily see the similarities. But just like the days of the week, note that, unlike English, Russian doesn't capitalize the names of the months:

✔ **январь** (een-*vahr'*) (*January*)

✔ **февраль** (feev-*rahl'*) (*February*)

✔ **март** (mahrt) (*March*)

✔ **апрель** (uhp-*ryehl'*) (*April*)

✔ **май** (mahy) (*May*)

✔ **июнь** (ee-*yoohn'*) (*June*)

✔ **июль** (ee-*yoohl'*) (*July*)

✔ **август** (*ahv*-goohst) (*August*)

✔ **сентябрь** (seen-*tyabr'*) (*September*)

✔ **октябрь** (ahk-*tyabr'*) (*October*)

✔ **ноябрь** (nah-*yabr'*) (*November*)

✔ **декабрь** (dee-*kahbr'*) (*December*)

When used in phrases like *in January, in February,* and so on, the words indicating months take the prepositional case. In other words, they all take the ending -e, as in **в январе** (v een-vuh-*ryeh*) (*in January*) or **в феврале** (v feev-ruh-*lyeh*) (*in February*). See Chapter 3 for full details on the prepositional case.

Although some places in the world just don't have **времена года** (vree-mee-*nah goh*-duh) (*seasons*) — take, for example, Florida or California — Russia sure does! Here they are:

✔ **зима** (zee-*mah*) (*winter*)

✔ **весна** (vees-*nah*) (*spring*)

✔ **лето** (*lyeh*-tah) (*summer*)

✔ **осень** (*oh*-seen') (*fall*)

Delving into dates

If you forgot today's *date* (**число**, which is pronounced chees-*loh*), ask somebody:

> **Какое сегодня число?** (kuh-*koh*-ee see-*vohd*-nyeh chees-*loh*?) (*What date it is today?*)

But be prepared to understand the answer. Most likely you'll hear something like this:

> **Сегодня двадцать пятое мая.** (see-*vohd*-nyeh *dvahd*-tsuht' *pya*-tah-ee *mah*-yeh.) (*Today is the 25th of May.*)

Look carefully at the preceding phrase. You may notice that the numeral 5 is in its neuter form (not in the nominative case) and has the ending **-ое**; that's because you ask about **число** (the date), which is a neuter noun. You may also note that May isn't translated as **май** but as **мая** — the genitive case form of the word **май**. (Flip to Chapter 3 for more about different cases.)

Make sure you know how to put down dates the Russian way. Compare how dates are written in the U.S. and Russia: In the U.S., the month comes before the day, as in 7/4/12 (July 4, 2012). In Russia, however, you write 4/7/12; the day comes before the month.

Saying years

Unless you're a history scholar, you probably don't have to talk about very distant history. Therefore, chances are most of your everyday conversations about any given *year* (**год**) (goht) won't go far beyond the second part of the 20th century or the beginning of the 21st. Here's a simple recipe for indicating years before the 21st century. To better illustrate it, we use the year 1985:

1. **Say the first number.**

   тысяча (*ti*-see-chuh) (*thousand*)

2. **Say the second number.**

   девятьсот (dee-veet'-*soht*) (*900*)

3. **Say the third number.**

   восемьдесят (*voh*-seem'-dee-syeht) (*80*)

4. **Say the last number as an ordinal number.**

   пятый (*pya*-tiy) (*the fifth*)

5. **Add the word for** *year.*

   год (goht)

The resulting phrase is **тысяча девятьсот восемьдесят пятый год** (*ti*-see-chuh dee-veet'-*soht voh*-seem'-dee-syeht *pya*-tiy goht) (*the year 1985*; Literally: *1985 year*).

To indicate a year in the 21st century, for instance, 2015, do this:

1. **Say the first number.**

   две тысячи (dvyeh *ti*-see-chee) (*2,000*)

2. **Say the second number as an ordinal number.**

   пятнадцатый (peet-*naht*-suh-tiy) (*15th*)

3. **Add the word for** *year*.

   год (goht)

So, here you have it: **две тысячи пятнадцатый год** (dvyeh *ti*-see-chee peet-*naht*-suh-tiy goht) (*the year 2015*; Literally: *2015 year*).

To say that something happened in a certain year, use the last ordinal number in the prepositional case (see Chapter 3) and change the word **год** to **году** (gah-*dooh*). Suppose you were born in 1978: The year itself is **тысяча девятьсот семьседят восьмой год.** Here's how you talk about the year in Russian:

Я родился в тысяча девятьсот семьдесят восьмом году. (Ya rah-*deel*-syeh v *ti*-see-chuh dee-veet'-*soht syehm*'-dee-syeht vahs'-*mohm* gah-*dooh*.) (*I was born in 1978.*)

Talkin' the Talk

 Two teenagers, Vera (**Вера**) and Natasha (**Наташа**), are talking about their birthdays. (Track 7)

Вера:	**Когда у тебя день рождения?** kahg-*dah* ooh tee-*bya* dyehn' rah-*zhdyeh*-nee-yeh? *When is your birthday?*
Наташа:	**28 февраля. А у тебя?** *dvaht*-suht' vahs'-*moh*-yeh feev-ruh-*lya*. ah ooh tee-*bya*? *February 28th. And yours?*
Вера:	**Я родилась восьмого мая.** ya rah-dee-*lahs*' vohs'-*moh*-vah *mah*-yeh. *I was born on the 8th of May.*
Наташа:	**А в каком году?** ah f kah-*kohm* gah-*dooh*? *In what year?*

Вера: **В 1997 году.**
v *ti*-see-chuh dee-veet-*soht* dee-vee-*nohs*-tah seed'-*mohm* gah-*dooh*.
In 1997.

Words to Know

Когда у тебя день рождения?	kahg-<u>dah</u> ooh tee-<u>bya</u> deen' rah-<u>zhdyeh</u>-nee-yeh?	When is your birthday?
А у тебя?	ah ooh tee-<u>bya</u>?	And yours?
Я родилась	ya rah-dee-<u>lahs</u>'	I was born
В каком году?	F kuh-<u>kohm</u> gah-<u>dooh</u>?	In what year?

The Long and Short of It: Familiarizing Yourself with Metric Measurements

Unlike people in some English-speaking countries, Russians use the elegant metric system, introduced at the time of the French Revolution. Its main or fundamental units are meters and kilograms. The system is extremely simple and convenient, but we don't get into that touchy subject. The important thing is that feet, yards, inches, miles, gallons, and ounces mean nothing to Russians. So whether you want to or not, prepare to convert. When in Rome, do as Romans do, or as Russians say, **В чужой монастырь со своим уставом не ходят.** (v chooh-*zhoy* mah-nuhs-*tir*' suh svah-*eem* oohs-*tah*-vuhm nee *khoh*-dyeht.) (*Don't go to a new monastery with your own laws.*)

Here are the terms you need to know for linear measurements:

- ✔ **сантиметр** (suhn-tee-*myehtr*) (*centimeter*)
- ✔ **метр** (myehtr) (*meter*)
- ✔ **километр** (kee-lah-*myehtr*) (*kilometer*)

You use the following terms for units of weight and volume:

- ✔ **грамм** (grahm) (*gram*)
- ✔ **килограмм** (kee-lah-*grahm*) (*kilogram*)
- ✔ **литр** (leetr) (*liter*)

Fun & Games

a.   b.   c.

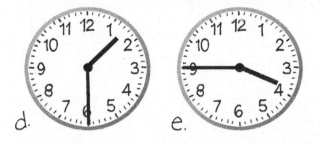

d.   e.

Select the phrase that indicates the time shown on each clock in the picture, and write the number of the correct phrase next to the corresponding letter. See Appendix D for the answers.

a. _____

1. Сейчас час

2. Сейчас два часа

3. Сейчас двенадцать часов

b. _____

1. Сейчас десять часов

2. Сейчас восемь часов

3. Сейчас четыре часа

c. _____

1. Сейчас десять часов

2. Сейчас восемь часов

3. Сейчас четыре часа

d. _____

1. Сейчас час тридцать

2. Сейчас два тридцать

3. Сейчас двенадцать тридцать

e. _____

1. Сейчас без пятнадцати десять

2. Сейчас без пятнадцати восемь

3. Сейчас без пятнадцати четыре

Chapter 6

Speaking Russian at Home

In This Chapter

▶ Naming the rooms and items in a home

▶ Dishing about eating and drinking

▶ Talking about your typical daily routine

Уou can start practicing your Russian language skills right away in your home, by naming the things that surround you every day. You can also practice talking about meals and listing routine activities you perform on a daily basis in Russian. This chapter helps you do it!

Taking a Tour of Your Home

Your home may be a **дом** (dohm) (*house*) or **квартира** (kvuhr-*tee*-ruh) (*apartment*). If you have a house, you may have a **подвал** (pahd-*vahl*) (*basement*). Each **комната** (*kohm*-nuh-tuh) (*room*) in your **дом** (dohm) (*home*) has a Russian name, and so does all the stuff those rooms contain.

In the following sections, we walk you through terms related to specific rooms, but to start, consider the following, more general residence-related vocabulary:

✔ **ковёр** (kah-*vyohr*) (*rug/carpet*)

✔ **лампа** (*lahm*-puh) (*lamp*)

✔ **мебель** (*myeh*-beel') (*furniture*)

✔ **выключатель** (vi-klyooh-*chah*-teel') (*light switch*)

✔ **дверь** (dvyehr') (*door*)

✔ **окно** (ahk-*noh*) (*window*)

✔ **пол** (pohl) (*floor*)

✔ **потолок** (pah-tah-*lohk*) (*ceiling*)

✔ **прихожая** (pree-*khoh*-zhuh-yeh) (*hall*)

High Russian standards: Ceilings and floors

Most Russians are fixated on high ceilings. A height of 4 to 5 meters (about 13 to 16 feet) is seen by many Russians as an acceptable norm. Russians also unequivocally prefer parquet floors everywhere in their home, except probably the kitchen and bathrooms. Wall-to-wall carpeting never took root in Russia, but Persian-type rugs often decorate walls. Well-to-do families today can afford to put them on the floor.

✔ стена (stee-*nah*) (*wall*)

✔ лестница (*lyehs*-nee-tsuh) (*stairs*)

✔ двор (dvohr) (*yard*)

One of the best proven ways to learn new words in a foreign language is to put stick-it notes labeling the objects around you in the foreign language. Every time you use a household item or just look at a piece of furniture, you'll be reminded of its Russian equivalent.

The kitchen

Your кухня (*kookh*-nyeh) (*kitchen*) probably has the following major appliances and features:

✔ холодильник (khah-lah-*deel'*-neek) (*refrigerator*)

✔ морозильник (mah-rah-*zeel'*-neek) (*freezer*)

✔ плита (plee-*tah*) (*stove*)

✔ духовка (dooh-*khohf*-kuh) (*oven*)

✔ микроволновка (meek-rah-vahl-*nohf*-kuh) (*microwave*)

✔ кухонный шкаф (*kooh*-khah-niy shkahf) (*kitchen cabinet*)

✔ раковина (*rah*-kah-vee-nuh) (*sink*)

✔ посудомоечная машина (pah-sooh-dah-*moh*-eech-nuh-yeh muh-*shi*-nuh) (*dishwasher*)

Kitchens also have a number of small appliances and gadgets, such as the following:

- ✔ **консервный нож** (kahn-*syehrv*-niy nohsh) (*can opener*)

- ✔ **взбивалка** (vzbee-*vahl*-kuh) (*whisk*)

- ✔ **шпатель** (*shpah*-teel') (*spatula*)

- ✔ **друшлак** (drooh-*shlahk*) (*colander*)

- ✔ **доска** (dahs-*kah*) (*cutting board*)

- ✔ **кофеварка** (koh-fee-*vahr*-kuh) (*coffee maker*)

- ✔ **кастрюля** (kuhs-*tryooh*-lyeh) (*pot*)

- ✔ **сковорода** (skah-vah-rah-*dah*) (*frying pan*)

- ✔ **смеситель** (smee-*see*-teel') (*blender*)

- ✔ **тостер** (*tohs*-teer) (*toaster*)

- ✔ **мусорное ведро** (*mooh*-sahr-nah-ee veed-*roh*) (*garbage can*)

The dining room

The following list provides you with words you may need while hanging out in the **столовая** (stah-*loh*-vuh-yeh) (*dining room*):

- ✔ **блюдечко** (*blyooh*-deech-kah) (*saucer*)

- ✔ **бокал** (bah-*kahl*) (*wine glass*)

- ✔ **буфет** (booh-*fyeht*) (*cupboard*)

- ✔ **вилка** (*veel*-kuh) (*fork*)

- ✔ **ложка** (*lohsh*-kuh) (*spoon*)

- ✔ **миска** (*mees*-kuh) (*bowl*)

- ✔ **нож** (nohsh) (*knife*)

- ✔ **обеденный стол** (ah-*byeh*-dee-niy stohl) (*dinner table*)

- ✔ **салфетка** (suhl-*fyeht*-kuh) (*napkin*)

- ✔ **стакан** (stuh-*kahn*) (*glass*)

- ✔ **стулья** (*stoohl'*-yeh) (*chairs*)

- ✔ **тарелка** (tuh-*ryehl*-kuh) (*plate*)

- ✔ **хлебница** (*khlyehb*-nee-tsuh) (*bread basket*)

- ✔ **чашка** (*chahsh*-kuh) (*cup*)

- ✔ **скатерть** (*skah*-teert') (*tablecloth*)

Apartment living in Russian cities

The majority of Russian families residing in the cities live in apartments. Many families have owned these apartments since the early 1990s, when the government began selling these apartments to private citizens. Russian apartments may consist of one room or, more often, two or three rooms, plus a kitchen, bathroom, and hallway. Note that a kitchen, bathroom facilities, and a hallway are not considered rooms — only bedrooms, living rooms, and dining rooms count.

The living room

What do people usually do in the **гостиная** (gahs-*tee*-nuh-yeh) (*living room*)? They watch TV and often fight for the *remote control* (Russians have not yet invented a Russian translation for this term, so they simply use the "Russified" version: **ремоут контрол** [ree-*moh*-ooht kahn-*trohl*]). Here's a list of some things you're likely to find in the living room:

- **диван** (dee-*vahn*) (*sofa*)
- **журнальный стол** (zhoohr-*nahl'*-niy stohl) (*coffee table*)
- **картина** (kuhr-*tee*-nuh) (*painting*)
- **кресло** (*kryehs*-lah) (*armchair*)
- **письменный стол** (*pees*-mee-niy stohl) (*desk*)
- **телевизор** (tee-lee-*vee*-zahr) (*TV set*)
- **телефон** (tee-lee-*fohn*) (*telephone*)
- **торшер** (tahr-*shehr*) (*floor lamp*)
- **камин** (kuh-*meen*) (*fireplace*)

The bedroom

Thinking in Russian when you're tired and sleepy or when you just woke up isn't easy. To help you out, here's vocabulary related to your **спальня** (*spahl'*-nyeh) (*bedroom*).

- **кровать** (krah-*vaht'*) (*bed*)
- **одеяло** (ah-dee-*ya*-lah) (*blanket*)
- **подушка** (pah-*doohsh*-kuh) (*pillow*)

- ✔ **простыня** (prahs-ti-*nya*) (*sheet*)

- ✔ **постельное бельё** (pahs-*tyehl'*-nah'-yeh beel'-*yoh*) (*bedding*)

- ✔ **будильник** (booh-*deel'*-neek) (*alarm clock*)

- ✔ **комод** (kah-*moht*) (*chest of drawers*)

- ✔ **ночной столик** (nahch-*nohy* stoh-leek) (*night table*)

- ✔ **шкаф** (shkahf) (*wardrobe*)

- ✔ **стенной шкаф** (stee-*nohy* shkahf) (*closet*)

- ✔ **зеркало** (*zyehr*-kuh-lah) (*mirror*)

Russians use only one lower bedsheet, which is fastened to the mattress with a stretchable string. Instead of the upper sheet, Russians use **пододяльник** (pah-dah-*d'yal'*-neek), a sort of envelope for the blanket. Square (rather than elongated) bed pillows — at least twice the size of those in the United States — are buttoned into pillowcases.

The bathroom

The things you're most likely to see in a Russian **ванная** (*vah*-nuh-yeh) (*bathroom*) are very similar to those found in your bathroom:

- ✔ **ванна** (*vah*-nuh) (*bathtub*)

- ✔ **душ** (doohsh) (*shower*)

- ✔ **мыло** (*mi*-lah) (*soap*)

- ✔ **полотенце** (pah-lah-*tyehn*-tseh) (*towel*)

- ✔ **туалетная бумага** (tooh-uh-*lyeht*-nuh-yeh booh-*mah*-guh) (*toilet paper*)

- ✔ **унитаз** (ooh-nee-*tahs*) (*toilet*)

- ✔ **раковина** (*rah*-kah-vee-nuh) (*sink*)

- ✔ **шампунь** (shuhm-*poohn'*) (*shampoo*)

- ✔ **щётка** (*sh'yoht*-kuh) (*brush*)

- ✔ **расчёска** (ruhs-*chyos*-kuh) (*comb*)

In Russian homes, you won't find a medicine cabinet in the bathroom. Medications are usually kept in one of the drawers in the kitchen; these drawers are called **аптечка** (uhp-*tyehch*-kuh) (*little pharmacy*).

The overflowing Russian wardrobe

Walk-in closets in Russian homes aren't very common and are very small. They're usually built in hallways rather than bedrooms. Usually, all clothes accumulated over the decades are kept in a large, movable wardrobe called a платяной шкаф (pluh-tee-*nohy* shkahf). As a rule, Russians have a hard time parting with pieces of clothing they used to wear years ago and tend to keep them in their wardrobes all their life.

One word from the preceding list deserves special attention, mostly to avoid embarrassment if you're a guest in a Russian home. If you ask your Russian host to take you to the bathroom, you probably won't see the appliance you're looking for — the toilet. In Russia, the bathroom is a room where you can take a bath or shower, but it may or may not have a toilet. The toilet may be located in a separate room. So, unless you indeed want to take a shower or a bath, don't ask for the bathroom; just ask straightforwardly:

Где туалет? (gdyeh tooh-uh-*lyeht?*) (*Where is the toilet?*)

Please note that "toilet" here means a room with a toilet and not a toilet itself. So, you're not asking for an actual toilet, but for a "toilet room." The word for a *toilet* in Russian is **унитаз** (ooh-nee-*tahs*).

The laundry room

Finding a laundry room in a Russian home is rather unlikely. In fact, Russian doesn't have an equivalent for the English term "laundry room." In most cases, the washing machine (though not necessarily the dryer) is found in the bathroom. Naturally, laundry detergent and bleach are also kept in the bathroom, in a cabinet or on a shelf.

Here's a list of words associated with doing laundry:

- ✔ **вешалка** (*vyeh*-shuhl-kuh) (*clothes hanger*)
- ✔ **гладильная доска** (gluh-*deel'*-nuh-yeh dahs-*kah*) (*ironing board*)
- ✔ **отбеливатель** (aht-*byeh*-lee-vuh-teel') (*bleach*)

- **стиральная машина** (stee-*rahl'*-nuh-yeh muh-*shi*-nuh) (*washer*)
- **стиральный порошок** (stee-*rahl'*-niy pah-rah-*shohk*) (*detergent*)
- **сушилка** (sooh-*shil*-kuh) (*dryer*)
- **утюг** (ooh-*tyoohk*) (*iron*)

The garage

You have to admit that your **гараж** (guh-*rahsh*) (*garage*) is a lot more than just the place where you park your car. It's also a place where you store your gardening and other household tools, your bicycles, and maybe some expensive fitness equipment you don't use any more. Garages are rare in Russian cities; people park their cars mostly outside on the street or in the huge inner yards of the houses built many years ago. Here are a few handy words to know when you talk about your garage:

- **велосипед** (vee-lah-see-*pyeht*) (*bicycle*)
- **винты** (veen-*ti*) (*screws*)
- **гаечный ключ** (*gah*-eech-niy klyoohch) (*wrench*)
- **гвозди** (*gvohz*-dee) (*nails*)
- **грузовик** (grooh-zah-*veek*) (*truck*)
- **машина** (muh-*shi*-nuh) (*car*)
- **молоток** (mah-lah-*tohk*) (*hammer*)
- **отвёртка** (aht-*vyohrt*-kuh) (*screwdriver*)
- **мини-автобус** (mee-nee uhf-*toh*-boohs) (*van*)
- **коробка для инструментов** (kah-*rohp*-kuh dlya een-strooh-*myehn*-tahf) (*toolbox*)
- **пила** (pee-*lah*) (*saw*)
- **сантиметр** (suhn-tee-*myehtr*) (*tape measure*)
- **плоскогубцы** (plahs-kah-*goohp*-tsi) (*pliers*)
- **травокосилка** (truh-vah-kah-*seel*-kuh) (*mower*)
- **удобрение** (ooh-dahb-*ryeh*-nee-ee) (*fertilizer*)

Talkin' the Talk

Mark's Russian friend Alexander (**Александр**) is staying with Mark (**Марк**) in his house in California. Mark is taking Alexander on a house tour. (Track 8)

Марк:	**Это наша кухня. Вот холодильник, микроволновка, и плита.**
	eh-tah *nah*-shuh *koohkh*-nyeh. voht khah-lah-*deel'*-neek, meek-rah-vahl-*nohf*-kuh, ee plee-*tah*.
	This is our kitchen. Here is the refrigerator, the microwave, and the stove.
Александр:	**У вас газовая или электрическая плита?**
	ooh vahs *gah*-zah-vuh-yeh ee-lee eh-leek-*tree*-chees-kuh-yeh plee-*tah*?
	Is it a gas or electric stove?
Марк:	**Газовая. Это посудомоечная машина. Тостер, кофеварка. Это дверь в гостиную. Это наша гостиная.**
	gah-zah-vah-yeh. *eh*-tah pah-sooh-dah-*moh*-eech-nuh-yeh mah-*shi*-nuh. *tohs*-teer, kah-fee-*vahr*-kuh *eh*-tuh dvyehr' v gahs-*tee*-nooh-yooh. *eh*-tah *nah*-shuh gahs-*tee*-nah-yeh.
	It's gas. This is the dishwasher. Toaster, coffee maker. Here is the door to the living room. This is our living room.
Александр:	**Какая большая комната! У вас есть камин!**
	kuh-*kah*-yeh bahl'-*shah*-yeh *kohm*-nuh-tuh! ooh vahs yehst' kuh-*meen*!
	What a big room! You have a fireplace!
Марк:	**Да, есть. Но мы его никогда не зажигаем. Только иногда на Рождество. А это столовая. Мы здесь очень редко едим. Мы едим в основном на кухне.**
	dah, est'. noh mi ee-*voh* nee-kahg-*dah* nee zuh-zhi-*gah*-eem. *tohl'*-kuh ee-nahg-*dah* nah rohzh-dees-*tvoh*. uh *eh*-tah stah-*loh*-vuh-yeh. mi zdyehs' *oh*-cheen' *ryehd*-kah ee-*deem*. mi ee-*deem* v ahs-nahv-*nohm* nah *koohkh*-nee.
	Yes, we do. But we never light it up. Only sometimes for Christmas. And this is the dining room. We don't eat here very often. We eat mostly in the kitchen.

Words to Know

кухня	<u>koohkh</u>-nyeh	kitchen
холодильник	khah-lah-<u>deel</u>'-neek	refrigerator
микроволновка	meek-rah-vahl-<u>nohf</u>-kuh	microwave
плита	plee-<u>tah</u>	stove
дверь	dvyehr'	door
гостиная	gahs-<u>tee</u>-nah-yeh	living room
Какая большая комната!	kuh-<u>kah</u>-yeh bahl'-<u>shah</u>-yeh <u>kohm</u>-nuh-tuh!	What a big room!
камин	kuh-<u>meen</u>	fireplace
только иногда	<u>tohl</u>'-kuh ee-nahg-<u>dah</u>	only/just sometimes
в основном	v ahs-nahv-<u>nohm</u>	mostly

Home Is Where the Food Is

Food is one of the first things that comes to mind when people talk about a foreign culture. In this section you discover Russian words and expressions associated with food, drinks, and meals; for details on dining out and shopping for food, check out Chapter 9.

Get cookin': The verb "to cook"

The word **щи** (shee) indicates one of the staples of Russian cuisine — a soup made of sauerkraut cooked in meat broth. In fact, it's considered the main indicator of a Russian housewife's culinary skills, according to this old proverb: "A good wife is not the one who speaks well but who cooks shee well." Actually, shee isn't that hard to cook, but it is a good excuse to introduce you to an important (and somewhat irregular) verb, **готовить** (gah-*toh*-veet') (*to cook*):

Conjugation	Pronunciation
я готовлю	ya gah-*tohv*-lyooh
ты готовишь	ti gah-*toh*-veesh'
он/она/оно готовит	ohn/ah-*nah*/ah-*noh* gah-*toh*-veet
мы готовим	mi gah-*toh*-veem
вы готовите	vi gah-*toh*-vee-tee
они готовят	ah-*nee* gah-*toh*-vyeht

You may have noticed that the verb has an additional letter -л in the first person singular. Many Russian verbs follow this kind of pattern: Just try to memorize their forms.

Eat up: The verb "to eat"

After you cook, you need to eat, of course. The verb **есть** (yehst') (*to eat*) is an irregular verb. It doesn't follow the regular present tense verb endings that we provide in Chapter 3, so you just have to memorize them:

Conjugation	Pronunciation
Я ем	ya yehm
Ты ешь	ti yehsh'
он/она/оно ест	ohn/ah-*nah*/ah-*noh* yehst
мы едим	mi ee-*deem*
вы едите	vi ee-*dee*-tee
они едят	ah-*nee* ee-*dyat*

Russians don't really use the phrase "I'm hungry"; more often, you hear **Я хочу есть** (ya khah-*chooh* yehst') (*I'm hungry*; Literally: *I want to eat*). To ask somebody formally whether he's hungry, you say **Вы хотите есть?** (vi khah-*tee*-tee yehst'?) (*Are you hungry?*). If you're asking your friend, a child, or your cat, you use the informal **Ты хочешь есть?** (ti *khoh*-cheesh yehst'?).

Drink up: The verb "to drink"

Eating and drinking are almost inseparable for North Americans, but they're not in Russia: It isn't customary to chase every morsel of food with a gulp of water or other beverage. Nevertheless, Russians need to drink like everyone

else! That said, here is the (quite unruly) conjugation of the verb **пить** (peet')
(*to drink*).

Conjugation	*Pronunciation*
Я пью	ya p'yooh
Ты пьёшь	ti p'yohsh'
он/она пьёт	ohn/ah-*nah* p'yoht
мы пьём	mi p'yohm
вы пьёте	vi *p'yoh*-tee
они пьют	ah-*nee* p'yooht

The phrase you use to announce that you wouldn't mind having a glass of
water follows the same pattern as the phrase you use to declare your hunger
(see the preceding section). You actually say **Я хочу пить** (ya khah-*chooh*
peet') (*I'm thirsty*, Literally: *I want to drink.*)

Enjoying different meals

Russians typically eat three meals a day, but the importance they place on
various mealtimes may differ from what you're accustomed to. A common
schedule includes the following meals:

- **завтрак** (*zahf*-truhk) (*breakfast*)
- **обед** (ah-*byeht*) (*dinner*)
- **ужин** (*ooh*-zhin) (*supper*)

What can you eat for Russian **завтрак**? The real question is what can't you
eat! In contrast to the American cereal, fruit, and bagels; the British porridge;
or the French croissant and jam; the Russian **завтрак** is very flexible. Some
Russian breakfast favorites include sandwiches with **колбаса** (kahl-buh-*sah*)
(*sausage*) or **сыр** (sir) (*cheese*), **кефир** (kee-*feer*) (*buttermilk*), and even
селёдка (see-*lyoht*-kuh) (*salted herring*), chased with **чай** (chahy) (*tea*) or
кофе (*koh*-fee) (*coffee*).

Обед is the midday meal (like lunch), usually eaten between 1 and 3 p.m., and
it's the main meal of the day. For this midday meal, Russians enjoy a four-
course dinner consisting of **закуски** (zuh-*koohs*-kee) (*appetizers*) — though
people may sometimes skip the appetizers and go directly to **суп** (soohp)
(*soup*), making it the first course — followed by **второе** (ftah-*roh*-ee) (*the main
course;* Literally: *second*) and **дессерт** (dee-*syehrt*) (*dessert*), also called **третье**
(*tryeh*-t'ee) (*the third course*; Literally: *third*). Tea may conclude this feast.

Minding your table manners in Russia

If you want to impress your Russian acquaintances, familiarize yourself with basic Russian table manners. Some of the most important rules are related to using table utensils:

✔ If you use a knife, hold your fork in your left hand at all times.

✔ If you don't need a knife to cut your food, hold your fork in your right hand. When Russians eat fish, for example, they don't use a knife, and they hold the fork in their right hand.

✔ When eating dessert, don't use a fork; use a teaspoon instead.

Russians often find the American habit of cutting food into pieces before eating it very amusing. In Russia, only mothers do this for their young children. So when you're in a Russian home or restaurant, never cut your food first with your knife and then put down the knife to hold your fork in the right hand. Always hold your knife in the right hand and your fork in the left hand, cutting one piece of food at a time as you eat.

The last meal of the day, **ужин**, is usually eaten with the family around the kitchen or dining room table. This meal is a feast of leftovers from today's or yesterday's lunch or even breakfast. And again . . . tea!

Russians believe that breakfast, the most important meal of the day, should be plentiful, whereas supper should be light. Russian folk wisdom says: "Eat your breakfast yourself, share your dinner with a friend, give your supper to your enemy." What may be new to you is the fact that Russians eat **обед** (*dinner*) as a midday — rather than late afternoon or evening — meal. The word **ланч** (*lahnch*) (*lunch*) is a token to new Westerns ways and is used (and eaten) only in important business situations.

Describing your food and drink preferences with the verb "to like"

The best way to express your food preferences is with the Russian verb **нравиться** (*nrah-*veet'-syeh) (*to like*). The following is the present tense conjugation:

Conjugation	Pronunciation
Я нравлюсь	ya _nrahv_-lyoohs'
Ты нравишься	ti _nrah_-veesh-syeh
Он/она/оно нравится	ohn/ah-_nah_/ah-_noh_ nrah-veet-syeh
Мы нравимся	mi _nrah_-veem-syeh
Вы нравитесь	vi _nrah_-vee-tees'
Они нравятся	ah-_nee_ nrah-vyeht-syeh

When you use the verb **нравиться,** Russian requires the subject of the sentence to take the dative case. **Я** (ya) (_I_) in the dative case, for example, is **мне** (mnyeh). The verb should agree in number with the thing or things it refers to, and those things should be in the nominative case. (Flip to Chapter 3 for full details on Russian cases.)

So, if you like tea, for example, you may say

Мне нравится чай. (mnyeh _nrah_-veet-syeh chahy.) (_I like tea._)

If you don't like tea, just add **не** (nee) (_do not_) before **нравится** to say

Мне не нравится чай. (mnyeh nee _nrah_-veet-syeh chahy.) (_I don't like tea._)

If you like both tea and coffee, use the verb in the plural form:

Мне нравятся чай и кофе. (mnyeh _nrah_-veet-syeh _koh_-fee.) (_I like tea and coffee._)

Talkin' the Talk

Syeryozha (**Серёжа**) comes home early from school because he has a stomachache. His mother (**Мама**) tries to discern the cause of his illness. (Track 9)

Мама:	**Серёжа, почему ты так рано пришёл из школы? Что случилось?**
	see-_ryoh_-zhuh, puh-chee-_mooh_ ti tahk _rah_-nuh pree-_shohl_ ees _shkoh_-li? shtoh slooh-_chee_-luhs'?
	Syeryozha, why did you come from school so early? What happened?

Серёжа: **Мама, у мена болит живот**
mah-muh, ooh mee-*nya* bah-*leet* zhi-*voht*.
Mom, I have a stomachache.

Мама: **Живот? Что ты сегодня ел на завтрак?**
zhi-*voht*? shtoh ti see-*vohd*-nyeh yehl nuh
zahf-truhk?
*Stomachache? What did you have for breakfast
today?*

Серёжа: **Я ел кашу и пил молоко.**
ya yehl *kah*-shooh ee peel mah-lah-*koh*.
I had hot cereal and drank milk.

Мама: **А что ты ел в школе на обед?**
uh shtoh ti yehl f *shkoh*-lee nuh ah-*byeht*?
And what did you eat for dinner at school?

Серёжа: **На обед я ел салат, котлеты с картошкой, и пил
кисель.**
nuh ah-*byeht* ya yehl suh-*laht*, kaht-*lyeh*-ti s kahr-
tohsh-kuhy ee peel kee-*syehl*'.
*For lunch I had salad, a meat patty with potatoes, and
drank kissel.*

Мама: **А что ты ел на первое?**
uh shtoh ti yehl nuh *pyehr*-vah-yeh?
And what did you eat for the first course?

Серёжа: **Я ничего не ел. Я не хотел суп.**
ya nee-chee-*voh* nee yehl. ya nee khah-*tyehl* soohp.
I did not eat anything. I did not want to eat soup.

Мама: **Серёжа, ты должен есть суп каждый день. Может
быть у тебя болит живот потому что ты не ешь
суп. Я сделаю чай и тебе будет лучше.**
see-*ryoh*-zhuh, ti *dohl*-zhin yehst' soohp *kahzh*-diy
dyehn'. *moh*-zhit bit' ooh tee-*bya* bah-*leet* zhi-*voht*
pah-tah-*mooh* shtah ti nee yehsh' soohp. ya *sdyeh*-
luh-yooh chahy ee tee-*byeh* booh-deet *loohch*-sheh.
*Syeryozha, you have to eat soup every day. Maybe
you have a stomachache because you don't eat soup.
I'll make some tea to help you feel better.*

Words to Know

Что случилось?	shtoh slooh-<u>chee</u>-luhs'?	What happened?
У меня болит живот.	ooh mee-<u>nya</u> bah-<u>leet</u> zhi-<u>voht.</u>	I have a stomachache.
завтрак	<u>zahf</u>-truhk	breakfast
каша	<u>kah</u>-shuh	hot cereal
молоко	mah-lah-<u>koh</u>	milk
обед	ah-<u>byeht</u>	dinner
салат	suh-<u>laht</u>	salad
первое	<u>pyehr</u>-vah-yeh	main course
Я ничего не ел.	ya nee-chee-<u>voh</u> nee yehl.	I didn't eat anything.
может быть	<u>moh</u>-zhit bit'	maybe
потому что	pah-tah-<u>mooh</u> shtah	because

Engaging in Daily Activities

People perform certain actions every day: They wake up, go to work or school, come home, do household chores, and go to bed so they can start the process all over again the next morning. This section helps you describe these activities in Russian.

Discussing your household chores

To show how hard you work at home, use these expressions:

Я убираю дом. (ya ooh-bee-*rah*-yooh dohm.) (*I clean/am cleaning the house.*)

Я вытираю пыль. (ya vi-tee-*rah*-yooh pil'.) (*I dust/am dusting furniture.*)

Я чищу ковры пылесосом. (ya *chee*-sh'ooh kahv-*ri* pi-lee-*soh*-sahm.) (*I vacuum/am vacuuming the floors.*)

Я занимаюсь садом. (ya zuh-nee-*mah*-yoohs' *sah*-dahm.) (*I garden/am gardening.*)

Я кошу траву. (ya kah-*shooh* truh-*vooh*.) (*I mow/am mowing the grass.*)

Note the dictionary forms of the above verbs: **убирать** (ooh-bee-*raht'*) (*to clean*), **вытирать пыль** (vi-tee-*raht'* pil') (*to dust*), **пылесосить** (pi-lee-*soh*-seet') (*to vacuum*), **заниматься садом** (zuh-nee-*maht'*-syeh *sah*-dahm) (*to garden*), and **косить траву** (kah-*seet'* truh-*vooh*) (*to mow*).

Talking about all the places you go

Chances are you don't stay at home all the time just doing your chores: sometimes you get out of the house, for example, to go to **школа** (*shkoh*-luh) (*school*) or **работа** ruh-*boh*-tuh) (*work*) — after all, somebody has to pay the bills. On weekends, you probably go out to eat or have fun. A very useful verb for all the preceding situations is **идти** (eed-*tee*) (*to go*), an irregular verb. See for yourself.

Conjugation	*Pronunciation*
Я иду	ya ee-*dooh*
ты идёшь	ti ee-*dyohsh*'
он/она идёт	ohn/ah-*nah* ee-*dyoht*
мы идём	mi ee-*dyohm*
вы идёте	vi ee-*dyoh*-tee
они идут	ah-*nee* ee-*dooht*

Now you can talk about a variety of places you go or are planning to go to. The important thing to know is that the place you're going to should be indicated by the accusative case with the appropriate preposition. Also, carefully select the form of the verb to go with the subject of your sentence.

For example, you can say the following:

Я обычно иду на работу в 8 часов. (ya ah-*bich*-nah ee-*dooh* nuh ruh-*boh*-tooh v *voh*-seem chuh-*sohf*.) (*I go to work at 8 o'clock.*)

Вечером мы идём в ресторан. (*vyeh*-chee-rahm mi ee-*dyohm* v rees-tah-*rahn*.) (*Tonight we are going to a restaurant.*)

Bantering about bedtime activities

After a long day of work, school, and chores, you probably spend a lot of time sleeping; the Russian translation of *to sleep* is **спать** (spat'), a second-conjugation verb that's conjugated as shown in the following table.

Conjugation	Pronunciation
Я сплю	ya splyooh
Ты спишь	ti speesh
Он/она спит	ohn/ah-*nah* speet
Мы спим	mi speem
Вы спите	vi *spee*-tee
Они спят	ah-*nee* spyat

But what do you do before you go to bed and after you get up? Most people would say they do the following:

> **Я чищу зубы.** (ya *chee*-sh'oo zoo-bi.) (*I brush/am brushing my teeth.*)

> **Я мою лицо.** (ya *moh*-yooh lee-*tsoh.*) (*I wash/am washing my face.*)

> **Я принимаю душ.** (ya pree-nee-*mah*-yooh doohsh.) (*I take/am taking a shower.*)

> **Я принимаю ванну.** (ya pree-nee-*mah*-yooh *vah*-nooh.) (*I take/am taking a bath.*)

> **Я одеваюсь.** (ya ah-dee-*vah*-yoohs'.) (*I get/am getting dressed.*)

> **Я раздеваюсь.** (ya *rahz*-dee-*vah*-yoohs'.) (*I get/am getting undressed.*)

The dictionary forms of the verbs we use in the preceding sentences are as follows: **причёсываться** (pree-*chyoh*-si-vuht'-syeh) (*to brush*), **мыться** (mit'-syeh) (*to wash*), **принимать душ** (pree-nee-*maht'* doohsh) (*to take a shower*), **принимать ванну** (pree-nee-*maht'* vah-nooh) (*to take a bath*), **одеваться** (ah-dee-*vaht'*-syeh) (*to get dressed*), and **раздеваться** (ruhz-dee-*vaht'*-syeh) (*to get undressed*). All of them are pretty regular verbs (some are reflexive).

In the following cutaway view of a home, match the Russian word for each room with the number of that room. Appendix D has the answers.

столовая	1.
кухня	2.
подвал	3.
спальня	4
ванная	5.
гостиная	6.

Part II
Russian in Action

The 5th Wave   By Rich Tennant

"If you're going to slurp your borscht, at least try to slurp it in Russian."

In this part . . .

Part II gives you all the Russian you need for ordinary, everyday living. You discover Russian phrases for making small talk, asking for directions, dining out, heading to the market, going shopping, and having fun on the town. You also find out how to talk about business and communication matters and how to discuss recreation and the outdoors.

Chapter 7

Getting to Know You: Making Small Talk

In This Chapter

▶ Breaking the ice by talking about yourself

▶ Knowing what to say when you don't understand something

▶ Exchanging contact information

The best way to start getting to know someone is through small talk. Imagine you're on a plane on your way to Russia. A fellow passenger, sitting next to you, looks Russian. What a wonderful opportunity to practice your new language skills! But what are you going to talk about? To break the ice, you probably want to state where you're from and mention your age, your job, and your family. Just before the flight lands, you may want to exchange contact information.

In this chapter, we show you how to do all these things in Russian as well as what to say when you don't understand something. You'll be ready for your first complete conversation with a real Russian! (For even more help during basic conversations, flip to Chapter 4, which tells you how to say hello and goodbye, make introductions, and use popular expressions.)

Let Me Tell You Something: Talking about Yourself

What do people talk about when they first meet? The topics are highly predictable: home, family, jobs, and even age. In the following sections, we deal with each of them.

The Western view of what one can ask about during the first casual conversation is quite different from the Russian view. The rules of Russian small talk are quite a bit looser and allow you to ask questions that the Western code of good manners considers quite forward, to say the least, including such topics as money, annual income, death, and illness. For instance, a 30-year-old man should expect to be asked why he's not yet married. And a recently married couple will probably be asked why they don't have children yet!

Stating where you're from

One of the topics that's bound to come up during your first conversations in Russian is your country of origin. Expect to hear this question:

Откуда вы? (aht-*kooh*-duh vi?) (*Where are you from?*)

If you're from the United States

✔ You can use the grammatical pattern the question calls for and say **Я из Америки** (ya eez uh-*myeh*-ree-kee) (*I am from America*), in which case the noun indicating the country you are from takes the genitive case. The preposition **из** (eez) (*from*) requires any noun that follows it to take the genitive case. (See Chapter 3 for full details on the genitive case and other cases.)

✔ You can say **Я живу в Америке** (ya zhi-*vooh* v uh-*myeh*-ree-kee) (*I live in America*). This structure requires the use of the prepositional case, because a noun following the preposition **в** (v) (*in*) to show location takes the prepositional case.

You can use this same grammatical pattern to add what city you live in. Just make sure you use the name of the city in the prepositional case. For example, if you live in Seattle, you can say

Я живу в Сиэттле. (ya zhi-*vooh* f see-*eht*-lee.) (*I live in Seattle.*)

Here, the word **Сиэтл** (see-*ehtl*) (*Seattle*) is in the prepositional case.

✔ You can say **Я американец** (ya uh-mee-ree-*kah*-neets) (*I am an American*) if you're a man or **Я американка** (ya uh-mee-ree-*kahn*-kuh) (*I am an American*) if you're a woman. (We talk more about this construction in the next section.)

Notice the wonderful fact that Russian doesn't require a "to be" verb (in this case, "am") or the article "an" in the present tense. What you're literally saying is *I American.* See how easy Russian is?

Naturally, if you're from a country other than the United States, just replace the references to America in the preceding examples with your own country.

Talking about your nationality and ethnicity

Russians generally tend to be very curious about people's nationalities and ethnicities. Chances are that sometime during your conversation with a native Russian you'll hear

> **А кто вы по-национальности?** (ah ktoh vi pah-nuh-tsi-ah-*nahl'*-nahs-tee?) (*And what is your nationality?*)

Literally, the question means *And who are you by nationality?* It seems that Russian grammar itself reflects how much importance is being attributed to nationality: You are what your nationality is.

Russian has three different types of words to indicate nationality. The choice of the word depends on the gender and number of the person or people whose nationality is being described:

- ✔ **Я американец.** (ya uh-mee-ree-*kahn*-neets.) (*I'm an American man.*)

- ✔ **Я американка.** (ya uh-mee-ree-*kahn*-kuh.) (*I'm an American woman.*)

- ✔ **Мы американцы.** (mi uh-mee-ree-*kahn*-tsi.) (*We're Americans.*)

  You use this phrase for a group of men, a group of women, or a group of men and women.

If you're a male, make sure you use the word indicating the nationality of a man, and if you're a female, make sure you use the word indicating the nationality of a woman. Imagine a man introducing himself as an American woman! Although people would understand what he was saying, they'd be quite amused — and if you were that man, you might be just a tad embarrassed.

Most Russians are educated enough to know that the United States, Canada, Australia, and Great Britain (among other countries) are ethnically diverse. Expect to be asked what your nationality is, especially if you don't look like a "typical American" — which, to a Russian, means a blue-eyed, blond, tall, and athletic-looking Anglo-Saxon. So if Russians seem to be asking you about your nationality a second time, they don't expect you to reiterate that you're American, Canadian, Australian, or British: They want to know your ethnic background. In this case, you can simply say something along the lines of the following:

> **Моя мама итальянка, а папа поляк.** (mah-*ya mah*-muh ee-tuhl'-*yan*-kuh, uh *pah*-puh pah-*lyak*.) (*My mom is Italian and my dad is Polish.*)

In Table 7-1, you find some adjectives you may want to use to describe your nationality and ethnicity.

Table 7-1	Words Denoting Nationality and Ethnicity		
Nationality of a Man	*Nationality of a Woman*	*Nationality of a Group*	*Translation*
африканец (uhf-ree-*kah*-neets)	**африканка** (uhf-ree-*kahn*-kuh)	**африканцы** (uhf-ree-*kahn*-tsi)	African
аргентинец (uhr-geen-*tee*-neets)	**аргентинка** (uhr-geen-*teen*-kuh)	**аргентинцы** (uhr-geen-*teen*-tsi)	Argentinean
китаец (kee-*tah*-eets)	**китаянка** (kee-tuh-*yan*-kuh)	**китайцы** (kee-*tahy*-tsi)	Chinese
индус (een-*doohs*)	**индианка** (een-dee-*ahn*-kuh)	**индусы** (een-*dooh*-si)	East Asian Indian
египтянин (ee-geep-*tya*-neen)	**египтянка** (ee-geep-*tyan*-kuh)	**египтяне** (ee-geep-*tya*-nee)	Egyptian
англичанин (uhn-glee-*chah*-neen)	**англичанка** (uhn-glee-*chahn*-kuh)	**англичане** (uhn-glee-*chah*-nee)	English
француз (fruhn-*tsoohz*)	**француженка** (fruhn-*tsooh*-zhin-kuh)	**французы** (fruhn-*tsooh*-zi)	French
немец (*nyeh*-meets)	**немка** (*nyehm*-kuh)	**немцы** (*nyehm*-tsi)	German
иранец (ee-*rah*-neets)	**иранка** (ee-*rahn*-kuh)	**иранцы** (ee-*rahn*-tsi)	Iranian
ирландец (eer-*lahn*-deets)	**ирландка** (eer-*lahnd*-kuh)	**ирландцы** (eer-*lahnd*-tsi)	Irish
итальянец (ee-tuhl'-*ya*-neets)	**итальянка** (ee-tuhl'-*yan*-kuh)	**итальянцы** (ee-tuhl'-*yan*-tsi)	Italian
японец (ee-*poh*-neets)	**японка** (ee-*pohn*-kuh)	**японцы** (ee-*pohn*-tsi)	Japanese
еврей (eev-*ryehy*)	**еврейка** (eev-*ryehy*-kuh)	**евреи** (eev-*ryeh*-ee)	Jewish
мексиканец (meek-see-*kah*-neets)	**мексиканка** (meek-see-*kahn*-kuh)	**мексиканцы** (meek-see-*kahn*-tsi)	Mexican
индеец (een-*dyeh*-eets)	**индианка** (een-dee-*ahn*-kuh)	**индейцы** (een-*dyehy*-tsi)	Native American

Nationality of a Man	Nationality of a Woman	Nationality of a Group	Translation
поляк (pah-*lyak*)	**полька** (*pohl'*-kuh)	**поляки** (pah-*lya*-kee)	Polish
русский (*roohs*-keey)	**русская** (*roohs*-kuh-yeh)	**русские** (*roohs*-kee-ee)	Russian
шотландец (shaht-*lahn*-deets)	**шотландка** (shaht-*lahnd*-kuh)	**шотландцы** (shaht-*lahnd*-tsi)	Scottish
испанец (ees-*pah*-neets)	**испанка** (ees-*pahn*-kuh)	**испанцы** (ees-*pahn*-tsi)	Spanish
турок (*tooh*-rahk)	**турчанка** (toohr-*chahn*-kuh)	**турки** (*toohr*-kee)	Turkish

Most words denoting the nationality of women have the ending **-ка**, as in **американка** (uh-mee-ree-*kahn*-kuh) (*American woman*). Many words denoting the nationality of men end in **-ец** (eets), such as **китаец** (kee-*tah*-eets) (*Chinese man*). Some words, however, divert from these general rules, such as those for *Russian*, *Jewish*, and *English*.

Talkin' the Talk

John (**Джон**) and Natasha (**Наташа**) are on board a flight from Frankfurt to Moscow. They're sitting next to each other, and John decides to strike up a conversation with Natasha. (Track 10)

Джон: **Извините, вы русская?**
eez-vee-*nee*-tee, vi *roohs*-kuh-yeh?
Excuse me, are you Russian?

Наташа: **Да, я русская. А вы наверное американец, да?**
dah, ya *roohs*-kuh-yeh. uh vi nuh-*vyehr*-nah-ee uh-mee-ree-*kah*-neets, dah?
Yes, I am Russian. And you must be American, right?

Джон: **Да, верно. Я американец. Я из Висконсина. Я живу в Мэдисоне.**
dah, *vyehr*-nuh. ya uh-mee-ree-*kah*-neets. ya eez vees-*kohn*-see-nuh. ya zhi-*vooh* v *meh*-dee-sah-nee.
Yes, that's true. I am American. I am from Wisconsin. I live in Madison.

Наташа:	**Вы не похожи на американца. Кто вы по-национальности?** vi nee puh-*khoh*-zhi nuh uh-mee-ree-*kahn*-tsuh. ktoh vi puh-nuh-tsi-uh-*nahl'*-nuhs-tee? *You don't look like an American. What is your nationality?*
Джон:	**Моя мама мексиканка, а папа итальянец.** muh-*ya mah*-muh meek-see-*kahn*-kuh, uh *pah*-puh ee-tuhl'-*ya*-neets. *My mother is Mexican, and my father is Italian.*
Наташа:	**Как интересно! Понятно.** kahk een-tee-*ryehs*-nah! puh-*nyat*-nah. *Interesting! I see.*

Words to Know

Извините	eez-vee-<u>nee</u>-tee	Excuse me
наверное	nuh-<u>vyehr</u>-nah-ee	must be, perhaps
Вы не похожи на . . .	vi *nee* puh-<u>khoh</u>-zhi nuh . . .	You don't look like . . .
Как интересно!	kahk *een*-tee-<u>ryehs</u>-nah!	Interesting!
Понятно	puh-<u>nyat</u>-nah	I see

Giving your age

To inquire about someone's **возраст** (*vohz*-ruhst) (*age*) in Russian, you ask:

Сколько вам лет? (*skohl'*-kah vahm lyeht?) (*How old are you?*)

The answer to this question is a little funny, though. In Russia, age is seen as something that happens to you (and this is, after all, very true). Maybe for this reason, the person whose age is stated takes the dative case. In Russian, you say literally "To me is 23 years old." You're not the subject in this sentence; the years are!

The translation of the words *year(s) old* depends on how old you are:

- If your age ends in 1, such as 21, 31, or 41, use the word **год** (goht) (*year*); for example, **Мне 21 год** (mnyeh *dvaht*-tsuht' ah-*deen* goht) (*I am 21 years old*).

- If your age ends in 2, 3, or 4, such as 22, 33, or 44, use the word **года** (goh-duh) (*years*); for example, **Мне 22 года** (mnyeh *dvaht*-tsuht' dvah goh-duh) (*I am 22 years old*).

- If your age ends in 5, 6, 7, 8, or 9, such as 25 or 59, use the word **лет** (lyeht) (*years*); for example, **Мне 25 лет** (mnyeh *dvaht*-tsuht' pyat' lyeht) (*I am 25 years old*).

- For ages that end in 0, such as 20, 30, or 40, use the word **лет** (lyeht) (*years*); for example, **Мне 20 лет** (mnyeh *dvaht*-tsuht' lyeht) (*I am 20 years old*).

Check out Chapter 3 for more information about cases and Chapter 5 for more about numbers.

Discussing your family

Family is a big part of Russian culture, so your Russian acquaintances will certainly be curious about yours. For example, they may ask

> **У вас большая семья?** (ooh vahs bahl'- *shah*-yeh seem-*ya*?) (*Do you have a big family?*)

At some point during a conversation with a new Russian friend, you may want to produce pictures of your family. Be prepared to state who the people in the pictures are!

The following words come in handy when talking about your family:

- **мать** (maht') (*mother*)
- **отец** (ah-*tyehts*) (*father*)
- **родители** (rah-*dee*-tee-lee) (*parents*)
- **сын** (sin) (*son*)
- **сыновья** (si-nah-*v'ya*) (*sons*)

- дочь (dohch') (*daughter*)

- дочери (*doh*-chee-ree) (*daughters*)

- жена (zhi-*nah*) (*wife*)

- муж (moosh) (*husband*)

- брат (braht) (*brother*)

- братья (*brah*-t'yeh) (*brothers*)

- сестра (sees-*trah*) (*sister*)

- сёстры (*syohs*-tri) (*sisters*)

- ребёнок (ree-*byoh*-nahk) (*child*)

- дети (*dyeh*-tee) (*children*)

- бабушка (*bah*-boohsh-kuh) (*grandmother*)

- дедушка (*dyeh*-doohsh-kuh) (*grandfather*)

- бабушка и дедушка (*bah*-boohsh-kuh ee *dyeh*-doohsh-kuh) (*grandparents*, Literally: *grandmother and grandfather*)

- внук (vnoohk) (*grandson*)

- внуки (*vnooh*-kee) (*grandsons*)

- внучка (*vnoohch*-kuh) (*granddaughter*)

- внучки (*vnoohch*-kee) (*granddaughters*)

- внуки (*vnooh*-kee) (*grandchildren*)

- дядя (*dya*-dyeh) (*uncle*)

- тётя (*tyoh*-tyeh) (*aunt*)

- кузен (kooh-*zehn*) (*male cousin*)

- кузина (kooh-*zee*-nuh) (*female cousin*)

- племянник (plee-*mya*-neek) (*nephew*)

- племянница (plee-*mya*-nee-tsuh) (*niece*)

- семья (seem'-*ya*) (*family*)

While you're proudly showing your family pictures, you may want to say something about the people who are in them. At the very least, you want to be able to say something like "This is my wife" or "These are my children." Saying *this/that is* or *these are* in Russian is extremely easy: Just say Это plus the person you're introducing, as shown in these examples:

Это моя мать. (*eh*-tah mah-*ya* maht'.) (*This is my mother.*)

Это мой отец. (*eh*-tah mohy ah-*tyehts*.) (*This is my father.*)

Telling what you do for a living

From the Russian perspective, what you do for a living is crucial to understanding who you are as a person. So be prepared to hear this question:

> **Кто вы по-профессии?** (ktoh vi pah-prah-*fyeh*-see-ee?) (*What do you do for a living?* Literally: *Who are you by profession?*)

To answer this question, all you need is the phrase **Я** plus your profession, as in these examples:

> **Я юрист.** (ya yooh-*reest*.) (*I am a lawyer.*)

> **Я преподаватель.** (ya pree-pah-duh-*vah*-teel'.) (*I am a professor.*)

The following is a list of some common occupations. Find the one that best fits you:

- **агент по недвижимости** (uh-*gyehnt* puh need-*vee*-zhi-mahs-tee) (*real estate agent*)
- **актёр** (uhk-*tyohr*) (*actor*)
- **актриса** (uhk-*tree*-suh) (*actress*)
- **архитектор** (uhr-khee-*tyehk*-tahr) (*architect*)
- **безработный** (beez-ruh-*boht*-niy) (*unemployed*)
- **библиотекарь** (beeb-lee-ah-*tyeh*-kuhr') (*librarian*)
- **бизнесмен** (beez-nehs-*mehn*) (*businessman*)
- **бизнесменка** (beez-nehs-*mehn*-kuh) (*businesswoman*)
- **бухгалтер** (boo-*gahl*-teer) (*accountant*)
- **домохозяйка** (dah-mah-khah-*zyay*-kuh) (*homemaker*)
- **инженер** (een-zhi-*nyehr*) (*engineer*)
- **художник** (khoo-*dohzh*-neek) (*artist*)
- **медбрат** (meed-*braht*) (*male nurse*)
- **музыкант** (mooh-zi-*kahnt*) (*musician*)
- **медсестра** (meed-sees-*trah*) (*female nurse*)
- **менеджер** (*myeh*-need-zhehr) (*manager*)
- **писатель** (pee-*sah*-teel') (*author, writer*)
- **программист** (prah-gruh-*meest*) (*programmer*)
- **преподаватель** (pree-pah-duh-*vah*-teel') (*college or university professor*)
- **студент** (stooh-*dyehnt*) (*male student*)

- студентка (stooh-*dyehnt*-kuh) (*female student*)

The Russian words **студент** and **студентка** refer only to college or university students. The Russian words for elementary, middle, and high school students are **школьник** (*shkohl'*-neek) (*schoolboy*) and **школьница** (*shkohl'*-nee-tsuh) (*schoolgirl*).

- учитель (ooh-*chee*-teel') (*male teacher*)

- учительница (ooh-*chee*-teel'-nee-tsuh) (*female teacher*)

- врач (vrahch) (*physician*)

- юрист (yooh-*reest*) (*attorney, lawyer*)

- журналист (zhoohr-nuh-*leest*) (*journalist*)

- зубной врач (zoohb-*nohy* vrahch) (*dentist*)

As you can see in the preceding list, some professions have separate versions for males and females, whereas others are used for both men and women.

You can also specify where you work when someone asks you this question:

Где вы работаете? (gdyeh vi ruh-*boh*-tuh-ee-tee?) (*Where do you work?*)

Russian doesn't have an equivalent for the English "I work for United" or "He works for FedEx." Instead of *for*, Russian uses its equivalent of *at*: The prepositions **в** (v) or **на** (nah) both correspond to the English *at* or *in*. Rather than saying "I work for United," a Russian says "I work at United."

The Russian prepositions **в** and **на** require the noun that denotes the place to take the prepositional case to show location (see Chapter 3). Following are some of the most common types of places people work. We include the right preposition and prepositional case, so you can start telling people where you work right away. Say **Я работаю** (ya rah-*boh*-tuh-yooh) (*I work*) plus one of these phrases:

- дома (*doh*-muh) (*from home*)

- на фабрике (nuh *fah*-bree-kee) (*at a light-industry factory*)

Use **на фабрике** if you work at an enterprise that manufactures clothing, for example, and **на заводе** (see the following bullet) if you engage in manufacturing tractors, cars, turbines, and the like.

- на заводе (nuh zuh-*voh*-dee) (*at a heavy-industry plant*)

- в банке (v *bahn*-kee) (*at a bank*)

- в библиотеке (v beeb-lee-ah-*tyeh*-kee) (*in a library*)

- в больнице (v bahl'-*nee*-tsee) (*at a hospital*)

- в бюро недвижимости (v byooh-*roh* need-*vee*-zhi-mahs-tee) (*at a real estate agency*)

- ✔ **в коммерческой фирме** (f kah-*myehr*-chees-kahy *feer*-mee) (*at a business firm, company*)
- ✔ **в магазине** (v muh-guh-*zee*-nee) (*at a store*)
- ✔ **в школе** (f *shkoh*-lee) (*at school*)
- ✔ **в учреждении** (v oohch-reezh-*dyeh*-nee-ee) (*at an office*)
- ✔ **в университете** (v ooh-nee-veer-see-*tyeh*-tee) (*at a university*)
- ✔ **в юридической фирме** (v yooh-ree-*dee*-chees-kahy *feer*-mee) (*at a law firm*)

I'm Sorry! Explaining that You Don't Understand Something

When you first start conversing in Russian, chances are you won't comprehend a lot of what you hear. You can signal that you don't understand something in several ways. Choose the phrase you like best, or use them all to really get the message across:

Извините, я не понял. (eez-vee-*nee*-tee, ya nee *poh*-nyehl.) (*Sorry, I didn't understand*; masculine)

Извините, я не поняла. (eez-vee-*nee*-tee, ya nee pah-nyeh-*lah*.) (*Sorry, I didn't understand*; feminine)

Говорите, пожалуйста, медленнее! (gah-vah-*ree*-tee, pah-*zhahl*-stuh, *myehd*-lee-nee-ee!) (*Speak more slowly, please!*)

Как вы сказали? (kahk vi skuh-*zah*-lee?) (*What did you say?*)

Повторите, пожалуйста? (pahf-tah-*ree*-tee, pah-*zhahl*-stuh?) (*Could you please repeat that?*)

Let's Get Together: Giving and Receiving Contact Information

When you're about to take your leave from a new Russian acquaintance, you may want to exchange contact information. The easiest way to do this is to just hand over your business card and say

Это моя карточка. (*eh*-tuh mah-*ya kahr*-tahch-kuh.) (*This is my card.*)

In the event that you don't have a business card, you need to know these phrases:

- **Мой адрес** (mohy *ah*-drees) (*My address is*)

- **Моя улица** (mah-*ya ooh*-lee-tsuh) (*My street is*)

- **Мой номер дома** (mohy *noh*-meer *doh*-muh) (*My house number is*)

- **Мой индекс** (mohy *een*-dehks) (*My zip code is*)

- **Мой номер телефона** (mohy *noh*-meer tee-lee-*foh*-nuh) (*My telephone number is*)

Russian telephone numbers are always written and spoken as XXX-XX-XX.

- **Мой адрес по имейлу** (mohy *ahd*-rees puh ee-*myeh*-ee-looh) (*My e-mail address is*)

When providing your phone number, you have two options: You can either dictate each number separately (the easy way) or use hundreds and tens. For example, if your phone number is 567-5544, you may want to say it like this: **пятьсот шестьдесят семь-пятьдесят пять-сорок четыре** (peet-*soht* shis-dee-*syat* syehm'-pee-dee-*syat* pyat'-*soh*-rahk chee-*ti*-ree). Note that the first section is a "hundred" number; the other two are "tens" (for more on numbers, see Chapter 5).

After you give your contact info, be sure to get your new friend's info in return. You can use these questions:

Какой у вас адрес? (kuh-*kohy* ooh vahs *ahd*-rees?) (*What is your address?*)

Какой у вас номер телефона? (kah-*kohy* ooh vahs *noh*-meer tee-lee-*foh*-nuh?) (*What is your phone number?*)

Какой у вас e-mail? (kah-*kohy* ooh vahs ee-*meh*-eel?) (*What is your e-mail address?*)

Talkin' the Talk

John (**Джон**) and Natasha (**Наташа**) have been talking for hours. Their plane has just landed at the Moscow airport and they're exchanging their contact information. (Track 11)

Джон: **Наташа, можно вам позвонить?**
nuh-*tah*-shuh, *mohzh*-nah vahm pahz-vah-*neet'*?
Natasha, can I call you?

Наташа: **Да. Мой телефон: 315-48-54.**
dah. mohy tee-lee-*fohn* tree ah-*deen* pyaht chee-*ti*-ree *voh*-seem pyaht' chee-*ti*-ree
Yes. My phone number is 315-48-54.

Джон: **А это номер мобильника. Это телефон в гостинице.**
ah *eh*-tah *noh*-meer mah-*beel'*-nee-kuh. *eh*-tah tee-lee-*fohn* v gahs-*tee*-nee-tseh.
And this is my cellphone number. This is my phone in the hotel.

Наташа: **Хорошо. Спасибо. Очень приятно было познакомиться!**
khah-rah-*shoh*. spuh-*see*-bah. *oh*-cheen' pree-*yat*-nah *bi*-lah pahz-nuh-*koh*-meet'-syeh!
Good. Thank you. It was nice to meet you!

Words to Know

Можно вам позвонить?	<u>mohzh</u>-nah vahm pahz-vah-<u>neet</u>'?	Can I call you?
номер телефона	<u>noh</u>-meer tee-lee-<u>foh</u>-nuh	phone number
Хорошо.	khah-rah-<u>shoh</u>.	Good.
Спасибо.	spuh-<u>see</u>-bah.	Thank you.
Очень приятно было познакомиться.	<u>oh</u>-cheen' pree-<u>yat</u>-nah <u>bi</u>-lah pahz-nuh-<u>koh</u>-meet'-syeh.	It was nice to meet you.

Fun & Games

Which of the two words in each line indicates a woman? See the answers in Appendix D.

1. a. **американец**   b. **американка**

2. a. **русские**   b. **русская**

3. a. **немцы**   b. **немка**

4. a. **еврейка**   b. **еврей**

5. a. **француженка**   b. **француз**

Chapter 8

Asking for Directions

· ·

In This Chapter

▶ Asking questions with "where" and "how"

▶ Understanding the directions you're given

· ·

For anyone in an unfamiliar place, asking for directions (and understanding them) is an indispensable skill. In this chapter, we give you the words and phrases you need in order to get to your destination without getting lost in the process. As exciting as exploring a new place may seem, being lost in a strange city can be scary. We give you the info you need to get wherever you want to go.

Using "Where" and "How" Questions

In Russia, most passers-by — who at first may seem to be preoccupied with their own business — are actually very happy to help you if you don't know where a place is or how to get there. As a matter of fact, you may even be doing them a favor by distracting their attention from their routine duties. When in doubt, just ask! In the following sections you discover how to ask for directions with two simple words: "where" and "how."

Asking where a place is

Russian uses two words to translate the English *where* — где (gdyeh) and куда (kooh-*dah*) — but you can't use these words interchangeably. The following is what you need to know about them:

✔ If "where" indicates *location* rather than direction of movement and you aren't using the so-called verbs of motion (to go, to walk, to drive, and so on), use the word где.

✔ If "where" indicates *direction* of movement rather than location or is used in a sentence with verbs of motion (to go, to walk, to drive, and so on), use the word куда.

Here are a couple examples:

> **Где Саша работает?** (gdyeh *sah*-shuh ruh-*boh*-tuh-yeht?) (*Where does Sasha work?*)

> **Куда Саша идёт?** (kooh-*dah* sah-shuh ee-*dyoht*?) (*Where is Sasha going?*)

When we say *verbs of motion,* we mean any verb that's associated with motion: going, walking, running, jogging, swimming, rowing, crawling, climbing, getting to, and so on. Flip to Chapter 16 for details on different verbs of motion.

Imagine you're looking for the nearest bus stop to get to a museum that's first on the list of places you want to see in a certain city. There you are, helplessly standing on the corner of a crowded street, looking for the person with the friendliest expression to approach with your question. You spot a young woman who seems nice. Why not ask her?

Hold on! What exactly do you intend to ask her? If you're planning to ask "Where is the bus stop?" first think about how you're going to translate the word "where." Are you inquiring about location or destination here? Obviously, your question is about location — the location of the bus stop. Go back to the rule we just provided you. In a sentence or question asking about location, you use **где**. Now you can go ahead and ask your question:

> **Где остановка автобуса?** (gdyeh ahs-tuh-*nohf*-kuh uhf-*toh*-booh-suh?) (*Where is the bus stop?*)

Now, imagine a slightly different situation. You're at the bus station. A bus has just arrived and you want to know where it's going. The best person to ask is probably the driver himself: He should know where the bus is headed, even if today is his first day on the job. Before you ask your question, think first about how to begin it: with **где** or **куда**? Is your question "Where is the bus going?" about location or destination? Yes, you're asking a question about the destination! Go back to the earlier rules: If the main point of your question is destination, you should use the word **куда**. Here's your question:

> **Куда идёт этот автобус?** (kooh-*dah* ee-*dyoht* eh-taht uhf-*toh*-boohs?) (*Where is this bus going?*)

Inquiring how to get to a place

You're standing at the corner of a crowded street, and a young woman is passing by. You want to ask her how you can get to the **музей** (mooh-*zyehy*) (*museum*) you planned to see today. To ask this question, you need the verb **попасть** (pah-*pahst'*) (*to get to*). The phrase *How do I get to* is **Как я отсюда могу попасть** (kahk ya aht-*syooh*-duh mah-*gooh* pah-*pahst'*). The following is what you want to ask:

Как я отсюда могу попасть в музей? (kahk ya aht-*syooh*-duh mah-*gooh* pah-*pahst'* v mooh-*zyehy*?) (*How do I get to the museum from here?*)

Russian uses the same prepositions, **в** and **на**, to express both "to (a place)" and "in/at (a place)." When you use **в** or **на** to indicate movement, the noun indicating the place of destination takes the accusative case. If you use **в** or **на** to denote location, the noun denoting location is used in the prepositional case. (For more on cases, see Chapter 3.)

At this point, you may be wondering when you use **на** and when you use **в**. The choice of the preposition depends on the noun it's used with. With most nouns, Russian uses **в** (to mean *to, into, in,* or *inside*). But a number of nouns require **на** (to mean *to, onto, at,* or *on*). Note that the meaning of **в** or **на** depends on the case: In the accusative case it means *to*; in the prepositional case, it means *at* or *in*. Here are a few useful phrases using **в** and **на** with the accusative case referring to destination:

- ✔ **в университет** (v ooh-nee-veer-see-*tyeht*) (*to the university*)
- ✔ **в школу** (v *shkoh*-looh) (*to school*)
- ✔ **в магазин** (v muh-guh-*zeen*) (*to the store*)
- ✔ **на стадион** (nuh stuh-dee-*ohn*) (*to the stadium*)
- ✔ **на вокзал** (nuh vahk-*zahl*) (*to the railway station*)
- ✔ **на фабрику** (nuh *fah*-bree-kooh) (*to the factory*)
- ✔ **на завод** (nuh zuh-*voht*) (*to the industrial plant*)
- ✔ **на площадь** (nuh *ploh*-sh'eet') (*to the square*)

The Next Step: Understanding Specific Directions

When you're asking for directions, it's important to understand what you're being told. In the following sections, you find out how to understand verbs in the imperative mood as well as prepositions and other phrases that often are used in giving and receiving directions.

Curiously enough, Russians don't like to indicate directions with the words **восток** (vahs-*tohk*) (*east*), **запад** (*zah*-puht) (*west*), **север** (*syeh*-veer) (*north*), and **юг** (yoohk) (*south*). They avoid them when explaining how you can reach your destination.

Making sense of commands in the imperative mood

Usually, when somebody gives you directions, they tell you where to go, not just where something is located. The *imperative mood* is the form of the verb in which you hear and give directions. It's indispensable for making polite requests, giving commands, and generally ordering people around.

Here are some useful phrases in the imperative mood that you may hear or want to use when giving and receiving directions:

- **Идите прямо** (ee-*dee*-tee *prya*-mah) (*Go straight*)

- **Идите обратно** (ee-*dee*-tee ahb-*raht*-nah) (*Go back*)

- **Идите прямо до** (ee-*dee*-tee *prya*-muh duh) (*Go as far as*) + the noun in the genitive case

- **Подойдите к** (pah-dahy-*dee*-tee k) (*Go up to*) + the noun in the dative case

- **Идите по** (ee-*dee*-tee puh) (*Go down along*) + the noun in the dative case

- **Пройдите мимо** (prahy-*dee*-tee *mee*-mah) (*Pass by*) + the noun in the genitive case

- **Поверните налево** (puh-veer-*nee*-tee nuh-*lyeh*-vah) (*Turn left* or *Take a left turn*)

- **Поверните направо** (pah-veer-*nee*-tee nuh-*prah*-vah) (*Turn right* or *Take a right turn*)

- **Заверните за угол** (zuh-veer-*nee*-tee *zah* ooh-gahl) (*Turn around the corner*)

- **Перейдите улицу** (pee-reey-*dee*-tee *ooh*-lee-tsooh) (*Cross the street*)

Listening for prepositions

When people provide you with directions, they often use prepositions that you need to recognize in order to understand the directions you're given:

- **около** (*oh*-kah-lah) (*near*) + a noun in the genitive case

- **рядом с** (*rya*-dahm s) (*next to*) + a noun in the instrumental case

- **напротив** (nuh-*proh*-teef) (*opposite, across from*) + a noun in the genitive case

- за (zah) (*beyond*) + a noun in the instrumental case

- позади (puh-zuh-*dee*) (*behind*) + a noun in the genitive case

- перед (*pyeh*-reet) (*in front of*) + a noun in the instrumental case

- между (*myehzh*-dooh) (*between*) + a noun in the instrumental case

- внутри (vnooh-*tree*) (*inside*) + a noun in the genitive case

- снаружи (snuh-*rooh*-zhih) (*outside*) + a noun in the genitive case

- над (naht) (*above*) + a noun in the instrumental case

- под (poht) (*below*) + a noun in the instrumental case

When you ask a simple question like **Где музей?** (gdyeh mooh-*zyehy*?) (*Where is the museum?*), you may get a response like this:

> **Музей рядом с театром, за магазином, между аптекой и почтой, напротив универмага.** (mooh-*zyehy rya*-dahm s tee-*aht*-rahm, zuh muh-guh-*zee*-nahm, *myehzh*-dooh uhp-*tyeh*-kahy ee *pohch*-tahy, nuh-*proh*-teef ooh-nee-veer-*mah*-guh.) (*The museum is next to the theater, beyond the store, between the pharmacy and the post office, opposite the department store.*)

Note that each of the prepositions in the preceding sentence requires a different case for the noun or phrase following it. Do we really expect you to be able to juggle all these cases? No, not at all. Your modest task for now is only to be able to understand the directions rather than provide them — unless, of course, you're planning on moving to Russia to become a traffic police officer. For more info on cases, see Chapter 3.

Keeping "right" and "left" straight

When people give you directions in Russian, they often use phrases that use the words *left* and *right*:

- справа от (*sprah*-vuh aht) (*to the right of*) + a noun in the genitive case

- направо (nuh-*prah*-vah) (*to the right*)

- слева от (*slyeh*-vuh aht) (*to the left of*) + a noun in the genitive case

- налево (nuh-*lyeh*-vuh) (*to the left*)

- на левой стороне (nuh *lyeh*-vahy stah-rah-*nyeh*) (*on the left side*)

- на правой стороне (nuh *prah*-vahy stah-rah-*nyeh*) (*on the right side*)

Peter the Great's training methods

Peter the Great, the creator of the regular Russian Army, often trained the new recruits himself. The young recruits, who were often illiterate peasants, had an extremely hard time distinguishing between the two military commands — **направо** (nuh-*prah*-vah) (*to the right*) and **налево** (nuh-*lyeh*-vah) (*to the left*). To overcome this problem, the great tsar was said to have invented a new method of training new soldiers. He used two words the young peasants could distinguish very well: **солома** (sah-*loh*-muh) (*straw*) to indicate **направо** and **сено** (*syeh*-nah) (*hay*) to indicate **налево**. And guess what? The method worked very well!

Here's a short exchange that may take place between you and a friendly-looking Russian woman:

You: **Извините, где магазин?** (eez-vee-*nee*-tee, gdyeh muh-guh-*zeen*?) (*Excuse me, where is the store?*)

The woman: **Магазин справа от аптеки.** (muh-guh-*zeen sprah*-vuh aht uhp-*tyeh*-kee.) (*The store is to the right of the pharmacy.*)

Talkin' the Talk

Two friends, Oleg (**Олег**) and Sergey (**Сергей**), are talking on the phone. It's Saturday night, and Oleg suggests that they go to a new restaurant. He has already been there and is now explaining to Sergey where the restaurant is located. (Track 12)

Олег:	**Давай пойдём в этот новый ресторан, Симфония.** duh-*vahy* pahy-*dyohm* v *eh*-taht *noh*-viy rees-tah-*rahn*, seem-*foh*-nee-yeh. *Let's go to this new restaurant, Symphony.*
Сергей:	**А, давай. Но я там ещё не был. Где это?** uh, duh-*vahy*. noh ya tahm ee-*shyoh* nyeh bil. gdyeh *eh*-tah? *Oh, okay. But I haven't been there yet. Where is it?*

Олег:	**Ты знаешь где кинотеатр Аврора?**
	ti *znah*-eesh' gdyeh kee-nah-tee-*ahtr* uhv-*roh*-ruh?
	Do you know where the Aurora movie theater is?

Сергей:	**Ну?**
	nooh?
	No, go on! (Literally: Well?)

Олег:	**Это недалеко от Авроры, на другой стороне.**
	eh-tuh nee-duh-lee-*koh* aht uhv-*roh*-ri, nuh drooh-*gohy* stah-rah-*nyeh*.
	It's not far from Aurora, on the other side of the street.

Сергей:	**Это что рядом с булочной?**
	eh-tuh shtoh *rya*-dahm s *booh*-lahch-nahy?
	Is it the one next to the bakery?

Олег:	**Да, справа от булочной и слева от аптеки.**
	dah, *sprah*-vuh aht *booh*-lahch-nahy ee *slyeh*-vuh aht uhp-*tyeh*-kee.
	Yes, to the right of the bakery, to the left of the pharmacy.

Сергей:	**Между булочной и аптекой?**
	myehzh-dooh *booh*-lahch-nahy ee uhp-*tyeh*-kahy?
	Between the bakery and the pharmacy?

Олег:	**Да, напротив бара Восток.**
	dah, nuh-*proh*-teef *bah*-ruh vahs-*tohk*.
	Yes, opposite Vostok bar.

Words to Know

Давай пойдём в	duh-_vahy_ pahy-_dyohm_ v	Let's go to
Я там ещё не был.	ya tahm ee-_shyoh_ nyeh bil.	I have not been there yet.
Где это?	gdyeh _eh_-tah?	Where is it?
Ну	nooh	Well (Go on!)
Это недалеко от	_eh_-tuh nee-duh-lee-_koh_ aht	It's not far from
на другой стороне	nuh drooh-_gohy_ stah-rah-_nyeh_	on the other side of the street
рядом с	_rya_-dahm s	next to
справа от	_sprah_-vuh aht	to the right of
слева от	_slyeh_-vuh aht	to the left of
между	_myehzh_-dooh	between
напротив	nuh-_proh_-teef	opposite

Going here and there

The English word _here_ has two different Russian equivalents:

- ✔ Use Здесь (zdyehs') to indicate location — in other words, when you're not dealing with a verb of motion.
- ✔ Use сюда (syooh-_dah_) if _here_ indicates destination and is used with a verb of motion, such as go, come, drive, and so forth.

Likewise, the word _there_ has two Russian equivalents:

- ✔ Use там (tahm) to indicate location.
- ✔ Use туда (too-_dah_) to indicate destination.

Compare these examples:

Остановка автобуса здесь. (ahs-tah-*nohf*-kuh uhf-*toh*-booh-suh zdyehs'.) (*The bus stop is here.*)

Иди сюда! (ee-*dee* syooh-*dah*!) (*Come here!*)

Магазин там. (muh-guh-*zeen* tahm.) (*The store is there.*)

Иди туда! (ee-*dee* tooh-*dah*!) (*Go there!*)

Talkin' the Talk

Tom (**Том**) is an American graduate student who is in St. Petersburg to study Russian literature. He asks a **работник обще-жития** (ruh-*boht*-neek ahp-sh'ee-*zhee*-tee-yeh) (*dorm employee*) how to get to the Dostoevsky museum. (Track 13)

Том:
Скажите пожалуйста, как мне отсюда попасть в музей Достоевского?
skuh-*zhi*-tee, pah-*zhahl*-stuh, kahk mnyeh aht-*syooh*-duh pah-*pahst'* v mooh-*zyehy* dahs-tah-*yehf*-skah-vah?
Could you please tell me how I can get to the Dostoevsky museum from here?

Работник
общежития:
Музей Достоевского находится на Кузнечном переулке, недалеко от Кузнечного рынка. Вы знаете где Кузнечный рынок?
mooh-*zyehy* dahs-tah-*yehf*-skah-vah nuh-*khoh*-deet-syeh nuh koohz-*nyehch*-nahm pee-ree-*oohl*-kee, nee-duh-lee-*koh* aht koohz-*nyehch*-nah-vah *rin*-kuh. vi *znah*-ee-tee gdyeh koohz-*nyehch*-niy *ri*-nahk?
The Dostoevsky museum is located on Kuznyechnyj Lane, not far from Kuznyechnyj market. Do you know where Kuznyechnyj market is?

Том:
Нет, я первый день в Петербурге.
nyeht, ya *pyehr*-viy dyehn' f pee-teer-*boohr*-gee.
No, it's my first day in St. Petersburg.

Работник
общежития:
Вам надо выйти на Невский проспект и повер-нуть направо. Идите прямо по Невскому проспекту, до Николаевской улицы. Там поверните направо. Когда дойдёте до Кузнечного переулка, поверните направо. Музей будет на левой стороне.

vahm *nah*-dah *viy*-tee nuh *nyehf*-skeey prahs-*pyehkt*
ee pah-veer-*nooht'* nuh-*prah*-vah. ee-*dee*-tee *prya*-
mah pah *nyehf*-skah-mooh prahs-*pyehk*-tooh, dah
nee-kah-*lah*-eev-skohy *ooh*-lee-tsi. tahm pah-veer-
nee-tee nuh-*prah*-vah. kahg-*dah* dahy-*dyoh*-tee dah
koohz-*nyehch*-nah-vah pee-ree-*oohl*-kuh, pah-veer-
nee-tee nuh-*prah*-vah. mooh-*zyehy* *booh*-deet nuh
lyeh-vahy stah-rah-*nyeh*.
*You need to go out to Nevsky Avenue and turn right.
Go straight along Nevsky Avenue, don't turn anywhere until you reach Marat Street. Turn right again
there. When you reach Kuznyechnyj Lane, turn right
again. The museum is on the left-hand side.*

Words to Know

Как мне отсюда попасть в...?	kahk mnyeh aht-<u>syooh</u>-duh pah-<u>pahst'</u> v...?	How can I get to ... from here?
находится	nuh-<u>khoh</u>-deet-syeh	is located
выйти на	<u>viy</u>-tee nuh	go out to
повернуть направо	pah-veer-<u>nooht'</u> nuh-<u>prah</u>-vah	turn right
идите прямо по	ee-<u>dee</u>-tee <u>prya</u>-mah pah	go straight along
когда дойдёте до	kahg-<u>dah</u> dahy-<u>dyoh</u>-tee dah	When you reach

Traveling near and far

Sometimes you don't want detailed information about directions. You just want to know whether someplace is near or far and how long it takes to get there. The Russian word for *near* is **близко** (*blees*-kah), and the Russian word for *far* is **далеко** (duh-lee-*koh*).

In giving directions, Russians usually like to indicate distance in terms of the time it takes to get there. Outdoorsy, younger people may say, for example:

> **Это близко. Минут пятнадцать пешком.** (*eh*-tah *blees*-kah. mee-*nooht* peet-*naht*-suht peesh-*kohm*.) (*It's near. About 15 minutes' walk.*)

Those people who don't fancy walking that much may see the same distance differently and say:

> **Это далеко. Минут пятнадцать пешком.** (*eh*-tah duh-lee-*koh*. mee-*nooht* peet-*naht*-suht' peesh-*kohm*.) (*It's far. About 15 minutes' walk.*)

You may notice that in both the preceding responses, the word **минут** (*minutes*) is placed before the numeral **пятнадцать** (*15*), and you may be wondering whether it's an error. Nope! Russian has a very special way of indicating approximate time, weight, distance, and even prices. Where English uses the word "about," Russian may simply reverse the order of words, as in **Минут пятнадцать пешком** (mee-*nooht* peet-*naht*-suht' peesh-*kohm*) (*About 15 minutes' walk*). To be more exact, a Russian would say **Пятнадцать минут пешком** (peet-*naht*-suht' mee-*nooht* peesh-*kohm*) (*Exactly 15 minutes' walk*).

A very popular way of indicating the distance in Russia is to count the number of bus, tram, trolleybus, or subway stops to the place you're inquiring about. If you think a 15-minute walk is a big deal, especially if you're tired, you may say in response:

> **Это довольно далеко. Две остановки на трамвае/автобусе/троллейбусе/метро.** (*eh*-tah dah-*vohl'*-nah duh-lee-*koh*. dvyeh ahs-tuh-*nohf*-kee nuh truhm-*vah*-ee/uhf-*toh*-booh-see/trah-*lyehy*-booh-see/meet-*roh*.) (*That's quite far away. Two stops by the tram/bus/trolleybus/metro.*)

Fun & Games

Match each picture indicated by a letter with one of the following phrases (see Appendix D for the answers). (*Note:* **дом** (dohm) means *house*; **на левой стороне** (nuh-*lyeh*-vahy stah-rah-*nyeh*) means *on the left-hand side*; **на правой стороне** (nuh *prah*-vohy stah-rah-*nyeh*) means *on the right-hand side*.)

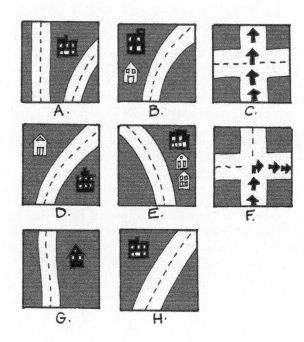

1. _____ **Дом напротив**

2. _____ **Дом на правой стороне**

3. _____ **Это третий дом на правой стороне**

4. _____ **Идите прямо**

5. _____ **Дом на левой стороне**

6. _____ **Это второй дом на левой стороне**

7. _____ **Дом между двумя улицами**

8. _____ **Поверните направо**

Chapter 9

Dining Out and Going to the Market

. . . .

In This Chapter

▶ Dining in restaurants and cafés

▶ Shopping for food

. . . .

Russians are famous for their bountiful cuisine. Whether you like to go out to restaurants or prefer homemade meals, knowing how to talk about food is helpful. In this chapter, we discuss dining out and shopping for groceries. For the basics on words used to discuss eating, drinking, and various meals, flip to Chapter 6; for the lowdown on non-food-oriented shopping, turn to Chapter 10.

Eating Out in Russia

Eating out at Russian restaurants and cafés can be a lot of fun, especially if you know Russian. In the following sections, we go over the different kinds of restaurants you can go to, how to reserve your table, the right way to order a meal, and how to pay your bill.

Finding a place to eat

You can find lots of different places to eat out Russian-style, depending on your mood and budget. If you're in the mood for a night of culinary delights with a full eight-course meal, lots of drinks, and live music, check out a fancy Russian **ресторан** (rees-tah-*rahn*) (*restaurant*). Make sure you have a healthy budget and are well-rested, because prices are steep and you won't be coming home 'til the wee hours of the morning!

A more affordable everyday option is a **кафе** (kuh-*feh*) (*café*), which may serve anything from coffee and ice cream to pancakes or pies. Cafés are privately owned and have such interesting names (often unrelated to food) that if you pass one of them on the street, you may not even recognize it as a place to eat!

Making reservations on the phone

After you decide which restaurant to go to, pick up the phone and make a reservation. (You don't need reservations for informal cafés, but for more upscale, popular restaurants, you do.)

✔ If you're a man, say **Я хотел бы заказать столик на сегодня** (ya khah-*tyehl* bi zuh-kuh-*zaht' stoh*-leek nuh see-*vohd*-nyeh) (*I'd like to reserve a table for tonight*).

✔ If you're a woman, say **Я хотела бы заказать столик на сегодня** (ya khah-*tyeh*-luh bi zuh-kuh-*zaht' stoh*-leek nuh see-*vohd*-nyeh) (*I'd like to reserve a table for tonight*).

When you say **я хотел(а) бы заказать**, you're using the Russian subjunctive mood — the easiest structure in Russian grammar. You just use the past tense of the verb plus the word **бы** (bi). Flip to Chapter 3 for an introduction to using the past tense.

If you want to reserve a table for tomorrow, just replace the phrase **на сегодня** (nuh see-*vohd*-nyeh) (*for tonight*) with the phrase **на завтра** (nuh *zahf*-truh) (*for tomorrow*). If you want to specify a day of the week, use the preposition **на** plus the day of the week in the accusative case. So, for example, if you want to make a reservation for Saturday and you're a male, you say

Я хотел бы заказать столик на субботу. (ya khah-*tyehl* bi zuh-kuh-*zaht' stoh*-leek nuh sooh-*boh*-tooh.) (*I'd like to reserve a table for Saturday.*)

We talk about the days of the week in Chapter 5; check out Chapter 3 for details on the accusative case.

You'll probably hear this in response: **На сколько человек?** (nuh *skohl'*-kah chee-lah-*vyehk*?) (*For how many people?*). To answer this question, use one of these phrases:

✔ **на одного** (nuh ahd-nah-*voh*) (*for one person*)

✔ **на двоих** (nuh dvah-*eekh*) (*for two*)

✔ **на троих** (nuh trah-*eekh*) (*for three*)

If you need reservations for more people, use **на** + the number of people:

✔ **на четыре человека** (nuh chee-*ti*-ree chee-lah-*vyeh*-kuh) (*for four people*)

✔ **на пять человек** (nuh pyaht' chee-lah-*vyehk*) (*for five people*)

✔ **на шесть человек** (nuh shehst' chee-lah-*vyehk*) (*for six people*)

The case for the word *people* depends on the number of people (see Chapter 3 for more info).

The person on the phone will probably want to know what time your table should be ready, in which case she'll ask **На какое время?** (nuh kuh-*koh*-ee *vryeh*-myeh?) (*For what time?*). To answer this question, use the preposition **на** (nah) (*for*) followed by the time you plan to arrive in the accusative case, which coincides here with the nominative case. For example, if you want a reservation for 7 o'clock, say **на семь часов** (nuh syehm' chuh-*sohf*) (*for 7 o'clock*). (See Chapter 5 for full details on talking about time.) Also be prepared to give your name (see Chapter 4).

Don't expect to be asked whether you want to sit in the smoking or nonsmoking section. Too many people in Russia smoke (especially when drinking alcoholic beverages), and smokers rule. Even those people who don't generally smoke tend to smoke in restaurants.

Ordering a meal

After you arrive at the restaurant and are seated by the **мэтрдотель** (mehtr-dah-*tehl'*) (*maitre d'hotel*), the **официант** (ah-fee-tsi-*ahnt*) (*waiter*) or **официантка** (ah-fee-tsee-*ahnt*-kuh) (*waitress*) will bring you a **меню** (mee-*nyooh*) (*menu*). In a nice restaurant, all the dishes on the menu are usually in English as well as Russian.

When you open the menu, you'll notice it's divided into several subsections, with items listed in the order in which they're usually eaten in a Russian restaurant:

- ✔ **закуски** (zuh-*koohs*-kee) (*appetizers*)

- ✔ **супы** (sooh-*pi*) (*soups*)

- ✔ **горячие блюда** (gah-*rya*-chee-ee blyooh-*dah*) (*main dishes*)

- ✔ **сладкие блюда** (*slaht*-kee-ee blyooh-*dah*) (*dessert*)

- ✔ **алкогольные напитки** (uhl-kah-*gohl'*-ni-ee nuh-*peet*-kee) (*alcoholic drinks*)

- ✔ **безалкогольные напитки** (beez-uhl-kah-*gohl'*-ni-ee nuh-*peet*-kee) (*nonalcoholic beverages*)

When the waiter asks **Что вы будете заказывать?** (shtoh vi *booh*-dee-tee zuh-*kah*-zi-vuht'?) (*What would you like to order?*), just say **Я буду** (ya *booh*-dooh) (*I will have*) followed by the name of the item you're ordering in the accusative case. (For details on forming the accusative case, see Chapter 3.) For example, you may say something like this:

> **Я буду котлету с картофелем и салат из помидоров.** (ya *booh*-dooh kaht-*lyeh*-tooh s kuhr-*toh*-fee-leem ee suh-*laht* ees pah-mee-*doh*-rahf.) (*I'll have the meat patty with potatoes and tomato salad.*)

The waiter may also ask specifically, **Что вы будете пить?** (shtoh vi *booh*-dee-tee peet'?) (*What would you like to drink?*) To answer, you simply say **Я буду** (ya *booh*-dooh) (*I will have*) plus the name of the drink(s) you want in the accusative case. So, if at dinner you're extremely thirsty (and you aren't the designated driver), you may say

> **Я буду водку и сок и бутылку вина.** (ya *booh*-dooh *vohd*-kooh ee sohk ee booh-*til*-kooh vee-*nah*.) (*I'll have vodka and juice and a bottle of wine.*)

Waiters and waitresses don't take your drink order before you start ordering your meal; expect to be asked what you want to drink at the end of your order. Also, having water or soda with your meal isn't as common as it is in the West. As a matter of fact, many Russians believe that one shouldn't chase food with water or any other beverage because it interferes with food digestion. But drinks will certainly be brought with your meal if you order them.

When you're done ordering, say **Всё!** (fsyoh!) (*That's it!*). Otherwise, the waiter will continue to stand next to you, waiting for you to order more.

Having handy phrases for the wait staff

In this section, we include more helpful phrases you may want to use when you're eating out to ensure your meal is satisfactory and to express your appreciation.

If you're a vegetarian, the best way to ask about vegetarian dishes is to say

> **Какие у вас есть вегетерианские блюда?** (kuh-*kee*-ee ooh vahs yehst' vee-gee-teh-ree-*ahns*-kee-ee blyooh-*duh*?) (*What vegetarian dishes do you have?*)

Note, however, that Russians still view vegetarianism as a very bizarre habit. Imagine that you're sitting in a restaurant waiting for the vegetarian dish you ordered. Instead, the waiter puts in front of you a steaming, juicy beefsteak with potatoes. What do you do? Before that waiter leaves your table, say **Я это не заказывал/заказывала!** (ya *eh*-tah nee zuh-*kah*-zi-vuhl/zuh-*kah*-zi-vuh-luh!) (*I did not order this!*). (Use **заказывал** if you're a man and **заказывала** if you're a woman.)

If you suddenly recall something you meant to include in your order or decide that you want something else, try getting the attention of your waiter with something along these lines:

Извините, вы не могли бы принести воду? (eez-vee-*nee*-tee, vi nee mahg-*lee* bi pree-nees-*tee voh*-dooh?) (*Excuse me, could you bring water?*).

Note that the name of any drink you want to ask for should be in the accusative case.

Other common problems you may come across can be resolved just by stating some facts about the meal that alert the waiter and make him take some countermeasures. For example, you may say

Это блюдо очень холодное. (*eh*-tah *blyooh*-dah *oh*-cheen' khah-*lohd*-nah-ee.) (*This dish is very cold.*)

If, on the other hand, you enjoyed your meal and service, be sure to say Всё было очень вкусно (fsyoh *bi*-lah *oh*-cheen' *fkoohs*-nah!) (*Everything was very tasty!*) and/or Спасибо за отличное обслуживание! (spuh-*see*-bah zuh aht-*leech*-nah-ee ahp-*slooh*-zhi-vuh-nee-ee!) (*Thank you for the excellent service!*)

Receiving and paying the bill

When it comes time to ask for the bill, don't expect the waiter to bring it automatically. When the waiter is in the vicinity, try to attract his attention either by waving or smiling at him or just saying (loudly, if necessary) Рассчитайте нас, пожалуйста! (ruh-chee-*tahy*-tee nahs, pah-*zhahl*-stuh!) (*Check, please!*)

Asking for several separate checks isn't common in Russia, and waiters aren't fond of splitting the bill. So ask for a check and then prepare to divide the amount by the number of eaters. If you're buying a meal for somebody or everybody at the table, announce it by saying one of the following:

Я заплачу. (Ya zuh-pluh-*chooh*.) (*I will pay.*)

Я плачу. (ya pluh-*chooh*.) (*I am paying.*)

Я угощаю. (ya ooh-gah-*shya*-yooh.) (*My treat.*)

Checks aren't accepted in Russia. You may be able to pay with a credit card, but ask first:

Вы принимаете кредитные карточки? (vih pree-nee-*mah*-ee-tee kree-*deet*-ni-ee *kahr*-tuhch-kee?) (*Do you take credit cards?*)

The tip (usually not included in your bill) is slightly lower than, say, in the United States and is about 10 percent of the price of the meal. Russian customers, though, don't tip unconditionally: A lot depends on how they liked the service.

Talkin' the Talk

Jack (**Джек**) is in a nice restaurant in downtown Moscow. He has just been seated at a table and is now ordering his meal from the waiter (**официант**). (Track 14)

Официант: **Что вы будете заказывать?**
shtoh vi *booh*-dee-tee zuh-*kah*-zi-vuht'?
What would you like to order?

Джек: **На закуску, я буду холодный язык. А потом шашлык.**
nuh zuh-*koohs*-kooh, ya *booh*-dooh khah-*lohd*-niy ee-*zik*. uh pah-*tohm* shuhsh-*lik*.
For the appetizer, I will have tongue. And after that kebab.

Официант: **Что вы будете пить?**
shtoh vi *booh*-dee-tee peet'?
What would you like to drink?

Джек: **Какое у вас есть хорошее вино?**
kuh-*koh*-ee ooh vahs yehst' khah-*roh*-shi-ee vee-*noh*?
What good wine do you have?

Официант: **Есть хорошее армянское вино.**
yehst' khah-*roh*-shi-ee uhr-*myan*-skah-ee vee-*noh*.
We have a nice Armenian wine.

Джек: **Хорошо, принесите бокал армянского вина.**
khah-rah-*shoh*, pree-*nee*-see-tee bah-*kahl* uhr-*myan*-skah-vah vee-*nah*.
Okay, bring a bottle of Armenian wine.

Официант: **Всё?**
fsyoh?
That's it?

Джек: **Всё.**
fsyoh.
That's it.

Words to Know

Что вы будете заказывать?	shtoh vi _booh-dee-tee zuh-kah-zi-vuht'_?	What would you like to order?
на закуску	nuh zah-_koohs_-kooh	as an appetizer
Я буду	ya _booh_-dooh	I will have
Что вы будете пить?	shtoh vi _booh-dee-tee peet'_?	What would you like to drink?
Какое у вас есть хорошее вино?	kuh-_koh_-ee ooh vahs yehst' khah-_roh_-shi-ee vee-_noh_?	What good wine do you have?
Всё.	fsyoh.	That's it.

Going Out for Groceries

If you want to make a quick trip to the **продуктовый магазин** (prah-doohk-_toh_-viy muh-guh-_zeen_) (_grocery store_), **супермаркет** (sooh-peer-_mahr_-keet) (_supermarket_), or **рынок** (_ri_-nahk) (_farmers' market_), you have to know the names of foods and drinks. We provide the Russian terms for these items in the following sections.

Meats and fish

The signs for **мясо** (_mya_-sah) (_meat_) and **рыба** (_ri_-buh) (_fish_) in a supermarket or on the front window of a smaller store help you identify these foods. If you want to make sure you're buying the right type of meat, you may want to know these words:

- **баранина** (buh-_rah_-nee-nuh) (_mutton_ or _lamb_)
- **ветчина** (veet-chee-_nah_) (_ham_)
- **говядина** (gah-_vya_-dee-nuh) (_beef_)
- **колбаса** (kahl-buh-_sah_) (_sausage_)

✔ **курица** (*kooh*-ree-tsuh) (*chicken*)

✔ **свинина** (svee-*nee*-nuh) (*pork*)

✔ **телятина** (tee-*lya*-tee-nuh) (*veal*)

Fruits and vegetables

No meal is complete without some healthy produce. Here are the Russian terms for some popular fruits and vegetables:

✔ **арбуз** (ahr-*boohs*) (*watermelon*)

✔ **виноград** (vee-nah-*graht*) (*grapes*)

✔ **горох** (gah-*rohkh*) (*peas*)

✔ **груши** (*grooh*-shi) (*pears*)

✔ **капуста** (kuh-*poohs*-tuh) (*cabbage*)

✔ **клубника** (kloohb-*nee*-kuh) (*strawberry*)

✔ **лук** (loohk) (*onion*)

✔ **морковь** (mahr-*kohf'*) (*carrots*)

✔ **малина** (muh-*lee*-nuh) (*raspberries*)

✔ **огурцы** (uh-goohr-*tsi*) (*cucumbers*)

✔ **перец** (*pyeh*-reets) (*pepper*)

✔ **помидоры** (pah-mee-*doh*-ri) (*tomatoes*)

✔ **редиска** (ree-*dees*-kuh) (*radish*)

✔ **свёкла** (*svyohk*-luh) (*beets*)

✔ **чеснок** (chees-*nohk*) (*garlic*)

✔ **яблоки** (*ya*-bluh-kee) (*apples*)

✔ **ежевика** (ee-zhi-*vee*-kuh) (*blueberries*)

✔ **вишня** (*veesh*-nyeh) (*cherries*)

✔ **баклажан** (buhk-luh-*zhahn*) (*eggplant*)

Dairy products and eggs

Dairy products on a shopping list in Russian look like this:

✔ **кефир** (kee-*feer*) (*buttermilk*)

✔ **масло** (*mahs*-lah) (*butter*)

- ✔ **молоко** (mah-lah-*koh*) (*milk*)
- ✔ **сливки** (*sleef*-kee) (*cream*)
- ✔ **сметана** (smee-*tah*-nuh) (*sour cream*)
- ✔ **йогурт** (*yoh*-goohrt) (*yogurt*)
- ✔ **сыр** (sir) (*cheese*)

You usually find *eggs* near the dairy products in a grocery store; you call them **яйца** (*yay*-tsuh) in Russian.

Baked goods

Baked goods in a Russian grocery store can be located by the sign **Хлеб** (khlyehp) (*Bread*) or **Выпечка** (*vi*-peech-kuh) (*Bakery*). Here, you find several different types of baked items:

- ✔ **белый хлеб** (*byeh*-liy khlyehp) (*white bread*)
- ✔ **бублики** (*boohb*-lee-kee) (*bagels*)
- ✔ **чёрный хлеб** (*chyohr*-niy khlyehp) (*black/rye bread*)

A Russian tradition: Hot cereal

Having **каша** (*kah*-shuh) (*hot cereal*) in the morning seems to be a uniquely Russian tradition. **Каша** is basically a hot cereal made of a wide variety of grains. Here we list the most popular kinds of grains that **каша** is made of:

- ✔ **гречневая крупа** (*gryehch*-nee-vuh-yeh krooh-*pah*) (*buckwheat*)
- ✔ **манная крупа** (*mahn*-nuh-yeh krooh-*pah*) (*semolina*)
- ✔ **овсянка** (ahf-*syan*-kuh) (*oats*)
- ✔ **рис** (rees) (*rice*)

Russian folk wisdom insists that eating **каша** every morning is a guarantee of good health, especially for young children.

Cold cereal eaten for breakfast in the U.S. or other English-speaking countries is simply translated as **сириал** (*see*-ree-uhl).

Beverages

A widely popular legend has it that in the year 987, Vladimir, one of the first rulers of Russia, sent envoys to study the religions of the neighboring countries in order to decide which one would best fit his subjects. When presented with the option of selecting Islam, with its taboo on alcoholic beverages, Vladimir said: "Drinking is the joy of the Russes. We cannot exist without this pleasure."

The greatest pleasure most Russians enjoy comes from three main sources:

- водка (*voht*-kuh) (*vodka*)
- вино (vee-*noh*) (*wine*)
- пиво (*pee*-vuh) (*beer*)

Are there nonalcoholic drinks in Russia? Yes, there are! They include

- вода (vah-*dah*) (*water*)
- минеральная вода (mee-nee-*rahl'*-nuh-yeh vah-*dah*) (*mineral water*)
- сок (sohk) (*juice*)
- кофе (*koh*-fee) (*coffee*)
- чай (chahy) (*tea*)

Talkin' the Talk

Irina (**Ирина**) is buying meat in the meat and fish department of the supermarket. She is talking to the sales associate (**продавец**). (Track 15)

Ирина:	**Скажите, это говядина?** skuh-*zhi*-tee, *eh*-tah gah-*vya*-dee-nuh? *Could you tell me if this is beef?*
Продавец:	**Нет, свинина.** nyeht, svee-*nee*-nuh. *No, it's pork.*
Ирина:	**А это что? Тоже свинина?** uh *eh*-tah shtoh? *toh*-zhi svee-*nee*-nuh? *And what is this? Is it also pork?*
Продавец:	**Да, свинина.** dah, svee-*nee*-nuh. *Yes, it is pork.*

Ирина: **Хорошо выглядит. Дайте мне пожалуйста кило-грамм. Она свежая?**
khah-rah-*shoh* vi-glyeh-deet. *dahy*-tee mnyeh pah-*zhahl*-stuh kee-lah-*grahm*. ah-*nah* svyeh-zhuh-yeh?
This looks good. Give me a kilogram, please. Is it fresh?

Продавец: **Да, очень свежая. Что-нибудь ещё?**
dah, *oh*-cheen' *svyeh*-zhuh-yeh. shtoh nee-*boohd'* ee-*sh'yoh*?
Yes, very fresh. Anything else?

Ирина: **Нет, всё. Спасибо.**
nyeht, fsyoh. spuh-*see*-bah.
No, that's it. Thanks.

Words to Know

скажите	skuh-<u>zhi</u>-tee	could you tell me
говядина	gah-<u>vya</u>-dee-nuh	beef
свинина	svee-<u>nee</u>-nuh	pork
А это что?	uh <u>eh</u>-tah shtoh?	And what is this?
тоже	<u>toh</u>-zhi	also
дайте мне	<u>dahy</u>-tee mnyeh	give me
Что-нибудь ещё?	shtoh nee-<u>boohd'</u> ee-<u>sh'yoh</u>?	Anything else?
спасибо	spuh-<u>see</u>-bah	thanks

Fun & Games

You are in Russia staying with a friend, and he's suddenly taken ill. He asks you to go to the grocery store and provides you with the following shopping list. Match each food listed to its number in the figure. See Appendix D for the answer key.

белый хлеб _____

молоко _____

сыр _____

масло _____

яйца _____

Chapter 10

Shopping Made Easy

. . . .

In This Chapter

▶ Getting comfortable with the verb "to buy"

▶ Finding out where to buy stuff

▶ Looking for clothes

▶ Selecting the items you want and paying for them

▶ Checking out great Russian souvenirs to buy

. . . .

Russians love to hunt for nice, mostly Western-made, goods. Buying anything new, whether it's a stereo, a sofa, or a coat, is a pleasant experience and an important event. So as an American (or other Westerner) shopping in Russian stores, you should feel right at home!

In this chapter, we help you find different kinds of stores, and we show you how to discover store hours and get assistance when you're there. We also instruct you in the art of clothes-shopping, Russian-style. We show you how to get the right color and size, how to ask to try things on, and what to say when you want to compare different items. You also find out how to pay for your selections in a Russian store.

Shopping with Confidence: The Verb "To Buy"

Before going shopping, you need to arm yourself with the verb **покупать** (pah-kooh-*pat'*) (*to buy*). Here's the conjugation of this verb in the present tense (it's a first conjugation verb):

Conjugation	*Pronunciation*
я покупаю	ya pah-kooh-*pah*-yooh
ты покупаешь	ti pah-kooh-*pah*-eesh'
он/она покупает	ohn/ah-*nah* pah-kooh-*pah*-eet
мы покупаем	mi pah-kooh-*pah*-eem
вы покупаете	vi pah-kooh-*pah*-ee-tee
они покупают	ah-*nee* pah-kooh-*pah*-yooht

Like any Russian verb, this verb has two forms to choose from: imperfective and perfective. Your choice depends on the meaning you intend to express. The preceding conjugation, like all Russian verbs in the present tense, uses the imperfective form. Very often, however, you use "to buy" in the infinitive (dictionary) form, in sentences like *I want to buy (a car, a couch, a parrot)*, in which case you need to use the perfective form: **Я хочу купить** (ya khah-*chooh* kooh-*peet'*) (*I want to buy*) followed by the name of the merchandise you want to buy in the accusative case (see Chapter 3 for more about cases).

"Why should I use the perfective infinitive in this instance?" you may ask. Good question! Using the imperfective infinitive — **Я хочу покупать** (ya khah-*chooh* pah-kooh-*paht'*) — tells those who are listening to you that you're interested in the *process* of buying rather than the *result* of buying. (For more info about perfective and imperfective forms, see Chapter 3.)

To brag about your new purchase, you need the verb in the past tense, again in its perfective form (**купить**):

Conjugation	*Pronunciation*
Я купил	ya kooh-*peel* (if you're a man)
Я купила	ya kooh-*pee*-luh (if you're a woman)
Ты купил/купила	ti kooh-*peel*/kooh-*pee*-luh
Он купил	ohn kooh-*peel*
Она купила	ah-*nah* kooh-*pee*-luh
Мы/вы/они купили	mi/vi/ah-*nee* kooh-*pee*-lee

To promise somebody that you will buy something, use the verb in the future tense, again in its perfective form (**купить**):

Conjugation	*Pronounciation*
я куплю	ya kooh-*plyooh*
ты купишь	ti *kooh*-peesh'
он/она купит	ohn/ah-*nah kooh*-peet
мы купим	mi *kooh*-peem
вы купите	vi kooh-*pee*-tee
они купят	ah-*nee kooh*-pyeht

So Many Stores, So Little Time: The Shopping Scene in Russia

In the grand scheme of things, Russian stores aren't too different from those in the United States. In the following sections, we describe many different kinds of stores and merchandise, as well as how to find a store's hours, navigate a store with ease, and accept (or decline) assistance.

Looking at different types of stores and merchandise

Stores that sell anything other than food can be divided into two major categories:

- ✔ **универмаги** (ooh-nee-veer-*mah*-gee) (*department stores*)
- ✔ Smaller, specialized **магазины** (muh-guh-*zee*-ni) (*stores*), which may specialize in anything from tableware to TVs.

What used to be huge department stores in downtown Moscow and St. Petersburg have gradually turned into a collection of unbelievably expensive little boutique stores, also known as **бутики** (booh-*tee*-kee) (*boutiques*), very rarely visited by average Russians who simply can't afford to buy anything there. Most **универмаги**, which are similar to big-box stores in the United States, both in the merchandise they offer and their organization, have moved to the newer districts of big cities and are more affordable.

Additionally, there are now multitudes of smaller, privately owned, specialized stores scattered all over cities. Whereas **бутики** sell mostly clothing, these smaller stores sell a variety of merchandise one may really need. Unfortunately, the secret of what these stores sell may often be hidden behind a fancy store name that has nothing to do with the merchandise the store offers — the only way to figure out what these stores actually sell is to go in and look around. The most efficient way to find a store you need is to use the Yellow Pages, which classify the stores into categories according to the goods they offer. Following are some typical classifications:

- **аптека** (uhp-*tyeh*-kuh) (*pharmacy*)
- **одежда** (ah-*dyehzh*-duh) (*clothes*)
- **мужская одежда** (moohzh-*skah*-yeh ah-*dyehzh*-duh) (*men's apparel*)
- **женская одежда** (*zhehn*-skuh-yeh ah-*dyehzh*-duh) (*women's apparel*)
- **бельё** (beel'-*yoh*) (*intimate apparel*)
- **детская одежда** (*dyeht*-skuh-yeh ah-*dyehzh*-duh) (*children's apparel*)
- **верхняя одежда** (*vyehrkh*-nee-yeh ah-*dyehzh*-duh) (*outerwear*)
- **спортивные товары** (spahr-*teev*-ni-ee tah-*vah*-ri) (*sports*)
- **музыкальные товары** (mooh-zi-*kahl'*-ni-ee tah-*vah*-ri) (*music*)
- **фототовары** (*foh*-tah-tah-*vah*-ri) (*photography*)
- **электротовары** (eh-*lyehk*-trah-tah-*vah*-ri) (*electrical goods*)
- **галантерея** (guh-luhn-tee-*ryeh*-yeh) (*haberdashery*)
- **головные уборы** (gah-lahv-*ni*-ee ooh-*boh*-ri) (*hats*)
- **косметика** (kahs-*myeh*-tee-kuh) (*makeup*)
- **парфюмерия** (puhr-fyooh-*myeh*-ree-yeh) (*perfume*)
- **ювелирные товары** (yooh-vee-*leer*-ni-ee tah-*vah*-ri) (*jewelry*)
- **газетный киоск** (guh-*zyeht*-niy kee-*ohsk*) (*newsstand*)
- **канцелярские товары** (kuhn-tsi-*lyar*-skee-ee tah-*vah*-ri) (*stationery products*)
- **хозяйственные товары** (khah-*zyay*-stvee-ni-ee tah-*vah*-ri) (*household goods* or *hardware*)
- **кухонные товары** (*kooh*-khah-ni-ee tah-*vah*-ri) (*kitchen and tableware*)
- **ткани** (*tkah*-nee) (*fabric*)
- **цветы** (tsvee-*ti*) (*flowers*)
- **антикварные магазины** (uhn-tee-*kvahr*-niy muh-guh-*zeen'*) (*antique store*)
- **комиссионный магазин** (kah-mee-see-*ohn*-iy muh-guh-*zeen*) (*second-hand store*)
- **сувениры** (soo-vee-*nee*-ri) (*souvenirs*)

Finding out when a store is open

The easiest way to find out whether a Russian store is open is to go there and look for a sign on the door that indicates the days and times when the store is open. You may see something like this:

>**Часы работы** (chuh-*si* ruh-*boh*-ti) (*hours of work*)

>**понедельник–пятница 10–18** (pah-nee-*dyehl'*-neek *pyat*-nee-tsuh s dee-see-tee dah vah-seem-*naht*-suh-tee) (*Monday through Friday, 10 a.m. to 6 p.m.*)

>**суббота, воскресенье 11–16** (sooh-*boh*-tuh, vahs-kree-*syehn'*-ee s ah-*dee*-nuht-suh-tee dah shis-*naht*-suh-tee) (*Saturday, Sunday, 11 a.m. to 4 p.m.*)

Note that the preceding times are based on the 24-hour clock, which is commonly used in Russia and other European countries; flip to Chapter 5 for the full scoop on times and dates.

Another way to find out whether a store is open is just to call. If nobody answers the phone, the store is probably closed. Problem solved! But if someone does answer, you may want to ask one of these questions:

>**Магазин открыт?** (muh-guh-*zeen* aht-*krit*?) (*Is the store open?*)

>**До какого часа открыт магазин?** (duh kuh-*koh*-vah *chah*-suh aht-*krit* muh-guh-*zeen*?) (*'Til what time is the store open?*)

You may hear these (quite abrupt) responses:

>**Да, открыт.** (dah, aht-*krit*.) (*Yes, it is.*)

>**До шести.** (dah-shis-*tee*.) (*'Til six.*)

Here's an example of what to say if you want to inquire whether the store is open on a particular day:

>**В воскресенье магазин открыт?** (v vahs-kree-*syehn'*-ee muh-guh-*zeen* aht-*krit*?) (*Is the store open on Sunday?*)

Note that the word indicating the day should be in the accusative case.

In response, you'll probably hear:

>**Нет, закрыт.** (nyeht, zuh-*krit*.) (*No, it's closed.*)

Some other ways to ask about store hours include the following:

>**Когда магазин закрывается?** (kahg-*dah* muh-guh-*zeen* zuh-kri-*vah*-eet-syeh?) (*When does the store close?*)

>**Когда завтра открывается магазин?** (kahg-*dah* *zahf*-truh aht-kri-*vah*-eet-syeh muh-guh-*zeen*?) (*When does the store open tomorrow?*)

And in response to these questions you'll hear something along the lines of **В семь** (v syehm') (*At seven*).

Navigating a department store

Today's Russian department stores are quite easy to navigate, especially if you refer to the list of goods we provide in the earlier section "Looking at different types of stores and merchandise." The signs indicating what's for sale are located exactly where you expect them to be: between the aisles.

If you feel lost, try to grab somebody who's wearing a store uniform and quickly ask him where to find what you're looking for. Here's an example:

Где сувениры? (gdyeh sooh-vee-*nee*-ri?) (*Where are souvenirs?*)

The word indicating the merchandise should be used in its dictionary (nominative case) form. (See Chapter 3 for more information on cases.)

Another way to locate an item is to ask **У вас продаются. . . ?** (ooh vahs prah-duh-*yooht*-syeh. . . ?) (*Do you sell. . . ?*), inserting the name of the merchandise you're looking for in the nominative case.

Talkin' the Talk

Boris (**Борис**) needs to buy new gloves and goes to a big department store. He has a short conversation with the **работник универмага** (ruh-*boht*-neek ooh-nee-veer-*mah*-guh) (*department store employee*). (Track 16)

Борис:	**Скажите, пожалуйста, где можно купить перчатки?** skuh-*zhi*-tee, pah-*zhahl*-stuh, gdyeh *mohzh*-nah koo-*peet'* peer-*chaht*-kee? *Tell me, please, where can I buy gloves?*
Работник универмага:	**В отделе галантереи. Вон там.** v aht-*dyeh*-lee guh-luhn-tee-*ryeh*-ee. vohn tahm. *In the haberdashery department.* *Over there.*
Борис:	**Понятно. спасибо.** pah-*nyat*-nuh. spuh-*see*-buh. *I see. Thank you.*

Words to Know

Где можно купить. . . ?	gdyeh <u>mohzh</u>-nah kooh-<u>peet'</u>. . . ?	Where can I buy. . . ?
в отделе галантереи	v aht-<u>dyeh</u>-lee guh-luhn-tee-<u>ryeh</u>-ee	in the haberdashery department
вон там	vohn tahm	over there
Понятно	pah-<u>nyat</u>-nuh	I see

You Are What You Wear: Shopping for Clothes

CULTURAL WISDOM Russian folk wisdom has it that people's first impression of you is based on the way you're dressed. That's why you're likely to see Russians well dressed in public, even in informal situations. Clothes-shopping is a big deal to Russians and is often a full-day affair. In the following sections, we tell you how to get the most out of your clothes-shopping by describing what you're looking for and getting and trying on the right size.

Seeking specific items of clothing and accessories

We assume that if you indeed go to Russia, you'll know what kind of weather to expect in different seasons and will bring the clothes and accessories that are appropriate for the time of the year. But what if you forget to pack a warm hat for winter or a pair of shorts for a hot Russian summer? (Yes, Russia gets warm weather, too.) Here we provide you with a list of words indicating some essential pieces of clothing you may find you left at home:

✔ пальто (puhl'-*toh*) (*coat*)

✔ куртка (*koohrt*-kuh) (*short coat* or *a warmer jacket*)

✔ плащ (plahsh') (*raincoat* or *trench coat*)

- сандалии (suhn-*dah*-lee-ee) (*sandals*)
- кроссовки (krah-*sohf*-kee) (*sneakers*)
- сапоги (suh-pah-*gee*) (*boots*)
- туфли (*toohf*-lee) (*lighter shoes for men and women*)

  Note: The term "lighter" includes dress shoes, casual shoes, high-heel shoes — anything but boots.

- рубашка (rooh-*bahsh*-kuh) (*shirt*)
- футболка (fooht-*bohl*-kuh) (*football jersey* or *sports shirt*)
- блузка (*bloohz*-kuh) (*blouse*)
- свитер (*svee*-tyehr) (*sweater*)
- кофта (*kohf*-tuh) (*cardigan*)
- брюки (*bryooh*-kee) (*pants*)
- джинсы (*dzhin*-si) (*jeans*)
- шорты (*shohr*-ti) (*shorts*)
- платье (*plaht'*-ee) (*dress*)
- юбка (*yoohp*-kuh) (*skirt*)
- костюм (kahs-*tyoohm*) (*suit*)
- пиджак (peed-*zhahk*) (*suit jacket*)
- галстук (*gahl*-stoohk) (*necktie*)
- носки (nahs-*kee*) (*socks*)
- колготки (kahl-*goht*-kee) (*pantyhose*)
- трусы (trooh-*si*) (*men's underwear*)
- женское бельё (*zhehn*-skah-ee beel'-*yoh*) (*women's underwear*)
- бюстгалтер (byoohst-*gahl*-tyehr) (*bra*)
- пижама (pee-*zhah*-muh) (*pajamas*)
- халат (khuh-*laht*) (*robe*)
- купальник (kooh-*pahl'*-neek) (*bathing suit*)
- плавки (*plahf*-kee) (*swimming trunks*)
- кепка (*kyehp*-kuh) (*cap*)
- шляпа (*shlya*-puh) (*hat*)
- шапка (*shahp*-kuh) (*warm winter hat*)
- шарф (shahrf) (*scarf*)
- платок (pluh-*tohk*) (*head scarf*)

✔ **перчатки** (peer-*chaht*-kee) (*gloves*)

✔ **платок** (pluh-*tohk*) (*handkerchief*)

✔ **пояс** (*poh*-ees) (*belt*)

✔ **сумка** (*soohm*-kuh) (*purse*)

✔ **очки** (ahch-*kee*) (*eyeglasses*)

✔ **зонтик** (*zohn*-teek) (*umbrella*)

Describing items in color

What's your favorite **цвет** (tsvyeht) (*color*)? So that you can get the color you want, here's a quick list of the most common colors:

✔ **белый** (*byeh*-liy) (*white*)

✔ **чёрный** (*chyohr*-niy) (*black*)

✔ **коричневый** (kah-*reech*-nee-viy) (*brown*)

✔ **серый** (*syeh*-riy) (*gray*)

✔ **синий** (*see*-neey) (*blue*)

✔ **голубой** (gah-looh-*bohy*) (*light blue*)

✔ **лиловый** (lee-*loh*-viy) (*purple*)

✔ **красный** (*krahs*-niy) (*red*)

✔ **розовый** (*roh*-zah-viy) (*pink*)

✔ **оранжевый** (ah-*rahn*-zhi-viy) (*orange*)

✔ **желтый** (*zhohl*-tiy) (*yellow*)

✔ **зелёный** (zee-*lyoh*-niy) (*green*)

The names for colors in Russian are adjectives. So when you describe the color of an item you want, make sure the color agrees in case, number, and gender with the noun it modifies. (For more on adjective-noun agreement, see Chapter 3.) For example, a *black suit* in the nominative case is **чёрный костюм** (*chyohr*-niy kahs-*tyoohm*).

If you want to ask for a different shade of a color, use these phrases:

А потемнее есть? (uh pah-teem-*nyeh*-ee yehst'?) (*Do you have it in a darker shade?*)

А посветлее есть? (uh pahs-veet-*lyeh*-ee yehst'?) (*Do you have it in a lighter shade?*)

Other words that may come in handy are **одного цвета** (ahd-nah-*voh* tsvyeh-tuh) (*solid*) and **цветной** (tsveet-*nohy*) (*patterned*).

Finding the right size

Shoe and clothing sizes differ from country to country, but you don't have to memorize them when you're traveling. You can usually find conversion charts in any travel book or even in your own pocket calendar. A great resource for shoe sizes is www.i18nguy.com/l10n/shoes.html#adult.

Sizes from different systems of measurement are often displayed on the items themselves. If you need to convert from inches to centimeters for an item of clothing (Russian sizes are given in centimeters), multiply the size in inches by 2.53 and you get the equivalent size in centimeters. But the best way to be certain something fits is to just try the item on!

Following are some words and phrases you may hear or say while searching for the right size:

- **размер** (ruhz-*myehr*) (*size*)
- **Я ношу . . . размер** (ya nah-*shooh* . . . ruhz-*myehr*) (*I wear size . . .*)

  To indicate your size, use an ordinal number before the word **размер** (see Chapter 5 for more about numbers).

- **Это мой размер.** (*eh*-tah mohy ruhz-*myehr*.) (*This is my size.*)
- **Какой у вас размер?** (kuh-*kohy* ooh vahs ruhz-*myehr*?) (*What's your size?*)

Trying on clothing

Before you decide to buy something, you probably want to try it on first. To ask to try something on, say

Можно померить? (*mohzh*-nuh pah-*myeh*-reet'?) (*May I try this on?*)

You'll most likely hear

Да, пожалуйста. (dah, pah-*zhahl*-stuh.) (*Yes, please.*)

Then, you may ask where the dressing room is:

Где примерочная? (gdeh pree-*myeh*-rahch-nuh-yeh?) (*Where is the fitting room?*)

Here are some adjectives you may use to describe clothing:

- хороший (khah-*roh*-shiy) (*good*)
- плохой (plah-*khohy*) (*bad*)
- большой (bahl'-*shohy*) (*big*)
- маленький (*mah*-leen'-keey) (*small*)
- длинный (*dlee*-niy) (*long*)
- короткий (kah-*roht*-keey) (*short*)

When you're done trying on and you walk out of the dressing room, the sales assistant may ask:

Ну, как? Подошло? (nooh, kahk? pah-dahsh-*loh*?) (*Well? Did it fit?*)

You can give either of the following responses:

Нет, спасибо. (nyeht, spuh-*see*-bah.) (*No, thank you.*)

Я хочу купить это. (ya khah-*chooh* kooh-*peet'* eh-tah.) (*I want to buy it.*)

This or That? Deciding What You Want

One of the most exciting things about shopping for clothes (or anything, for that matter) is talking about the advantages and disadvantages of your potential purchase. In this section we give you all the words, phrases, and grammatical constructions you need to do just that. We tell you how to compare items and specify which one you like best. (Check out Chapter 6 if you need a refresher on how to express likes and dislikes.)

Using demonstrative pronouns

When comparing items, you almost always use demonstrative pronouns, such as *this, these, that,* and *those,* in the nominative case, so here are all the forms you need to know:

- этот (*eh*-taht) (*this* or *this one*) for masculine nouns
- эта (*eh*-tuh) (*this* or *this one*) for feminine nouns
- это (*eh*-tah) (*this* or *this one*) for neuter nouns
- эти (*eh*-tee) (*these* or *these ones*) for plural nouns
- тот (toht) (*that* or *that one*) for masculine nouns

- ✔ **та** (tah) (*that* or *that one*) for feminine nouns
- ✔ **то** (toh) (*that* or *that one*) for neuter nouns
- ✔ **те** (tyeh) (*those* or *those ones*) for plural nouns

Using these words, you can say something like this:

> **Это платье лучше чем то.** (*eh*-tah *plaht'*-yeh *loohch*-sheh chyehm toh.) (*This dress is better than that one.*)

Flip to Chapter 3 for full details on masculine, feminine, neuter, and plural nouns and pronouns.

Comparing two items

To compare things, Russian uses adjectives that express comparative degrees. Here is the list of those that may be used in reference to clothing:

- ✔ **больше** (*bohl'*-shi) (*bigger*)
- ✔ **меньше** (*myehn'*-shi) (*smaller*)
- ✔ **лучше** (*loohch*-shi) (*better*)
- ✔ **хуже** (*khooh*-zhi) (*worse*)
- ✔ **длиннее** (dlee-*nyeh*-ee) (*longer*)
- ✔ **короче** (kah-*roh*-chee) (*shorter*)
- ✔ **дороже** (dah-*roh*-zheh) (*more expensive*)
- ✔ **дешевле** (dee-*shehv*-lyeh) (*cheaper*)
- ✔ **красивее** (kruh-*see*-vee-ee) (*more beautiful*)
- ✔ **удобнее** (ooh-*dohb*-nee-ee) (*more comfortable*)
- ✔ **толще** (*tohl*-sh'ee) (*thicker*)
- ✔ **тоньше** (*tohn'*-shi) (*thinner*)
- ✔ **тяжелее** (tee-zhi-*lyeh*-ee) (*heavier*)
- ✔ **легче** (*lyehk*-chee) (*lighter*)

Just as in English, the equation for creating a comparative sentence looks like this: the name of the item + the comparative adjective (for instance, "bigger" or "smaller") + the word **чем** (chyehm) (*than*) + the other item. Say you're trying on two pairs of shoes. You like the second pair better: It's not only more comfortable but cheaper too. You may be thinking the following to yourself (in Russian!):

Эти туфли удобнее и дешевле чем те. (*eh*-tee *toohf*-lee ooh-*dohb*-nee-ee ee dee-*shyehv*-lee chyehm tyeh.) (*These shoes are more comfortable and cheaper than those.*)

The noun **туфли** should be in the nominative case.

Talking about what you like most (or least)

When you look at several items (or people or things), you may like one of them best of all. To communicate this preference, you may use the phrase **Больше всего мне нравится . . .** (*bohl'*-sheh fsee-*voh* mnyeh *nrah*-veet-syeh . . .) (*I like . . . best of all*), replacing the ellipsis with the one you like best. Another way to do it is to place the object of liking at the very beginning of the sentence:

Этот сувенир мне нравится больше всего. (*eh*-toht sooh-vee-*neer* mnyeh *nrah*-veet-syeh *bohl'*-sheh fsee-*voh*.) (*I like this souvenir best of all.*)

If you feel the urge to use the words "most" or "least" to express your emotions about a pending purchase, you should know that Russian uses the adjective **самый** (*sah*-miy) for both. Because it is an adjective, it should agree with the noun it's used with in gender and number. So, for example, if, after trying a dozen dresses, you conclude, *This is the most beautiful dress*, in Russian you say **Это самое красивое платье** (*eh*-tah *sah*-mah-ee krah-*see*-vah-ee *plaht'*-ee).

You Gotta Pay to Play: Buying Items

After you decide on an item of clothing or any other piece of merchandise, you want to make sure the price is right. In the following sections, we show you how to ask how much something costs, how to indicate that you'll take it, and how to find out how to pay for it.

How much does it cost?

If you're buying one item and you want to find out how much it costs, use the phrase **Сколько стоит. . . ?** (*skohl'*-kah *stoh*-eet. . . ?) (*How much does . . . cost?*), inserting the name of the item in the nominative case. If you want to know the price of an umbrella, for example, ask:

Сколько стоит этот зонтик? (*skohl'*-kah *stoh*-eet *eh*-taht *zohn*-teek?) (*How much is this umbrella?*)

Note the order of words in this Russian question: It begins with "How much costs" and ends with the merchandise you're interested in.

If you're buying more than one of an item, ask **Сколько стоят . . .?** (*skohl'*-kah *stoh*-yeht. . . ?) (*How much do . . . cost?*), adding the name of the item in the nominative plural. For example, if you want to know the price of several umbrellas, you ask

> **Сколько стоят эти зонтики?** (skohl'-kah *stoh*-yat *eh*-tee *zohn*-tee-kee?) (*How much do these umbrellas cost?*)

I'll take it! How do I pay?

The simplest way to express your intention to buy something is to say

> **Я возьму это.** (ya vahz'-*mooh eh*-tuh.) (*I'll take it.*)

You can also use a form of the verb **купить** (kooh-*peet'*) (*to buy*):

> **Я это куплю.** (ya *eh*-tuh kooh-*plyooh*.) (*I'll buy it.*)

If you're buying more than one item, say one of the following:

> **Я возьму их.** (ya vahz'-*mooh* eekh.) (*I'll take them.*)
>
> **Я их куплю.** (ya eekh kooh-*plyooh*.) (*I'll buy them.*)

We give you the complete conjugation of this verb in the future tense in the earlier section "Shopping with Confidence: The Verb 'To Buy.'"

The best way to pay for anything is certainly with a credit card. However, not all stores in Russia accept credit cards. If you're unsure whether the store accepts credit cards, you can ask:

> **Вы принимаете кредитные карточки?** (vi pree-nee-*mah*-ee-tee kree-*deet*-ni-ee *kahr*-tahch-kee?) (*Do you accept credit cards?*)

The answer will be similar to one of the following:

> **Да, принимаем.** (dah, pree-nee-*mah*-eem.) (*Yes, we do.*)
>
> **Нет, не принимаем, только наличные.** (nyeht, nee pree-nee-*mah*-eem, *tohl'*-kah nah-*leech*-ni-ee.) (*No, we don't, only cash.*)

Check out Chapter 15 for more information on handling money.

Talkin' the Talk

Zina (**Зина**) and Nina (**Нина**) are best friends. They call each other every day. Today Zina bought a new dress, and she calls Nina to share this exciting news. (Track 17)

Зина:	**Нина, я сегодня купила платье!** *nee-nuh, ya see-vohd-nyeh kooh-pee-luh plaht'-ee!* *Nina, I bought a dress today!*
Нина:	**Где?** gdyeh? *Where?*
Зина:	**В магазине на Садовой улице.** *v muh-guh-zee-nee nah suh-doh-vohy ooh-lee-tsyeh.* *At the store on Sadovaya street.*
Нина:	**А за сколько ты купила платье?** *uh zah skohl'-kah ti kooh-pee-luh plaht'-ee?* *And for how much did you buy the dress?*
Зина:	**Дёшево. За тысячу пятьсот рублей.** *dyoh-shi-vah. zah ti-see-chooh peet'-soht roohb-lyehy.* *Cheap. For one thousand five hundred rubles.*

Words to Know

Я купила платье.	ya kooh-<u>pee</u>-luh <u>plaht</u>'-yee.	I bought a dress.
в магазине	v muh-guh-<u>zee</u>-nee	at the store
на … улице	nah … <u>ooh</u>-lee-tseh	on … street
за сколько?	zah <u>skohl</u>'-kah?	for how much?
дёшево	<u>dyoh</u>-shi-vah	cheap

Fun & Games

Match the name of each piece of clothing in the following figure to its Russian term in the right column. See Appendix D for the answer key.

a. belt	**брюки**
b. blouse	**пояс**
c. skirt	**носки**
d. pants	**пиджак**
e. shirt	**блузка**
f. socks	**рубашка**
g. necktie	**галстук**
h. suit jacket	**юбка**

Chapter 11

Going Out on the Town

. . . .

In This Chapter

▶ Arranging an outing

▶ Catching a flick

▶ Getting the most out of the ballet and theater

▶ Checking out a museum

▶ Sharing your impressions about an event

. . . .

This chapter is all about going out on the town the Russian way. We take you to the movies, the theater, the ballet, and museums — the most popular entertainment venues among Russians. We show you how to make plans with friends, how and where to buy tickets, how to find your seat, and what to say when you want to share your impressions of an event with your friends.

Together Wherever We Go: Making Plans to Go Out

Going out on the town is always more fun with friends and family. Here is what you may hear when people invite you to do things with them:

> ✔ **Informal:** Давай пойдём в . . . (duh-*vahy* pahy-*dyohm* v . . .) (*Let's go to the . . .*)
>
> ✔ **Formal or plural:** Давайте пойдём в . . . (duh-*vahy*-tee pahy-*dyohm* v . . .) (*Let's go to the . . .*)

Note that after the preposition в you need to use the noun indicating destination in the accusative case. In the preceding examples, however, it really doesn't matter because masculine nouns are the same in the accusative and nominative cases. (See Chapter 3 for details on cases.)

Another way to extend an invitation is by using what's known in grammar as the subjunctive mood, which roughly corresponds to the English phrase *Would you like to go. . . ?* In Russian, you say **Вы не хотели бы пойти в** (vi nee khah-*tyeh*-lee bi pahy-*tee* v) and then add the name of the place you're suggesting, using the accusative case. For example, when inviting somebody with whom you're still on formal **вы** (vi) (*you*) terms to go to a restaurant, you can say

> **Вы не хотели бы пойти в ресторан?** (vi nee khah-*tyeh*-lee bi pahy-*tee* v rees-tah-*rahn*?) (*Would you like to go to a restaurant?*)

The **вы** form is very appropriate here because this phrasing has a formal tone. When talking to your friend or a member of your family (who turned out to be Russian!) say

> **Ты не хочешь пойти в ресторан?** (ti nee *khoh*-cheesh pahy-*tee* v rees-tah-*rahn*?) (*Do you want to go to a restaurant?*)

A more casual way to ask the same thing is to simply say:

- ✔ **Formal: Вы хотите . . .** (vi khah-*tee*-tee . . .) (*Do you want to . . .*)
- ✔ **Informal: Ты хочешь . . .** (ti *khoh*-cheesh' . . .) (*Do you want to . . .*)

In either case, you end the phrase with a verb in its infinitive form. For example, to invite someone with whom you're on informal terms to watch a movie, you can say:

> **Ты хочешь посмотреть фильм?** (ti *khoh*-cheesh' pah-smah-*tryeht'* feel'm?) (*Do you want to watch a movie?*)

Flip to Chapter 4 for full details on using formal and informal "you."

To specify a day of the week in your question, add **в** plus the day of the week in the accusative case:

> **Ты не хочешь пойти в кино в субботу?** (ti nee *khoh*-cheesh pahy-*tee* v kee-noh v sooh-*boh*-tooh?) (*Would you like to go to the movies on Saturday?*)

After someone invites you to make plans, you need to decline or accept.

- ✔ **To say no:** Declining an invitation isn't as easy as you may think: Russians don't easily take **нет** (nyeht) (*no*) for an answer and may continue to insist that you join them! So, if you need to decline an invitation, we recommend that you offer a convincing reason to explain why you can't go. For example, you can use one of the following, depending on your gender:

> **If you're a man: Я не могу, я занят.** (ya nee mah-*gooh*, ya *zah*-nyeht.) (*I can't, I am busy.*)

> **If you're a woman: Я не могу, я занята.** (ya nee-mah-*gooh*, ya zuh-nee-*tah*.) (*I can't, I am busy.*)

To soften your response, you can add:

> **Может быть в другой раз.** (*Moh*-zhit bit' v drooh-*gohy* rahs.) (*Maybe next time.*)

✔ **To say yes:** To accept the invitation, say this (almost unpronounceable) phrase:

> **Спасибо, с удовольствием!** (spuh-*see*-bah, s ooh-dah-*vohl'*-stvee-eem!) (*Thank you, with pleasure!*)

A simple reply of **Да!** (dah!) (*Yes!*) will do, too.

You may need to know what time an event starts before you can decline or accept an invitation. If you want to know when an event (such as a movie or a performance) begins, this is how you ask: **Когда начинается. . . ?** (kahg-*dah* nuh-chee-*nah*-eet-syeh. . . ?) (*When does . . . start?*) The event you're asking about goes into the nominative case. Consider this example:

> **Когда начинается фильм?** (kahg-*dah* nuh-chee-*nah*-eet-syeh feel'm?) (*When does the film start?*)

Note that you begin this Russian question with "When begins . . ." and end it with the word indicating the event.

On the Big Screen: Going to the Movies

Going to see a **фильм** (feel'm) (*movie*) in Russia may be somewhat challenging because most Russian movies are — you guessed it! — in Russian (even American movies are dubbed in loud Russian voiceovers). Unless you just want to enjoy the music of the language or pick up some phrases and words here and there, your best bet is to rent Russian movies with subtitles or find a **кино** (kee-*noh*) (*movie theater*) that features movies with subtitles. If, however, you want to check out a real Russian film, in the following sections we show you different types of movies, how to buy a ticket, and how to find your seat at the movie theater.

Whereas English uses the word "theater" for a movie theater, Russian is more exact in expressing the difference between a movie theater and a play, opera, or ballet theater. The word **кино** or the more formal **кинотеатр** (kee-nah-tee-*ahtr*) are the only words you can use to denote a movie theater in Russian.

Picking a particular type of movie

Check out the following list for the names of different film genres in Russian:

✔ **детектив** (deh-tehk-*teef*) (*mystery movie*)

✔ **экранизация художественной литературы** (eh-kruh-nee-*zah*-tsi-yeh khooh-*doh*-zhis-tvee-nahy lee-tee-ruh-*tooh*-ri) (*screen version of a book*)

- **фильм ужасов** (feel'm *ooh*-zhuh-sahf) (*horror film*)

- **комедия** (kah-*myeh*-dee-yeh) (*comedy*)

- **мьюзикл** (*m'yooh*-zeekl) (*musical*)

- **мультфильм** (mool't-*feel'm*) (*cartoon*)

- **научная фантастика** (nuh-*oohch*-nuh-yeh fuhn-*tahs*-tee-kuh) (*science fiction*)

- **приключенческий фильм** (pree-klyooh-*chyehn*-chees-keey feel'm) (*adventure film*)

- **триллер** (*tree*-leer) (*thriller*)

- **вестерн** (*vehs*-tehrn) (*western*)

- **боевик** (bah-ee-*veek*) (*action movie*)

What genres do Russians prefer? It's hard to generalize. We should mention one thing, though: Russians don't seem to like happy endings as much as most Americans do, and they tend to prefer harsh reality to beautiful dreams in their movies.

Buying tickets

If you decide to go to the movies, you'll need a **билет** (bee-*lyeht*) (*ticket*). You can easily buy one online. But if you want to practice your Russian language skills, go to the ticket office, which is generally near the entrance to the movie theater. Most likely it has a sign that says **Касса** (*kah*-suh) (*ticket office*) or **Касса кинотеатра** (*kah*-suh kee-nah-tee-*aht*-ruh) (*ticket office of the movie theater*).

To ask for a ticket, customers often use a kind of stenographic language. **Кассиры** (kuh-*see*-ri) (*cashiers*) are generally impatient people, and you may have a line behind you. So try to make your request for a ticket as brief as you can; simply state the number of tickets you need plus the time of the movie. If you want to go to the 2:30 p.m. show, for example, you can say one of these phrases:

> **Один на четырнадцать тридцать.** (ah-*deen* nah chee-*tir*-nuhd-tsuht' *treet*-tsuht'.) (*One for 2:30.*)

> **Два на четырнадцать тридцать.** (dvah nah chee-*tir*-nuhd-tsuht' *treet*-tsuht'.) (*Two for 2:30.*)

If two movies happen to be showing at the same time, or if you want to make sure that you get tickets to the right movie, you can simply add the phrase **на** (nah) (*to*) plus the title of the movie to your request.

Choosing a place to sit and watch

In Russia, when you buy a ticket to the movie, you're assigned a specific seat, so the **кассир** (kuh-*seer*) (*cashier*) may ask you where exactly you want to sit. You may hear one of these questions:

> **Где вы хотите сидеть?** (gdyeh vi khah-*tee*-tee see-*dyeht'*?) (*Where do you want to sit?*)

> **Какой ряд?** (kuh-*kohy* ryat?) (*Which row?*)

The best answer is **В середине** (f see-ree-*dee*-nee) (*in the middle*). If you're far-sighted, you may want to say **Подальше** (pah-*dahl'*-sheh) (*farther away from the screen*). On the other hand, if you want to sit closer, say **поближе** (pah-*blee*-zheh) (*closer to the screen*). You may also specify a row by saying **первый ряд** (*pyehr*-viy ryat) (*first row*), **второй ряд** (vtah-*rohy* ryat) (*second row*), and so forth. (See Chapter 5 for more about ordinal numbers.)

When you finally get your ticket, you must be able to read and understand what it says. Look for the words **ряд** (ryat) (*row*) and **место** (*myehs*-tah) (*seat*). For example, you may see **Ряд: 5, Место: 14**. That's where you're expected to sit: in Row 5, Seat 14!

In the following sections, we cover two handy verbs to know at the movies: "to sit" and "to watch."

The verb "to sit"

The verb **сидеть** (see-*dyeht'*) (*to sit*) is a second-conjugation verb; the **д** changes to **ж** in the first person singular. Because you'll use this verb a lot, it's a good idea to know the full conjugation, as shown in the following table.

Conjugation	Pronunciation
Я сижу	ya see-*zhooh*
ты сидишь (informal singular)	ti see-*deesh*
он/она/оно сидит	ohn/ah-*nah*/ah-*noh* see-*deet*
мы сидим	mi see-*deem*
вы сидите (formal singular or plural)	vi see-*dee*-tee
они сидят	ah-*nee* see-*dyat*

The verb "to watch"

The verb **смотреть** (smah-*tryeht'*) (*to watch*) is another useful word when you go to the movies. The following table shows how to conjugate it in the present tense.

Conjugation	Pronunciation
я смотрю	ya smah-*tryooh*
ты смотришь (informal singular)	ti *smoht*-reesh'
он/она смотрит	ohn/ah-*nah smoht*-reet
мы смотрим	mi *smoht*-reem
вы смотрите (formal singular or plural)	vi *smoht*-ree-tee
они смотрят	ah-*nee smoht*-ryeht

Talkin' the Talk

Igor (**Игорь**) and Pyehtya (**Петя**), two high-school friends, are discussing their plans for the evening. (Track 18)

Игорь: **Давай пойдём в кино сегодня вечером!**
duh-*vahy* pahy-*dyohm* f kee-*noh* see-*vohd*-nyeh
vyeh-chee-rahm!
Let's go to the movies tonight!

Петя: **Давай! А какой фильм ты хочешь посмотреть?**
duh-*vahy*! uh kuh-*kohy* feel'm ti *khoh*-cheesh
pah-smaht-*ryeht'*?
Let's (go)! But what movie do you want to see?

Игорь: **Я не знаю. Я люблю боевики. А ты?**
ya nee *znah*-yooh. ya lyoohb-*lyooh* bah-ee-vee-*kee*.
uh ti?
I don't know. I like action movies. And you?

Петя: **Я тоже!**
ya *toh*-zhi!
Me too!

Игорь: **Здорово!**
zdoh-rah-vah!
Cool!

Words to Know

Давай пойдём в . . .	duh-_vahy_ pahy-_dyohm_ f . . .	Let's go to . . .
кино	kee-_noh_	movies (Literally: movie theater)
сегодня вечером	see-_vohd_-nyeh _vyeh_-chee-rahm	tonight
Я не знаю	ya nee _znah_-yooh	I don't know
А ты?	uh ti?	And you?
Я тоже	ya _toh_-zhi	Me too
Здорово!	_zdoh_-rah-vah!	Cool!

It's Classic: Taking in the Russian Ballet and Theater

If a Russian ballet company happens to be in your area, don't miss it! And if you're in Russia, don't even think of leaving without seeing at least one performance either in Moscow's **Большой Театр** (bahl'-_shohy_ tee-ahtr) (_Bol'shoy Theater_) or St. Petersburg's **Мариинский Театр** (muh-ree-_een_-skeey tee-_ahtr_) (_Mariinsky Theater_). No ballet in the world can compare with the Russian **балет** (buh-_lyeht_) (_ballet_), with its grand, powerful style; lavish decor; impeccable technique; and proud preservation of the classical tradition.

The Russian **театр** (tee-_ahtr_) (_theater_) is just as famous and impressive as the ballet, but most theater performances are in Russian, so you may not understand a lot until you work on your Russian for a while. Still, if you want to see great acting and test your Russian knowledge, by all means, check out the theater, too!

You can always buy tickets for ballet and theater performances online, but buying them in person is a great way to practice your Russian skills. The technique of buying a ticket to the ballet or theater is basically the same as it is for the movie theater (see the earlier sections "Buying tickets" and "Choosing a place to sit and watch" for more information). Each performance hall has a **касса** (_kah_-suh) (_ticket office_) and a **кассир** (kuh-_seer_) (_cashier_). In addition, you find quite a few **театральные кассы** (tee-uht-_rahl_'-ni-ee _kah_-si) (_theater ticket offices_) in the downtown area of any big city.

When you go to buy a ticket, the cashier may ask you one of these questions:

Где вы хотите сидеть? (gdyeh vi khah-*tee*-tee see-*dyeht'*?) (*Where do you want to sit?*)

Какой ряд? (kah-*kohy* ryat?) (*Which row?*)

Your answer is a little bit different than the reply you give when buying a movie ticket. A Russian ballet hall is more complicated than a movie theater, and it has many seating options you may want to consider, depending on your budget and taste:

- **в партере** (f puhr-*tyeh*-ree) (*in the orchestra seats*)
- **ложа** (*loh*-zhuh) (*box seat*)
- **бенуар** (bee-nooh-*ahr*) (*lower boxes*)
- **бэльэтаж** (behl'-eh-*tahzh* (*the tier above* **бенуар**)
- **ярус** (*ya*-roohs) (*the tier above* **бельэтаж**)
- **галерея** (guh-lee-*ryeh*-yeh) (*the last balcony*)
- **балкон** (buhl-*kohn*) (*the balcony*)

Next, you'll most likely hear **На какое число?** (nah kah-*koh*-ee chees-*loh*?) (*For what date?*) Your response should begin with **на** (nah) (*for*) followed by the date you want to attend the performance, such as **на пятое мая** (nuh *pya*-tah-ee *mah*-yeh) (*for May 5*). You can also say things like **на сегодня** (nah see-*vohd*-nyeh) (*for today*) or **на завтра** (nuh *zahf*-truh) (*for tomorrow*). And if you want to buy a ticket for a specific day of the week, say **на** plus the day of the week in the accusative case. For example, *for Friday* is **на пятницу** (nuh *pyat*-nee-tsooh).

Enjoying (or just plain surviving) the Philharmonic

Are you a classical music lover? If so, then the Russian Philharmonic may be just what you're looking for. But if not, we recommend you try to avoid the Philharmonic, even if tickets are free. If you're not used to classical music or if you can tolerate it only for a limited amount of time, going to the Philharmonic may be a very trying experience. For one thing, you have to sit almost motionless for over two hours, staring at the **оркестр** (ahr-*kyehstr*) (*orchestra*) or **исполнитель** (ees-pahl-*nee*-teel') (*performer/soloist*).

Secondly, you're not allowed to talk with your friend sitting next to you, eat candy, chew gum, or produce any sound that may disturb your fellow music lovers.

When you're at the Philharmonic, you're expected to do one thing and one thing only: **слушать музыку!** (*slooh*-shuht' *mooh*-zi-kooh!) (*to listen to the music!*) Whether you actually hear the music is up to you.

When you indicate a date, use the ordinal number and the name of the month in the genitive case. For more information on ordinal numerals and months, see Chapter 5.

Culture Club: Visiting a Museum

Russians are a nation of museum-goers. Visiting a **музей** (mooh-*zyehy*) (*museum*) is seen as a "culture" trip. This view explains why Russian parents consider their first duty to be taking their kids to all kinds of museums on the weekends. Apart from the fact that Russian cities and even villages usually have a lot of museums, whenever Russians go abroad they immediately start looking for museums they can go to.

In almost every city, you're likely to find the following museums to satisfy your hunger for culture:

- **музей истории города** (mooh-*zyehy* ees-*toh*-ree-ee *goh*-rah-duh) (*museum of the town history*)

- **музей истории края** (mooh-*zyehy* ees-*toh*-ree-ee *krah*-yeh) (*regional history museum*)

- **исторический музей** (ee-stah-*ree*-chees-keey mooh-*zyehy*) (*historical museum*)

- **картинная галерея** (kuhr-*tee*-nuh-yeh guh-lee-*ryeh*-yeh) (*art gallery*)

A special decree of the new Soviet government after the October Revolution of 1917 converted a lot of former tsar residences into museums. At that time, one of the main purposes of this action was to show the working people of Russia the revolting luxury that the former Russian rulers lived in by exploiting their people. The most popular ones are **Екатерининский Дворец** (ee-kuh-tee-*ree*-neen-skeey dvah-*ryehts*) (*Catherine's Palace*), **Павловский Дворец** (*pahv*-luhf-skeey dvah-*ryehts*) (*Paul's Palace*), and **Петродворец** (peet-rah-dvah-*ryehts*) (*Peter's Palace*) in Peterhof. There's also a little palace of Peter the Great in St. Petersburg you may want to see.

No matter what museum you visit, you'll most likely find these things there:

- **тур** (toohr) (*tour*)

- **гид** (geed) (*tour guide*)

- **путеводитель** (pooh-tee-vah-*dee*-teel') (*guidebook*)

- **экспонат** (ehks-pah-*naht*) (*exhibit*)

- **выставка** (*vis*-tuhv-kuh) (*exhibition*)

- **зал** (zahl) (*exhibition hall*)

✔ **экспозиция** (ehks-pah-*zee*-tsi-yeh) (*display*)

✔ **картина** (kuhr-*tee*-nuh) (*painting*)

✔ **скульптура** (skoohl'-*ptooh*-ruh) (*sculpture* or *piece of sculpture*)

How Was It? Talking about Entertainment

After you've been out to the ballet, theater, museum, or a movie, you'll probably want to share your impressions with others. The best way to share your opinions is by using a form of the verb **нравиться** (*nrah*-veet'-syeh) (*to like*). (For details on the present tense of this verb, see Chapter 6.)

✔ To say that you liked what you saw, say **Мне понравился** (mnyeh pahn-*rah*-veel-syeh) plus the name of what you saw in the nominative case. For example, you may want to say

> **Мне понравился спектакль/фильм.** (mnyeh pahn-*rah*-veel-syeh speek-*tahkl'*/feel'm.) (*I liked the performance/movie.*)

✔ If you didn't like the production, just add the particle **не** (nee) before the verb:

> **Мне не понравился спектакль/фильм.** (mnyeh nee pahn-*rah*-veel-syeh speek-*tahkl'*/feel'm.) (*I did not like the performance/movie.*)

If you want to elaborate on your opinion, you may want to use words and phrases like these:

✔ **Потрясающе!** (puh-tree-*sah*-yooh-sh'ee!) (*Amazing!*)

✔ **хороший балет/спектакль/концерт/фильм** (khah-*roh*-shiy buh-*lyeht*/speek-*tahkl'*/kahn-*tsyehrt*/feel'm) (*a good ballet/performance/concert/film*)

✔ **плохой балет/спектакль/концерт/фильм** (plah-*khohy* buh-*lyeht*/speek-*tahkl'*/kahn-*tsehrt*/feel'm) (a bad ballet/performance/concert/film)

To ask a friend whether she liked an event, you can ask:

> **Тебе/Вам понравился спектакль/фильм?** (tee-*byeh*/*vahm* pahn-*rah*-veel-syeh speek-*tahkl'*/feel'm?) (*Did you like the performance/movie?*)

Use the informal **тебе** or the formal **вам** in accordance with the situation.

Another way to ask for an opinion of an event is simple:

> **Ну, как?** (nooh, kahk?) (*How was it?*)

Talkin' the Talk

Natasha (**Наташа**) and John (**Джон**) have just attended a classical ballet at the St. Petersburg Mariinsky Theater and exchange their opinions of the performance. (Track 19)

Наташа:	**Ну, как? Тебе понравился спектакль?** nooh kahk? tee-*byeh* pahn-*rah*-veel-syeh speek-*tahkl*'? *How was it? Did you like the performance?*
Джон:	**Очень. Потрясающе. Очень красивый балет. А тебе?** oh-cheen'. puh-tree-*sah*-yooh-sh'ee. oh-cheen' kruh-*see*-viy buh-*lyeht*. uh tee-*byeh*? *A lot. It was amazing. A very beautiful ballet. And you?*
Наташа:	**мне очень понравился.** mnyeh oh-cheen' pahn-*rah*-veel-syeh. *I liked the performance a lot.*

Words to Know

Ну, как?	*nooh kahk?*	How was it?
Тебе понравился спектакль?	*tee-byeh pahn-rah-veel-syeh speek-tahkl'?*	Did you like the performance?
Очень	*oh-cheen'*	A lot
потрясающе	*puh-tree-sah-yooh-sh'ee*	amazing
красивый	*kruh-see-viy*	beautiful
А тебе?	*uh tee-byeh?*	And you?

Fun & Games

Which of the following phrases would you probably use to express that you liked a show or performance you attended? Find the correct answers in Appendix D.

1. **Мне понравился спектакль.**

2. **Потрясающе!**

3. **Очень скучный фильм.**

4. **Неинтересный фильм.**

5. **Очень красивый балет.**

Chapter 12

Taking Care of Business and Telecommunications

In This Chapter

▶ Checking out basic office vocabulary

▶ Talking on the phone

▶ Using your computer

▶ Handling correspondence

*T*he workplace may be pretty different when you're working in a foreign country or even at home for a foreign company. This chapter equips you with the necessary vocabulary and phrases to thrive in a Russian workspace. We also provide you with the basics on communicating via phone and computer, both in and out of the office.

Looking Around Your Office

All the special gadgets and rooms in an office building can make anyone dizzy, even if you don't need to refer to them in a foreign language. In the following sections, we tell you how to navigate your office with maximum ease; we also give you pointers on basic office etiquette.

Indispensable office supplies

When you're **в офисе** (v *oh*-fee-see) (*at the office*), you definitely have a huge advantage as an English speaker: Out of the zillion little things inhabiting the office, a good portion has highly recognizable, English-borrowed names. Even if you knew no Russian whatsoever, you'd probably suspect something if you heard this sentence:

Мне нужен катридж для принтера. (mnyeh *nooh*-zhin *kah*-treedzh dlya *preen*-teh-ruh.) (*I need a cartridge for my printer.*)

Here's a list of common office supplies to know:

- **компьютер** (kahm-*p'yooh*-teer) (*computer*)
- **ноутбук** (nah-ooht-*boohk*) (*laptop*)
- **монитор** (mah-nee-*tohr*) (*monitor*)
- **принтер** (*preen*-tehr) (*printer*)
- **факс** (fahks) (*fax*)
- **ксерокс** (*ksyeh*-rahks) (*copy machine*)
- **скэннер** (*skeh*-nehr) (*scanner*)
- **модэм** (*moh*-dehm) (*modem*)
- **письменный стол** (*pees'*-mee-niy stohl) (*desk*)
- **стул** (stoohl) (*chair*)
- **настольная лампа** (nuhs-*tohl'*-nuh-yeh *lahm*-puh) (*desk lamp*)
- **календарь** (kuh-leen-*dahr'*) (*calendar*)
- **книжные полки** (*kneezh*-ni-ee *pohl*-kee) (*bookshelves*)
- **корзина для мусора** (kahr-*zee*-nuh dlya *mooh*-sah-ruh) (*wastebasket*)
- **телефон** (tee-lee-*fohn*) (*telephone*)
- **ручка** (*roohch*-kuh) (*pen*)
- **карандаш** (kuh-ruhn-*dahsh*) (*pencil*)
- **стёрка** (*styohr*-kuh) (*eraser*)
- **точилка** (tah-*cheel*-kuh) (*pencil sharpener*)
- **тетрадь** (teet-*raht'*) (*notebook*)
- **папка** (*pahp*-kuh) (*file*)
- **бумага** (booh-*mah*-guh) (*paper*)
- **замазка** (zuh-*mahs*-kuh) (*liquid corrector*)
- **скрепки** (*skryehp*-kee) (*paper clips*)
- **клейкая лента** (*klyehy*-kuh-yeh *lyehn*-tuh) (*tape*)
- **стейплер** (*stehyp*-leer) (*stapler*)

Rooms around the office

In addition to the **кабинет** (kuh-bee-*nyeht*) (*office*), you may want to know the names for other important rooms at work, such as the **столовая** (stah-*loh*-vuh-yeh) (*cafeteria*), **комната отдыха** (*kohm*-nuh-tuh *oht*-di-khuh) (*lounge*), and **курилка** (kooh-*reel*-kuh), a room designated for smoking, where you'll see most of your colleagues.

Although smoking is prohibited in most public places in the U.S. and smokers are treated almost as lepers, this is certainly not the case in Russia. Besides, smoking in Russia is a form of escapism — an "escaping from work" strategy.

Financial matters can be settled in the **бухгалтерия** (boohkh-guhl-*tyeh*-ree-yeh) (*accounts office*). The room everybody wants to avoid is the **кабинет начальника** (kuh-bee-*nyeht* nuh-*chahl'*-nee-kuh) (*boss's office*). Your actual work is usually done in a **кабинет** (kuh-bee-*nyeht*) (*office room*) and a **конференцзал** (kahn-fee-*ryehnts*-zuhl) (*meeting room*). American cubicles have not yet taken root in Russia. Most offices are rooms with closed doors. Before entering somebody's office, you need to knock.

Simple office etiquette

One thing about the workplace is that you're never alone. You often need to talk to a **сотрудник** (saht-*roohd*-neek) (*co-worker*), your **начальник** (nuh-*chahl'*-neek) (*boss*), or a **клиент** (klee-*yehnt*) (*client*).

Here are examples of standard phrases used to **назначить встречу** (nuhz-*nah*-cheet' fstryeh-chooh) (*make an appointment*):

> **Давайте встретимся в 9 часов утра.** (duh-*vahy*-tee fstryeh-teem-syeh v *dyeh*-veet' chuh-*sohf* ooht-rah.) (*Let's meet at 9 a.m.*)

> **Я вас буду ждать в три часа.** (ya vahs *booh*-dooh zhdaht' v tree chuh-sah.) (*I'll be waiting for you at 3 p.m.*)

If you're arranging a phone call, you may say the following:

> **Я вам позвоню в два часа.** (Ya vahm pah-zvah-*nyooh* v dvah chuh-sah.) (*I'll call you at 2 p.m.*)

> **Я буду ждать вашего звонка в десять часов.** (Ya *booh*-dooh zhdaht' *vah*-sheh-vuh zvahn-*kah* v *dyeh*-syat' chuh-*sohf*.) (*I'll be waiting for your phone call at 10 a.m.*)

Russian business etiquette is not as strict as that of some other cultures. Just garnish your speech generously with **пожалуйста** (pah-*zhahl*-stuh) (*please*) and **спасибо** (spuh-*see*-bah) (*thank you*), and you'll already sound more formal than an average Russian in the workplace.

Always use the formal **вы** (vi) (*you,* formal singular or plural) whenever you communicate with anyone in the workplace. If your co-workers and your boss want to switch to less formal terms, they'll tell you so.

To avoid uncomfortable situations, always use the first name plus the patronymic form to address your colleagues. If they want to switch to the Western first-name manner, they'll tell you:

Можно просто Саша. (*mohzh*-nah *prohs*-tah *sah*-shuh.) (*You can call me Sasha.*)

For more information on Russian names, see Chapter 4.

Ringing Up Telephone Basics

Telephones are an indispensable part of people's busy lives. In the following sections, you find out basic phone vocabulary.

Brushing up on phone vocabulary

Before you make a phone call, you need to know a number of important words associated with the use of the **телефон** (tee-lee-*fohn*) (*telephone*). When somebody wants to talk to you, he may want to **звонить** (zvah-*neet'*) (*call*) you. The caller needs to **набирать** (nuh-bee-*raht'*) (*dial*) your **номер телефона** (*noh*-meer tee-lee-*foh*-nuh) (*telephone number*) — when the call goes through, you hear a **звонок** (zvah-*nohk*) (*ring*).

The main part of the telephone is the **трубка** (*troohp*-kuh) (*receiver*). On your landline, the **трубка** rests on the **телефонный аппарат** (tee-lee-*fohn*-niy uh-puh-*raht*) (*body of the phone*).

You can do a lot of things with the **трубка**. You can **поднимать трубку** (pahd-nee-*maht' troohp*-kooh) (*pick up the receiver*), **вешать трубку** (*vyeh*-shuht' *troohp*-kooh) (*hang up the receiver*), or **класть трубку** (klahst' *troohp*-kooh) (*put down the receiver*). Other words related to phones include the following:

- ✔ **кнопка** (*knohp*-kuh) (*button*)
- ✔ **гудок** (gooh-*dohk*) (*beep, tone*)
- ✔ **долгий гудок** (*dohl*-geey gooh-*dohk*) (*dial tone*; Literally: *long tone*)
- ✔ **короткие гудки** (kah-*roht*-kee-ee goohd-*kee*) (*busy signal*; Literally: *short tones*)
- ✔ **код города** (koht *goh*-rah-duh) (*area code*)
- ✔ **телефонная книга** (tee-lee-*fohn*-nuh-yeh *knee*-guh) (*telephone book*)

You also need to be able to give other people your phone number and to understand the phone numbers dictated to you. Usually, Russians give phone numbers in chunks. For instance, if your phone number is 123-45-67, you say it like this: **сто двадцать три, сорок пять, шестьдесят семь** (stoh *dvaht*-tsuht' tree, *soh*-rahk pyat', shis-dee-*syat'* syehm') (*one hundred twenty-three, forty-five, sixty-seven*). Check out Chapter 5 for an introduction to numbers in Russian.

Distinguishing different types of phones

In addition to the standard **телефон** (tee-lee-*fohn*) (*landline*), most people today in Russia have a **сотовый телефон** (*soh*-tah-viy tee-lee-*fohn*) (*cellphone*) and seem to enjoy it more than any other people in the world. A cellphone may also be called a **мобильный телефон** (mah-*beel'*-niy tee-lee-*fohn*) (*mobile phone*); a **мобильник** (mah-*beel'*-neek) (*mobile phone*); or, more frequently (and affectionately), a **трубка** (*troohp*-kuh) (Literally: *receiver*). Other specific types of phones include these:

- **дисковый телефон** (*dees*-kah-viy tee-lee-*fohn*) (*rotary phone*)

- **кнопочный телефон** (*knoh*-pahch-niy tee-lee-*fohn*) (*touch-tone phone*)

- **беспроводной телефон** (bees-prah-vahd-*nohy* tee-lee-*fohn*) (*cordless phone*)

Before you leave for Russia, call your cellphone company to make sure it offers phone coverage in Russia. Ask to be upgraded to international roaming. If your cellphone company doesn't offer coverage in Russia, which is often the case, you may consider renting a cellphone; however, doing so may be quite costly. Our recommendation: If you're planning mostly to make calls within Russia, consider buying a cellphone with a SIM-card that will work in Russia. Another option is to buy a new SIM-card in Russia and insert it in your existing phone. The SIM-card will come with a new phone number and can be bought in one of the numerous cellphone stores. Don't lose your existing SIM-card — you'll need it when you return to the U.S. Cellphones usually work on a prepay basis, and the minutes are more expensive in Russia than they are in the U.S.

Knowing different kinds of phone calls

If you call somebody in your calling area, you make a **местный звонок** (*myehst*-niy zvah-*nohk*) (*local call*), and you aren't charged. If the person or institution you call is in a different city, you make a **междугородный звонок** (meezh-dooh-gah-*rohd*-niy zvah-*nohk*) (*long-distance call*; Literally: *intercity*). If you want to call back home from Russia, you make a **международный звонок** (meezh-dooh-nuh-*rohd*-niy zvah-*nohk*) (*international call*).

Russia has no collect or operator-assisted calls. So when you're in Russia and you want to make a call, be sure to have a Russian-speaking friend around!

Dialing the Number and Making the Call

When you want to make a phone call, you can't translate your desire into reality without first dialing the number of the person or institution you're calling. In order to **набрать номер** (nuh-*braht' noh*-meer) (*dial the number*), use a **циферблат** (tsi-feer-*blaht*) (*dial-plate*), which, in many Russian homes, is still rotary rather than push-button. To help you handle this task, we provide you with the conjugation of the verb **набрать** (nuh-*braht'*) (*to dial*) in the present tense (see Chapter 3 for an introduction to present-tense verb conjugations, including first-conjugation verbs like the following).

Conjugation	*Pronunciation*
я набираю	ya nuh-bee-*rah*-yooh
ты набираешь (informal singular)	ti nuh-bee-*rah*-eesh'
он/она набирает	ohn/ah-*nah* nuh-bee-*rah*-eet
мы набираем	mi nuh-bee-*rah*-eem
вы набираете (formal singular or plural)	vi nuh-bee-*rah*-ee-tee
они набирают	ah-*nee* nuh-bee-*rah*-yooht

Russian makes a grammatical distinction between calling a person, an institution, and a different city or country. The following rules apply (see Chapter 3 for more details about cases):

✔ If you're calling a person, use the dative case, for example:

> **Я хочу позвонить Наташе.** (ya khah-*chooh* pah-zvah-*neet'* nuh-*tah*-shi.) (*I want to call Natasha.*)

Note that you should use the perfective verb here (**позвонить** rather than **звонить**) because you intend to call Natasha just once instead of calling her incessantly.

✔ If you're calling an institution, after the verb, use the preposition **в** or **на** plus the accusative case to indicate the institution you're calling, as in these examples:

> **позвонить на работу** (pah-zvah-*neet'* nuh ruh-*boh*-tooh) (*to call work*)
>
> **позвонить в магазин** (pah-zvah-*neet'* v muh-guh-*zeen*) (*to call a store*)

✔ If you're calling another city or a foreign country, after the verb use **в** plus the accusative form of the city or country you're calling, like this:

> **позвонить в Америку** (pah-zvah-*neet'* v uh-*myeh*-ree-kooh) (*to call the U.S.*)

Unfortunately, **звонить** is nothing but an infinitive, and you can't do much with infinitives if you intend to engage in serious conversation about telephone matters. So in the following table, we provide you with the present tense of this important verb.

Conjugation	*Pronunciation*
я звоню	ya zvah-*nyooh*
ты звонишь (informal singular)	ti zvah-*neesh'*
он/она звонит	ohn/ah-*nah* zvah-*neet*
мы звоним	mi zvah-*neem*
вы звоните (formal singular or plural)	vi zvah-*nee*-tee
они звонят	ah-*nee* zvah-*nyat*

As you can see, the verb **по/звонить** is a second-conjugation verb.

Now, imagine that you head to the phone and pick up the receiver. If you hear a **долгие гудки** (*dohl*-gee-ee gooht-*kee*) (*long tone*) after you dial, it means that the phone is ringing and is **свободен** (svah-*boh*-deen) (*not busy*); you need to be patient until somebody answers the phone. While you're waiting for somebody to answer, you may think to yourself:

> **Никто не подходит к телефону.** (neek-*toh* nee paht-*khoh*-deet k tee-lee-*foh*-nooh.) (*Nobody is picking up the phone.*)

After waiting for a couple minutes (depending on the amount of patience you have), you may say

> **Никто не подошёл к телефону.** (neek-*toh* nee pah-dah-*shohl* k tee-lee-*foh*-nooh.) (*Nobody answered the phone.*)

If the person you're calling is already talking on the phone with somebody else, you hear a **короткие гудки** (kah-*roht*-kee-ee gooht-*kee*) (*busy signal*; Literally: *short tones*). This signal means the phone is busy, and you need to **повесить трубку** (pah-*vyeh*-seet' troohp-kooh) (*hang up*) and **перезвонить** (pee-ree-zvah-*neet'*) (*call back*). See the next section for details on what to do when you reach the person you want to speak to.

Arming Yourself with Basic Telephone Etiquette

Every culture has its own telephone etiquette, and Russia is no exception. In the following sections, you discover how to ask for the person you want to speak to, what you may hear in response, and how to leave a message with a person or an answering machine.

Saving time by not introducing yourself

When you make a phone call in Russia, you may get the impression that the person who answers is an extremely impatient individual who can't afford the luxury of wasting time answering the phone. That's why the person's **Аллё!** (uh-*lyoh*!) (*Hello!*) — a standard way to answer the phone — may sound abrupt, unfriendly, or even angry. You may also hear just **Да** (dah) (*Yes*) or **Слушаю** (*slooh*-shuh-yooh) (*I'm listening*). Don't waste time introducing yourself (even if it's a business call). Hurry up and tell the person your business right away.

Asking for the person you want to speak to

In English, you often say something like "Is John there?" Not so in Russian. In fact, a Russian may not even understand what you mean by that question. Instead, get to your request right away, using the phrase **Можно. . . ?** (*mohzh*-nah. . . ?) (*Can I talk to. . . ?*), inserting the name of the person you want to talk to in the accusative case. If you want to talk to a woman named **Наталья Ивановна**, you say

> **Можно Наталью Ивановну?** (*mohzh*-nah nuh-*tahl'*-yooh ee-*vah*-nahv-nooh?) (*Can I talk to Natalya Ivanovna?*)

You have to use the name of the person you want to talk to in the accusative case because what you're saying is an abbreviated version of **Можно позвать к телефону Наталью Ивановну?** (*mohzh*-nah pahz-*vaht'* k tee-lee-*foh*-nooh nuh-*tahl'*-yooh ee-*vah*-nahv-nooh?) (*Can you call to the phone Natalya Ivanovna?*), and the verb **позвать** (pahz-*vaht'*) (*to call*) requires the noun after it to be in the accusative case. (For more on the accusative case, see Chapter 3.) You can make this phrase more polite by adding the phrase **Будьте добры** (*boohd'*-tee dahb-*ri*) (*Will you be so kind*) at the beginning.

Anticipating different responses

Here are some of the more common things you may hear in response to your request to speak to someone:

- If you call somebody at home and he or she isn't at home, you'll most likely hear

    Его/её нет дома. (ee-*voh*/ee-*yoh* nyeht *doh*-muh.) (*He/she is not at home.*)

- If the person you call is at home but he or she isn't the one who answered the phone, you'll hear one of these responses:

    Сейчас. (seey-*chahs*.) (*Hold on.*)

    Сейчас, позову. (seey-*chahs*, pah-zah-*vooh*.) (*Hold on, I'll get him/her.*)

- When the person you want finally answers the phone (or if he or she actually picked up the phone when you called), he or she will say one of the following: **Аллё** (uh-*lyoh*) (*Hello*), **Слушаю** (*slooh*-shuh-yooh) (*Speaking*), or simply **Да** (dah) (*Yes*).

- You probably have the wrong number if you hear **Кого?** (kah-*voh*?) (*Whom?*) If the person knows you called the wrong number, you'll most likely be told

    Вы не туда попали. (vi nee tooh-*dah* pah-*pah*-lee.) (*You dialed the wrong number.*)

You can check to make sure you dialed the right number by saying something like

       Это пятьсот девяносто восемь сорок пять двадцать один? (*eh*-tah peet'-*soht* dee-vee-*nohs*-tah *voh*-seem' *soh*-rahk pyat' *dvaht*-tsuht' ah-*deen*?) (*Is this five nine eight four five two one?* Literally: *Is this five hundred ninety-eight forty-five twenty-one?*)

If you dialed another number, you may hear

       Нет, вы неправильно набираете. (nyeht, vi nee-*prah*-veel'-nah nuh-bee-*rah*-ee-tee.) (*No, you've dialed the wrong number.*)

Talkin' the Talk

Jack (**Джек**) met Boris at a party, and they exchanged phone numbers. It's Sunday night, and Jack decides to call his new friend. **Женщина** (*zhehn*-sh'ee-nuh) (*a woman*) answers the phone. (Track 20)

Женщина:	**Аллё!**
	uh-*lyoh*!
	Hello!

Джек:	**Можно Бориса?**
	mohzh-nah bah-*ree*-suh?
	Can I talk to Boris?

Женшина:	**Кого?**
	kah-*voh*?
	Who?

Джек:	**Бориса.**
	bah-*ree*-suh.
	Boris.

Женщина:	**Здесь таких нет.**
	zdyehs' tuh-*keekh* nyeht.
	There's nobody by that name here.

Джек:	**Извините, я не понял. Что вы сказали?**
	eez-vee-*nee*-tee, ya nee *poh*-nyehl. shtoh vi
	skuh-*zah*-lee?
	Sorry, I did not understand. What did you say?

Женщина:	**Молодой человек, я сказала, что здесь таких нет! Вы не туда попали!**
	mah-lah-*dohy* chee-lah-*vyehk*, ya skuh-*zah*-luh, shtoh
	zdyehs' tuh-*keekh* nyeht! vi nee tooh-*dah* pah-*pah*-lee!
	Young man, I said there is no Boris here! You dialed the wrong number!

Джек:	**Не туда попал?**
	nee tooh-*dah* pah-*pahl*?
	I got the wrong number?

Женщина:	**Молодой человек, какой номер телефона вы набираете?**
	mah-lah-*dohy* chee-lah-*vyehk*, kuh-*kohy* noh-meer
	tee-lee-*foh*-nuh vi nuh-bee-*rah*-ee-tee?
	Young man, what phone number are you dialing?

Джек:	**Я набираю двести сорок восемь двенадцать девяносто три.**
	ya nuh-bee-*rah*-yooh *dvyehs*-tee *soh*-rahk *voh*-seem'
	dvee-*naht*-tsuht' dee-vee-*nohs*-tah tree.
	I am dialing 248-12-93.

Женщина:	**это двести сорок восемь двенадцать девяносто два.**
	eh-tah *dvyehs*-tee *soh*-rahk *voh*-seem' dvee-*naht*-tsuht' dee-vee-*nohs*-tah dvah.
	This is 248-12-92.

Джек:	**Ой, извините!**
	ohy eez-vee-*nee*-tee!
	Oh, sorry!

Женщина:	**Ничего.**
	nee-chee-*voh.*
	That's okay.

Words to Know

Можно . . .	mohzh-nah . . .	Can I talk to . . .
Здесь таких нет.	zdyehs' tuh-keekh nyeht.	There's nobody by that name here.
Извините.	eez-vee-nee-tee.	Sorry.
Я не понял.	ya nee poh-nyehl.	I didn't understand.
Что вы сказали?	shtoh vi skuh-zah-lee?	What did you say?
Вы не туда попали!	vi nee tooh-dah pah-pah-lee!	You dialed the wrong number!
Не туда попал?	nee tooh-dah pah-pahl?	I got the wrong number?
Какой номер телефона вы набираете?	kuh-kohy noh-meer tee-lee-foh-nuh vi nuh-bee-rah-ee-tee?	What phone number are you dialing?
Ничего.	nee-chee-voh.	That's okay.

Leaving a message with a person

If you call and ask for somebody who isn't available, you'll probably hear one of these responses, depending on the gender of the person you're trying to reach:

✔ **If the person you're asking for is a man:** You may hear **А кто его спрашивает?** (uh ktoh ee-*voh sprah*-shi-vuh-eet?) (*And who is asking for him?*) or **А что ему передать?** (uh shtoh ee-*mooh* pee-ree-*daht'?*) (*Can I take a message?*)

✔ **If the person you're asking for is a woman:** You may hear **А кто её спрашивает?** (uh ktoh ee-*yoh sprah*-shi-vuh-eet?) (*And who is asking for her?*) or **А что ей передать?** (uh shtoh yehy pee-ree-*daht'?*) (*Can I take a message?*)

When asked who is calling, say: **Это звонит** plus your name in the nominative case (*eh*-tah zvah-*neet*) (*This is . . . calling*). Then you may simply want to give your phone number and say **Спасибо** (spuh-*see*-bah) (*thank you*).

To ask to leave a message, begin your request with

> **А вы не можете ему/ей передать?** (uh vi nee *moh*-zhi-tee ee-*mooh*/yehy pee-ree-*daht'?*) (*Can I leave a message for him/her?*)

No matter what your message is, it should begin with the phrase **Передайте, пожалуйста. . .** (pee-ree-*dahy*-tee, pah-*zhahl*-stuh . . .) (*Please tell him/her . . .*) Most likely, you want to say one of the following:

✔ **If you're a man:** Say **Передайте, пожалуйста, что звонил** plus your name (pee-ree-*dahy*-tee, pah-*zhahl*-stuh shtoh zvah-*neel*) (*Please tell him/her that . . . called*).

✔ **If you're a woman:** Say **Передайте, пожалуйста, что звонила** plus your name (pee-ree-*dahy*-tee, pah-*zhahl*-stuh shtoh zvah-*nee*-luh) (*Please tell him/her that . . . called*).

Talkin' the Talk

Kira (**Кира**) and Vera are school friends. Kira calls Vera to suggest going to the movies together. Vera's mother, Olga Nikolayevna (**Ольга Николаевна**), answers the phone. (Track 21)

Ольга Николаевна: **Аллё!**
                              uh-*lyoh*!
                              Hello!

Кира:	**Можно Веру?**
	mohzh-nah *vyeh*-rooh?
	Can I talk to Vyera?

Ольга Николаевна:	**Веры нет дома. кто её спрашивает? Это её мама.**
	vyeh-ri nyeht *doh*-muh. ktoh ee-*yoh* sprah-shi-vuh-eet? *eh*-tah ee-*yoh mah*-muh.
	Vyera is not at home. Who is it? This is her mother speaking.

Кира:	**Это её подруга Кира. Здравствуйте! Вы не знаете, где она?**
	eh-tah ee-*yoh* pahd-*rooh*-guh *kee*-ruh. *zdrahs*-tvoohy-tee! vi nee *znah*-ee-tee, gdyeh ah-*nah*?
	It's her friend Kira. Hello! Do you happen to know where she is?

Ольга Николаевна:	**А, Кира? Кира, а Вера пошла в бассейн.**
	ah, *kee*-ruh? *kee*-ruh, uh *vyeh* ruh pahsh-*lah* v buh-*seh*-een.
	Oh, Kira? Kira, Vyera went to the swimming pool.

Кира:	**Когда она будет дома?**
	kahg-*dah* ah-*nah booh*-deet *doh*-muh?
	When will she be home?

Ольга Николаевна:	**Она должна вернуться через полчаса. Может быть, что-нибудь передать?**
	ah-*nah* dahl-*zhnah* veer-*nooht'*-syeh *chee*-rees puhl-chuh-*sah*. *moh*-zhit bit' *shtoh*-nee-booht' pee-ree-*daht'*?
	She should be back in half an hour. Would you like to leave a message?

Кира:	**Нет, спасибо. Я перезвоню.**
	nyeht, spuh-*see*-bah. ya pee-reez-vah-*nyooh*.
	No, thanks. I'll call back.

Ольга Николаевна:	**Ну, хорошо. Я ей скажу, что ты звонила.**
	nooh, khah-rah-*shoh*. ya yehy skuh-*zhooh*, shtoh ti zvah-*nee*-luh.
	Okay. I will tell her that you called.

Кира:	**Спасибо.**
	spuh-*see*-bah.
	Thanks.

Words to Know

Вы не знаете, где она?	vi nee <u>znah</u>-ee-tee, gdyeh ah-<u>nah</u>?	Do you happen to know where she is?
Когда она будет дома?	kahg-<u>dah</u> ah-<u>nah</u> <u>booh</u>-deet doh-muh?	When will she be home?
Она должна вернуться . . .	ah-<u>nah</u> dahl-<u>zhnah</u> veer-<u>nooht'</u>-syeh . . .	She should be back . . .
Может быть, что-нибудь передать?	<u>moh</u>-zhit bit', <u>shtoh</u>-nee-booht' pee-ree-<u>daht'</u>?	Would you like to leave a message?
Я перезвоню.	ya pee-reez-vah-<u>nyooh</u>.	I'll call back.
Я ей скажу, что ты звонила.	ya yehy skuh-<u>zhooh</u>, shtoh ti zvah-<u>nee</u>-luh.	I will tell her that you called.

Talking to an answering machine

If your call is answered by **автоответчик** (ahf-tah-aht-*vyeht*-cheek) (*voice mail*), the first thing you'll probably hear is this:

> **Здравствуйте, нас нет дома. Оставьте, пожалуйста, сообщение после гудка.** (*zdrah*-stvoohy-tee, nahs nyeht *doh*-muh. ahs-*tahf*-tee, pah-*zhahl*-stuh, sah-ahp-*sh'yeh*-nee-ee *pohs*-lee gooht-*kah*.) (*Hello, we're not home. Please leave your message after the beep.*)

A cellphone's message is likely to be slightly different. It typically sounds like this:

> **Абонент не доступен. Оставьте сообщение после сигнала.** (uh-bah-*nyehnt* nee dahs-*tooh*-peen. ahs-*tahf*-tee sah-ahp-*sh'yeh*-nee-ee *pohs*-lee seeg-*nah*-luh.) (*The person you are calling is not available. Leave a message after the beep.*)

When leaving a message, you can begin by saying: **Здравствуйте! Это** (*zdrah*-stvoohy-tee! *eh*-tah) (*Hello! This is*) followed by your name in the nominative case (see Chapter 3 for details). Then add: **Позвоните мне, пожалуйста. Мой номер телефона** (pahz-vah-*nee*-tee mnyeh, pah-*zhahl*-stuh. mohy *noh*-meer tee-lee-*foh*-nuh) (*Call me please. My phone number is*) followed by your phone number.

Using a Computer

Using a computer is an important aspect of working and communicating. In the following sections, we provide Russian terms related to e-mail and the Internet.

If you're traveling to Russia with your computer, make sure your computer's power supply is compatible with Russian voltage. Russia uses the European standard of 220 volts of electricity rather than the 110-volt version used in the United States. Most laptops' power supplies automatically convert the power, but you still need to purchase an adapter that fits Russian (European) electric plugs.

Are there wireless hotspots in Russia? A few years ago, that would have been an absurd question to ask, but today the situation is very different. Most chain hotels and restaurants have a solid wireless connection available for you.

Familiarizing yourself with computer terms

Any office you walk into has at least one **компьютер** (kahm-p'*yooh*-tehr) (*computer*). Here are some important computer terms to understand:

- **вебкамера** (vehb-*kah*-mee-ruh) (*webcam*)
- **интернет** (een-tehr-*neht*) (*Internet*)
- **колонка** (kah-*lohn*-kuh) (*speaker*)
- **клавиатура** (kluh-vee-uh-*tooh*-ruh) (*keyboard*)
- **модем** (mah-*dehm*) (*modem*)
- **монитор** (mah-nee-*tohr*) (*monitor*)
- **принтер** (*preen*-tehr) (*printer*)
- **программа** (prah-*grah*-muh) (*program*)
- **мышь** (mish) (*mouse*)
- **СД диск** (see dee deesk) (*CD drive*)
- **файл** (*fah*-eel) (*file*)

One way to get a taste of Russia while you're still at home is to browse the Internet with www.google.ru. Try it and see how the English text on your computer is replaced by Russian. To help you get oriented, we provide you with the translation of the Cyrillic words in the left top corner of Google's home page:

- ✔ **Веб** (vehp) (*Web*)
- ✔ **Картинки** (kuhr-*teen*-kee) (*Images*; Literally: *little pictures*)
- ✔ **Видео** (*vee*-dee-oh) (*Video*)
- ✔ **Карты** (*kahr*-ti) (*Maps*)
- ✔ **Новости** (*noh*-vahs-tee) (*News*)
- ✔ **Почта** (*pohch*-tuh) (*Gmail*)
- ✔ **Ещё** (ee-*sh'yoh*) (*More*)

The word in the upper-right corner, **Войти** (vahy-*tee*), means *log-in* (Literally: *to come in*).

Sending e-mail

The official word for *e-mail* in Russian is **электронная почта** (eh-leek-*troh*-nah-yeh *pohch*-tuh), but few people use it in everyday casual communication: They either use the English word *e-mail* or just the word **электронка** (eh-leek-*trohn*-kuh) (Literally: *the electronic*). **Прикрепление** (pree-kree-*plyeh*-nee-ee) is the Russian (and very clumsy-sounding) equivalent for the English word *attachment*.

If you want to ask somebody what her e-mail address is, just say

> **Какой у вас e-mail?** (kuh-*kohy* ooh vahs ee-*meh*-eel?) (*What is your e-mail address?* Literally: *What is your e-mail?*)

But before you ask this question, you may want to make sure that this person has an e-mail account by asking

> **У вас есть e-mail?** (ooh vahs yehst' ee-*meh*-eel?) (*Do you have e-mail?*)

When you talk about e-mail, use the verb pair **посылать** (pah-si-*laht'*) and **послать** (pahs-*laht'*), which both mean *to send*. The imperfective verb **посылать** and its perfective counterpart **послать** have different patterns of conjugation. Whereas **посылать** is a nice regular verb and **послать** has nothing special about it in the past tense, the verb **послать** has a peculiar pattern of conjugation in the future tense, as shown in the following table. You may need to know the future tense so you can promise your new Russian friends that you'll send them e-mail. (Check out Chapter 3 for more about verbs in general, including imperfective and perfective verbs.)

Conjugation	Pronunciation
я пошлю	ya pahsh-*lyooh*
ты пошлёшь (informal singular)	ti pahsh-*lyohsh'*
он/она пошлёт	ohn/ah-*nah* pahsh-*lyoht*
мы пошлём	mi pahsh-*lyohm*
вы пошлёте (formal singular or plural)	vi pah-*shlyoh*-tee
они пошлют	ah-*nee* pahsh-*lyooht*

Sending Correspondence

With all the technology that people have now (cellphones, texting, and the like), amazingly, they still exchange letters. Just as in English, when sending written correspondence in Russian, it's customary to address the person you're writing to with a salutation. The word "dear" is appropriate for writing to relatives or exchanging some amorous correspondence:

✔ **If the person you're writing to is male:** Use дорогой (dah-rah-*gohy*) (*dear*, masculine) + the person's name in the nominative case.

✔ **If the person you're writing to is female:** Use дорогая (dah-rah-*gah*-yeh) (*dear*, feminine) + the person's name in the nominative case.

✔ **If you're writing to more than one person:** Use дорогие (dah-rah-*gee*-ee) (*dear*, plural) + the people's names in the nominative case.

In a formal letter, the word to use is уважаемый (esteemed):

✔ **If the person you're writing to is male:** Use уважаемый (ooh-vuh-*zhah*-ee-miy) (*dear*, Literally: *esteemed;* masculine) + the person's name.

✔ **If the person you're writing to is female:** Use уважаемая (ooh-vuh-*zhah*-ee-muh-yeh) (*dear*, Literally: *esteemed;* feminine) + the person's name.

✔ **If you're writing to more than one person:** Use уважаемые (ooh-vuh-*zhah*-ee-mi-ee) (*dear*, Literally: *esteemed;* plural) + the people's names.

The close of your письмо (pees'-*moh*) (*letter*) may include the standard ваш (vahsh) (*yours;* formal, masculine)/ваша (*vah*-shuh) (*yours;* formal, feminine) or твой (tvohy) (*yours;* informal, masculine)/твоя (tvah-*ya*) (*yours;* informal, feminine) plus your name. Or, you may use one of the following phrases, depending on your intention and relationship with the recipient:

✔ с уважением (s ooh-vuh-*zheh*-nee-eem) (*respectfully*)

✔ с любовью (s lyooh-*bohv'*-yooh) (*with love*)

✔ целую (tsi-*looh*-yooh) (*love;* Literally: *I kiss you*)

Fun & Games

In the following figure, match the various objects found in a typical office with their Russian names. See Appendix D for the answer key.

a. chair	письменный стол
b. desk lamp	книжные полки
c. calendar	настольная лампа
d. computer	ручка
e. telephone	стейплер
f. pencil sharpener	корзина для мусора
g. pen	стул
h. bookshelves	компьютер
i. wastebasket	календарь
j. desk	точилка
k. stapler	телефон

Chapter 13

Recreation and the Great Outdoors

- -

In This Chapter

▶ Discussing plans

▶ Chatting about sports

▶ Reading and enjoying music

▶ Making crafts

▶ Taking in the joys of nature

- -

The art of conversation isn't a forgotten skill among Russians. They love trading stories, relating their experiences, and exchanging opinions. And what's a better conversation starter than asking people about the things they like to do? Go ahead and tell your new acquaintances about your sports obsession or your reading habits. In this chapter, we show you how to talk about hobbies and recreation. You discover some activities that Russians especially enjoy and find out what to say when you're participating in them.

Shootin' the Breeze about Recreational Plans

Before getting to the nitty-gritty of your **хобби** (*khoh*-bee) (*hobby* or *hobbies*) — the word is used for both the singular and plural forms — you probably want to know how to talk about hobbies and recreation in general terms. In the following sections, you find out how to talk about your latest adventures, your plans for the coming weekend, and your general likes and dislikes.

What did you do last night?

The easiest way to ask someone about recent adventures is to ask one of the following questions, depending on whether you're asking in the singular or plural and the formal or informal form:

✔ To use the informal singular (masculine and feminine) form, ask

> **Что ты делал/делала вчера вечером?** (shtoh ti *dyeh*-luhl/*dyeh*-luh-luh fchee-*rah vyeh*-chee-rahm?) (*What did you do last night?*)

✔ To use the formal singular or plural (formal and informal) form, ask

> **Что вы делали вчера вечером?** (shtoh vi *dyeh*-luh-lee fchee-*rah vyeh*-chee-rahm?) (*What did you do last night?*)

If you're asked this question, you may find one of these responses appropriate:

✔ If you have nothing to report, you can simply say **Ничего** (nee-chee-*voh*) (*Nothing*).

✔ To say *I was at home*, say **Я был дома** (ya bil *doh*-muh) if you're a male or **Я была дома** (ya bi-*lah doh*-muh) if you're a female.

If you're talking to someone you happen to know was out the previous day, you can ask one of the following, depending on who you're addressing:

✔ If you're speaking to a male and you want to use the informal, singular form, ask **Куда ты вчера ходил?** (kooh-*dah* ti fchee-*rah* khah-*deel*?) *Where did you go yesterday?*)

✔ If you're speaking to a female and you want to use the informal, singular form, ask **Куда ты вчера ходила?** (kooh-*dah* ti fchee-*rah* khah-*dee*-luh?) (*Where did you go yesterday?*)

✔ If you're speaking to more than one person or you want to use the formal singular form (gender isn't an issue in this case), ask **Куда вы вчера ходили?** (kooh-*dah* vi fchee-*rah* khah-*dee*-lee?) (*Where did you go yesterday?*)

To reply to questions like these, you can say the following (see Chapter 3 for more about cases):

✔ To say *I was in/at*, begin your sentence with **Я был в** (ya bil v) if you're a male or **Я была в** (ya bi-*lah* v) if you're a female. Then finish the sentence with a noun in the prepositional case:

> **Я была вчера в театре.** (ya bi-*lah* fchee-*rah* v tee-*aht*-ree.) (*I was at the theater yesterday.*)

✔ To say *I went to*, begin the sentence with **Я ходил в** (ya khah-*deel* v) if you're a male or **Я ходила в** (ya khah-*dee*-luh v) if you're a female. Then complete the sentence by adding a noun in the accusative case:

> **Я ходил вчера в музей.** (ya khah-*deel* fchee-*rah* v mooh-*zyehy*.) (*I went to the museum yesterday.*)

To specify other times when you may have done something, these phrases may come in handy:

✔ **вчера вечером** (fchee-*rah vyeh*-chee-rahm) (*last night*)

✔ **на прошлой неделе** (nuh *prohsh*-lohy nee-*dyeh*-lee) (*last week*)

✔ **в выходные** (v vi-khad-*ni*-ee) (*over the weekend*)

What are you doing this weekend?

You may try to get the most out of your weeknights, but the weekend is the time for real adventure. Find out what your Russian friends do on the weekends using the following phrases:

✔ **Using the informal singular form:**

Что ты планируешь делать в выходные? (shtoh ti pluh-*nee*-rooh-eesh' *dyeh*-luht' v vi-khahd-*ni*-ee?) (*What are you doing this weekend?* Literally: *What do you plan to do this weekend?*)

Что ты обычно делаешь на выходные? (shtoh ti ah-*bich*-nah *dyeh*-luh-eesh' nuh vi-khahd-*ni*-ee?) (*What do you usually do on the weekend?*)

Что ты делаешь сегодня вечером? (shtoh ti *dyeh*-luh-eesh' see-*vohd*-nyeh *vyeh*-chee-rahm?) (*What are you doing tonight?*)

✔ **Using the formal singular or plural form:**

Что вы планируете делать в выходные? (shtoh vi pluh-*nee*-rooh-ee-tee *dyeh*-luht' v vi-khahd-*ni*-ee?) (*What are you doing this weekend?* Literally: *What do you plan to do this weekend?*)

Что вы обычно делаете в выходные? (shtoh vi ah-*bich*-nah *dyeh*-luh-ee-tee v vi-khahd-*ni*-ee?) (*What do you usually do on the weekend?*)

Что вы делаете сегодня вечером? (shtoh vi *dyeh*-luh-ee-tee see-*vohd*-nyeh *vyeh*-chee-rahm?) (*What are you doing tonight?*)

To answer these questions, you may say

✔ **Я планирую . . .** (ya pluh-*nee*-rooh-yooh . . .) (*I plan to . . .*) + the imperfective infinitive of a verb

✔ **Мы планируем . . .** (mi pluh-*nee*-rooh-eem . . .) (*We plan to . . .*) + the imperfective infinitive of a verb

✔ **Я буду . . .** (ya *booh*-dooh . . .) (*I will . . .*) + the imperfective infinitive of a verb

✔ **Мы будем . . .** (mi *booh*-deem . . .) (*We will . . .*) + the imperfective infinitive of a verb

✔ **Я обычно . . .** (ya ah-*bich*-nah . . .) (*I usually . . .*) + an imperfective verb in the first-person singular ("I") form

> ✔ **Мы обычно . . .** (mi ah-*bich*-nah . . .) (*We usually . . .*) + an imperfective verb in the first-person plural form

For full details about imperfective verbs, see Chapter 3.

If you don't have any particular plans, you may want to simply say one of the following:

> **Я буду дома.** (ya *booh*-dooh *doh*-muh.) (*I'll be at home.*)

> **Мы будем дома.** (mi *booh*-deem *doh*-muh.) (*We'll be at home.*).

What do you like to do?

In conversation, you can easily switch from talking about your private life to discussing your general likes and dislikes, which Russians like to do a lot. To discover someone's likes or dislikes, you can ask one of the following questions:

> ✔ **Using the informal singular form:**
>
> • **Чем ты любишь заниматься?** (chyehm ti *lyooh*-beesh' zuh-nee-*maht'*-syeh?) (*What do you like to do?*)
>
> • **Ты любишь. . . ?** (ti *lyooh*-beesh'. . . ?) (*Do you like. . . ?*) + the imperfective infinitive of a verb or a noun in the accusative case
>
> ✔ **Using the formal singular or plural form:**
>
> • **Чем вы любите заниматься?** (chyehm vi *lyooh*-bee-tee zuh-nee-*maht'*-syeh?) (*What do you like to do?*)
>
> • **Вы любите. . . ?** (vi *lyooh*-bee-tee. . . ?) (*Do you like. . . ?*) + the imperfective infinitive of a verb or a noun in the accusative case

For details about infinitives and cases, see Chapter 3.

Just like in English, the activity you like is expressed by the infinitive of a verb after the verb **любить** (lyooh-*beet'*) (*to like*). Here's an example:

> **Я люблю читать.** (ya lyooh-*blyooh* chee-*taht'*.) (*I like to read.*)

With nouns, however, the rule is different. To describe a person or object you love or like, put the noun in the accusative case, like this:

> **Я люблю музыку.** (ya lyooh-*blyooh* *mooh*-zi-kooh.) (*I love music.*)

The following table shows how the verb **любить** conjugates.

Conjugation	Pronunciation
я люблю	ya lyooh-*blyooh*
ты любишь (informal singular)	ti *lyooh*-beesh'
он/она любит	ohn/ah-*nah lyooh*-beet
мы любим	mi *lyooh*-beem
вы любите (formal singular or plural)	vi *lyooh*-bee-tee
они любят	ah-*nee lyooh*-byeht

Любить is a second-conjugation verb (see Chapter 3 for more info). Note, too, that its first-person form is **люблю**.

Interestingly enough, the word **любить**, which literally means *to love*, is often used in place of **нравиться** (*nrah*-veet'-syeh) (*to like*) when used before infinitives indicating things one likes to do.

Surveying the World of Sports

Whatever your relationship with sports is (whether you play and/or watch them), the following sections equip you with the necessary tools to talk about them. The word for *sports* is **спорт** (spohrt); it's always singular.

Listing a few popular sports

You may notice that the Russian words for various sports are easily recognizable because they sound very much like their English counterparts. Here's a list of words for some popular sports you may like to play or watch:

- **футбол** (fooht-*bohl*) (*soccer*)
- **волейбол** (vah-leey-*bohl*) (*volleyball*)
- **американский футбол** (uh-mee-ree-*kahn*-skeey fooht-*bohl*) (*football*)
- **бейсбол** (beeys-*bohl*) (*baseball*)
- **баскетбол** (buhs-keet-*bohl*) (*basketball*)
- **гольф** (gohl'f) (*golf*)
- **теннис** (*teh*-nees) (*tennis*)
- **гимнастика** (geem-*nahs*-tee-kuh) (*gymnastics*)
- **хоккей** (khah-*kyehy*) (*hockey*)

Using the verb "to play"

To talk about playing sports, you need the verb **играть** (eeg-*raht'*) (*to play*). The following table shows you how it conjugates in the present tense (it's a first conjugation verb; see Chapter 3).

Conjugation	Pronunciation
я играю	ya eeg-*rah*-yooh
ты играешь	ti eeg-*rah*-eesh'
он/она играет	ohn/ah-*nah* eeg-*rah*-eet
мы играем	mi eeg-*rah*-eem
вы играете	vi eeg-*rah*-ee-tee
они играют	ah-*nee* eeg-*rah*-yooht

Nothing is easier than stating what sports you play: Just use **Я играю в** followed by the names of the sports you play in the accusative case (see Chapter 3). For example, suppose you want to say that you play soccer. This is how you do it:

> **Я играю в футбол.** (ya eeg-*rah*-yooh v fooht-*bohl*.) (*I play soccer.*)

You can ask somebody whether they play sports by asking

> **Ты занимаешься спортом?** (ti zuh-nee-*mah*-eesh'-syeh *spohr*-tahm?)
> (*Do you play sports?* Literally: *Do you engage in sports?*)

If someone asks you this question, you can answer using one of these two phrases:

- ✔ **Да, я занимаюсь . . .** (dah, ya zuh-nee-*mah*-yoohs' . . .) (*Yes, I play . . .*) + the name of the sport in the instrumental case

- ✔ **Нет, я не занимаюсь спортом.** (nyeht, ya nee zuh-nee-*mah*-yoohs' *spohr*-tahm.) (*No, I don't play sports.*)

Before you tell someone you don't play sports, take a gander at the following section. By Russian standards, you may be more athletic than you think you are!

Talking about other athletic activities

Biking, jogging, walking, and swimming are regarded as sports in Russia. So, when someone asks **Вы занимаетесь спортом?** (vi zuh-nee-*mah*-ee-tees' *spohr*-tahm?) (*Do you engage in sports?*), you can talk about any of these activities to indicate your athletic prowess.

Soccer and hockey: Russians' favorite sports

Soccer and hockey are two absolute winners in the hearts of Russian fans. When national — and especially international — championship soccer and hockey tournaments are on TV, big cities literally turn into ghost towns: The streets are empty because people are glued to TV screens watching their favorite team winning (or losing) in the most important game of the year.

A word of caution: Before you use the word **футбол** (fooht-*bohl*), make sure you know the specific game you're talking about. **футбол** in Russian is *soccer*; what you may mean to say is **американский футбол** (uh-mee-ree-*kahn*-skeey fooht-*bohl*) (*football*; Literally: *American*

football). In this instance, you have to deal with an important cultural difference between Russians and Americans: Russians don't play "football" in the American sense of the word (and even somewhat despise it); instead they play **футбол**, which translates to "soccer" in English.

Russians' attachment to hockey is somewhat similar to that of Canadians, Finns, and other nations known for their long, cold winters. The origin of this sentiment is quite obvious: Children begin to play hockey in these countries everywhere the rivers or ponds are frozen for extended periods of time.

Following are some examples:

> **Я езжу на велосипеде.** (ya *yehz*-zhooh nuh vee-lah-see-*pyeh*-dee.) (*I ride a bike.*)

> **Я бегаю.** (ya *byeh*-guh-yooh.) (*I jog.*)

> **Я гуляю.** (ya gooh-*lyah*-yooh.) (*I walk.*)

> **Я плаваю.** (ya *plah*-vuh-yooh.) (*I swim.*)

And don't forget about winter sports! Prepare to hear (or say) the following phrases if you're speaking to a native Russian:

> **Я занимаюсь фигурным катанием** (ya zuh-nee-*mah*-yoohs' fee-*goohr*-nim kuh-*tah*-nee-eem.) (*I do figure skating.*)

> **Я катаюсь на лыжах.** (ya kuh-*tah*-yoohs' nuh *li*-zhukh.) (*I ski.*)

> **Я катаюсь на коньках.** (ya kuh-*tah*-yoohs' nuh kahn'-*kahkh*.) (*I skate.*)

Talkin' the Talk

Greg (**Грег**) and Vladimir (**Владимир**) meet at a party. Vladimir immediately starts talking about his favorite pastime, sports. (Track 22)

Владимир: **Ты занимаешься спортом?**
ti zuh-nee-*mah*-eesh'-syeh *spohr*-tahm?
Do you play sports?

Грег: **Да, я занимаюсь теннисом. А ты?**
dah, ya zuh-nee-*mah*-yoohs' *teh*-nee-sahm. ah ti?
Yes, I play tennis. What about you?

Владимир: **Я играю в футбол. Ты любишь футбол?**
ya eeg-*rah*-yooh f fooht-*bohl*. ti *lyooh*-beesh'
fooht-*bohl*?
I play soccer. Do you like soccer?

Грег: **Не очень. Я люблю американский футбол.**
nee *oh*-cheen'. ya lyooh-*blyooh* uh-mee-ree-*kahn*-
skeey fooht-*bohl*.
Not really. I like football.

Words to Know

Ты занимаешься спортом?	ti zuh-nee-<u>mah</u>-eesh'-syeh <u>spohr</u>-tahm?	Do you play sports?
А ты?	ah ti?	What about you?
Я играю	ya eeg-<u>rah</u>-yooh	I play
футбол	fooht-<u>bohl</u>	soccer
Не очень	nee <u>oh</u>-cheen'	Not really
американский футбол	uh-mee-ree-<u>kahn</u>-skeey fooht-<u>bohl</u>	football

Reading All about It

One American who has traveled in Russia observed that on the Moscow metro, half the people are reading books, and the other half are holding beer bottles. But we don't agree with such a sharp division. Some Russians can hold a book in one hand and a beer bottle in the other!

But, all joking aside, Russians are still reported to read more than any other nation in the world. So, get ready to discuss your reading habits using phrases we introduce in the following sections.

Talking about what you're reading

When you talk about reading, **читать** (chee-*taht'*) (*to read*) is a handy verb to know. This verb is a regular first-conjugation verb (see Chapter 3 for more information). Here are some essential phrases you need to hold a conversation about reading:

- ✔ **Я читаю . . .** (ya chee-*tah*-yooh . . .) (*I read/am reading . . .*) + a noun in the accusative case

- ✔ **Что ты читаешь?** (shtoh ti chee-*tah*-eesh'?) (*What are you reading?*; informal singular)

- ✔ **Что вы читаете?** (shtoh vi chee-*tah*-ee-tee?) (*What are you reading?*; formal singular or plural)

- ✔ **Ты читал. . . ?** (ti chee-*tahl*. . .) (*Have you read. . . ?*; informal singular) + a noun in the accusative case when speaking to a male

- ✔ **Ты читала. . . ?** (ti chee-*tah*-luh. . . ?) (*Have you read. . . ?*; informal singular) + a noun in the accusative case when speaking to a female

- ✔ **Вы читали. . . ?** (vi chee-*tah*-lee. . . ?) (*Have you read . . . ?*; formal singular or plural) + a noun in the accusative case

Discussing genres

So you're ready to talk about your favorite **книга** (*knee*-guh) (*book*) or **книги** (*knee*-gee) (*books*). Here are some words to outline your general preferences in literature, some of which may sound very familiar:

- ✔ **литература** (lee-tee-ruh-*tooh*-ruh) (*literature*)

- ✔ **проза** (*proh*-zuh) (*prose*)

- ✔ **поэзия** (pah-*eh*-zee-yeh) (*poetry*)

- ✔ **романы** (rah-*mah*-ni) (*novels*)

- ✔ **повести** (*poh*-vees-tee) (*novellas*)

- ✔ **рассказы** (ruhs-*kah*-zi) (*short stories*)

- ✔ **пьесы** (*p'yeh*-si) (*plays*)

- ✔ **стихи** (stee-*khee*) (*poems*)

Russian writers you just gotta know

A reading nation has to have some outstanding authors, and Russia certainly does. Russia is famous for the following writers:

✔ **Anton Chekhov**, or **А.П. Чехов** (*chyeh-khahf*) in Russian, is up there with Shakespeare and Ibsen on the Olympus of world dramaturgy. Chekhov's plays *The Cherry Orchard* and *The Seagull* are some of the most heartbreaking comedies you'll ever see.

✔ **Fyodor Dostoevsky**, or **Ф.М. Достоевский** (*dah-stah-yehf-skeey*) in Russian, is the reason 50 percent of foreigners decide to learn Russian. Dostoevsky was a highly intense, philosophical, 19th-century writer, whose tormented and yet strangely lovable characters search for truth while throwing unbelievably scandalous scenes in public places. "The Grand Inquisitor" from his *Brothers Karamazov* is probably the most frequently cited "favorite literary passage" of politicians all over the world.

✔ **Alexander Pushkin**, or **А.С. Пушкин** (*poohsh-keen*) in Russian, is someone you can mention if you want to soften any Russian's heart. Pushkin did for Russian what Shakespeare did for English, and thankful Russians keep celebrating his birthday and putting up more and more of his statues in every town.

✔ **Leo Tolstoy**, or **Л.Н. Толстой** (*tahl-stohy*) in Russian, was a subtle psychologist and connoisseur of the human soul. His characters are so vivid, you may feel like you know them better than you do your own family members. Reading Tolstoy's *Anna Karenina* or *War and Peace* is the best-discovered equivalent of living a lifetime in 19th-century Russia.

When someone asks **Что вы любите читать?** (shtoh vi *lyooh*-bee-tee chee-*taht'*?) (*What do you like to read?*), the conversation probably won't end with you saying **Я люблю читать романы** (ya lyooh*bl-yooh* chee-*taht'* rah-*mah*-ni) (*I like to read novels*). The next question is likely to be **А какие романы вы любите?** (ah kuh-*kee*-ee rah-*mah*-ni vi *lyooh*-bee-tee?) (*And what kind of novels do you like?*) To answer this question, you can simply say **Я люблю** (ya lyooh-*blyooh* . . .) (*I like* . . .) plus one of the following genres in the accusative case:

✔ **современная проза** (suhv-ree-*myeh*-nuh-yeh *proh*-zuh) (*contemporary fiction*)

✔ **детективы** (deh-tehk-*tee*-vi) (*mysteries*)

✔ **историческая проза** (ees-tah-*ree*-chees-kuh-yeh *proh*-zuh) (*historical fiction*)

✔ **фантастика** (fuhn-*tahs*-tee-kuh) (*science fiction*)

✔ **любовные романы** (lyooh-*bohv*-ni-ee rah-*mah*-ni) (*romance*)

✔ **биографии** (bee-ahg-*rah*-fee-ee) (*biographies*)

✔ **исторические исследования** (ees-tah-*ree*-chees-kee-ee ees-*lyeh*-dah-vuh-nee-yeh) (*history*; Literally: *historical research*)

✔ **мемуары** (mee-mooh-*ah*-ri) (*memoirs*)

Now you're well prepared to talk about literature, but what about the news, political commentary, and celebrity gossip? These phrases can help:

✔ **журнал** (zhoohr-*nahl*) (*magazine*)

✔ **газета** (guh-*zyeh*-tuh) (*newspaper*)

✔ **новости на интернете** (*noh*-vahs-tee nuh een-tehr-*neh*-tee) (*news on the Internet*)

✔ **новости** (*noh*-vahs-tee) (*the news*)

✔ **статья** (stuht'-*ya*) (*article*)

✔ **комиксы** (*koh*-mcek-si) (*comic books*)

Talkin' the Talk

Claire (**Клэр**) is visiting a Russian library for the first time. A friendly **библиотекарь** (beeb-lee-ah-*tyeh*-kuhr') (*librarian*) starts a conversation with Claire. (Track 23)

Библиотекарь:	**Вы любите читать?** vi *lyooh*-bee-tee chee-*taht*'? *Do you like to read?*
Клэр:	**Да, очень люблю. Особенно романы.** dah, *oh*-cheen' lyooh-*blyooh*. ah-*soh*-bee-nah rah-*mah*-ni. *Yes, I like it very much. Especially novels.*
Библиотекарь:	**А какие романы, исторические или детективы?** ah kuh-*kee*-ee rah-*mah*-ni, ees-tah-*ree*-chees-kee-ee *ee*-lee deh-tehk-*tee*-vi? *And what kind of novels, historical or mysteries?*
Клэр:	**Больше всего я люблю фантастику.** *bohl'*-shi vsee-*voh* ya lyooh-*blyooh* fuhn-*tahs*-tee-kooh. *Most of all, I like science fiction.*

Words to Know

Вы любите читать?	vi <u>lyooh</u>-bee-tee chee-<u>taht</u>'?	Do you like to read?
особенно	ah-<u>soh</u>-bee-nah	especially
романы	rah-<u>mah</u>-ni	novels
исторические	ees-tah-<u>ree</u>-chees-kee-ee	historical
детективы	deh-tehk-<u>tee</u>-vi	mystery
больше всего	<u>bohl</u>'-shi vsee-<u>voh</u>	most of all
фантастика	fuhn-<u>tahs</u>-tee-kuh	science fiction

Sounding Off about Music

If you love music, you'll want to read through the following sections. We list some popular musical instruments in Russian and provide you with some handy expressions related to the world of music.

Taking note of a few popular instruments

Whether or not you play a musical instrument, you may want to talk about instruments and the sounds they produce. Some musical instruments you may want to mention include the following:

- **пианино** (pee-uh-*nee*-nah) (*piano*)
- **скрипка** (*skreep*-kuh) (*violin*)
- **флейта** (*flyehy*-tuh) (*flute*)
- **кларнет** (kluhr-*nyeht*) (*clarinet*)
- **барабан** (buh-ruh-*bahn*) (*drum*)
- **гитара** (gee-*tah*-ruh) (*guitar*)

- **саксофон** (suhk-sah-*fohn*) (*saxophone*)
- **тромбон** (trahm-*bohn*) (*trombone*)
- **труба** (trooh-*bah*) (*trumpet*)

If, for example, you like the violin, you can say

Я люблю скрипку. (ya lyooh-*blyooh skreep*-kooh.) (*I like violin.*)

Note that in this sentence the word **скрипка** is used in the accusative case. That's because the verb **люблю** requires a direct object, and a direct object in Russian is expressed by the accusative case (for more info on cases, go to Chapter 3).

Asking about instruments that others play

To talk about playing a **музыкальный инструмент** (mooh-zi-*kahl'*-niy een-strooh-*myehnt*) (*musical instrument*), use the verb **играть** (eeg-*raht'*) (*to play*) plus the preposition **на** (nah) (*on*) and the name of the instrument in the prepositional case. (We discuss the verb "to play" earlier in this chapter; for prepositional case endings, see Chapter 3.) Here's an example:

Я играю на пианино. (ya eeg-*rah*-yooh nuh pee-uh-*nee*-nah.) (*I play piano.*)

To ask others whether they play an instrument, you can ask one of the following questions, depending on who you're talking to:

- **To use the informal singular form:** Ask **Ты умеешь играть на. . . ?** (ti ooh-*myeh*-eesh' eeg-*raht'* nah. . . ?) (*Can you play. . . ?*) followed by the name of the instrument in the prepositional case.
- **To use the formal singular or plural form:** Ask **Вы умеете играть на. . . ?** (vi ooh-*myeh*-ee-tee eeg-*raht'* nah. . . ?) (*Can you play. . . ?*) followed by the name of the instrument in the prepositional case.

Wondering what kinds of music others like

You don't have to play a musical instrument to be a music lover. To characterize your musical preferences, use these words:

- **классическая музыка** (kluh-*see*-chees-kuh-yeh *mooh*-zi-kuh) (*classical music*)
- **рок** (rohk) (*rock*)

- **кантри** (*kahn*-tree) (*country music*)
- **танцевальная музыка** (tahn-tsi-*vahl'*-nuh-yeh *mooh*-zi-kah) (*dance music*)
- **народная музыка** (nuh-*rohd*-nuh-yeh *mooh*-zi-kuh) (*folk music*)
- **джаз** (dzhahz) (*jazz*)

For example, if you like classical music, you can say

> **Я люблю классическую музыку.** (ya lyooh-*blyooh* kluh-*see*-chees-kooh-yooh *mooh*-zi-kooh.) (*I like classical music.*)

If you like rock music, you can say

> **Я люблю рок.** (ya lyooh-*blyooh* rohk.) (*I like rock.*)

Be sure to use the accusative case for the type of music you like! (See Chapter 3 for details.)

To ask *What kind of music do you like?*, say **Какую музыку вы любите?** (kuh-*kooh*-yooh *mooh*-zi-kooh vi *lyooh*-bee-tee?)

Being Crafty

If you're one of those lucky people who can create things with your hands, don't hesitate to tell Russians about it! They'll be very impressed. The following are some words you may want to know:

- **вязать** (vee-*zaht'*) (*to knit*)
- **шить** (shit') (*to sew*)
- **рисовать** (ree-sah-*vaht'*) (*to draw*)
- **писать маслом** (pee-*saht'* *mahs*-lahm) (*to paint*)
- **лепить** (lee-*peet'*) (*to sculpt*)
- **лепить из глины** (lee-*peet'* eez *glee*-ni) (*to make pottery*)

To ask someone whether she can do one of these crafts, use the verb **уметь** (ooh-*myeht'*) (*can*) plus the infinitive:

> **Ты умеешь писать маслом?** (ti ooh-*myeh*-eesh' pee-*saht'* *mahs*-lahm?) (*Can you paint?*; informal singular)

> **Вы умеете вязать?** (vi ooh-*myeh*-ee-tee vee-*zaht'*?) (*Can you knit?*; formal singular or plural)

You may want to use the verb **уметь** (ooh-*myeht'*) (*can, know how to do something*) in numerous other situations. Luckily for you, it's a very regular first-conjugation verb (for more info, see Chapter 3).

Rejoicing in the Lap of Nature

Russians love nature. Every city in Russia has big parks where numerous urban dwellers take walks, enjoy picnics, and swim in suspicious-smelling ponds. Even more so, Russians like to get out of town and enjoy nature in the wild. Luckily, the country's diverse geography offers a wide variety of opportunities to do so.

Almost every Russian family has a **дача** (*dah*-chuh), a country house not far from a big city. **Дачи** (*dah*-chee) (dachas) have existed for centuries, surviving revolutions, wars, and purges. They remain an integral, if at times hard-to-define, part of Russian life. **Дачи** come in all shapes and sizes, from modest huts to large, modern homes. On Friday evenings and Sunday afternoons, local trains are usually overcrowded with people of every social class riding to and from their **дачи**. For many Russians, the **дача** is still a simple home away from home. Every weekend, many put on large rubber boots to weed and care for their vegetable patches. **Поехать на дачу** (pah-*yeh*-khuht' nuh *dah*-chooh) (*to go to the dacha*) usually implies an overnight visit that includes barbecuing, dining in the fresh air, and, if you're lucky, **баня** (*bah*-nyeh) — the Russian-style sauna.

Some phrases to use during your **дача** experience include the following:

- **жарить шашлык** (*zhah*-reet' shuh-*shlik*) (*to barbecue*)
- **разводить костёр** (ruhz-vah-*deet'* kahs-*tyohr*) (*to make a campfire*)
- **натопить баню** (nuh-tah-*peet'* bah-nyooh) (*to prepare the sauna*)
- **сад** (saht) (*orchard* or *garden*)
- **огород** (ah-gah-*roht*) (*vegetable garden*)
- **собирать овощи** (sah-bee-*raht'* oh-vah-sh'ee) (*to pick vegetables*)
- **работать в саду** (ruh-*boh*-tuht' f suh-*dooh*) (*to garden*)

Only the verbs **работать** and **собирать** are first-conjugation verbs; the others are second-conjugation verbs.

Fun & Games

The following images depict different sports. Write the letter of each sport next to its name. You can find the answers in Appendix D.

Гимнастика _____

американский футбол _____

теннис _____

футбол _____

волейбол _____

Part III
Russian on the Go

The 5th Wave · By Rich Tennant

"What I can't say in Russian I hope to express in the universal language of music."

In this part . . .

If you're the kind of person who's constantly on the go, then Part III is for you. In this part, you find the phrases you need to plan a trip; deal with foreign currency; get around the city and the world on planes, trains, and more; and make the most of your hotel experience. You also discover the best way to handle emergencies in Russian. By the time you're done with Part III, you'll be armed with all the Russian you need to travel nearly anywhere on Earth!

Chapter 14

Planning a Trip

. . . .

In This Chapter

▶ Selecting a destination

▶ Working with a travel agency

▶ Getting your passport and visa

▶ Knowing what to pack

. . . .

Do you like to **путешествовать** (poo-tee-*shehs*-tvah-vuht') (*to travel*)? If so, then this chapter is for you! In this chapter, you discover how to express where you want to travel, how to speak to a travel agent, and how to secure a passport and a visa. We also give you packing tips for a **путешествие** (pooh-tee-*shehs*-tvee-ee) (*trip*) to Russia. And now, as Russians often say, **Поехали!** (pah-*yeh*-khuh-lee!) (*Let's go!* or *Let's roll!*)

Where Do You Want to Go? Picking a Place for Your Trip

The first question to consider when you're planning a trip is this:

> **Куда ты хочешь поехать?** (kooh-*dah* ti *khoh*-cheesh' pah-*yeh*-khuht'?) (*Where do you want to go?*)

In the following sections, you find out how to talk about different countries in Russian. We also give you some pointers for places in Russia to visit.

Checking out continents and countries

You may want to know the name of each **континент** (kahn-tee-*nyehnt*) (*continent*) in Russian. The seven **континенты** (kuhn-tee-*nyen*-ti) (*continents*) appear in the following list:

- **Австралия** (uhf-*strah*-lee-yeh) (*Australia*)

- **Азия** (*ah*-zee-yeh) (*Asia*)

- **Антарктика** (uhn-*tahrk*-tee-kuh) (*Antarctica*)

- **Африка** (*ahf*-ree-kuh) (*Africa*)

- **Европа** (eev-*roh*-puh) (*Europe*)

- **Северная Америка** (*syeh*-veer-nuh-yeh uh-*myeh*-ree-kuh) (*North America*)

- **Южная Америка** (*yoohzh*-nuh-yeh uh-*myeh*-ree-kuh) (*South America*)

Here we list some **страны** (*strah*-ni) (*countries*) that tourists often visit:

- **Австрия** (*ahv*-stree-yeh) (*Austria*)

- **Англия** (*ahn*-glee-yeh) (*England*)

- **Франция** (*frahn*-tsi-yeh) (*France*)

- **Германия** (geer-*mah*-nee-yeh) (*Germany*)

- **Голландия** (gah-*lahnd*-dee-yeh) (*Holland*)

- **Италия** (ee-*tah*-lee-yeh) (*Italy*)

- **Испания** (ees-*pah*-nee-yeh) (*Spain*)

- **Америка** (uh-*myeh*-ree-kuh) (*the United States*)

- **Канада** (kuh-*nah*-duh) (*Canada*)

- **Мексика** (*myehk*-see-kuh) (*Mexico*)

- **Аргентина** (uhr-geen-*tee*-nuh) (*Argentina*)

- **Бразилия** (bruh-*zee*-lee-yeh) (*Brazil*)

- **Египет** (ee-*gee*-peet) (*Egypt*)

- **Израиль** (eez-*rah*-eel') (*Israel*)

- **Морокко** (mah-*roh*-kah) (*Morocco*)

- **Турция** (*toohr*-tsi-yeh) (*Turkey*)

- **Китай** (kee-*tahy*) (*China*)

- **Индия** (*een*-dee-yeh) (*India*)

- **Япония** (ee-*poh*-nee-yeh) (*Japan*)

- **Новая Зеландия** (*noh*-vuh-yeh zee-*lahn*-dee-yeh) (*New Zealand*)

Visiting Russia

If you're reading this book, you may be considering a trip to **Россия** (rah-*see*-yeh) (*Russia*). Great idea! You won't regret it. Where would you like to go first? We recommend that you begin with **Москва** (mahs-*kvah*) (*Moscow*), Russia's bustling **столица** (stah-*lee*-tsuh) (*capital*), and **Санкт-Петербург** (sahnkt-pee-teer-*boohrk*) (*St. Petersburg*).

You'll find quite a few things to see in Moscow, including the following:

- **Кремль** (kryehml') (*Kremlin*), the walled-in old town and the seat of the Russian government

- **Красная площадь** (*krahs*-nuh-yeh *ploh*-sh'uht') (*Red Square*), the main square in Moscow just outside the Kremlin where all the military parades take place during national holidays

- **Третьяковская галерея** (tree-t'ee-*kohf*-skuh-yeh guh-lee-*ryeh*-yeh) (*Tretyakoff art gallery*)

- **Пушкинский музей** (*poosh*-keen-skeey mooh-*zyehy*) (*Pushkin art museum*)

- **Коломенское** (kah-*loh*-meen-skah-ee), the former tsars' estate

- **Новодевичье кладбище** (*noh*-vah-*dyeh*-veech-ee *klaht*-bee-sh'ee) (*Novodevich'ye cemetery*), the burial place of many famous Russian people

If you have a particular interest in staring at dead bodies, go to the **Мавзолей** (muhv-zah-*lyehy*) (*mausoleum*). Vladimir Lenin's mummy is still there on display.

If you like Russian history, literature, and culture, **Санкт-Петербург** is a must. Our advice: Visit St. Petersburg at the end of May and the beginning of June, during the **белые ночи** (*byeh*-li-ee *noh*-chee) (*white nights*). That's what Russians call the short period in early summer when it almost never gets dark in the north. **Санкт-Петербург** is the city where, as **петербуржцы** (pee-teer-*boohrzh*-tsi) (people born and living in St. Petersburg) say, **Каждый дом музей** (*kahzh*-diy dohm mooh-*zyehy*) (*Every building is a museum*). Here's a list of a few of the places we recommend you see in **Санкт-Петербург:**

- **Эрмитаж** (ehr-mee-*tahsh*) (the *Hermitage* museum)

- **Русский музей** (*roohs*-keey mooh-*zyehy*) (*Russian Museum*)

- **Пушкин** (*poohsh*-keen) (the town of *Pushkin*)

- **Царское Село** (*tsahr*-skuh-ee see-*loh*) (*the tsars' village*, a former summer residence of the Russian tsars)

- **Павловск** (*pahv*-lahvsk) (*Pavlovsk*, another former residence of the Russian tsars)

- **Петродворец** (*pyeht*-rah-dvah-*ryehts*) (Russian Versailles, founded by *Peter the Great*)

- **Петропавловская крепость** (peet-rah-*pahv*-luhf-skuh-yeh *kryeh*-pahst') (*Peter and Paul's Fortress*, the burial place of the Russian tsars and a former political prison)

   ✔ **Исаакиевский собор** (ee-suh-*ah*-kee-eef-skeey sah-*bohr*) (*St. Isaak's Cathedral*, the world's third largest one-cupola cathedral)

   ✔ **Пискарёвское кладбище** (pees-kuh-*ryohf*-skah-ee *klaht*-bee-sh'ee) (*Piskarev memorial cemetery*, a museum of the Leningrad 900-day siege)

Those of you with a more adventurous nature, may want to go to the Asiatic part of Russia, which is the part of Russia lying beyond the **Уральские горы** (ooh-*rahl'*-skee-ee *goh*-ri) (*Ural Mountains*). How about going to **Сибирь** (see-*beer'*) (*Siberia*)? **Сибирь** is a beautiful region, and contrary to popular belief, it's not always cold there. In fact, the summers are quite hot.

How Do We Get There? Booking a Trip

After you decide where you want to go, you need to book your trip. Of course, you can make plans online, but another option is to call a **бюро путешествий** (byooh-*roh* pooh-tee-*shehs*-tveey) (*travel agency*) and talk to an **агент** (uh-*gyehnt*) (*agent*). If you're planning a trip, you may want to say something like the following:

   Я хотел/хотела бы поехать в Россию в мае. (ya khah-*tyehl*/khah-*tyeh*-luh bi pah-*yeh*-khuht' v rah-*see*-yooh v *mah*-ee.) (*I would like to go to Russia in May.*)

Use the first verb option if you're a man and the second option if you're a woman. Place the month in which you want to travel in the prepositional case (see Chapter 3 for more info).

While you're talking to the travel agent, be sure to add:

   Что вы можете предложить? (shtoh vi *moh*-zhi-tee preed-lah-*zhit'*?) (*What can you offer?* or *What do you have available?*)

In response, you'll most likely hear:

   А куда именно вы хотите поехать? (uh kooh-*dah* ee-mee-nah vi khah-*tee*-tee pah-*yeh*-khuht'?) (*And where exactly would you like to travel?*)

To answer this question, use the expression **Я хотел/хотела бы поехать в** (ya khah-*tyehl*/khah-*tyeh*-luh bi pah-*yeh*-khuht' v) (*I'd like to go to*), followed by the name of the city you want to see in the accusative case. Here's an example:

   Я хотел/хотела бы поехать в Москву и в Петербург. (ya khah-*tyehl*/khah-*tyeh*-luh bi pah-*yeh*-khuht' v mahs-*kvooh* ee f pee-teer-*boohrk*.) (*I would like to go to Moscow and St. Petersburg.*)

Use the first verb option if you're a man and the second option if you're a woman.

Now listen carefully as the travel agent lists available **туры** (*tooh*-ri) (*tours*). If anything sounds appealing to you, your next question may be about what the package includes:

> **Что это включает?** (shtoh *eh*-tah fklyooh-*chah*-eet?) (*What does it include?*)

Naturally, you also want to know how much the trip will cost. You may hear the following price-related terms:

- ✔ **гостиница первого/второго/третьего класса** (gahs-*tee*-nee-tsuh *pyehr*-vah-vah/ftah-*roh*-vah/*tryeht'*-ee-vah *klah*-suh) (*one/two/three star hotel*)

- ✔ **трёх/двух разовое питание** (*tryohkh/dvoohkh* rah-zah-vah-ee pee-*tah*-nee-ee) (*three/two meals a day*)

- ✔ **экскурсии** (ehks-*koohr*-see-ee) (*excursions*)

- ✔ **самолёт туда и обратно** (suh-mah-*lyoht* tooh-*dah* ee ahb-*raht*-nah) (*round-trip flight*)

Finally, as you book your trip, you may find that these terms come in handy:

- ✔ **билет туда и обратно** (bee-*lyeht* tooh-*dah* ee ahb-*raht*-nah) (*one-way ticket*)

- ✔ **дата прилёта** (*dah*-tuh pree-*lyoh*-tuh) (*arrival date*)

- ✔ **время прилёта** (*vryeh*-myeh pree-*lyoh*-tuh) (*arrival time*)

- ✔ **дата отлёта** (*dah*-tah aht-*lyoh*-tuh) (*departure date*)

- ✔ **время отлёта** (*vreh*-myeh aht-*lyoh*-tuh) (*departure time*)

- ✔ **пересадки** (pyeh-ree-*saht*-kee) (*flight with stopovers*)

- ✔ **прямой рейс** (pryeh-*mohy* rehys) (*direct flight*)

Talkin' the Talk

Tom (**Том**) teaches English in a public school in Perm, a city beyond the Urals. It is May, the school year is almost over, and he wants to go to St. Petersburg and Moscow. The following conversation takes place when Tom meets with a **турагент** (travel agent). (Track 24)

Турагент: **Куда вы хотели бы поехать?**
kooh-*dah* vi khah-*tyeh*-lee bi pah-*yeh*-khuht'?
Where would you like to go?

Том:	**Я хотел бы посмотреть Москву и Петербург.** ya khah-*tyehl* bi pahs-maht-*ryeht'* mahs-*kvooh* ee pee-teer-*boohrk*. *I would like to see Moscow and St. Petersburg.*
Турагент:	**Когда и на сколько дней?** kahg-*dah* ee nuh *skohl'*-kah dnyehy? *When and for how many days?*
Том:	**В июне или в июле. На неделю или десять дней.** v ee-*yooh*-nee ee-lee v ee-*yooh*-lee. nuh nee-*dyeh*-lyooh ee-lee *dyeh*-syeht' dnyehy. *In June or July. For a week or ten days.*
Турагент:	**Вот есть очень хороший тур. Он включает Москву и Петербург. С пятнадцатого июня по двадцать пятое июня.** voht yehst' *oh*-cheen' khah-*roh*-shiy toohr. ohn fklyooh-*chah*-eet mahs-*kvooh* ee pee-teer-*boohrk*. s peet-*naht*-suh-tah-vah ee-*yooh*-nyeh pah dvaht-*suht'* *pya*-tah-ee ee-*yooh*-nyeh. *Here is a very good tour. It includes Moscow and St. Peterburg. From June 15th to June 25th.*
Том:	**Да, это хороший тур. Пожалуй, я куплю его.** dah, *eh*-tah khah-*roh*-shiy toohr. pah-*zhah*-loohy, ya koohp-*lyooh* ee-*voh*. *Yes, it's a nice tour. I think I will buy it.*

Words to Know

Куда вы хотели бы поехать?	kooh-<u>dah</u> vi khah-<u>tyeh</u>-lee bi pah-<u>yeh</u>-khuht'?	Where would you like to go?
Я хотел бы посмотреть...	ya khah-<u>tyehl</u> bi pahs-maht-<u>ryeht'</u>...	I would like to see...
На сколько дней?	nuh <u>skohl'</u>-kah dnyehy?	For how many days?
Пожалуй, я куплю его.	pah-<u>zhah</u>-loohy, ya koop-<u>lyooh</u> ee-<u>voh</u>.	I think I will buy it.

Don't Leave Home without Them: Dealing with Passports and Visas

If you're planning to go to Russia, read this section carefully! Here you find out about the all-important documents without which you aren't allowed into (or out of!) Russia: a **паспорт** (*pahs*-pahrt) (*passport*) and a **виза** (*vee*-zuh) (*visa*).

If you're an American citizen who has already been abroad, you know that to travel to other countries, you need a U.S. passport. If this trip isn't your first **путешествие за границу** (pooh-tee-*shehs*-tvee-ee zuh gruh-*nee*-tsooh) (*trip abroad*), make sure to have your passport updated. For some countries, though, this document isn't enough. To go to Russia, you also need a visa that states that you're allowed to cross the Russian border and return home within the time period indicated on the visa. In other words, if you decide to arrive in Russia a day before the date indicated on your visa, the law-abiding customs officer in the Russian airport has the legal right not to let you enter the country. Likewise, if your visa states that you have to leave Russia on May 1, 2012, don't even think of leaving on May 15. You may have to pay a fine and spend a lot more time at the airport than you expected, and you may even miss your flight while explaining to the officials why you stayed in Russia longer than your visa permits.

The million-dollar question for anybody wanting to travel to Russia concerns **как достать визу** (kahk dahs-*taht'* vee-zooh) (*how to get a visa*). You have three options, depending on which of these circumstances best describes your situation:

- ✔ Your travel agent arranges the trip for you, and you're officially a **турист** (tooh-*reest*) (*tourist*) who stays in a hotel.

- ✔ You're going to Russia **в командировку** (f kah-muhn-dee-*rohf*-kooh) (*on business*) and have an **официальное приглашение** (ah-fee-tsi-*ahl'*-nah-ee pree-gluh-*sheh*-nee-ee) (*official invitation*) from an organization in Russia approved by the Russian Ministry of Internal Affairs.

- ✔ You have friends or relatives in Russia who are officially inviting you. These people must be extremely devoted to you and willing to state that you'll be staying with them at all times until you leave and that they agree to feed you while you're there. They also have to go to the Department of Visas and Invitations (OVIR) and prove that they have enough space in their apartment/house to host an additional person.

Which of the three situations gives you the easiest chance to get a visa? Certainly, the first one. All you have to do is call your travel agency, and they take care of it for you. Be sure to plan ahead; it can take some time to get a visa, unless you're willing to pay extra for speedy processing.

Here's the list of documents you need in order to **подать заявление на визу** (pah-*daht'* zuh-yehv-*lyeh*-nee-ee nuh *vee*-zooh) (*to apply for a visa*):

- **паспорт** (*pahs*-pahrt) (*passport*)

- **две фотографии** (dvyeh fah-tah-*grah*-fee-ee) (*two photos*)

- **денежный ордер** (*dyeh*-neezh-niy *ohr*-deer) (*money order*)

- **заявление на визу** (zuh-yehv-*lyeh*-nee-yeh nuh *vee*-zooh) (*visa application*)

- **официальное приглашение** (ah-fee-tsi-*ahl'*-nah-ee pree-gluh-*shyeh*-nee-ee) (*official invitation*)

Talkin' the Talk

Eric (**Эрик**) is going to Russia on a business trip. He calls the Russian Consulate to ask how he can get a business visa. Here is his conversation with the **работник консульства** (ruh-*boht*-neek *kohn*-soohl'-stvuh) (*consulate employee*) in the visa department. (Track 25)

Эрик:	**Я еду в Москву в командировку. Как я могу получить визу?** ya *yeh*-dooh v mahs-*kvooh* f kah-muhn-dee-*rohf*-kooh. kahk ya mah-*gooh* pah-looh-*cheet'* *vee*-zooh? *I am going to Moscow for a business trip. How can I get a visa?*
Работник консульства:	**Пришлите нам паспорт, приглашение, заявление, одну фотографию, и денежный ордер на сто сорок долларов.** preesh-*lee*-tee nahm *pahs*-pahrt, pree-gluh-*sheh*-nee-ee, zuh-eev-*lyeh*-nee-ee, ahd-*nooh* fah-tah-*grah*-fee-yooh, ee *dyeh*-neezh-niy *ohr*-deer nuh stoh *soh*-rahk *doh*-luh-rohf. *You need to send us your passport, invitation, application, one picture, and a money order for $140.*
Эрик:	**Хорошо, спасибо.** khah-rah-*shoh*, spuh-*see*-bah. *Okay, thank you.*

Words to Know

в командировку	f kuh-muhn-dee-rohf-kooh	for a business trip
Как я могу получить визу?	kahk ya mah-gooh pah-looh-cheet' vee-zooh?	How can I get a visa?
паспорт	pahs-pahrt	passport
приглашение	pree-gluh-sheh-nee-yeh	invitation
заявление	zuh-eev-lyeh-nee-ee	application

Taking It with You: Packing Tips

When your trip is quickly approaching, it's time to start packing. No matter when and where you travel, you'll most likely take the following items with you:

- ✔ чемодан (chee-mah-*dahn*) (*suitcase*)
- ✔ сумка (*soohm*-kuh) (*bag*)
- ✔ рюкзак (ryoohk-*zahk*) (*backpack*)
- ✔ карта (*kahr*-tuh) (*map*)
- ✔ фотоаппарат (fah-tah-uh-puh-*raht*) (*camera*)
- ✔ видеокамера (*vee*-dee-ah-*kah*-mee-ruh) (*video camera*)
- ✔ мыло (*mi*-lah) (*soap*)
- ✔ шампунь (shuhm-*poohn'*) (*shampoo*)
- ✔ деодорант (dyeh-ah-dah-*rahnt*) (*deodorant*)
- ✔ зубная щётка (zoohb-*nah*-yeh sh'*yoht*-kuh) (*toothbrush*)
- ✔ зубная паста (zoohb-*nah*-yeh *pahs*-tuh) (*toothpaste*)
- ✔ косметика (kahs-*myeh*-tee-kuh) (*makeup*)

Fun & Games

In the right column, find the English equivalents for the Russian words indicating countries in the left column.

Америка	Spain
Россия	Russia
Украина	Germany
Германия	France
Франция	Italy
Испания	Ukraine
Италия	the United States

Chapter 15

Dealing with Money in a Foreign Land

. . . .

In This Chapter

▶ Deciphering different currencies

▶ Exchanging your money

▶ Getting the gist of basic banking

▶ Spotting bargains and paying for your purchases

. . . .

What do traveling, shopping, dining, going out, and moving into a new place all have in common? They all require **деньги** (*dyehn'*-gee) (*money*). This chapter takes you on a tour of the Russian monetary business. You find out about Russian currency and how to exchange the money you have for the currency you want. You also discover phrases to use at the bank and while making payments. It pays to be prepared!

Paying Attention to Currency

In spite of ubiquitous dollar signs in fancy restaurant menus and "for rent" ads, the official Russian currency is not the U.S. dollar. In the following sections, you discover the names and denominations of Russian and international forms of money.

Rubles and kopecks

REMEMBER

The official Russian currency is the **рубль** (roohbl') (*ruble*). Much like a dollar equals 100 cents, one **рубль** equals 100 **копейки** (kah-*pyehy*-kee) (*kopecks*).

How a kopeck can save a ruble

Although Russians take pride in being extravagant with money, a Russian proverb teaches otherwise:

Копейка рубль бережёт. (kah-*pyehy*-kuh roohbl' bee-ree-*zhoht*.) (*A kopeck saves a ruble.*)

Apparently, Russian folk wisdom fully agrees with the familiar "Take care of your pennies, and the pounds will take care of themselves." In other words, being careful about spending little sums of money leads to big savings.

With prices these days, pennies are of little consequence, and the same is true of **копейки** — in Russia, they almost never appear in prices anymore.

To talk about different numbers of rubles, you need to use different cases. For example, **два рубля** (dvah roohb-*lya*) (*2 rubles*) is in the genitive singular case, **пять рублей** (pyat' roohb-*lyehy*) (*5 rubles*) is in the genitive plural case, and **двадцать один рубль** (*dvaht*-tsuht' ah-*deen* roohbl') (*21 rubles*) is in the nominative singular case. For more info on numbers followed by nouns, see Chapter 5.

Dollars, euros, and other international currencies

Although the official Russian currency is the ruble, some foreign currencies, such as U.S. dollars and European euros, are widely used to indicate the price but are not accepted officially in payments. Here's a list of foreign currencies that you may need to exchange when you're in Russia:

- **доллар Ю.С.** (*doh*-luhr yooh. *ehs*.) (*U.S. dollar*)
- **канадский доллар** (kuh-*nahts*-keey *doh*-luhr) (*Canadian dollar*)
- **австралийский доллар** (uhf-struh-*leey*-skeey *doh*-luhr) (*Australian dollar*)
- **евро** (*yehv*-rah) (*euros*)
- **фунт стерлингов** (foohnt *styehr*-leen-gahf) (*British pound*)
- **японская йена** (ee-*pohns*-kuh-yeh *yeh*-nuh) (*Japanese yen*)

Changing Money

Upon arriving in Russia, you have to immediately jump into the "ruble zone." Big Russian cities are saturated with **пункты обмена** (*poohnk*-ti ahb-*myeh*-nuh) (*currency exchange offices*), which are also called **обмен валют** (ahb-*myehn* vuh-*lyooht*). You can usually find a **пункт обмена** in any hotel. The best **курс обмена** (koohrs ahb-*myeh*-nuh) (*exchange rate*), however, is offered by **банки** (*bahn*-kee) (*banks*).

Some handy phrases to use when you exchange currency include the following:

Я хочу обменять деньги. (ya khah-*chooh* ahb-mee-*nyat'* dyehn'-gee.) (*I want to exchange money.*)

Я хочу обменять доллары на рубли. (ya khah-*chooh* ahb-mee-*nyat'* *doh*-luh-ri nuh roohb-*lee*.) (*I want to exchange dollars for rubles.*)

Я хочу обменять рубли на доллары. (ya khah-*chooh* ahb-mee-*nyat'* roohb-*lee* nuh *doh*-luh-ri.) (*I want to exchange rubles for dollars.*)

Какой курс обмена? (kuh-*kohy* koohrs ahb-*myeh*-nuh?) (*What is the exchange rate?*)

Надо платить коммиссию? (*nah*-dah pluh-*teet'* kah-*mee*-see-yooh?) (*Do I have to pay a fee?*)

Most exchange offices require some kind of identification to allow you to exchange money; showing your passport is the safest bet.

Talkin' the Talk

Jim (**Джим**) stops by a bank in Russia to exchange U.S. dollars for rubles. He needs to talk to a **работник банка** (ruh-*boht*-neek *bahn*-kuh) (*bank employee*). (Track 26)

Джим: **У вас можно обменять доллары на рубли?**
ooh vahs *mohzh*-nah ahb-mee-*nyat'* *doh*-luh-ri nuh roohb-*lee*?
Can I exchange dollars for rubles here?

Работник банка: **Да. Курс обмена — один к тридцати.**
dah. koohrs ahb-*myeh*-nuh — ah-*deen* k tree-tsuh-*tee*.
Yes. The exchange rate is 1 for 30.

Джим:	**Я хочу обменять сорок долларов.** ya khah-*chooh* ahb-mee-*nyat' soh*-rahk *doh*-luh-rahf. *I want to exchange 40 dollars.*
Работник банка:	**Хорошо. Ваш паспорт, пожалуйста.** khah-rah-*shoh*. vahsh *pahs*-pahrt, pah-*zhahl*-stuh *Okay. Your passport, please.*

Words to Know

У вас можно обменять доллары на рубли?	ooh vahs <u>mohzh</u>-nah ahb-mee-<u>nyat'</u> <u>doh</u>-luh-ri nuh roohb-<u>lee</u>?	Can I exchange dollars for rubles here?
курс обмена	koohrs ahb-<u>myeh</u>-nuh	exchange rate
Я хочу обменять...	ya khah-<u>chooh</u> ahb-mee-<u>nyat'</u>...	I want to exchange...

Using Banks

Opening a bank account is a useful thing to do if you want to have payments deposited directly to your account, make money transfers easier, or get rid of the nerve-wracking obligation of thinking about your cash's safety. The following sections show you how to open and manage a bank account in Russian.

Opening an account at the bank of your choice

The first thing you need to do is decide on the type of bank you want to work with: Do you prefer a **коммерческий банк** (kah-*myehr*-chees-keey bahnk) (*commercial bank*) or a **госбанк** (gahs-*bahnk*) (*state bank*)? A privately owned **коммерческий банк** offers a much better **процент** (prah-*tsehnt*) (*interest rate*).

Your next decision concerns the type of **счёт** (sch'yoht) (*account*) you want to open. Although **сберегательный** (sbee-ree-*gah*-teel'-niy) literally translates as *savings*, this type of **счёт** corresponds to the English *checking account*. The accounts that involve a minimal term of investment are called **срочные вклады** (*srohch*-ni-ee *fklah*-di); they correspond to *savings accounts*.

To open an account, you need to talk to a **работник банка** (ruh-*boht*-neek *bahn*-kuh) (*bank employee*). Simply say

> **Я хочу открыть счёт.** (ya khah-*chooh* aht-*krit'* sch'yoht.) (*I want to open an account.*)

You'll need to **показать паспорт** (pah-kuh-*zaht' pahs*-pahrt) (*show your passport*) and to **заполнить заявление** (zuh-*pohl*-neet' zuh-ee-*vlyeh*-nee-ee) (*fill out forms*). On a **заявление** (zuh-eev-*lyeh*-nee-ee) (*application*), you'll need to provide your **имя** (*ee*-myeh) (*given name*), **фамилия** (fuh-*mee*-lee-yeh) (*last name*), **адрес** (*ahd*-rees) (*address*), **номер паспорта** (*noh*-meer *pahs*-pahr-tuh) (*passport number*), and the type of **счёт** you want to open.

Talkin' the Talk

Laura (**Лора**) is a student at Moscow State University. She decides to open an account with a Russian bank and talks to a **работник банка** (ruh-*boht*-neek *bahn*-kuh) (*bank employee*). (Track 27)

Лора: **Я хотела бы открыть счёт в банке.**
ya khah-*tyeh*-luh bi aht-*krit'* sch'yoht v *bahn*-kee.
I would like to open an account with your bank.

Работник банка: **Пожалуйста. Посмотрите эту брошюру и выберите, какой счёт вы хотите открыть.**
pah-*zhahl*-stuh. pah-smah-*tree*-tee *eh*-tooh brah-*shyooh*-rooh ee *vi*-bee-ree-tee, kuh-*kohy* sch'yoht vi khah-*tee*-tee aht-*krit'*.
Here you go. Look at this booklet and choose the kind of account you would like to open.

Лора: **Мне подходит сберегательный счёт.**
mnyeh pahd-*khoh*-deet sbee-ree-*gah*-teel'-niy sch'yoht.
The savings account suits me best.

Работник банак: **Отлично. Минимальный вклад двести рублей.**
aht-*leech*-nah. Mee-nee-*mahl'*-niy fklaht — *dvyehs*-tee roohb-*lyehy*.
Great. The minimum deposit is 200 rubles.

Words to Know

открыть счёт	aht-_krit'_ sch'yoht	_to open an account_
брошюра	brah-_shyooh_-ruh	_booklet_
сберегательный счёт	sbee-ree-_gah_-teel'-niy sch'yoht	_savings account_
минимальный вклад	mee-nee-_mahl_-niy fklaht	_minimum deposit_

Making deposits and withdrawals

You have several ways to **сделать вклад** (_sdyeh_-luht' fklaht) (_deposit money_) into your account:

✔ **класть деньги на счёт** (klahst' _dyehn'_-gee nuh sch'yoht) (_to deposit money directly at the bank or ATM_; Literally: _to put money into an account_)

✔ **перечислять деньги на счёт** (pee-ree-chees-_lyat'_ _dyehn'_-gee nuh sch'yoht) (_to deposit money into an account_)

✔ **переводить деньги на счёт** (pee-ree-vah-_deet'_ _dyehn'_-gee nuh sch'yoht) (_to transfer money from a different account or have it deposited by a third party_; Literally: _to transfer money to an account_)

✔ **получать перевод** (pah-looh-_chaht'_ pee-ree-_voht_) (_to have money wired to your account_; Literally: _to receive a transfer_)

The imperfective verb **класть** (klahst') (_to put_) pairs with the perfective verb **положить** (pah-_lah_-zhit') (_to put, to deposit_). Because the two verbs sound nothing like each other and the frequency of their usage in conversation is so high, a good number of native speakers of Russian attempt to create an imperfective form of the verb **положить** and use it in conversation. You may hear it a lot, but don't be tempted to pick it up; this form is both the most common and the most frowned upon grammatical mistake made by Russians themselves. (For more information on imperfective and perfective verbs, see Chapter 3.)

When you fill out a deposit slip, you need to enter the **сумма вклада** (_sooh_-muh _fklah_-duh) (_deposit amount_) and the **номер счёта** (_noh_-meer sch'yoh-tuh) (_account number_).

Now that you have some money in your account, you can

- ✔ **снять деньги со счёта** (snyat' _dyehn'_-gee sah _sch'yoh_-tuh) (_withdraw money from an account_)

- ✔ **перевести деньги на другой счёт** (pee-ree-vees-_tee dyehn'_-gee nuh drooh-_gohy_ sch'yoht) (_transfer money to a different account_)

- ✔ **послать деньги переводом** (pahs-_laht' dyehn'_-gee pee-ree-_voh_-dahm (_wire money_; Literally: _to send a money transfer_)

And, finally, if you no longer need your bank account, you can just **закрыть счёт** (zuhk-_rit'_ sch'yoht) (_close the account_).

Heading to the ATM

The fastest way to access your account is via the **банкомат** (buhn-kah-_maht_) (_ATM_). **Банкоматы** (buhn-kah-_mah_-ti) (_ATMs_) are less ubiquitous in small cities; they're usually found in banks. Keep in mind that you have to pay a **комиссия** (kah-_mee_-see-yeh) (_ATM fee_) each time you use a **банкомат** that belongs to a bank other than your own. The **комиссия** is usually 1.5 percent of the sum you're withdrawing, but no less than $3–$6 depending on the type of card. So, it probably makes sense to withdraw larger sums of money to avoid numerous **комиссии** (kah-_mee_-see-ee) (_fees_) for smaller withdrawals.

Before inserting your card, make sure that the **логотип** (lah-gah-_teep_) (_symbol_) of the card you're about to use (such as Visa or American Express) is on the **банкомат**. Otherwise, the **банкомат** may not recognize the card and may even swallow it for security purposes.

Here's your guide to the phrases you see on the **банкомат** screen:

- ✔ **вставьте карту** (_fstahf'_-tee _kahr_-tooh) (_insert the card_)
- ✔ **введите ПИН-код** (vee-_dee_-tee peen-_koht_) (_enter your PIN_)
- ✔ **введите сумму** (vee-_dee_-tee _sooh_-mooh) (_enter the amount_)
- ✔ **снять наличные** (snyat' nuh-_leech_-ni-ee) (_withdraw cash_)
- ✔ **квитанция** (kvee-_tahn_-tsee-yeh) (_receipt_)
- ✔ **заберите карту** (zuh-bee-_ree_-tee _kahr_-tooh) (_remove the card_)

By the way, the card you use to withdraw cash from the ATM is called a **дебитная карта** (dee-_beet_-nuh-yeh _kahr_-tuh) (_debit card_). In addition to this card, you may also have a **кредитная карта** (kree-_deet_-nuh-yeh _kahr_-tuh) (_credit card_).

Spending Money

The best thing about money is spending it. In the following sections, you discover what to do and what to say while making payments two different ways: by cash or by using a credit card.

Before you run out and spend your money, you may find it helpful to know the verb **платить** (pluh-*teet'*) (*to pay*). Its conjugation is in the following table.

Conjugation	Pronunciation
я плачу	ya pluh-*chooh*
ты платишь (informal singular)	ti *plah*-teesh'
он/она платит	ohn/ah-*nah plah*-teet
мы платим	mi *plah*-teem
вы платите (formal singular or plural)	vi *plah*-tee-tee
они платят	ah-*nee plah*-tyeht

This verb is a second-conjugation verb. Just note the ending in the first-person singular (see Chapter 3).

Using cash

Наличные (nuh-*leech*-ni-ee) (*cash*) is still widely used in Russia. Many stores and ticket offices accept cash only, as do such places as the **рынок** (*ri*-nahk) (*market*) or a small **кафе** (kuh-*feh*) (*café*). The general rule of thumb is this: The fancier and more expensive the place is, the higher the chances that you'll be able to pay with a credit card (see the following section). Otherwise, prepare a stack of those rubles before you head out! To find out whether you can pay with cash, ask

> **У вас можно заплатить наличными?** (ooh vahs *mohzh*-nah zuh-pluh-*teet'* nuh-*leech*-ni-mee?) (*Can I pay with cash here?*)

In fact, this last question may be superfluous: Cash is always preferable in the country where checks and credit cards are still looked upon with suspicion.

Russian rubles come both in **купюры** (kooh-*pyooh*-ri) (*bills*) and **монеты** (mah-*nyeh*-ti) (*coins*). Kopecks always come in coins, but they're virtually extinct now (see "Rubles and kopecks" earlier in this chapter for more info). Here's a list of Russian bills and coins in use (so you know to be a little suspicious if you receive change in 15-ruble bills and 25-kopeck coins):

✔ **купюры** (kooh-*pyooh*-ri) (*bills*):

- десять рублей (*dyeh*-seet' roohb-*lyehy*) (*10 rubles*)
- пятьдесят рублей (pee-dee-*syat* roohb-*lyehy*) (*50 rubles*)
- сто рублей (stoh roohb-*lyehy*) (*100 rubles*)
- пятьсот рублей (peet'-*soht* roohb-*lyehy*) (*500 rubles*)
- тысяча рублей (*ti*-see-chuh roohb-*lyehy*) (*1,000 rubles*)

✔ **монеты** (mah-*nyeh*-ti) (*coins*):

- десять копеек (*dyeh*-seet' kah-*pyeh*-eek) (*10 kopecks*)
- пятьдесят копеек (pee-dee-*syat* kah-*pyeh*-eek) (*50 kopecks*)
- один рубль (ah-*deen* roohbl') (*1 ruble*)
- два рубля (dvah roohb-*lya*) (*2 rubles*)
- пять рублей (pyat' roohb-*lyehy*) (*5 rubles*)

When paying **наличными** (nuh-*leech*-ni-mee) (*with cash*) in Russia, putting money into the other person's hand isn't customary. Instead, you're supposed to put the cash into a little plate that's usually found on the counter.

Traveler's checks may seem like a convenient way to transport money, but not in Russia. There, you may have a really hard time finding a place to exchange them. Russian doesn't even have an equivalent for "traveler's checks"; in those few places where they're recognized, they're referred to in English.

Paying with credit cards

Although **кредитные карточки** (kree-*deet*-ni-ee *kahr*-tahch-kee) (*credit cards*) and **банковские карточки** (*bahn*-kahf-skee-ee *kahr*-tahch-kee) (*debit cards*) have long been established in cities like Moscow and St. Petersburg, in other cities your attempts to pay with a credit card may not be as welcome. When making plans to pay with a credit card, asking one of the following questions is worthwhile:

> **У вас можно заплатить кредитной карточкой?** (ooh vahs *mohzh*-nah zuh-pluh-*teet'* kree-*deet*-nahy *kahr*-tahch-kahy?) (*Can I pay with a credit card here?*)

> **Вы принимаете кредитные карточки?** (vi pree-nee-*mah*-ee-tee kree-*deet*-ni-ee *kahr*-tahch-kee?) (*Do you accept credit cards?*)

Some places, such as travel agencies, may charge you a fee when accepting payment by credit card. To find out where this is the case, you may want to ask

> **Вы берёте комиссионный сбор за оплату кредитной карточкой?** (vi bee-*ryoh*-tee kah-mee-see-*oh*-niy zbohr zuh ahp-*lah*-tooh kree-*deet*-nahy *kahr*-tahch-kahy?) (*Do you charge a fee for paying with a credit card?*)

Fun & Games

Match each Russian sentence in Column A with the corresponding English translation in Column B. Then check out the answers in Appendix D.

A

1. **Я хочу обменять деньги.**

2. **Я хочу обменять доллары на рубли.**

3. **Я хочу обменять рубли на доллары.**

4. **Какой курс обмена?**

5. **Я хочу открыть счёт.**

6. **Вы принимаете кредитные карточки?**

B

a. I want to exchange rubles for dollars.

b. I want to exchange money.

c. I want to exchange dollars for rubles.

d. What is the exchange rate?

e. Do you accept credit cards?

f. I want to open an account.

Chapter 16

Getting Around: Planes, Trains, Taxis, and More

In This Chapter

▶ Moving along with motion verbs

▶ Making your way through the airport

▶ Exploring public transportation

▶ Traveling by train

As the Russian proverb has it, **Язык до Киева доведёт** (ee-*zik* dah *kee*-ee-vuh dah-vee-*dyoht*), which translates to "Your tongue will lead you to Kiev," and basically means "Ask questions, and you'll get anywhere." With the help of this chapter, you'll be able to ask your way into the most well-concealed corners of the Russian land (or any land where Russian is spoken, for that matter!) via several different modes of transportation.

Understanding Verbs of Motion

For one very simple and straightforward English infinitive, *to go*, Russian has several equivalents, also called verbs of motion: **ходить, ездить, идти,** and **ехать.** Each of these verbs has its own (and, we should note, erratic) conjugation pattern. Your choice of verb for the Russian equivalent of *to go* depends on a number of factors, which we talk about in the following sections. We also show you how to talk about the exact places you're going.

Going by foot or vehicle habitually

Russians use the verbs **ходить** (khah-*deet'*) and **ездить** (*yehz*-deet') when they talk about repeated trips to and from a particular place, such as school or work:

> **Я хожу в школу.** (ya khah-*zhooh* f *shkoh*-looh.) (*I go to school.*)

> **Он ездит на работу.** (ohn *yehz*-deet nah ruh-*boh*-tooh.) (*He goes to work by vehicle.*)

Use **ходить** when you go on foot and **ездить** when you go via transportation, be it your own bike, a car, a bus, a taxi, or another vehicle. For an example of how to use these verbs, think of places that you go to once a week, every day, two times a month, once a year, or every weekend. Most folks, for instance, have to go to work every day.

The verb **ходить** is a second-conjugation verb with a change in the first person singular form as shown in the following table.

Conjugation	Pronunciation
я хожу	ya khah-*zhooh*
ты ходишь (informal singular)	ti *khoh*-deesh'
он/она ходит	ohn/ah-*nah khoh*-deet
мы ходим	mi *khoh*-deem
вы ходите (formal singular or plural)	vi *khoh*-dee-tee
они ходят	ah-*nee kho*-dyeht

And this is how the verb **ездить** conjugates (it has a similar pattern, too).

Conjugation	Pronunciation
я езжу	ya *yehz*-zhooh
ты ездишь (informal singular)	ti *yehz*-deesh'
он/она ездит	ohn/ah-*nah yehz*-deet
мы ездим	mi *yehz*-deem
вы ездите (formal singular or plural)	vi *yehz*-dee-tee
они ездят	ah-*nee yehz*-dyeht

Going by foot or vehicle at the present time

To talk about moving in a specific direction or to a specific place at the present time, use the verb идти (eed-*tee*) when you go on foot or the verb ехать (*yeh*-khuht') when you use a vehicle. For an example of how to use these verbs, imagine that you're informing somebody that you're going home after work:

> **Я иду домой.** (ya ee-*dooh* dah-*mohy*.) (*I am going home.*)

You use иду because your home is in a very specific direction. Likewise, if your plans for the future include going to Russia (obviously, you're not going to walk there), you say

> **Я еду в Россию.** (ya ee-*dooh* v rah-*see*-yooh.) (*I am going to Russia.*)

Here's the conjugation of идти (which is irregular).

Conjugation	*Pronunciation*
Я иду	ya ee-*dooh*
Ты идёшь (informal singular)	ti ee-*dyohsh'*
Он/она идёт	ohn/ah-*nah* ee-*dyoht*
Мы идём	mi ee-*dyohm*
Вы идёте (formal singular or plural)	vi ee-*dyoh*-tee
Они идут	ah-*nee* ee-*dooht*

Here's the irregular conjugation of ехать:

Conjugation	*Pronunciation*
Я еду	ya *yeh*-dooh
Ты едешь (informal singular)	ti *yeh*-deesh'
Он/она едет	ohn/ah-*nah yeh*-deet
Мы едем	mi *yeh*-deem
Вы едете (formal singular or plural)	vi *yeh*-dee-tee
Они едут	ah-*nee yeh*-dooht

Explaining where you're going

To tell someone specifically where you're going, use the prepositions **в** (v) (*to*) or **на** (nah) (*to*) plus the accusative case of the place you're going (see Chapter 3 for details on cases). Here are a couple of examples:

Я иду в театр. (ya ee-*dooh* v tee-*ahtr*.) (*I am going to the theater.*)

Она идёт на концерт. (ah-*nah* ee-*dyoht* nuh kahn-*tsehrt*.) (*She is going to the concert.*)

Did you notice that we used different prepositions in the preceding examples? Russian generally uses **в** in place of *to*, but in some cases, when a noun indicates an activity rather than an institution or place, Russian uses **на** for *to*. The word *concert* is seen as an activity, so the preposition **на** is used.

For walking or driving around a place, use the preposition **по** (pah) (*around*) plus the dative case:

Она ходит по Москве. (ah-*nah* *khoh*-deet pah mahsk-*vyeh*.) (*She walks around Moscow.*)

Мы ездим по центру города. (mi *yehz*-deem pah *tsehnt*-rooh *goh*-rah-duh.) (*We drive around downtown.*)

Talkin' the Talk

Sarah (**Сара**) gets a new job in Moscow. On the way to work, she bumps into her Russian friend Kolya (**Коля**). (Track 28)

Сара:	**Привет! Куда идёшь?** pree-*vyeht*! kooh-*dah* ee-*dyohsh'*? *Hi! Where are [you] going?*
Коля:	**На работу. Я хожу на работу пешком каждый день.** nuh ruh-*boh*-tooh. ya khah-*zhooh* nuh ruh-*boh*-tooh peesh-*kohm* kahzh-diy dyehn'. *To work. I walk to work every day.*
Сара:	**А я езжу на метро. Я сейчас иду на станцию метро. Счастливо!** uh ya *yehz*-zhooh nuh meet-*roh*. ya seey-*chahs* ee-*dooh* nuh *stahn*-tsi-yooh meet-*roh*. Schuhst-*lee*-vah! *And I take the subway. I'm walking to the subway station right now. Have a good day!*

Words to Know

Привет!	pree-_vyeht_!	Hi!
Куда идёшь?	_kooh_-dah ee-_dyohsh_?	Where are you going?
На работу.	nuh ruh-_boh_-tooh.	To work.
Я езжу на метро.	ya _yehz_-zhoo nuh meet-_roh._	I take the subway.
Счастливо!	schuhst-_lee_-vah!	Have a nice day!

Navigating the Airport

Chances are, if you visit Russia, you enter by **самолёт** (suh-mah-_lyot_) (_plane_). The vocabulary you find in the following sections helps you plan and enjoy your trip by air.

Using the verb "to fly"

You use a special verb of motion when you talk about flying: **лететь** (lee-_tyeht'_) (_to fly_). Here's the conjugation of this verb (which is a second-conjugation verb with a change in the first-person singular form).

Conjugation	_Pronunciation_
Я лечу	ya lee-_chooh_
Ты летишь (informal singular)	ti lee-_teesh'_
он/она летит	ohn/ah-_nah_ lee-_teet_
мы летим	mi lee-_teem_
вы летите (formal singular or plural)	vi lee-_tee_-tee
они летят	ah-_nee_ lee-_tyat_

Checking in and boarding your flight

After you arrive at the **аэропорт** (ah-eh-rah-*pohrt*) (*airport*), you want to make sure your **рейс** (rehys) (*flight*) hasn't been cancelled or delayed. To find out the status of your flight, look at the **информационное табло** (een-fahr-muh-tsi-*oh*-nah-yeh tuhb-*loh*) (*departures and arrivals display*). *Arrivals* are called **прибытие** (pree-*bi*-tee-ee) and *departures* are called **отправление** (aht-pruhv-*lyeh*-nee-ee).

When you come for **регистрация** (ree-geest-*rah*-tsee-yeh) (*check-in*), you need to have your **билет** (bee-*lyeht*) (*ticket*) and your **паспорт** (*pahs*-pahrt) (*passport*). Also, be prepared to answer these questions:

> **Вы будете сдавать багаж?** (vi *booh*-dee-tee sduh-*vaht'* buh-*gahsh*?) (*Are you checking any luggage?*)

> **Вы оставляли ваш багаж без присмотра?** (vi ahs-tahv-*lya*-lee vahsh buh-*gahsh* byehs pree-*smoh*-truh?) (*Have you left your luggage unattended?*)

At the end of the transaction, you receive a **посадочный талон** (pah-*sah*-duhch-niy tuh-*lohn*) (*boarding pass*) with your **место** (*myehs*-tah) (*seat*) indicated on it.

Be prepared to go through the **контроль безопасности** (kahn-*trohl'* bee-zah-*pahs*-nahs-tee) (*security check*) and pass through a **металлодетектор** (mee-*tah*-lah-deh-*tehk*-tahr) (*metal detector*). If you forget your gate number, you can ask **Какой у меня выход?** (kuh-*kohy* ooh mee-*nya* vi-khaht?) (*What is my gate number?*). At the **выход** (*vi*-khaht) (*gate*), you may ask the **бортпроводник** (*bohrt*-prah-vahd-*neek*) (*male flight attendant*) or **бортпроводница** (*bohrt*-prah-vahd-*nee*-tsuh) (*female flight attendant*) this question: **Это рейс на. . . ?** (*eh*-tah ryehys nuh. . . ?) (*Is this the flight to. . . ?*). When **посадка** (pah-*saht*-kuh) (*boarding*) begins, don't forget your **ручной багаж** (roohch-*nohy* buh-*gahsh*) (*carry-on*).

Handling customs and passport control

If you're taking an international flight, you need to fill out a **таможенная декларация** (tuh-*moh*-zhi-nuh-yeh deek-luh-*rah*-tsi-yeh) (*customs declaration*) before you arrive. This task is very easy because the form has both Russian text and its (very clumsy) English translation. Fill it out on the plane to save yourself time in the chaos at the airport.

After leaving the plane and walking through a corridor maze, you see a crowded hall with **паспортный контроль** (*pahs*-pahrt-niy kahnt-*rohl'*) (*passport control*). To save yourself some frustration, make sure you get in the right line: One line is for **граждан России** (*grahzh*-duhn rah-*see*-ee) (*Russian citizens*), and one is for **иностранные граждане** (ee-nahs-*trah*-ni-ee grahzh-duh-nee) (*foreign citizens*). At passport control, you show your **паспорт** (*pahs*-pahrt) (*passport*) and **виза** (*vee*-zuh) (*visa*); see Chapter 14 for details about these documents. While standing in front of the customs officer, you can remain silent. He just looks at your face to compare it with your passport picture, and puts a stamp on your passport.

After you're done with passport control, it's time to pick up your luggage. To find the baggage claim, just follow the signs that say **БАГАЖ** (buh-*gahsh*) (*luggage*).

The moment you step out of customs, you're attacked by an aggressive mob of cab drivers. They speak numerous foreign languages and offer ungodly fares to take you to the city. Ignore them and move toward the **выход** (*vi*-khaht) (*exit*), where the more timid (and usually more honest) cab drivers reside. See the later section "Taking a taxi" for more information.

Talkin' the Talk

Tony (**Тони**) just arrived in Moscow by plane. He's going through passport control at the airport. He has a short exchange with a **таможенник** (tuh-*moh*-zhee-neek) (*customs officer*). (Track 29)

Тони:	**Добрый день. Вот мой паспорт.** *dohb*-riy dyehn'. voht mohy *pahs*-pahrt. *Good afternoon. Here's my passport.*
Таможенник:	**Хорошо. А где виза?** khah-rah-*shoh*. uh gdyeh *vee*-zuh? *Great. And where is your visa?*
Тони:	**Вот она.** voht ah-*nah*. *Here it is.*
Таможенник:	**Проходите!** prah-khah-*dee*-tee! *You can pass!*
Тони:	**Спасибо!** spuh-*see*-bah! *Thank you!*

Words to Know

Вот мой паспорт.	voht mohy <u>pahs</u>-pahrt.	Here's my passport.
А где виза?	uh gdyeh <u>vee</u>-zuh?	And where is your visa?
Вот она.	voht ah-<u>nah</u>.	Here it is.
Проходите!	prah-khah-<u>dee</u>-tee!	You can pass!

Conquering Public Transportation

Russians hop around their humongous cities with the ease of a butterfly, changing their means of **общественный транспорт** (ahp-*sh'es*-tvee-niy *trahn*-spahrt) (*public transportation*) two or three times during a one-way trip to work. And so can you, with the help of the following sections.

Taking a taxi

The easiest way to get around unfamiliar cities and have your share of good conversation with interesting personalities is to take a cab. Russian **такси** (tuhk-*see*) (*cabs*) don't always look like cabs. Whereas the official ones are decorated with a checkered design or have **ТАКСИ** in large print on their sides, you also see plenty of regular-looking cars that stop when you raise your arm to hail a cab. Those cars are neither cabs in disguise nor necessarily serial killers; they're just regular citizens trying to make an extra buck — sorry, ruble — on the way to work. Most Russians feel safe riding with them. However, if you're a foreigner, you can easily be taken advantage of and asked to pay a lot more than a regular Russian passenger.

To be on the safe side, just call a **служба такси** (*sloohzh*-buh tuhk-*see*) (*cab service*). Be prepared to answer these questions:

- **Ваш адрес?** (vahsh *ahd*-rees?) (*Your address?*)
- **Куда едете?** (kooh-*dah yeh*-dee-tee?) (*Where are you going?*)

The last question is asked because the cab service intends to provide you with information about the cost of your ride, which, you surely agree, is very convenient. If you want to ask for your fare directly while you're ordering your cab, just say the following:

> **Сколько это будет стоить?** (*skohl'*-kah *eh*-tah *booh*-deet *stoh*-eet'?) (*How much would that be?*)

This fare is usually non-negotiable.

You don't have to **давать чаевые** (duh-*vaht'* chuh-ee-*vi*-ee) (*to give a tip*) to cab drivers in Russia, but it's nice if you do.

Using minivans

One especially convenient type of transportation in today's Russia is the **маршрутка** (muhr-*shrooht*-kuh), a *minivan* with a set route. **Маршрутки** (muhr-*shrooht*-kee) (*minivans*) stop only where passengers need to get off, so make sure you tell the driver something like the following:

> **Остановите, пожалуйста, у вокзала?** (ah-stuh-nah-*vee*-tee pah-*zhahl*-stuh, ooh vahk-*zah*-luh?) (*Would you please stop at the railway station?*)

Маршрутки have different routes, marked by numbers. To board a **маршрутка**, you need to go to a place where it stops. When in doubt ask a local:

> **Где остановка маршрутки?** (gdyeh ahs-tuh-*nohf*-kuh mahr-*shrooht*-kee?) (*Where do the minivans stop?*)

Маршрутки have a set fare, which is usually written on a piece of paper above the driver's head, and you need to pay in cash.

Catching buses, trolley buses, and trams

In English, buses, trolley buses, and trams are simply called "buses." But in Russia, these vehicles have very different names. Here's a short, comprehensive guide on how to tell one vehicle from another:

- **автобус** (uhf-*toh*-boohs): This is a bus as you know it.

- **троллейбус** (trah-*lyehy*-boohs): This bus (also known as a *trolley bus*) is connected to electric wires above it.

- **трамвай** (truhm-*vahy*): This bus (also known as a *tram*) is connected to electric wires and runs on rails.

You can catch a **автобус**, **троллейбус**, or **трамвай** at a **автобусная остановка** (uhf-*toh*-boohs-nuh-yeh ahs-tuh-*nohf*-kuh) (*bus stop*), **троллейбусная остановка** (trah-*lyehy*-boohs-nuh-yeh ahs-tuh-*nohf*-kuh) (*trolley bus stop*), or **трамвайная остановка** (truhm-*vahy*-nuh-yeh ahs-tuh-*nohf*-kuh) (*tram stop*), respectively. Look for a sign with an **A** for **автобус** or a **T** for **троллейбус** or **трамвай.**

The best way to find your route is to ask the locals. They're usually extremely friendly and happy to provide you with more information than you even want. The general formula for the question to ask is: **Как мне доехать до. . . ?** (kahk mnyeh dah-*yeh*-khuht' dah. . . ?) (*How can I get to. . . ?*) Your destination should be indicated by the genitive case.

In most big cities you pay the fee to the **кондуктор** (kahn-*doohk*-tahr) (*bus conductor*) when you board the bus.

Hopping on the subway

The Russian **метро** (meet-*roh*) (*subway*) is beautiful, clean, and cheap. It connects the most distant parts of such humongous cities as Moscow, and it's impenetrable to traffic complications. During the day, trains come every two to three minutes at each **остановка метро** (ahs-tah-*nohf*-kuh meet-*roh*) (*subway station*). Expect to wait longer in the evening: 10 or 15 minutes.

To take the **метро**, you need to buy a **жетон** (zhi-*tohn*) (*token*), which you just drop into a machine at the entrance. You can buy tokens at any of the little windows right inside the station where you see lines of people.

Embarking on a Railway Adventure

Taking a **поезд** (*poh*-eest) (*train*) is probably one of the best adventures you can have in Russia. In the following sections, you find out how to read a train schedule, choose the type of train that's just right for you, buy a ticket, and board the train.

Making sense of a train schedule

As you're standing in front of a giant timetable tableau **на вокзале** (nuh vahk-*zah*-lee) (*at a railway station*), you'll probably be thinking that it provides more information than you want to have. You'll see the following details:

- **станция отправления** (*stahn*-tsi-yeh aht-pruhv-*lyeh*-nee-yeh) (*departure station*)

✔ **станция прибытия** (*stahn*-tsi-yeh pree-*bi*-tee-yeh) (*arrival station*)

✔ **время в пути** (*vryeh*-myeh f poo-*tee*) (*travel time*)

✔ **номер поезда** (*noh*-meer *poh*-eez-duh) (*train number*)

The column with a bunch of unfamiliar words divided by commas is probably the list of stations where the train stops. You also see **время отправления** (*vryeh*-myeh aht-prahv-*lyeh*-nee-yeh) (*departure time*) and **время прибытия** (*vryeh*-myeh pree-*bi*-tee-yeh) (*arrival time*).

The abbreviation **Ч** stands for **чётные дни** (*chyoht*-ni-ee dnee) (*even-numbered days*) and the abbreviation **Неч** stands for **нечётные дни** (nee-*chyoht*-ni-ee dnee) (*odd-numbered days*), which are the days on which the trains run.

Surveying types of trains and cars

Three types of trains are available in Russia. We list them from lowest to highest in terms of price and quality:

✔ **электричка** (eh-leek-*treech*-kuh) (*a suburban train*)

✔ **скорый поезд** (*skoh*-riy *poh*-eest) (*a faster and more expensive train*)

✔ **фирменный поезд** (*feer*-mee-niy *poh*-eest) (*a premium train*; Literally: *company train*)

Unless you're traveling to the suburbs, the **фирменный поезд** is your best choice; you'll be surprised with its speed and service. If you are going to the suburbs, the **электричка** is a good alternative to a bus.

After you pick a train, you need to pick the right kind of **вагон** (vuh-*gohn*) (*train car*). Every train, except for the **электричка**, has the following types of cars (in order of increasing cost):

✔ **общий вагон** (*ohp*-sch'eey vuh-*gohn*): A train car consisting of just benches with a bunch of people sitting around. We recommend it only if your travel time is only a couple hours.

✔ **плацкарт** (pluhts-*kahrt*): A no-privacy sleeping car with way too many people; not divided into compartments. We don't recommend it, unless you're into extreme sociological experiments.

✔ **купе** (kooh-*peh*): A good, affordable sleeping car with four-person compartments.

✔ **спальный вагон** (*spahl'*-niy vuh-*gohn*): The granddaddy of them all; a two-person sleeping compartment. This one may be pricey.

Buying tickets

You can **купить билеты** (kooh-*peet'* bee-*lyeh*-ti) (*buy tickets*) directly at the railway station, at a travel agency, or in a **железнодорожные кассы** (zhi-*lyehz*-nah-dah-*rohzh*-ni-ee *kah*-si) (*railway ticket office*). Ticket offices are located throughout the city. Remember to bring your **паспорт** (*pahs*-pahrt) (*passport*).

You can start your dialogue with **Мне нужен билет в** (mnyeh *nooh*-zhin bee-*lyeht* v) (*I need a ticket to*), followed by the name of the city you're heading for in the accusative case (see Chapter 3 for more about cases). The ticket salesperson will probably ask you the following questions:

> **На какое число?** (nuh kuh-*koh*-ee chees-*loh*?) (*For what date?*)

> **Вам купе или плацкарт?** (vahm kooh-*peh* ee-lee pluhts-*kahrt*?) (*Would you like a compartment car or a reserved berth?*)

> **В одну сторону или туда и обратно?** (v ahd-*nooh* stoh-rah-nooh *ee*-lee tooh-*dah* ee ah-*braht*-nah?) (*One way or round trip?*)

You can also tell the ticket salesperson what kind of seat you prefer: а **верхняя полка** (*vyehrkh*-nee-yeh *pohl*-kuh) (*top fold-down bed*) or а **нижняя полка** (*neezh*-nee-yeh *pohl*-kuh) (*bottom fold-down bed*). On **электрички** (eh-leek-*treech*-kee) (*suburban trains*), which don't have fold-down beds, seats aren't assigned.

Stocking up on essentials for your ride

After you find out what **перрон** (pee-*rohn*) (*platform*) your train is departing from, you can take care of important things, such as stocking up on food and reading materials. Both of these resources are readily available on the train itself; you can always buy food in the **вагон-ресторан** (vuh-*gohn*-rees-tah-rahn) (*restaurant car*). Numerous vendors also walk through the train offering snacks.

On the train, have a lot of small bills ready to pay for your **постельное бельё** (pahs-*tyehl'*-nah-ee beel'-*yoh*) (*bed sheets*), **чай** (chahy) (*tea*), and any food you may want to buy.

Boarding the train and enjoying your trip

You can find your **номер вагона** (_noh_-meer vuh-_goh_-nuh) (_car number_) on your **билет** (bee-_lyeht_) (_ticket_). When you approach your train car (it's a good idea to start moving in that direction about half an hour before the departure time), you'll see a friendly (or not) **проводник** (prah-vahd-_neek_) (_male train attendant_) or **проводница** (prah-vahd-_nee_-tsuh) (_female train attendant_) who will want to see your **билет** and **паспорт**.

Shortly after the train starts, the **проводник** will bring **постельное бельё** (pah-styehl'-nah-ee beel'-_yoh_) (_bed sheets_). You have to pay for these sheets if you don't want to sleep directly on a hard, plastic board.

Russians tend to treat a train trip like a small vacation. Even before the train takes off, they change into comfortable clothes and **тапочки** (_tah_-pahch-kee) (_slippers_) to make it easier to get in and out of "bed." Before the train leaves the city limits, they take out plentiful snacks and start the first of a long procession of on-the-train meals. People in your compartment will definitely invite you to share their meal, so make sure you offer them something, too. A **проводник** or **проводница** drops by throughout the ride to offer hot tea and coffee. Take the attendant up on the offer, if only for the joy of holding unique Russian **подстаканники** (paht-stuh-_kah_-nee-kee) (_glass holders_) — they can't be found anywhere else except in rarity collections.

Fun & Games

Look at these sentences with motion verbs. Which of them just don't make sense? See Appendix D for the answers.

1. **Я иду в школу.**

2. **Я еду пешком.**

3. **Он идёт на вокзал.**

4. **Мы идём в Россию.**

5. **Они едут в театр.**

Chapter 17

Finding a Place to Stay

Staying in a comfortable **гостиница** (gahs-*tee*-nee-tsuh) (*hotel*) while you travel is extremely important. If you have a nice, comfy hotel room, life will be good and you'll probably love the country you're in. If, however, you stay in an old, dilapidated hotel, you may feel miserable and sorry that you ever came. To make your stay in a Russian hotel more pleasurable, in this chapter we show you how to find and book the right hotel room, what to say and do when checking in, how to resolve service problems, and how to check out and pay your bill.

Finding a Hotel that's Right for You

To ensure the hotel you're staying in doesn't disappoint you, make sure the room meets your needs and has the amenities you want. In the following sections, you discover different types of hotels to choose from and find out to how to make reservations in Russian.

Distinguishing different types of hotels

Two main types of hotels exist in Russia:

✔ The more expensive, more comfortable **пятизвёздочные гостиницы** (pee-tee-*zvyohz*-dahch-ni-ee- gahs-*tee*-nee-tsi) (*five-star hotels*)

✔ The less expensive, less comfortable **однозвёздные гостиницы** (ahd-nah-*zvyohzd*-ni-ee gahs-*tee*-nee-tsi) (*one-star hotels*)

But don't be surprised if one- or two-star hotels in Russia charge you as much as four- or even five-star hotels. Another Russian puzzle for you!

You don't just stay at a hotel; you live there

What do people do in hotels? They stay there. Although Russian does have an equivalent for this verb — **останавливаться** (ahs-tuh-nahv-lee-vuht'-syeh) (*to stay*), Russians perfer using the verb **жить** (zhit') (*to live*) to indicate the same notion. For example, when you're describing where you stayed, saying something along these lines is very common:

> **Мы жили в гостинице Москва.** (mi zhi-lee v gahs-*tee*-nee-tseh mahs-*kvah*.) (*We stayed in the Moscow Hotel;* Literally: *We lived in Hotel Moscow.*)

Russian today has two words for the English *hotel*:

> ✔ One of them is a good old Russian word, **гостиница** (gahs-*tee*-nee-tsuh) (*hotel*, Literally: *a place for the guests*).

> ✔ The other word is **отель** (ah-*tehl'*) (*hotel*), an offspring from the foreign word.

Although from a linguistic point of view both words are interchangeable, they're charged with slightly different meanings. Nobody in Russia uses the word **отель** in reference to a little, old, shabby hotel. In this situation, the word **гостиница** is more appropriate. On the other hand, when speaking about luxurious four- or five-star hotels, Russians use both words interchangeably.

Making a reservation

If you're making a reservation online, the forms that you fill out are self-explanatory. If, however, you prefer to make a reservation on the phone, you want to begin by saying

> **Я хотел/хотела бы забронировать номер.** (ya khah-*tyehl*/khah-*tyeh*-luh bi zuh-brah-*nee*-rah-vuht' *noh*-meer.) (*I would like to make a reservation for a room.*)

Use **хотел** if you're a man and **хотела** if you're a woman.

When they talk about hotel rooms, Russians use the word **номер**, which also means *number*. In a way it makes sense, because all rooms in a hotel have numbers!

You have to provide some important information when you make a hotel reservation on the phone. We steer you through the process in the following sections.

Saying when and how long you want to stay

After you state that you want to make a reservation on the phone, the person you're talking to will probably ask:

> **На какое число?** (nuh kuh-*koh*-ee chees-*loh*?) (*For what date?*)

To answer this very predictable question, use this formula: **На** (nah) (*for*) + the ordinal numeral indicating the date in its neuter form + the name of the month in the genitive case. (Flip to Chapter 5 for details on ordinal numbers and Chapter 3 for details on the genitive case.) For example, if you're planning to arrive on September 15, you say

> **На пятнадцатое сентября** (nuh peet-*naht*-tsuh-tah-ee seen-teeb-*rya*) (*For September 15*)

You may also be asked for the range of dates during which you want to stay in the hotel:

> **С какого по какое число?** (s kuh-*koh*-vah pah kuh-*koh*-ee chees-*loh*?) (*From what date to what date?*)

To answer this question, use **с** (s) (*from*) + the genitive case of the ordinal number indicating the date + the genitive case of the word indicating the month + **по** (pah) (*until*) + the ordinal numeral indicating the date in its neuter form (and accusative case) + the name of the month in the genitive case. Got that? If, for example, you're planning to stay in the hotel from June 21 to June 25, you say

> **С двадцать первого июня по двадцать пятое июня.** (s *dvaht*-tsuht' *pyehr*-vah-vah ee-*yooh*-nyeh pah *dvaht*-tsuht' *pya*-tah-ee ee-*yooh*-nyeh.) (*From June 21 to June 25.*)

Alternately, you can simply state how many nights you plan to stay in the hotel. If you're checking in on June 21 at 3 p.m. and leaving on June 25 at 11 a.m., you'll be staying in the hotel **четыре ночи** (chee-*ti*-ree *noh*-chee) (*four nights*). For more info about numbers with nouns, check out Chapter 5.

Choosing your room: Double or single?

When you're done talking about dates, you may hear

Вы хотите одноместный номер или двух-местный номер? (vi khah-*tee*-tee ahd-nah-*myehst*-niy *noh*-meer *ee*-lee dvoohkh-*myehst*-niy *noh*-meer?) (*Do you want a single or double accommodation?*)

Most rooms in hotels are either **одноместные** (ahd-nah-*myehst*-ni-ee) (*single accommodation*) or **двухместные** (dvoohkh-*myehst*-ni-ee) (*double accommodation*). If you have a third person, such as a child, you may get a **раскладушка** (ruhs-kluh-*doohsh*-kuh) (*cot*). And if you're the happy parent of two kids, you probably want to spring for an extra room.

In a Russian hotel room, you won't find king- or queen-sized beds, only **односпальные** (ahd-nah-*spahl'*-ni-ee) (*twins*) or **двуспальные** (dvooh-*spahl'*-ni-ee) (*doubles*).

Asking about amenities

One very important thing you need to ask about is whether the room has a **ванная** (*vah*-nuh-yeh) (*bathtub*), **душ** (doosh) (*shower*), or even a **туалет** (tooh-uh-*lyeht*) (*toilet*). In an inexpensive hotel in a small provincial city, showers and toilets may be located **на этаже** (nuh eh-tuh-*zheh*) (*on the floor*) rather than **в номере** (v *noh*-mee-ree) (*in the hotel room*). To avoid any disappointments, you can ask

> **В номере есть ванная, душ и туалет?** (v *noh*-mee-ree yehst' *vah*-nuh-yeh doohsh ee tooh-uh-*lyeht*?) (*Is there a bathtub, shower, and toilet in the room?*)

Note that although the word **туалет** best translates as *toilet*, it really refers to the room in which a toilet is found. The actual toilet itself is called an **унитаз** (ooh-nee-*tahs*).

Understanding how much your room is going to cost you

Certainly an important question to ask is

> **Сколько стоит номер?** (*skohl'*-kah *stoh*-eet *noh*-meer?) (*How much is the room?*)

If the hotel you're calling has a number of vacancies, chances are the rates may be different for different rooms. If this is the case, you may hear something like this:

> **Есть номера за семьдесят евро, за восемьдесят евро, за сто евро.** (yehst' nah-mee-*rah* zuh *syehm'*-dee-syeht *yehv*-rah, zuh *voh*-seem'-dee- syeht *yehv*-rah, zuh stoh *yehv*-rah.) (*There are rooms for 70 euros, for 80 euros, for 100 euros.*)

When you decide which room you want, express it like this:

> **Я возьму номер за восемьдесят евро.** (ya vahz'-*mooh noh*-meer zuh *voh*-seem-dee- syeht *yehv*-rah.) (*I will take a room for 80 euros.*)

You may also want to inquire whether this amount includes breakfast:

Это включает завтрак? (*eh*-tah fklyooh-*chah*-eet *zahf*-truhk?) (*Does it include breakfast?*)

Talkin' the Talk

Nancy (**Нэнси**) is calling a hotel in St. Petersburg to make a reservation. She is traveling alone and is on a budget. A **работник гостиницы** (ruh-*boht*-neek gahs-*tee*-nee-tsi) (*hotel employee*) answers the phone. (Track 30)

Нэнси:	**Я хотела бы забронировать номер.**
	ya khah-*tyeh*-luh bi zuh-brah-*nee*-rah-vuht' *noh*-meer.
	I would like to make a reservation for a room.

Работник гостиницы:	**На какое число?**
	nuh kuh-*koh*-ee chees-*loh*?
	For what date?

Нэнси:	**На двадцатое ноября.**
	nuh dvuht-*tsah*-tah-ee nuh-eeb-*rya*.
	For November 20.

Работник гостиницы:	**Один номер? На сколько дней?**
	ah-*deen noh*-meer? nuh *skohl'*-kah dnyehy?
	One room? For how many days?

Нэнси:	**Да, один. На две ночи. Одноместный номер.**
	dah, ah-*deen*. nuh dvyeh *noh*-chee. ahd-nah-*myehst*-niy *noh*-meer.
	Yes, one. For two nights. Single accommodation.

Работник гостиницы:	**Есть номер за сто евро и за семьде-сят евро.**
	yehst' *noh*-meer zuh stoh *yehv*-rah, ee zuh *syehm'*-dee-syeht *yehv*-rah.
	There is a room for 100 euros, and one for 70 euros.

Нэнси:	**Я возьму номер за семьдесят евро. В номере есть душ и туалет?** ya vahz'-*mooh noh*-meer zuh *syehm'*-dee-syeht *yehv*-rah. v *noh*-mee-ree yehst' doohsh ee tooh-uh-*lyeht*? *I will take the room for 70 euros. Is there a shower and toilet in the room?*
Работник гостиницы:	**Да, есть. Будете бронировать?** dah, *yehst'. booh*-dee-tee brah-*nee*-rah-vuht'? *Yes, there are. Will you be making a reservation?*
Нэнси:	**Да, буду.** Dah, *booh*-dooh. *Yes, I will.*

Words to Know

Я хотела бы забронировать номер.	ya khah-<u>tyeh</u>-luh bi zuh-brah-<u>nee</u>-rah-vuht' <u>noh</u>-meer.	I would like to make a reservation for a room.
На какое число?	nuh kuh-<u>koh</u>-ee chees-<u>loh</u>?	For what date?
На сколько дней?	nuh <u>skohl</u>'-kah dnyehy?	For how many days?
одноместный номер	ahd-nah-<u>myehst</u>-niy <u>noh</u>-meer	single accommodation
Будете бронировать?	<u>booh</u>-dee-tee brah-<u>nee</u>-rah-vuht'?	Will you be making a reservation?
Да, буду.	dah, <u>booh</u>-dooh.	Yes, I will.

Checking In

Congratulations! You made it to your hotel. To make your check-in process as smooth as possible, in the following sections, we tell you what to say when checking in, what to expect in your room, and how to find the services you're looking for in the hotel. We also tell you about the names of important hotel employees you may want to know.

Enduring the registration process

When you arrive at your hotel, you're likely to be greeted by a **швейцар** (shveey-*tsahr*) (*doorman*) and a **носильщик** (nah-*seel'*-scheek) (*porter*), especially if you're at a nice hotel.

Look for a sign with the word **регистрация** (ree-gee-*strah*-tsee-yeh) (*check-in*). That's where you report upon your arrival. Simply say

> **У меня забронирован номер.** (ooh mee-*nya* zuh-brah-*nee* rah vuhn *noh*-meer.) (*I made a reservation for a room today*; Literally: *I have a room reserved.*)

Expect to be asked for your name:

> **Как ваша фамилия?** (kahk *vah*-shuh fuh-*mee*-lee-yeh.) (*What is your last name?*)

Keep your passport ready — you need it for registration. To ask for your passport, the **регистратор** (ree-gee *strah*-tahr) (*receptionist*) says **Ваш паспорт** (vahsh *pahs*-pahrt) (*Your passport*).

Beware: Your driver's license (be it Russian or foreign) isn't a valid ID in Russia. We suggest that you carry your passport with you at all times, just in case you need ID.

The next step in registration is filling out the **регистрационная карточка** (ree-gee-struh-tsi-*oh*-nuh-yeh *kahr*-tahch-kuh) (*registration form*). The **регистратор** may say

> **Заполните, пожалуйста, регистрационную карточку.** (zuh-*pohl*-nee-tee, pah-*zhahl*-stuh, ree-gee-struh-tsi-*ohn*-nooh-yooh *kahr*-tahch-kooh.) (*Please fill out the registration form.*)

In most cases, this form requires you to provide the following information:

- **Имя** (*ee*-myeh) *First name*)
- **Фамилия** (fuh-*mee*-lee-yeh) (*Last name*)
- **Адрес** (*ahd*-rees) (*Address*)
- **Домашний/рабочий телефон** (dah-*mahsh*-neey/ruh-*boh*-cheey tee-lee-*fohn*) (*Home/work phone number*)
- **Срок пребывания в гостинице с . . . по . . .** (srohk pree-bi-*vah*-nee-yeh v gahs-*tee*-nee-tseh s . . . pah . . .) (*Period of stay in the hotel, from . . . to . . .*)
- **Номер паспорта** (*noh*-meer *pahs*-pahr-tuh) (*Passport number*)

Next, you'll be asked if you have to register, a procedure that's different from a hotel's registration. If you're staying in Russia for longer than 72 hours from the moment of arrival, you have to register. If you're changing locations and your new stay is also longer than 72 hours, you have to register again, so the answer is almost always **Да** (dah) (*Yes*). Your passport will be taken by the hotel's personnel and returned with the registration card within the next 24 hours, or you can pick it up at the registration desk. Make sure that you have a colored copy of your passport with you. Like your passport, you should carry it everywhere while your passport is being used for registration.

The beauty of staying in a hotel is that all the registration procedures are fulfilled by the hotel personnel; otherwise, you or your hosts have to do it — a very time-consuming adventure.

After you fill out all the forms and give the receptionist your passport, you receive the all-important **ключ от комнаты** (klyoohch aht *kohm*-nuh-ti) (*key to your room*) and your **карточка гостя** (*kahr*-tahch-kuh *gohs*-tyeh) or **визитка** (vee-*zeet*-kuh) (*hotel guest card*).

Don't assume that your room number is related to the floor number. For example, if the **номер комнаты** (*noh*-meer *kohm*-nuh-ti) (*room number*) is 235, it doesn't mean that the room is on the second floor; it can actually be on any floor of the hotel. Before you leave check-in, ask:

> **На каком этаже мой номер?** (nuh kuh-*kohm* eh-tuh-*zheh* mohy *noh*-meer?) (*On what floor is my room?*)

Make sure you drop off your key with the reception desk each time you leave the hotel (and certainly pick it up when you come back). If you take your key with you, the administration of the hotel can't be held responsible for your personal belongings if anything of value left in your room mysteriously disappears.

Never leave the hotel without your **карточка гостя** or **визитка** if you want to be let into the hotel when you come back after a long day of sightseeing. In most cases, you need to present your **визитка** to the security officer that most Russian hotels are staffed with today.

Talkin' the Talk

Greg Brown (**Грег Браун**) has made a reservation for a hotel room in Yaroslavl' and is now checking in. Here is his conversation with the **регистратор** (ree-gee-*strah*-tahr) (*receptionist*). (Track 31)

Грег Браун:	**У меня забронирован номер на сегодня.** ooh mee-*nya* zuh-brah-*nee*-rah-vuhn *noh*-meer nuh see-*vohd*-nyeh. *I made a reservation for a room for today.*
Регистратор:	**Как ваша фамилия?** kahk *vah*-shuh fuh-*mee*-lee-yeh? *What is your last name?*
Грег Браун:	**Браун.** *brah*-oohn. *Brown.*
Регистратор:	**Грег Браун? Ваш паспорт, пожалуйста.** grehg *brah*-oohn? vahsh *pahs*-pahrt, pah-*zhahl*-stuh. *Greg Brown? Your passport, please.*
Грег Браун:	**Вот пожалуйста.** voht pah-*zhahl*-stuh. *Here it is.*
Регистратор:	**Заполните, пожалуйста, регистрационную карточку** zuh-*pohl*-nee-tee, pah-*zhahl*-stuh, ree-gee-struh-tsi-*oh*-nooh-yooh *kahr*-tahch-kooh. *Please fill out the registration form.*
Грег Браун:	**Хорошо.** khah-rah-*shoh*. *Okay.* (Greg fills out the form and hands it to the receptionist.) **Вот я заполнил.** voht ya zuh-*pohl*-neel. *Here, I filled it out.*

Регистратор:	**Вот ваш ключ. Номер триста пятнадцать. Вы выписываетесь восьмого? Рассчётный час двенадцать часов дня.**
	voht vahsh klyoohch. *noh*-meer *trees*-tuh peet-*naht*-tsuht'. vi vi-*pee*-si-vuh-ee-tees' vahs'-*moh*-vah? ruhs-*chyoht*-niy chahs dvee-*naht*-tsuht' chuh-*sohf* dnya.
	Here is your key. You room number is 350. Are you checking out on the 8th? Check-out time is 12 p.m.
Грег:	**Да, восьмого. Спасибо.**
	da, vahs'-*moh*-vah. spah-*see*-bah.
	Yes, on the 8th, thank you.

Words to Know

У меня забронирован номер.	ooh mee-_nya_ zuh-brah-_nee_-rah-vuhn _noh_-meer.	I have reserved a room.
на сегодня	nuh see-_vohd_-nyeh	for today
Как ваша фамилия?	kahk _vah_-shuh fuh-_mee_-lee-yeh?	What is your last name?
Ваш паспорт	vahsh _pahs_-pahrt	Your passport
Вот пожалуйста.	voht pah-_zhahl_-stuh.	Here it is.
заполните	zuh-_pohl_-nee-tee	fill out
Вот, я заполнил.	Voht, ya zuh-_pohl_-neel.	Here, I filled it out.
Вот ваш ключ.	voht vahsh klyoohch.	Here is your key.
расчётный час	ruhs-_chyoht_-niy chahs	check-out time

Taking a tour of your room

What can you expect to find in your hotel room? Most likely, you'll see a **двуспальная кровать** (dvoohkh-*spahl'*-nuh-yeh krah-*vaht'*) (*double bed*) or an **односпальная кровать** (ahd-nah-*spahl'*-nuh-yeh krah-*vaht'*) (*twin bed*) if you have a **номер на одного** (*noh*-meer nuh ahd-nah-*voh*) (*single room*).

You may also see some or all of the following items, depending on the quality of the hotel:

- **торшер** (tahr-*shehr*) (*standing lamp*)
- **тумбочки** (*toohm*-bahch-kee) (*nightstands*)
- **письменный стол и стул** (*pees'*-mee-niy stohl ee stoohl) (*desk and chair*)
- **шкаф** (shkahf) (*wardrobe*)
- **вешалки** (*vyeh*-shuhl-kee) (*hangers*)
- **телефон** (tee-lee-*fohn*) (*telephone*)
- **телевизор** (tee-lee-*vee*-zahr) (*TV set*)
- **будильник** (boo-*deel'*-neek) (*alarm clock*)
- **телефонный справочник** (tee-lee-*foh*-niy *sprah*-vahch-neek) (*phone book containing hotel numbers*)

If you have a bathroom in your room, you find an **унитаз** (ooh-nee-*tahs*) (*toilet*) and a **душ** (doohsh) (*shower*) or **ванная** (*vah*-nuh-yeh) (*bathtub*). Check to make sure you have **полотенца** (pah-lah-*tyehn*-tsuh) (*towels*). Don't expect to see towels of various sizes in the bathroom of your hotel room. In the best-case scenario, you find two kinds of towels: a **банное полотенце** (*bah*-nah-ee puh-lah-*tyehn*-tseh) (*bath towel*) and a smaller **личное полотенце** (leech-*noh*-ee pah-lah-*tyehn*-tseh) (*face towel*).

Familiarizing yourself with the facilities

To idle away time in the hotel, you may want to explore. Here's what you may find:

- **гардероб** (guhr-dee-*rohp*) (*cloak room*)
- **почта** (*pohch*-tuh) (*post office*)
- **сувенирный киоск** (sooh-vee-*neer*-niy kee-*ohsk*) (*souvenir kiosk*)
- **камера хранения** (*kah*-mee-ruh khruh-*nyeh*-nee-yeh) (*storeroom*)

- **бюро обслуживания** (byooh-*roh* ahp-*slooh*-zhi-vuh-nee-yeh) (*customer service*)

- **ресторан** (rees-tah-*rahn*) (*restaurant*)

- **бар** (bahr) (*bar*)

To inquire where a certain service is, go to **бюро обслуживания** and ask the following question, substituting the service you need for the one shown here:

> **Скажите, пожалуйста, где камера хранения?** (skuh-*zhi*-tee, pah-*zhahl*-stuh, gdyeh *kah*-mee-ruh khruh-*nyeh*-nee-yeh?) (*Could you tell me where the storeroom is?*)

If you aren't staying in the hotel but are just visiting somebody or having lunch in one of the hotel bars or restaurants, leaving your coat and hat in the **гардероб** is customary.

Meeting the staff

Looking for a particular type of staff member? People who work in various hotel positions include the following:

- **администратор** (uhd-mee-nee-*strah*-tahr) (*manager, person working at the front desk,* or *concierge*)

- **гардеробщик/гардеробщица** (guhr-dee-*rohp*-sh'eek/guhr-dee-*rohp*-sh'ee-tsuh) (*person working in the cloak room*)

- **носильщик** (nah-*seel'*-sh'eek) (*porter*)

- **швейцар** (shveey-*tsahr*) (*doorman*)

- **горничная** (*gohr*-neech-nuh-yeh) (*maid*)

Resolving Service Problems Successfully

Experienced travelers know that something almost always goes wrong when you stay in a foreign country. In the following sections, we show you how to resolve some of the most common problems, including reporting a broken item, asking for missing items, and requesting a room change.

Reporting a broken item

A very common problem is that something in your room doesn't work. The key refuses to open the door, the phone is silent when you pick it up, or the shower pours only cold water on you. You need to speak to a **работник** (ruh-*boht*-neek) (*employee*) in **бюро обслуживания** (byooh-*roh* ahp-*slooh*-zhi-vuh-nee-yeh) (*customer service*) to get help with these problems.

To report the problem, use the phrase **У меня в комнате не работает. . . .** (ooh mee-*nya* f *kohm*-nuh-tee nee ruh-*boh*-tuh-eet) (*The . . . in my room is not working*), inserting the item that's not working in the nominative case (see Chapter 3 for details on this case). If your telephone is broken, for instance, you say

> **У меня в комнате не работает телефон.** (ooh mee-*nya* f *kohm*-nuh-tee nee ruh-*boh*-tuh-eet tee-lee-*fohn*.) (*The telephone in my room is not working.*)

Requesting missing items

The formula you need to know to report that something is missing is **У меня в номере нет** (ooh mee-*nya* v *noh*-mee-ree nyeht) (*In my room I don't have a*) plus the word denoting the missing item in the genitive case. (For more information on forming the genitive case, see Chapter 3.)

Imagine that you've just taken a shower and are now reaching for the **банное полотенце** (*bah*-nuh-ee pah-lah-*tyehn*-tseh) (*bath towel*), only to discover you don't have one! Shivering from cold and dripping water, you rush to the phone to call customer service. You say

> **У меня в номере нет банного полотенца.** (ooh mee-*nya* v *noh*-mee-ree nyeht *bah*-nah-vah pah-lah-*tyehn*-tsuh.) (*I don't have a bath towel in my room.*)

Other things you may want to request include

- **подушка** (pah-*doohsh*-kuh) (*pillow*)
- **одеяло** (ah-dee-*ya*-lah) (*blanket*)
- **вешалка** (*vyeh*-shuhl-kuh) (*hanger*)
- **туалетная бумага** (tooh-uh-*lyeht*-nuh-yeh booh-*mah*-guh) (*toilet paper*)

Asking to change rooms

To be honest, changing rooms isn't the easiest thing to do in a Russian hotel, but as they say in Russia:

> **Попытка не пытка!** (pah-*pit*-kuh nee *pit*-kuh) (*It doesn't hurt to try!* Literally: *An attempt is not a torture!*)

To give it a whirl, call customer service and say

> **Я хотел/хотела бы поменять номер.** (ya khah-*tyehl*/khah-*tyeh*-luh bi pah-mee-*nyat' noh*-meer.) (*I would like to change my room.*)

Use **хотел** if you're a man and **хотела** if you're a woman. Then give some convincing reasons for wanting a room change, such as

> **В комнате очень шумно.** (f *kohm*-nuh-tee *oh*-cheen' *shoohm*-nah.) (*It is very noisy in my room.*)

> **В комнате очень холодно/жарко.** (f *kohm*-nuh-tee *oh*-cheen' *khoh*-lahd-nah/*zhahr*-kah.) (*It is very cold/hot in my room.*)

> **В комнате нет света.** (f *kohm*-nuh-tee nyeht *svyeh*-tuh.) (*There is no light in my room.*)

Checking Out and Paying Your Bill

Your stay has come to an end, and now you have to pay. Or as Russians like to say:

> **Наступил час расплаты.** (nuh-stooh-*peel* chahs ruhs-*plah*-ti.) (*It's time to pay;* Literally: *The hour of reckoning has arrived.*)

In order to **заплатить за гостиницу** (zuh-pluh-*teet'* zuh gahs-*tee*-nee-tsooh) (*pay for your hotel stay*), go to **регистрация** (ree-gee-*strah*-tsi-yeh) (*check-in*) and say

> **Я выписываюсь. Я хочу заплатить.** (ya vi-*pee*-si-vuh-yoohs'. ya khah-*chooh* zuh-pluh-*teet'*.) (*I am checking out. I want to pay for my stay.*)

You may also want to ask whether the hotel takes credit cards:

> **Вы принимаете кредитные карточки?** (vi pree-nee-*mah*-ee-tee kree-*deet*-ni-ee *kahr*-tahch-kee?) (*Do you accept credit cards?*)

If the hotel does, ask which cards it accepts:

> **Какие кредитные карточки вы принимаете?** (kuh-*kee*-ee kree-*deet*-ni-ee *kahr*-tahch-kee vi pree-nee-*mah*-ee-tee?) (*What credit cards do you take?*)

See to it that everything is correct on your receipt. It may include a **телефон-ный разговор** (tee-lee-*foh*-niy ruhz-gah-*vohr*) (*telephone call*) you made from your room, or maybe **стирка** (*steer*-kuh) (*laundry service*). If you feel you've been overcharged for some service you didn't use, point it out to the receptionist and politely ask

> **А это за что?** (uh *eh*-tah zah shtoh?) (*And what is this for?*)

And don't forget to **получить квитанцию** (pah-looh-*cheet'* kvee-*tahn*-tsi-yooh) (*get a receipt*) before you hurry out of the hotel to catch your train or plane.

As in most hotels throughout the world, the **рассчётный час** (ruhs-*chyoht*-niy chahs) (*check-out time*) is **полдень** (*pohl*-deen') (*noon*) or **двенадцать часов дня** (dvee-*nahd*-tsuht' chuh-*sohf* dnya) (*12 p.m.*). So where do you put your luggage if your plane doesn't leave until midnight? Most hotels have a **камера хранения** (*kah*-mee-ruh khruh-*nyeh*-nee-yeh) (*storeroom*).

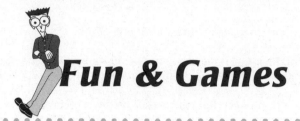

Fun & Games

Using the following figure and the information in the right-hand column, help John Evans fill out his hotel registration form in the left column. See Appendix D for the right answers.

ГОСТИНИЦА "МОСКВА"
РЕГИСТРАЦИОННАЯ КАРТОЧКА

ИМЯ_____

ФАМИЛИЯ_____

АДРЕС: _____

_____

ТЕЛЕФОН: _____

НОМЕР ПАСПОРТА:

_____

СРОК ПРЕБЫВАНИЯ В ГОСТИНИЦЕ_____

С_____ ПО_____

имя _____   a. 4446678

фамилия _____   b. from June 16th to June 17th

адрес _____   c. John

телефон _____   d. 123 Highpoint Drive, Chicago, Illinois, USA

Срок пребывания в гостинице с . . . по _____   e. 815-555-5544

Номер паспорта _____   f. Evans

Chapter 18

Handling Emergencies

• •

In This Chapter

▶ Knowing how to ask for help

▶ Getting medical attention

▶ Dealing with the police

• •

An emergency would be called something else if it were possible to be fully prepared for it. However, you can avoid some panic if you have a convenient reference guide that gives you just the right things to say in case an emergency interrupts your plans. In this chapter, you find out how to explain yourself in various unpleasant situations: asking for help during an emergency, getting help with a health concern, and talking to the police. Enjoy this emergency guide; we hope you never need to use it!

Finding Help in Case of Accidents and Other Emergencies

Dealing with accidents and emergencies in your native language is enough of a headache; problems seem twice as bad when you have to speak a foreign language to resolve them. But if you know how to ask for help, chances are you'll find somebody who makes resolving your problems much easier. In the following sections, you find out how to request help, call the Russian equivalent of 911, and explain your problem. And just in case your Russian fails you in a time of need, you discover the way to find somebody who speaks English!

Hollering for help

The first thing you need to know is how to ask for help. If you aren't feeling well or don't know what to do during an emergency, address someone with one of these sentences:

Извините, мне нужна помощь! (eez-vee-*nee*-tee, mnyeh noohzh-*nah* poh-mahsh'!) (*Excuse me, I need help!*)

Помогите мне, пожалуйста? (pah-mah-*gee*-tee mnyeh, pah-*zhahl*-stuh?) (*Will you please help me?*)

Make sure you explain what your problem is immediately after you ask for help so that the person you're talking to doesn't think you're a scam artist. Phrases you may want to say include the following:

Я себя плохо чувствую. (ya see-*bya ploh*-khah *choohs*-tvooh-yooh.) (*I am not feeling well.*)

Мне плохо. (mnyeh *ploh*-khah.) (*I am not feeling well.*)

Позвоните в скорую помощь! (pahz-vah-*nee*-tee v *skoh*-rooh-yooh *poh*-mahsh'!) (*Call an ambulance!*)

Помогите! (pah-mah-*gee*-tee!) (*Help!*)

Позовите на помощь! (pah-zah-*vee*-tee nuh *poh*-mahsh'!) (*Call for help!*)

Позвоните в полицию! (pahz-vah-*nee*-tee f pah-*lee*-tsi-yooh!) (*Call the police!*)

Держите вора! (deer-*zhi*-tee *voh*-ruh!) (*Stop the thief!*)

Пожар! (pah-*zhahr*!) (*Fire!*)

Making an emergency phone call

In the United States, calling 911 is the answer to almost any emergency question, but it's not this way in Russia. There, you have three different numbers to call in cases of fire, crime, or health problems. The numbers are easy, and any Russian knows them by heart:

- ✔ **01: пожарная служба** (pah-*zhahr*-nuh-yeh *sloohzh*-buh) (*fire brigade*)
- ✔ **02: полиция** (pah-*lee*-tsi-yeh) (*police*)
- ✔ **03: скорая помощь** (*skoh*-ruh-yeh *poh*-mahsh') (*ambulance;* Literally: *urgent help*)

Reporting a problem

When reporting an accident or an emergency, a good verb to use is **происходить** (prah-ees-khah-*deet'*) (*to happen*). To talk about something that is happening or has happened, you need only the third person singular form in the present tense — **происходит** (prah-ees-*khoh*-deet) (*is happening*) — or one of these past-tense forms of *has happened*:

- ✔ **произошёл** (prah-ee-zah-*shohl*); masculine singular
- ✔ **произошла** (prah-ee-zah-*shlah*); feminine singular
- ✔ **произошло** (prah-ee-zah-*shloh*); neuter singular
- ✔ **произошли** (prah-ee-zah-*shlee*); plural

Problems that you may have to report include the following:

- ✔ **авария** (uh-*vah*-ree-yeh) (*car accident*)
- ✔ **несчастный случай** (nees-*chahs*-niy *slooh*-chuhy) (*accident*)
- ✔ **пожар** (pah-*zhahr*) (*fire*)
- ✔ **ограбление** (ahg-ruhb-*lyeh*-nee-ee) (*robbery*)
- ✔ **отравление** (aht-ruhv-*lyeh*-nee-ee) (*poisoning*)
- ✔ **инфаркт** (een-*fahrkt*) (*heart attack*)
- ✔ **ранение** (ruh-*nyeh*-nee-ee) (*injury*)

If you've witnessed an accident, you may be asked one of these two interchangeable questions:

Что произошло? (shtoh prah-ee-zah-*shloh*?) (*What happened?*)

Что случилось? (shtoh slooh-*chee*-lahs') (*What happened?*)

When responding to this question, you may want to say one of the following:

Здесь произошла авария. (zdyehs' prah-ee-zahsh-*lah* uh-*vah*-ree-yeh.) (*A car accident took place here.*)

Здесь прозошёл несчастный случай. (zdyehs' prah-ee-zah-*shohl* nees-*chahs*-niy *slooh*-chuhy.) (*An accident took place here.*)

Note that the verb agrees with the noun in gender.

Talkin' the Talk

While walking along a street in Moscow, Stacy (**Стаси**) witnesses an accident. He calls 03 and talks to the **оператор** (ah-pee-*rah*-tahr) (*operator*). (Track 32)

Оператор: **Скорая помощь. Слушаю.**
skoh-ruh-yeh *poh*-mahsh'. *slooh*-shuh-yooh.
Ambulance. How can I help you? (Literally: *I am listening.*)

Стаси:	**Тут произошла авария. Человек попал под машину.** tooht prah-ee-zah-*shlah* uh-*vah*-ree-yeh. chee-lah-*vyehk* pah-*pahl* pahd mah-*shi*-nooh. *A road accident happened here. A person was hit by a car.*
Оператор:	**Где произошла авария? Адрес?** gdyeh prah-ee-zah-*shlah* uh-*vah*-ree-yeh? *ahd*-rees? *Where did the accident happen? What is the address?*
Стаси:	**На углу улицы Тверской и Пушкинского бульвара.** nuh oohg-*looh* ooh-*lee*-tsi tveer-*skohy* ee *poohsh*-keen-skah-vah boohl'-*vah*-ruh. *At the corner of Tverskaya Street and Pushkinskiy Avenue.*
Оператор:	**В каком состоянии потерпевший?** f kah-*kohm* sahs-tah-*ya*-nee-ee pah-teer-*pyehf*-shiy? *What's the condition of the victim?*
Стаси:	**Без сознания.** byehs sahz-*nah*-nee-yeh. *Unconscious.*
Оператор:	**Вы родственник потерпевшего?** vi *roht*-stvee-neek pah-teer-*pyehf*-shi-vah? *Are you a relative of the victim?*
Стаси:	**Нет, я просто прохожий, случайный свидетель.** nyeht, ya *prohs*-tah prah-*khoh*-zhiy, slooh-*chahy*-niy svee-*dyeh*-teel'. *No, I'm just a passerby, an accidental witness.*
Оператор:	**Бригада выезжает.** bree-*gah*-duh vi-eez-*zhah*-eet. *An ambulance is on its way.*

Words to Know

скорая помощь	<u>skoh</u>-ruh-yeh <u>poh</u>-mahsh'	ambulance
Слушаю?	<u>slooh</u>-shuh-yooh?	How can I help you? (Literally: I am listening.)
Где произошла авария?	gdyeh prah-ee-zah-<u>shlah</u> uh-<u>vah</u>-ree-yeh?	Where did the accident happen?
В каком состоянии потерпевший?	f kah-<u>kohm</u> sahs-tah-<u>ya</u>-nee-ee pah-teer-<u>pyehf</u>-sheey?	What is the condition of the victim?
без сознания	byehs sahz-<u>nah</u>-nee-yeh	unconscious
прохожий	prah-<u>khoh</u>-zhiy	passerby
свидетель	svee-<u>dyeh</u>-teel'	witness
Бригада выезжает.	bree-<u>gah</u>-duh vi-eez-<u>zhah</u>-eet.	An ambulance is on its way.

Requesting English-speaking help

In case you don't feel like practicing your Russian in the midst of an emergency — or if you just want to speed up the process — you may want to ask for English-speaking help. The question you want to use is

Здесь есть кто-нибудь, кто говорит по-английски? (zdyehs' yehst' *ktoh*-nee-booht', ktoh gah-vah-*reet* pah-uhng-*leey*-skee?) (*Is there anybody here who speaks English?*)

If you want to insist on finding somebody who can help you in English, say

> **Мне нужен кто-нибудь, кто говорит по-английски!** (mnyeh *nooh*-zhehn *ktoh*-nee-booht' ktoh guh-vah-*reet* pah-uhng-*leey*-skee!) (*I need somebody who speaks English!*)

If you're making this request at a hospital or some other place staffed with highly educated people, you have a good chance of finding somebody who speaks English; many Russians study English in school and college.

In Moscow and St. Petersburg, you can find clinics with American and British doctors. Here are a few such clinics:

> **American Clinic**, 31 Grokholskij Pyeryeulok, 129090 Moscow; phone 095-937-5757; e-mail info@americanclinic.ru.

> **European Medical Center**, 5 Spiridonievskiy Per., Bldg. 1, Moscow; phone 095-933-6655; e-mail emcinfo@emcmos.ru.

> **American Medical Clinic,** Mojka Embankment #78, 190000 St.Petersburg; phone 812-740 2090, fax 812-310-4664; e-mail info@amclinic.ru.

Receiving Medical Care

If "an apple a day" doesn't work, you may need to **пойти к врачу** (pahy-*tee* k vruh-*chooh*) (*see a doctor*). Every culture has different beliefs and procedures related to **здоровье** (zdah-*rohv'*-ee) (*health*) and **медицина** (mee-dee-*tsi*-nuh) (*medicine*), and knowing what they are before you visit a doctor helps. In the following sections, you find out how to talk about medical problems in Russian, how to understand your diagnosis, and what to say and do in a pharmacy.

To make an appointment with your doctor at a big **поликлиника** (pah-lee-*klee*-nee-kuh) (*an outpatient facility*), you need to go to the **регистратура** (ree-gees-truh-*tooh*-ruh) (*check-in desk*) and say **Мне надо записаться на приём к . . .** (mnyeh *nah*-duh zuh-pee-*saht'*-syeh nuh pree-*yohm* k . . .) (*I need to make an appointment with . . .*), followed by the type of doctor you want to see in the dative case (for more info on case endings, see Chapter 3). At some **поликлиники** (pah-lee-*klee*-nee-kee) (*clinics*), you may be able to make an appointment over the phone; at others, you always have to show up in person. To find out which is the case, you can call the **поликлиника** and ask:

> **Можно записаться на приём?** (*mohzh*-nah zuh-pee-*saht'*-syeh nuh pree-*yohm*?) (*Can I make an appointment?*)

For an emergency, call a **скорая помощь** (*skoh*-ruh-yeh *poh*-mahsh') (*ambulance*) by dialing 03. The ambulance will come and take the patient to the *emergency room*, which is also called **скорая помощь.**

Health is more valuable than money

According to a Russian proverb, **здоровье дороже денег** (zdah-*rohv'*-ee dah-*roh*-zheh *dyeh*-neek) (*health is more valuable than money*). Believing this bit of folk wisdom was easy during the times of the Soviet Union, when medicine was free for all Soviet citizens. Nowadays, numerous **частные клиники**

(*chahs*-ni-ee *klee*-nee-kee) (*private medical offices*) offer a variety of **платные услуги** (*plaht*-ni-ee oohs-*looh*-gee) (*services for a fee*). State-owned hospitals and medical offices are still free, but you're expected to pay for your medicine, and a monetary donation to the doctor is strongly encouraged.

Knowing parts of the body

When you go to a doctor, you want to know how to talk about your **тело** (tyeh-*lah*) (*body*). In the following sections, we provide the Russian terms for visible body parts and internal organs.

Visible body parts

The following list names visible parts of the body from the top down:

- ✔ **голова** (gah-lah-*vah*) (*head*)
- ✔ **шея** (*sheh*-yeh (*neck*)
- ✔ **горло** (*gohr*-lah) (*throat*)
- ✔ **плечо** (plee-*choh*) (*shoulder*)
- ✔ **грудь** (grooht') (*chest/breast*)
- ✔ **спина** (spee-*nah*) (*back*)
- ✔ **рука** (rooh-*kah*) (*arm/hand*)
- ✔ **локоть** (*loh*-kaht') (*elbow*)
- ✔ **запястье** (zuh-*pyast'*-ee) (*wrist*)
- ✔ **палец** (*pah*-leets) (*finger*)
- ✔ **ногти** (*nohk*-tee) (*nails*)
- ✔ **живот** (zhi-*voht*) (*stomach*)
- ✔ **половые органы** (pah-lah-*vi*-ee *ohr*-guh-ni) (*genitals*)
- ✔ **нога** (nah-*gah*) (*leg/foot*)
- ✔ **колено** (kah-*lyeh*-nah) (*knee*)

✔ **лодыжка** (lah-*dish*-kuh) (*ankle*)

✔ **кожа** (*koh*-zhuh) (*skin*)

In Russian, no distinction exists between the arm and the hand; for both body parts, you use the word **рука**. Similarly, for both the leg and the foot, you use the word **нога**.

Parts of your head that you may seek treatment for include the following:

✔ **лицо** (lee-*tsoh*) (*face*)

✔ **глаз** (glahs) (*eye*)

✔ **ухо** (*ooh*-khah) (*ear*)

✔ **нос** (nohs) (*nose*)

✔ **рот** (roht) (*mouth*)

✔ **зуб** (zoohp) (*tooth*)

✔ **язык** (ee-*zik*) (*tongue*)

✔ **подбородок** (pahd-bah-*roh*-dahk) (*chin*)

Internal organs

The internal organs you may need to talk about include these body parts:

✔ **сердце** (*syehr*-tseh) (*heart*)

✔ **печень** (*pyeh*-cheen') (*liver*)

✔ **желудок** (zhi-*looh*-dahk) (*stomach*)

✔ **мозг** (mohzk) (*brain*)

✔ **лёгкие** (*lyohkh*-kee-ee) (*lungs*)

✔ **кость** (kohst') (*bone*)

✔ **мышцы** (*mish*-tsi) (*muscles*)

✔ **почка** (*pohch*-kuh) (*kidney*)

✔ **нервы** (*nyehr*-vi) (*nerves*)

Describing your symptoms

The best way to start describing your symptoms if you're in pain is with the verb **болеть** (bah-*lyeht'*) (*to hurt*): Say **У меня болит . . .** (ooh mee-*nya* bah-leet . . .) (*. . . is hurting*), adding the name of the organ that hurts in the nominative case (see Chapter 3 for details on cases).

You can also point to the place where it hurts and say

> **У меня болит здесь.** (ooh mee-*nya* bah-*leet* zdyehs'.) (*It hurts me here.*)

You may want to specify whether it hurts **внутри** (vnooh-*tree*) (*inside*) or **снаружи** (snuh-*rooh*-zhee) (*on the outside*).

To describe other specific symptoms, you can say **У меня . . .** (ooh mee-*nya . . .*) (*I have . . .*) followed by one of the phrases from the following list:

- ✔ **температура** (teem-pee-ruh-*tooh*-ruh) (*fever*)
- ✔ **понос** (pah-*nohs*) (*diarrhea*)
- ✔ **запор** (zuh-*pohr*) (*constipation*)
- ✔ **тошнота** (tahsh-nah-*tah*) (*nausea*)
- ✔ **рвота** (*rvoh*-tuh) (*vomiting*)
- ✔ **головокружение** (gah-lah-vah-krooh-*zheh*-nee-ee) (*dizziness*)
- ✔ **болит горло** (bah-*leet* gohr-lah) (*sore throat*)
- ✔ **болит голова** (bah-*leet* gah-lah-*vah*) (*headache*)
- ✔ **болит живот** (bah-*leet* zhi-*voht*) (*stomachache*)
- ✔ **болит ухо** (bah-*leet* ooh-khuh) (*earache*)
- ✔ **кашель** (*kah*-sheel') (*cough*)
- ✔ **насморк** (*nahs*-mahrk) (*runny nose*)
- ✔ **сыпь** (sip') (*rash*)
- ✔ **ожог** (ah-*zhohk*) (*burn*)
- ✔ **боль** (bohl') (*pain*)

In Russia, temperature is measured in degrees Celsius (C). Normal body temperature is 36.6°C. Anything higher than that is a **высокая температура** (vi-*soh*-kuh-yeh teem-pee-ruh-*tooh*-ruh) (*high fever*).

Understanding questions a doctor asks

The first question you hear from a **врач** (vrahch) (*doctor*) is usually one of these two:

> **Что у вас болит?** (shtoh ooh vahs bah-*leet*?) (*What is hurting you?*)

> **Что вас беспокоит?** (shtoh vahs bees-pah-*koh*-eet?) (*What brought you here?* Literally: *What is bothering you?*)

Your doctor will want to find out when the pain started to bother you by asking

> **Когда это началось?** (kahg-*dah eh*-tah nuh-chuh-*lohs'*?) (*When did it start?*)

The doctor may also ask about your temperature:

> **Температура есть?** (teem-pee-ruh-*tooh*-ruh yehst'?) (*Do you have a fever?*)

While examining you, the doctor may ask for specifics about your pain by asking

> **Здесь болит?** (zdyehs' bah-*leet*?) (*Does it hurt here?*)

Talkin' the Talk

 Kate (**Кейт**) is spending her vacation in St. Petersburg. She starts to feel sick, so she goes to see a **врач** (vrahch) (*doctor*). (Track 33)

Кейт:	**Доктор, я себя плохо чуствую.**
	dohk-tahr, ya see-*bya ploh*-khah *choohs*-tvooh-yooh.
	Doctor, I am not feeling well.

Врач:	**Что вас беспокоит?**
	shtoh vahs bees-pah-*koh*-eet?
	What is bothering you?

Кейт:	**У меня болит живот.**
	ooh mee-*nya* bah-*leet* zhi-*voht*.
	My stomach is hurting.

Врач:	**Боль резкая или ноющая?**
	bohl' *ryehs*-kuh-yeh ee-lee *noh*-yooh-sh'uh-yeh?
	Is the pain sharp or dull?

Кейт:	**Ноющая. И ещё у меня температура.**
	noh-yooh-sh'uh-yeh. ee ee-*sh'yoh* ooh mee-*nya* teem-pee-ruh-*tooh*-ruh.
	It's dull. I also have a fever.

Врач:	**Тошнота или рвота есть?**
	tahsh-nah-*tah* ee-lee *rvoh*-tuh yehst'?
	Do you have nausea or vomiting?

Кейт:	**Нет. Но немного кружится голова.**
	nyeht. noh neem-*noh*-gah *krooh*-zhit-syeh gah-lah-*vah*.
	No. But I am a little dizzy.

Врач: **Будем проводить осмотр. Раздевайтесь.**
             booh-deem prah-vah-*deet'* ahs-*mohtr.*
             ruhz-dee-*vahy*-tees'.
             Let's examine you. Undress.
_____

Words to Know

Я себя плохо чуствую.	ya see-<u>bya</u> <u>ploh</u>-khah <u>choohs</u>-tvooh-yooh.	I am not feeling well.
Что вас беспокоит?	shtoh vahs bees-pah-<u>koh</u>-eet?	What is bothering you?
резкая боль	<u>ryehs</u>-kuh-yeh bohl'	sharp pain
ноющая боль	<u>noh</u>-yooh-shuh-yeh bohl'	dull pain
ещё	ee-<u>shyoh</u>	also
Но немного кружится голова.	noh neem-<u>noh</u>-gah <u>krooh</u>-zhit-syeh gah-lah-<u>vah</u>.	But I am a little dizzy.
проводить осмотр	prah-vah-<u>deet'</u> ahs-<u>mohtr</u>	to examine
раздевайтесь	ruhz-dee-<u>vahy</u>-tees'	undress

Communicating allergies or special conditions

Asking about allergies and special conditions isn't always part of a Russian doctor's routine. Make sure you take the initiative and tell the doctor if you have an allergy. Say **У меня аллергия на . . .** (ooh mee-*nya* uh-leer-*gee*-yeh nuh . . .) (*I am allergic to . . .*) followed by the word naming the cause of the allergy in the accusative case (see Chapter 3 for details on cases). Common causes of allergies include

✔ **пенициллин** (pee-nee-tsi-*leen*) (*penicillin*)

✔ **орехи** (ah-*ryeh*-khee) (*nuts*)

✔ **обезболивающие** (ah-beez-*boh*-lee-vuh-yooh-shee-ee) (*painkillers*)

✔ **укус пчелы** (ooh-*koohs* pchee-*li*) (*bee stings*)

✔ **кошки** (*kohsh*-kee) (*cats*)

✔ **собаки** (sah-*bah*-kee) (*dogs*)

✔ **яйца** (*yay*-tsuh) (*eggs*)

✔ **пыльца** (pil'-*tsah*) (*pollen*)

✔ **молоко** (mah-lah-*koh*) (*milk*)

✔ **моллюски** (mah-*lyoohs*-kee) (*shellfish*)

✔ **рыба** (*ri*-buh) (*fish*)

If you're on some kind of medication, tell your doctor **Я принимаю . . .** (ya pree-nee-*mah*-yooh . . .) (*I am on . . .*) followed by the name of the medication in the accusative case. Some other special conditions that you may need to announce to the doctor include the following:

> **У меня астма.** (ooh mee-*nya* ahst-muh.) (*I have asthma.*)
>
> **Я эпилептик.** (ya eh-pee-*lyehp*-teek.) (*I have epilepsy.*)
>
> **Я диабетик.** (ya dee-uh-*byeh*-teek.) (*I have diabetes.*)
>
> **Я беременна.** (ya bee-*ryeh*-mee-nuh-yeh.) (*I am pregnant.*)

Seeing a specialist

In Russia, each doctor specializes in a type of organ (for instance, the skin, bones, or nerves). If you go to a Russian physician and say that your foot hurts, he doesn't send you to a foot doctor. Instead, he finds out what type of problem you have and then sends you to a **дерматолог** (dehr-muh-*toh*-lahk) (*dermatologist*) if your problem concerns the skin of your foot, to a **хирург** (khee-*roohrk*) (*surgeon*) if you've broken a bone in your foot, or to a **невропатолог** (neev-rah-puh-*toh*-lahk) (*neurologist*) if your problem stems from nerve connections.

Some other doctors and their areas of specialization include

✔ **ухо/горло/нос** (*ooh*-khah/*gohr*-la/nohs) (*ear/throat/nose*)

✔ **дантист** (duhn-*teest*) (*dentist*)

✔ **венеролог** (vee-nee-*roh*-lahk) (*a specialist in venereal diseases*)

✔ **терапевт** (tee-ruh-*pyehft*) (*internist*)

- ✔ глазной врач (gluhz-*nohy* vrahch) (*eye doctor*)

- ✔ гинеколог (gee-nee-*koh*-lahk) (*gynecologist/obstetrician*)

- ✔ ортопед (ahr-tah-*pyeht*) (*orthopedist*)

- ✔ педиатр (pee-dee-*ahtr*) (*pediatrician*)

- ✔ психиатр (psee-khee-*ahtr*) (*psychiatrist*)

- ✔ кардиолог (kuhr-dee-*oh*-lahk) (*cardiologist*)

Undergoing an examination and getting a diagnosis

During a medical examination, you may hear the following phrases:

> **Разденьтесь до пояса.** (ruhz-*dyehn'*-tees' dah *poh*-ee-suh.) (*Undress from your waist up.*)

> **Разденьтесь полностью.** (ruhz-*dyehn'*-tees' *pohl*-nahst'-yooh.) (*Take off all your clothes.*)

> **Закатите рукав.** (zuh-kuh-*tee*-tee rooh-*kahf*.) (*Please roll up your sleeve.*)

> **Глубоко вдохните.** (glooh-bah-*koh* vdahkh-*nee*-tee.) (*Take a deep breath.*)

> **Ложитесь.** (lah-*zhi*-tees'.) (*Please lie down.*)

> **Откройте рот.** (aht-*krohy*-tee roht.) (*Open your mouth.*)

> **Покажите язык.** (pah-kuh-*zhi*-tee ee-*zik*.) (*Stick out your tongue.*)

You also may have to undergo the following tests:

- ✔ анализ крови (uh-*nah*-lees *kroh*-vee) (*blood test*)

- ✔ анализ мочи (uh-*nah*-lees mah-*chee*) (*urine test*)

- ✔ рентген (reen-*gyehn*) (*X-ray*)

- ✔ электрокардиограмма (eh-*lyehkt*-rah-kuhr-dee-ahg-*rah*-muh) (*electrocardiogram*)

- ✔ сонограмма (sah-nah-*grah*-muh) (*sonogram*)

- ✔ ультразвук (oohl'-truh-*zvoohk*) (*ultrasound*)

After all the turmoil of going through the **осмотр** (ahs-*mohtr*) (*medical examination*), you're ready to hear your **диагноз** (dee-*ahg*-nahs) (*diagnosis*). The doctor will probably phrase it this way: **У вас . . .** (ooh vahs . . .) (*You have . . .*) plus the diagnosis itself. For instance, you may hear that you have one of the following:

- ✔ **простуда** (prahs-*tooh*-duh) (*cold*)

- ✔ **ангина** (uhn-*gee*-nuh) (*sore throat*)

- ✔ **грипп** (greep) (*flu*)

- ✔ **бронхит** (brahn-*kheet*) (*bronchitis*)

- ✔ **инфекция** (een-*fyehk*-tsi-yeh) (*infection*)

- ✔ **пневмония** (pneev-mah-*nee*-yeh) (*pneumonia*)

- ✔ **сенная лихорадка** (*syeh*-nah-yeh lee-khah-*raht*-kuh) (*hay fever*)

- ✔ **растяжение связок** (ruhs-tee-*zheh*-nee-ee *svya*-zahk) (*sprain*)

Russian doctors aren't in the habit of explaining what they're doing, either during the examination or while prescribing treatment. If you want to know what's actually wrong with you, you may need to ask:

А что у меня? (ah shtoh ooh mee-*nya*?) (*What do I have?*)

If the doctor recommends that you go to the **ложиться в больницу** (lah-*zhit'*-syeh v bahl'-*nee*-tsooh) (*hospital*), you have a more serious condition. Maybe you have **аппендицит** (ah-peen-dee-*tsit*) (*appendicitis*), **перелом** (pee-ree-*lohm*) (*a broken bone*), or **пищевое отравление** (pee-shee-*voh*-ee aht-ruhv-*lyeh*-nee-ee) (*food poisoning*).

Don't panic if the doctor recommends that you go to the hospital; it doesn't necessarily mean that your condition is critical. Russians tend to go to the hospital more often and stay there longer than Americans generally do. For example, a new mother with a baby stays in the hospital for at least a week in Russia versus only 48 hours in the United States.

Your doctor may recommend that you **ходить на процедуры** (khah-*deet'* nuh prah-tsi-*dooh*-ri) (*take treatment*). This type of recommendation doesn't necessarily imply that you have to stay at the hospital; you may need to come to the hospital daily or several times a week for a certain type of treatment. In this case, the doctor gives you a **направление** (nuh-pruhv-*lyeh*-nee-ee) (*written treatment authorization*).

Visiting a pharmacy

In most cases, a doctor will **прописать лекарство** (prah-pee-*saht'* lee-*kahrst*-vah) (*prescribe medicine*) for you. The Russian word for *prescription* is **рецепт** (ree-*tsehpt*).

To get your **лекарство**, you need to go to the **аптека** (uhp-*tyeh*-kuh) (*pharmacy*). Unlike in the United States, a Russian pharmacy isn't usually part of a big department store; it's a separate little store where only medicine is sold. To get your **лекарство**, you simply hand your **рецепт** to the **аптекарь** (uhp-*tyeh*-kuhr') (*pharmacist*).

You can buy many drugs that require prescriptions in the United States as over-the-counter drugs in Russia. So, to save the time you might otherwise spend going to the doctor, you can just ask the pharmacist for what you need. For example, you may ask for **что-нибудь от простуды** (shtoh nee-*booht'* aht prahs-*tooh*-di) (*something for a cold*). Even if you don't have a prescription, chances are there will be something you can buy without one. For example, for a high fever you'll be offered dry raspberries, an excellent folk remedy that you can consume with hot tea.

Some common medicines include

- **нейтрализующее кислоту средство** (neey-truh-lee-*zooh*-yooh-shee-ee kees-lah-*tooh sryehts*-tvah) (*antacid*)
- **аспирин** (uhs-pee-*reen*) (*aspirin*)
- **капли от кашля** (*kahp*-lee aht *kahsh*-lyeh) (*cough drops*)
- **сироп от кашля** (see-*rohp* aht *kahsh*-lyeh) (*cough syrup*)
- **средство для снижения температуры** (*sryehts*-tvah dlya snee-*zhch*-ncc-yeh teem-pee-ruh-*tooh*-ri) (*fever reducer*)
- **болсутоляющее** (bah-lee-ooh-tah-*lya*-yooh-shee-ee) (*pain reliever*)
- **средство от изжоги** (*sryehts*-tvah aht eez-*zhoh*-gee) (*heartburn reliever*)

Calling the Police When You're the Victim of a Crime

In the difficult situation of becoming a victim of crime, you need to know where to turn for help and what to say to the people assisting you. In the following sections, you find out how to talk to the police about different crimes and answer their questions.

If the crime is serious, you should try to contact your embassy before contacting the police. A person at the embassy will advise you on what to do and help you through the difficult situation.

Talking to the police

You can contact the **полиция** (pah-*lee*-tsee-yeh) (*police*) by calling 02 (see the section "Making an emergency phone call" earlier in this chapter) or by going directly **в отделение полиции** (v aht-dee-*lyeh*-nee-ee pah-*lee*-tsee-ee) (*to the police station*). To find the nearest police station, you can ask a passerby:

> **Где ближайшее отделение полиции?** (gdyeh blee-*zhahy*-shi-ee aht-dee-*lyeh*-nee-ee pah-*lee*-tsi-ee?) (*Where is the nearest police station?*)

Here are some useful sentences you can use to describe different types of crime to the police:

> **Меня ограбили.** (mee-*nya* ah-*grah*-bee-lee.) (*I was robbed.*)
>
> **Меня обокрали.** (mee-*nya* ah-bah-*krah*-lee.) (*I became a victim of a theft.*)
>
> **На меня было совершено нападение.** (nuh mee-*nya* bi-lah sah-veer-shi-*noh* nuh-puh-*dyeh*-nee-ee.) (*I was attacked.*)
>
> **Мою квартиру обокрали.** (mah-*yooh* kvuhr-*tee*-rooh ah-bah-*krah*-lee.) (*My apartment was broken into.*)
>
> **Мою машину обокрали.** (mah-*yooh* muh-*shi*-nooh ah-bah-*krah*-lee.) (*My car was broken into*; Literally: *My car was robbed.*)

In order to report a specific item that's stolen from you, use the phrase **У меня украли . . .** (ooh mee-*nya* ooh-*krah*-lee . . .) (*They stole . . .*) plus the name of the item in the accusative case. (For more info on case endings, see Chapter 3.)

Answering questions from the police

When a crime is reported, the police want to gather more information about the **преступление** (prees-toohp-*lyeh*-nee-ee) (*crime*) and the **преступник** (prees-*toohp*-neek) (*criminal*).

When talking to the police and describing the incident, you may need to use the words **вор** (vohr) (*thief*), **карманник** (kuhr-*mah*-neek) (*pickpocket*), or **бандит** (buhn-*deet*) (*gangster*) to refer to the criminal.

The police may want to know the **время** (*vryeh*-myeh) (*time*) and **место** (*myehs*-tah) (*place*) of the **происшествие** (prah-ee-*shehst*-vee-ee) (*incident*). They may ask you to describe the **внешность** (*vnyehsh*-nahst') (*appearance*) of the criminal, and **куда он скрылся** (kooh-*dah* ohn *skril*-syeh) (*in what direction he escaped*). They may also ask whether he was **один** (ah-*deen*) (*alone*) or **с сообщниками** (s sah-*ohp*-shnee-kuh-mee) (*with accomplices*).

If you're physically assaulted or threatened with an **оружие** (ah-*rooh*-zhee-ee) (*weapon*), the police may ask

> **Чем вас ударили?** (chyehm vahs ooh-*dah*-ree-lee?) (*What were you hit with?*)

> **Чем вам угрожали?** (chyehm vahm oohg-rah-*zhah*-lee?) (*What were you threatened with?*)

To answer the preceding questions, use the noun in the instrumental case, because this case expresses the means or tool with which something is done: **ударили рукой** (ooh-*dah*-ree-lee rooh-*kohy*) (*hit with a hand*) or **угрожали пистолетом** (oohg-rah-*zhah*-lee pees-tah-*lyeh*-tahm) (*threatened with a gun*), for example. (For details on the instrumental case, see Chapter 3.)

After answering the questions, you may need to state the same information in a **заявление** (zuh-eev-*lyeh*-nee-ee) (*police report*).

Fun & Games

The following figure points out five major parts of the body. Match the body parts in English to their corresponding terms in Russian (see Appendix D for the answers).

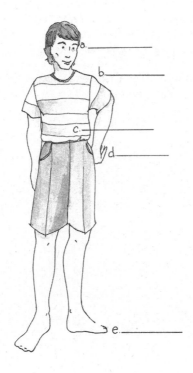

a. head   **рука**

b. shoulder   **живот**

c. stomach   **голова**

d. hand   **нога**

e. foot   **плечо**

Part IV
The Part of Tens

The 5th Wave
By Rich Tennant

"I've learned a lot of common American phrases in Russian, like 'Bon voyage,' 'Hasta la vista,' and 'Gesundheit.'"

In this part . . .

Part IV gives you short but valuable lists of practical
information. To help you pick up Russian, we give
you ten tried-and-true tips that have worked for many
others, including one of the authors of this book. We warn
you about ten things you never want to say in Russian.
We tell you ten favorite Russian expressions that are sure
to warm the heart of any Russian you say them to. And
finally, we give you ten Russian phrases that are bound to
win you "native speaker" points. If you follow the sugges-
tions in this part, you're sure to win the minds and hearts
of most Russians you meet!

Chapter 19

Ten Ways to Pick Up Russian Quickly

In This Chapter

▶ Engaging in activities that will advance your Russian

▶ Practicing Russian in the right places

We're not breaking any news to you by saying that the best way to learn a language is to use it. You have a much better chance of remembering **Как дела?** (kahk dee-*lah*?) (*How are you?*) after you say it to a Russian and actually hear **Нормально!** (nahr-*mahl'*-nah!) (*Fine!*) in response than you have of remembering this expression just by reading about it in Chapter 4. Actually speaking a language makes you feel that your skills are more advanced.

Coming up with new and fun ways to practice your Russian isn't always easy, though. That's why we give you some ideas in this chapter for creative ways to bring Russian into your life. Try them and feel free to come up with your own! After all, your life can contain only as much Russian as you let into it.

Check Out Russian TV, Movies, and Music

Whether you're into independent cinema or action movies, classical ballet or rock music, Russians have something to offer every taste. Browse the foreign section of an online DVD rental service and the world music shelf of your local library to find something with which to practice your Russian. As far as movies go, be sure to get a Russian-language version with subtitles rather than a dubbed one. And plenty of Russian-language TV channels exist in America — your cable service may even come with one!

Listen to Russian Radio Programs

You can advance your Russian without sitting down and giving it your undivided attention — just listen to a Russian radio program in the car, during a walk, or while doing the dishes (such programs are usually available on satellite radio). Who knows how much of that new vocabulary will get stuck in your subconscious?

A variety of Russian radio stations broadcast on the Internet. For a comprehensive guide to Russian radio online, go to www.multilingualbooks.com/online-radio-russian.html.

Read Russian Publications

Seeing a phrase in a phrase book, even if it's your favorite *Russian For Dummies,* is one thing. Seeing a phrase in a real Russian newspaper and actually recognizing it is a totally different experience.

Pick up copies of Russian publications, which are available in many libraries. Russian immigrant establishments, such as law offices and stores, often have local Russian-language newspapers lying around; the bonus of reading those papers is finding out what's going on locally with Russian social and cultural life. Reading such publications also is a good way to practice recognizing and "decoding" Cyrillic.

Surf the Internet

Because the Internet exists, no one can complain about a lack of ways to practice Russian. Just remember that Russian websites end in "ru." You may want to start your exploitation from some of these websites:

- gazeta.ru
- lenta.ru
- list.mail.ru/index.html
- menu.ru
- www.piter.ru
- www.theatre.ru/emain.html

And on blogs.mail.ru, you can read **блоги** (*bloh*-gee) (*blogs*) in Russian or even create your own.

Sometimes, Russian characters don't show properly on the Internet. If, instead of Cyrillic, you see a bunch of characters that look like $$##%%&&, change the encoding to Cyrillic. To do that, click on View → Encoding in your browser's toolbar, and try different Cyrillic encodings until you find the one that works.

Visit a Russian Restaurant

Most major American cities have at least one Russian restaurant. You may get more out of your visit than just a bowl of steaming **борщ** (bohrsh') and a plate of aromatic **голубцы** (gah-loohp-*tsi*) (*rice and ground beef rolled in cabbage leaves*). Be ambitious, and talk to the staff exclusively in Russian. You may be pleasantly surprised by how supportive Russians can be when people try to speak their language. And who knows, your language skills may even get you a bargain! See Chapter 9 for details on visiting a restaurant.

Find a Russian Pen Pal

If you strike a personal connection with someone in a Russian chat room, you may get the chance to not only practice your Russian but also find an interesting interlocutor, and even a good friend. Some Russian **чаты** (*chah*-ti) (*chat rooms*) to go to are my.mail.ru/corp/chat/, www.divan.ru, and www.games.ru/chat. You may even want to open your own Russian e-mail account to exchange messages with your new friend; good places to do so are mail.ru and www.rambler.ru.

If you want to type in Russian but don't have a Russian keyboard, you can either put stickers with Russian letters on your regular English keyboard or use an online Russian keyboard, such as the one at keyboard.yandex.ru. Another option is to go to www.translit.ru. Today, all word processing software comes with Russian fonts, and you can choose a configuration that corresponds very closely to the English keyboard.

Teach English to a Russian Immigrant

Because learning is a mutual experience, teaching English to a Russian speaker may be a great way to advance your Russian. If you don't know anybody from the local Russian community, you can post an ad in a Russian store or restaurant. Writing that ad can be your first Russian exercise!

Seek out a Russian establishment; then you can just ask people who work there about other Russian restaurants and stores. Make sure to explain that the reason you're looking for them is to practice your language skills.

Russians will be flattered by your interest in their culture and will happily share the information with you. You may even make some friends right there.

Visit a Jewish Community Center

A number of Jewish immigrants came to America throughout the 20th century and into the 21st century; many of them came from the former Soviet Union, where Russian was their native language. For many of them — especially the older generations — the Russian language is a part of their cultural heritage, and some events at a Jewish community center may be held in Russian.

You can find a Jewish community center through the Internet or in the phone book. Pay a visit there; you'll find out whether you can attend any Russian-language events. If you're willing to donate your time, offer to volunteer. Elderly immigrants may appreciate some help from someone who speaks English, and it's a great opportunity for you to practice your Russian.

Travel to Russia

Nothing beats traveling to the country of your interest. Whether you're going to Russia for a year of teaching English to Moscow high school students, a week of sightseeing, or a walk through the streets of St. Petersburg while your cruise ship is waiting in the port, no place makes practicing Russian easier than, well, Russia. See Chapter 14 for details on planning a trip.

Marry a Russian!

If you're really set on the idea of speaking Russian like a native, you gotta do what you gotta do. Marry (or at least date) a Russian, and convince him or her to teach you the language. Of course, we're being a little tongue-in-cheek. We don't advocate that you go out and find yourself a Russian spouse just to improve your language skills. But if you do decide to date or marry a Russian, you should know that you have a great opportunity to dramatically improve your Russian. So take advantage of it! Watch out, though: Russians assimilate quickly, and you may end up spending much more time teaching English than being taught Russian. Then you'll have to resort to the secret weapon: learning Russian from your mother-in-law!

Chapter 20

Ten Things Never to Say in Russian

Sometimes, knowing what *not* to do ... ...g what to do if you want to fit in or ... to find out about ten things you

Us... ...ou"

... ...u have to be extremely careful ... ...). To be on the safe side, ..., older than 14 years ... ...y saying

... ...ты *with me.*)

... ...tion is

... ...*dress you with* ты?)

... ...addressing somebody.

... ...Russian speech ethics. It even ... ...e beginning of a new friendship. ... ...nversation in which you and ... ..., he or she suddenly interrupts

... ...*et's switch to* ты!)

Barnes & Noble Booksellers #2554
960 S Colorado Blvd
Glendale, CO 80246
303-691-2998

...554 REG:001 TRN:8670 CSHR:Lena T

...ian For Dummies
...781118127698   T1
...1 @ 24.99)   24.99

...ubtotal   24.99
Sales Tax T1 (8.000%)   2.00
TOTAL   26.99
VISA DEBIT   26.99
  Card#: XXXXXXXXXXXX2034

  Application Label: US DEBIT
  AID: a0000000980840
  PIN Verified
  TVR: 8080048000
  TSI: 6800

A MEMBER WOULD HAVE SAVED   2.50

Thanks for shopping at
Barnes & Noble

101.42A   01/16/2017 02:39PM

CUSTOMER COPY

You should interpret this suggestion as "Let's become pals." Heaven forbid you should say "no"! That would put an end to your friendly relationship. Say **Давайте!** (duh-*vahy*-tee!) (*Let's do it!*, used with **вы**) or even **Давай!** (duh-*vahy*!) (*Let's do it!*, used with **ты**) to indicate that you are more than happy to abandon this formality.

A curious tradition is associated with the phrase **Давай на ты!** (duh-*vahy* nuh ti!) (*Let's switch to ты!*). It's called drinking Brudershaft. If you happen to know German, you may recognize the word *Brudershaft,* which means "brotherhood." People follow this tradition quite often when, well, they drink (alcoholic beverages) together. Usually one of the two, already sufficiently inebriated, suggests:

> **Давай выпьем на брудершафт!** (duh-*vahy* vi-p'eem nuh brooh-dehr-shahft!) (*Let's drink for Brudershaft!*)

This means that you're invited to pour drinks (again!), and link arms while drinking them to the bottom, after which you have to kiss two times. From that point on, you and your co-drinker can use **ты** when addressing each other. Oh, those Russians!

Don't Rush to Say "Hi!"

The Russian word for the informal English greeting *Hi* is **Привет** (pree-*vyeht*). Yes, we have to admit it is much shorter and easier to pronounce than the bulky, almost endless words **Здравствуйте** (*zdrah*-stvoohy-tee) (*Hello*, used with the formal you, **вы**) or **Здравствуй** (*zdrah*-stvoohy; *Hello* used with **ты**). But please do not rush to use it, especially in a formal situation or with people you do not know very well or people who are considerably older than yourself. It is inconceivable, for example, for a university student to use **Привет!** when greeting a professor. Likewise, professors can't use it with their students: Any official situation prohibits using it, unlike the widely used English *Hi.*

Don't Switch to First Names Prematurely

Russian full names consist of three distinct parts: a first name, a patronymic, and a last name. A *patronymic* is the name of a person's father — slightly transformed — and it's different for men and women. For example, if a woman's name is **Ирина** (ee-*ree*-nuh) (*Irene*) and her father's name is **Иван** (ee-*vahn*) (*Ivan*), her full name is **Ирина Ивановна** (ee-*ree*-nuh ee-*vah*-nahv-nuh). If her brother's name is **Алексей** (uh-leek-*syehy*) (*Alexi*), his full name is **Алексей Иванович** (uh-leek-*syehy* ee-*vah*-nah-veech).

Chapter 20

Ten Things Never to Say in Russian

In This Chapter

▶ Avoiding embarrassment when addressing and greeting people

▶ Taking care with certain words and phrases

*E*very culture has its do's and don'ts. Sometimes, knowing what *not* to do is even more important than knowing what to do if you want to fit in or at least make a good impression. Read on to find out about ten things you should never say in Russian.

Use the Right Form of "You"

If you've read Chapter 4, you know that you have to be extremely careful about using the familiar form of address **ты** (ti) (*you*). To be on the safe side, use the formal **вы** (vi) (*you*) with anybody who is, say, older than 14 years old. You can let someone know to use **ты** with you by saying

Можно на ты. (*mohzh*-nah nuh ti.) (*You can use* **ты** *with me.*)

The same phrase used with an interrogative intonation is

Можно на ты? (*mohzh*-nah nuh ti?) (*Can I address you with* **ты**?)

You can use it to ask whether you can use **ты** in addressing somebody.

 The **ты/вы** threshold is extremely important in Russian speech ethics. It even has a somewhat symbolic meaning signifying the beginning of a new friendship. So don't be surprised if in the middle of the conversation in which you and your conversational partner have been using **вы**, he or she suddenly interrupts it by saying

Давайте на ты! (duh-*vahy*-tee nuh ti!) (*Let's switch to* **ты**!)

You should interpret this suggestion as "Let's become pals." Heaven forbid you should say "no"! That would put an end to your friendly relationship. Say Давайте! (duh-*vahy*-tee!) (*Let's do it!*, used with вы) or even Давай! (duh-*vahy*!) (*Let's do it!*, used with ты) to indicate that you are more than happy to abandon this formality.

A curious tradition is associated with the phrase Давай на ты! (duh-*vahy* nuh ti!) (*Let's switch to* ты!). It's called drinking Brudershaft. If you happen to know German, you may recognize the word *Brudershaft,* which means "brotherhood." People follow this tradition quite often when, well, they drink (alcoholic beverages) together. Usually one of the two, already sufficiently inebriated, suggests:

> Давай выпьем на брудершафт! (duh-*vahy vi*-p'eem nuh brooh-dehr-shahft!) (*Let's drink for Brudershaft!*)

This means that you're invited to pour drinks (again!), and link arms while drinking them to the bottom, after which you have to kiss two times. From that point on, you and your co-drinker can use ты when addressing each other. Oh, those Russians!

Don't Rush to Say "Hi!"

The Russian word for the informal English greeting *Hi* is Привет (pree-*vyeht*). Yes, we have to admit it is much shorter and easier to pronounce than the bulky, almost endless words Здравствуйте (*zdrah*-stvoohy-tee) (*Hello*, used with the formal you, вы) or Здравствуй (*zdrah*-stvoohy; *Hello* used with ты). But please do not rush to use it, especially in a formal situation or with people you do not know very well or people who are considerably older than yourself. It is inconceivable, for example, for a university student to use Привет! when greeting a professor. Likewise, professors can't use it with their students: Any official situation prohibits using it, unlike the widely used English *Hi*.

Don't Switch to First Names Prematurely

Russian full names consist of three distinct parts: a first name, a patronymic, and a last name. A *patronymic* is the name of a person's father — slightly transformed — and it's different for men and women. For example, if a woman's name is Ирина (ee-*ree*-nuh) (*Irene*) and her father's name is Иван (ee-*vahn*) (*Ivan*), her full name is Ирина Ивановна (ee-*ree*-nuh ee-*vah*-nahv-nuh). If her brother's name is Алексей (uh-leek-*syehy*) (*Alexi*), his full name is Алексей Иванович (uh-leek-*syehy* ee-*vah*-nah-veech).

If **Алексей Иванович** happens to be your co-worker, business partner, or just an acquaintance, don't address him with just **Алексей** unless he encourages you to start doing so. He'll say something like

> **Зовите меня просто Алексей.** (zah-*vee*-tee mee-*nyah prohs*-tah uh-leek-*syehy*.) (*Call me just Alexi*.)

Flip to Chapter 4 for more details about using Russian names.

Use "How Are You?" with Caution

Russians do say **Как дела?** (kahk dee-*lah*?) (*How are you?*), but the truth is they don't use it as often as Americans. And this is why: Americans use "How are you?" mostly as a formulaic greeting. Not so in Russian. In Russian, when people ask how you are, they indeed want to know, and they expect a sincere account of how things are going for you. When they hear the question, they believe that the same sort of account is expected from them. So, reserve the question for situations in which you are indeed prepared to spend a while listening to what is happening in your Russian friend's life. (See Chapter 4 for more about this greeting.)

When Russians ask **Как дела?**, they're in fact using an abbreviated version of the phrase **Как у вас дела?** (Kahk ooh vahs dee-*lah*?) (*How are things with you?*) To politely respond to this question with your own question, you need to use the same grammatical structure. The proper way to answer is with **А у вас?** (uh ooh vahs?) (Literally: *And with you?*) rather than **А вы?** (uh vi) (Literally: *And you?*).

Respond to "How Are You?" in a Culturally Appropriate Manner

When responding to "How are you?" Americans tend to say things like "great," "fantastic," or "pretty good," even when it's not exactly true. Unlike optimistic Americans, though, Russians see life as an endless flow of misfortunes and problems. Russians tend to be considerably more reserved or honest, if you will, and usually say **Ничего** (nee-chee-*voh*) (*So-so*). Overusing **очень хорошо** (*oh*-cheen' khah-rah-*shoh*) (*very good*) or **прекрасно** (pree-*krahs*-nah) (*excellent*) may be misunderstood and even make Russians suspicious or jealous, causing them to wonder, "Why is this guy always happy?"

Choose the Right Form of "Happy"

The Russian word for *happy* is **счастлив** (*schahst*-leef) or **счастлива** (*schahst*-lee-vuh), and these words indicate feelings equal to exaltation. In Russian mentality, the sentiment is appropriate only for life events such as weddings, falling in love, the birth of a child, and so on. The more appropriate Russian word for *happy* to use in more mundane situations is **рад/рада** (rahd/*rah*-duh). For example, you can say

> **Я был/была рад/рада с вами познакомиться** (ya bil/bi-*lah* rahd/*rah*-duh s *vah*-mee pah-znuh-*koh*-meet'-syeh) (*I was happy to meet you*).

Use the first set of words if you're a man and the second set of words if you're a woman.

Watch Out When You Talk about Studying

The verb *to study* has two Russian equivalents: **изучать** (ee-zoh-*chaht'*) and **учиться** (ooh-*cheet'*-syeh):

- ✔ If the verb *to study* has a direct object, as in *I study Russian*, use the verb **изучать**: Я изучаю русский язык (ya ee-zoh-*chah*-yooh *roohs*-keey ee-*zik*).

- ✔ If the verb *to study* is used in a construction describing where you study, use the verb **учиться**: Я учусь в университете. (ya ooh-*choohs'* v ooh-nee-veer-see-*tyeh*-tee) (*I study at the university*).

Accent a Certain Verb Carefully

There are two verbs in Russian that have exactly the same spelling in their infinitive forms. The verb is **писать.** Stressing this verb on the second syllable (pee-*saht'*) means *to write,* but stressing it on the first syllable (*pee*-suht') means something completely different: *to urinate!* So be careful!

Know the Difference between a Bathroom and a Restroom

A very common mistake made by beginning Russian speakers is to ask **Где ванная?** (Gdyeh *vah*-nuh-yeh?) (*Where is the bathroom?*) when looking for a restroom or toilet. The fact is that in many Russian homes, the bathroom and the restroom/toilet are located in two different places. The Russian philosophy of life claims that it's not hygienic to wash up and, well, perform other bodily functions in the same room. So, we recommend that you use two different phrases to make perfectly clear what your intentions are:

> **Где можно помыть руки?** (Gdyeh *mohzh*-nah pah-*mit'* rooh-kee?) (*Where can I wash my hands?*)

> **Где туалет?** (Gdyeh tooh-uh-*lyeht*?) (*Where is the restroom?*; Literally: *Where is the toilet?*)

Don't Toast with the Wrong Phrase

People who don't speak Russian usually think that they know one Russian phrase: a toast, **На здоровье!** Little do they know that **На здоровье!** (nuh zdah-*rohv'*-ee!) (*For health!*) is what Russians say when somebody thanks them for a meal. In Polish, indeed, **На здоровье** (or something close to it) is a traditional toast. Russians, on the other hand, like to make up something long and complex, such as **За дружбу между народами!** (zah *droohzh*-booh *myehzh*-dooh nuh-*roh*-duh-mee!) (*To friendship between nations!*)

If you want a simpler Russian toast, go with **За вас!** (zuh vahs!) (*To you!*)

Chapter 21

Ten Favorite Russian Expressions

In This Chapter

▶ Exploring phrases beyond their dictionary definitions

▶ Discovering the most popular Russian quotes and proverbs

Every culture has a way of taking familiar words and turning them into something else. The most diligent student can flip through his dictionary and, based on the literal translation, still have no idea what an expression means or why everybody is laughing. This chapter brings together ten words and expressions that Russians use a lot, and whose meanings aren't always intuitive. Recognizing these expressions in speech and using them with ease can make you sound really Russian!

Proverbs represent a large part of the Russian language. You can find whole dictionaries devoted to Russian proverbs. We strongly encourage everyone interested in Russian language to study them.

Showing Strong Feelings

To express surprise, dismay, admiration, gratitude, or even pain — pretty much any strong feeling — Russians say **Ой!** (ohy!) Use **Ой!** when in English you would say "oops," "ouch," or "wow," or make a facial expression. You can confidently use **Ой!** in any of the following sentences:

> **Ой, как красиво!** (ohy, kahk kruh-*see*-vah!) (*Wow, how beautiful!*)

> **Ой, спасибо!** (ohy, spuh-*see*-bah!) (*Thank you so much!*)

> **Ой, кто это?** (ohy, ktoh *eh*-tah?) (*Who in the world is this?*)

> **Ой, как приятно слышать твой голос!** (ohy, kahk pree-*yat*-nah *sli*-shuht' tvohy *goh*-lahs!) (*Oh, it's so nice to hear your voice!*)

Russians consider **Ой!** a more feminine exclamation; men, on the other hand, are supposed to grind their teeth and keep their emotions to themselves.

Using "Give" in Various Situations

If you look up **давай** (duh-*vahy*) in the dictionary, you find the translation *give*. Russians, however, use the word in all kinds of situations. It's a popular way to suggest doing something, as in **Давай пойдём в кино** (duh-*vahy* pahy-*dyohm* f kee-*noh*) (*Let's go to the movies*), and to answer *Sure, let's do it!* (**Давай!**) Used by itself, **давай** means *bye, take care*.

Starting a Story

Although the verb **представьте** (preed-*stahf'*-tee) can mean *imagine*, *picture*, or even *introduce*, **представьте себе** (preed-*stahf'*-tee see-*byeh*) means *Can you believe it?* or *Imagine that!* It's a good way to begin telling a story or to open a conversation on a subject you feel strongly about.

Taking "Listen!" to the Next Level

Although the literal translation of **Послушайте!** (pahs-*looh*-shuhy-tee!) is *Listen!*, this translation doesn't do the expression justice. Saying "Listen!" in English sounds pushy and aggressive; in Russian, **Послушайте!** is a good and nice way to attract attention to your arguments. Here are some examples:

> **Послушайте, давайте пойдём на прогулку!** (pahs-*looh*-shuhy-tee, duh-*vahy*-tee pahy-*dyohm* nuh prah-*goohl*-kooh!) (*You know what? Let's go for a walk!* Literally: *Listen, let's go for a walk!*)

> **Послушайте, но это прекрасный фильм!** (pahs-*looh*-shuhy-tee, noh *eh*-tah preek-*rahs*-niy feel'm!) (*But it's a wonderful movie!* Literally: *Listen, but it's a wonderful movie!*)

A less formal variant of the same expression is **Послушай!** (pahs-*looh*-shuhy!). You can use it with someone you're on familiar terms with, someone you normally say **Ты** (ti) (*you; informal*) to; see Chapter 4 for details on the informal "you." And if you want to be even more informal, you can use the conversational variant **Слушай!** (*slooh*-shuhy!) Just make sure the person you say it to is a good friend who will take this informality the right way. Otherwise, stick to **Послушай!**

Describing Amazement about Food

You may be at a loss to describe the grand abundance of Russian dinner parties and holiday tables. This expression, then, is useful: **пир горой** (peer gah-*rohy*) (Literally: *feast with food piled up like a mountain*). If you're hungry for more food info, check out Chapters 5 and 9.

Insisting that the Good Times Continue

The following phrase is a quote from one of Russia's most beloved comedies, **"Иван Васильевич меняет профессию"** (ee-*vahn* vah-*seel'*-ee-veech mee-*nya*-eet prah-*fyeh*-see-yooh) (*Ivan Vasil'yevich Changes His Occupation*) and is sure to make any Russian smile. Say **Я требую продолжения банкета!** (ya *tryeh*-booh-yooh prah-dahl-*zheh*-nee-yeh buhn-*kyeh*-tuh!) (Literally: *I insist on the continuation of the banquet!*) when a party or a trip is going well, when somebody invites you to come over again, or when you suggest doing some fun activity yet another time.

"Иван Васильевич меняет профессию" is an old Russian movie about a bland accountant, Ivan Vasil'yevich, who switches places with Tsar Ivan the Terrible with the help of a time machine invented by his neighbor. Confused, at first, to find himself in the position of Russia's 16th-century tsar (who turns out to be his identical twin), Ivan Vasil'yevich quickly takes to the tsar's lifestyle. Sitting in an ornate banquet hall of the old Kremlin, at the head of a huge table with endless delicacies, and watching a performance of his court dancers, Ivan Vasil'yevich, drunk from the rare wines and the attention of the beautiful tsarina, raises a precious goblet and exclaims, **Я требую продолжения банкета!**

Noting the Benefit of Silence

Russians love proverbs and use them a lot. **Слово-серебро, а молчание золото** (*sloh*-vah see-reeb-*roh*, uh mahl-*chah*-nee-ee *zoh*-lah-tah) (*A word is silver, but silence is gold*) can be loosely translated as *Speaking is nice, but silence is supreme.* This phrase is nice to say after you make a mistake speaking Russian or when you, or somebody else, says something that would have been better off left unsaid.

Saying that Two Heads Are Better Than One

Одна голова хорошо, а две лучше (ahd-*nah* gah-lah-*vah* khah-rah-*shoh*, ah dvyeh *loohch*-shi) (*one head is good, but two heads are better*) doesn't refer to science fiction mutants. Rather, it's a manifestation of the international belief that two heads are better than one. You can say this phrase when you invite somebody to do something together or when you ask for, or offer, help or advice.

Expressing that a Friend in Need Is a Friend Indeed

Друг познаётся в беде (droohk pahz-nuh-*yoht*-syeh v bee-*dyeh*) (*A friend is tested by hardship*) is the Russian equivalent of the saying, "A friend in need is a friend indeed."

Russians take friendship seriously. Their definition of a friend is not just a person you know (as in, "This is my new friend . . . what's your name again?"). Such a person would be called a **знакомый** (znuh-*koh*-miy) (*acquaintance*). A **друг** (droohk) (*friend*), on the other hand, is someone who cares for you. And the best way to find out whether a certain person is a friend or just an acquaintance is to see how they behave when things aren't going so great.

Understanding the Importance of Old Friends

Старый друг лучше новых двух (*stah*-riy droohk *loohch*-shi *noh*-vikh dvoohkh) (*An old friend is better than two new ones*) is another speculation on the theme of friendship. An old friend (not referring to age) is better because he or she has already been tested, possibly by hardships, as mentioned in the preceding section. New friends, on the other hand, are dark horses; when a bad moment strikes, they may turn out to be just acquaintances.

Chapter 22

Ten Phrases That Make You Sound Fluent in Russian

In This Chapter

▶ Finding out what to say to really fit in with Russians

▶ Discovering traditions that help you understand Russians better

Some phrases aren't really important in a conversation. They don't really mean anything, and you can get your point across without using them. Not coincidentally, these phrases also make native speakers hit you approvingly on the back and say, "Yeah, buddy, you're one of us." A book doesn't teach you these phrases — unless the book is *Russian For Dummies,* 2nd Edition. In this chapter, you find insider information on ten phrases that make you sound fluent in Russian.

Showing Off Your Excellent Manners

Oh, dear Old World! Russians still believe in opening doors for each other and letting others go first. If you want to be especially polite, absolutely refuse to go through a door if somebody else is aiming for it. Instead of just walking through and getting it over with, stand by the door for 15 minutes repeating **Только после вас!** (*tohl'*-kah *pohs*-lee vahs!) (*Only after you!*) while your counterpart stands by the other side of the door repeating the same phrase. It may be time consuming, but it's very rewarding in the long run; you'll be recognized as a well-bred and very nice individual.

Paying a Compliment

Russians, for some reason, don't believe that giving compliments is considered sexual harassment. So, if you start a conversation with a Russian woman by saying **Вы сегодня прекрасно выглядите!** (vi see-*vohd*-nyeh pree-*krahs*-nah *vig*-lee-dee-tee!) (*You look great today!*), she may actually treat you nicer instead of reporting you to the authorities. It's hard to believe, but this exact phrase is considered appropriate with colleagues, shop assistants, and hotel receptionists.

If someone says **Вы сегодня прекрасно выглядите!** to you, the appropriate response isn't **спасибо** (spuh-*see*-bah) (*thank you*); you should say **Ну, что вы!** (noo, shtoh vi!) (*Ah, what are you talking about!*). You have to show your modesty and disagree.

Inviting Someone Over for Tea

Making a Russian friend is very easy. When you meet someone (and if you like this person enough to want to be his or her friend), don't think too hard about finding a way to create a social connection. Just say

> **Заходите на чай!** (zuh-khah-*dee*-tee nuh chahy!) (*Stop by for some tea!*)

The person won't think you're a freak or a serial killer; he or she will most likely take your offer at face value. Keep in mind, though, that unlike "Let's do lunch," Russians take **Заходите на чай** seriously and usually accept your offer. That being said, you should actually have some tea and cookies at home, because **Заходите на чай!** implies drinking tea and conversing, unlike the American version: "Would you like to stop by my place for a drink?"

Saying "Help Yourself"

When you invite a new friend over for tea and whip out your strategically prepared box of cookies, a nice thing to say is

> **Угощайтесь!** (ooh-gah-*sh'ahy*-tees'!) (*Help yourself!* Literally: *Treat yourself!*)

Besides being friendly and polite, this word is just long enough to scare off foreigners. Which is, of course, a good enough reason to learn it and stand out in the crowd.

Wishing "Bon Appétit!"

Unless you want to strike people as a gloomy, misanthropic sociopath, don't start eating without wishing others **Приятного аппетита!** (pree-*yat*-nah-vah uh-pee-*tee*-tuh!) (*Bon appétit!*) Don't hesitate to say this phrase to people you don't know and are seeing for the first time in your life after your waiter sits them down at your table in an overcrowded restaurant.

Embracing the Tradition of Sitting Down Before Leaving

Before departing on a trip, surprise everybody by looking around thoughtfully and saying

> **Сядем на дорожку!** (*sya*-deem nuh dah-*rohsh*-kooh!) (*Let's sit down before hitting the road!*)

Essentially a superstition, this tradition is actually useful; sitting down and staying silent for a minute before you head out the door gives you an opportunity to remember what's important. Maybe your packed lunch is still in the fridge, and your plane tickets with a sticker that proclaims "Don't forget!" are still on your bedside table!

Offering Hospitality

Sitting down is a big deal for Russians, which is, of course, understandable: With those vast lands, they must have had to walk a lot (especially before the invention of trains). That's why when you're sitting with somebody standing before you, or when somebody stops by and hangs out in the doorway, claiming to be leaving in a minute, you can say

> **Садись, в ногах правды нет** (suh-*dees'*, v nah-*gahkh prahv*-di nyeht) (*Sit down, there is no truth in feet.*)

This phrase doesn't make much sense in English. And Russians most likely don't believe that more truth exists in other parts of the body than in the feet. The phrase, however, is a nice hospitality token, and it definitely wins you some "native speaker" points.

Wishing Good Luck

Although English has its own cute little "Break a leg" phrase, the expression is rarely used. Russians, on the other hand, never let anyone depart on a mission — whether a lady leaves to interview for a job or a guy goes to ask a girl out — without saying **Ни пуха, ни пера!** (nee *pooh*-khuh, nee pee-*rah!*) (*Good luck! Literally: Have neither fluff nor plume!*)

The appropriate response isn't **спасибо** (spuh-*see*-bah) (*thank you*); you should say **К чёрту!** (k *chyohr*-tooh!) (*To the devil!*) We have no clear explanation for where this response came from. The **чёрт** (chyohrt) (*petty devil*) part of the phrase represents a very popular character in Russian folklore. He's mentioned in a variety of expressions, such as **у чёрта на куличках** (ooh *chyohr*-tuh nuh kooh-*leech*-kuhkh) (*far away;* Literally: *at the devil's Easter celebration*) or **чёртова дюжина** (*chyohr*-tah-vuh *dyooh*-zhi-nuh) (*number 13;* Literally: *devil's dozen*). The most common way **чёрт** appears is in this phrase:

> **Иди к чёрту!** (ee-*dee* k *chyohr*-tooh!) (*Go to the devil!*)

As you can tell, **К чёрту!** sounds suspiciously close to an insult and is generally considered offensive. Responding to **Ни пуха, ни пера!** in this manner, however, is a precious opportunity to send to the devil someone you always wanted to get rid of but were afraid to. Just be sure to smile while responding!

Signing Off with Kisses

Russians sign their letters, e-mails, and cellphone text messages with **Целую** (tseh-*looh*-yooh) (*love;* Literally: *I kiss you*). You can also say **Целую** at the end of a phone conversation. We don't recommend saying it in person, though: If you're face to face with someone, you may as well kiss the person instead of talking about it!

Russians are known for kissing socially. Like folks in France, Russians kiss on the cheek; unlike folks in France, Russians do it three times (because three, much like seven, is a lucky number). Social kissing is such an accepted practice in Russia that one Soviet leader caused a considerable international scandal when he wholeheartedly kissed a Western leader. Doesn't sound too scandalous? Well, being old and clumsy, the Soviet leader missed the cheek and kissed his counterpart on the mouth!

Offering Unusual Congratulations

Here's a weird one: When Russians see someone who just came out of a shower, a sauna, or any place where you can supposedly clean yourself, they say **С лёгким паром!** (s *lyohkh*-keem pah-ruhm!) (Literally: *Congratulations on a light steam!*) This phrase is very popular, especially after it became the title of the token Russian New Year's night movie **"Ирония судьбы, или с лёгким паром!"** (ee-*roh*-nee-yeh soohd'-bi, *ee*-lee s *lyohkh*-keem *pah*-ruhm!) (*The Irony of Fate, or Congratulations on a Light Steam!*) This romantic comedy, shown by pretty much every Russian television channel on December 31, starts in a Russian **баня** (*bah*-nyeh) (*steam bath*), which triggers all the adventures that follow.

You can use **С лёгким паром!** humorously: Say it to someone who got caught in the rain or someone who spilled a drink. Yes, it sounds mean, but Russians have a dark sense of humor.

Part V
Appendixes

" ...and remember, no more Russian tongue twisters until you know the language better."

In this part . . .

The appendixes in Part V give you easy-to-use Russian reference sources. We provide you with a mini-dictionary with some of the words you use most often. We include a sample list of commonly used regular and irregular Russian verbs with their conjugations. We list the audio tracks of real-world conversations of native Russian speakers so you can read along and practice. And finally, we give you an answer key to all the Fun & Games sections that appear at the end of the chapters in this book.

Russian-English Mini-Dictionary

А

а (ah): and

август (*ahv*-goohst) m: August

автобус (uhf-*toh*-boohs) m: bus

адрес (*ahd*-rees) m: address

апрель (uhp-*ryehl'*) m: April

аптека (uhp-*tyeh*-kuh) f: drugstore, pharmacy

аэропорт (uh-eh-rah-*pohrt*) m: airport

Б

бабушка (*bah*-boohsh-kuh) f: grandmother

багаж (buh-*gahsh*) m: baggage, luggage

балет (buh-*lyeht*) m: ballet

банк (bahnk) m: bank

бедный (*byehd*-niy): poor

бежать/бегать (bee-*zhaht'*/*byeh*-guht'): to run

белый (*byeh*-liy): white

бензин (been-*zeen*) m: gas

билет (bee-*lyeht*) m: ticket

блин (bleen) m: pancake

богатый (bah-*gah*-tiy): rich

болен (*boh*-leen): ill

больница (bahl'-*nee*-tsuh) f: hospital

большой (bahl'-*shohy*): big

брат (braht) m: brother

брать/взять (braht'/vzyat'): to take

брюки (*bryooh*-kee): pants

бумага (booh-*mah*-guh) f: paper

бутылка (booh-*til*-kuh) f: bottle

быстрый (*bis*-triy): quick

быть (bit'): to be

В

в (v): at, in

важный (*vahzh*-niy): important

ванная (*vahn*-nuh-yeh) f: bathroom

валюта (vuh-*lyooh*-tuh) f: currency

ваш (vahsh): your

великий (vee-*lee*-keey): great

весна (vees-*nah*) f: spring

вечер (*vyeh*-cheer) m: evening

вечеринка (vee-chee-*reen*-kuh) f: party

вещь (vyehsh'): f: thing

видеть/увидеть (*vee*-deet'/ooh-*vee*-deet'): to see

виза (*vee*-zuh) f: visa

вилка (*veel*-kuh) f: fork

вино (vee-*noh*) n: wine

вместе (*vmyehs*-tee): together

внук (vnoohk) m: grandson

внучка (*vnoohch*-kuh) f: granddaughter

восемь (*voh*-seem'): eight

вода (vah-*dah*) f: water

водить/вести машину (vah-*deet'*/vees-*tee* muh-*shi*-nooh): to drive

вокзал (vahk-*zahl*) m: station

волосы (*voh*-lah-si) pl: hair

вопрос (vahp-*rohs*) m: question

воскресенье (vahs-kree-*syehn'*-ee) n: Sunday

восток (vahs-*tohk*) m: east

врач (vrahch) m: doctor

время (*vryeh*-myeh) n: time

все (fsyeh): everybody

всегда (vseeg-*dah*): always

всё (fsyoh): everything

встреча (fstryeh-chuh) f: meeting

вторник (*ftohr*-neek) m: Tuesday

второй (ftah-*rohy*): second (adj)

вход (vkhoht) m: entrance

входить/войти (vkhah-*deet'*/vahy-*tee*): to enter

вчера (fchee-*rah*): yesterday

вы (vi): you (formal singular or plural)

выход (*vi*-khaht) m: exit

высокий (vi-*soh*-keey): high, tall

Г

газета (guh-*zyeh*-tuh) f: newspaper

галерея (guh-lee-*ryeh*-yeh) f: gallery

галстук (*gahls*-toohk) m: tie

гараж (guh-*rahzh*) m: garage

где (gdyeh): where

гид (geet) m: guide

главный (*glahv*-niy): main

глаз (glahs) m: eye

говорить/сказать (gah-vah-*reet'*/skuh-*zaht'*): to say, to speak

говядина (gah-*vya*-dee-nuh) f: beef

год (goht) m: year

голова (gah-lah-*vah*) f: head

голодный (gah-*lohd*-niy): hungry

гора (gah-*rah*) f: mountain

город (*goh*-raht) m: city, town

гостиная (gahs-*tee*-nuh-yeh) f: living room

гостиница (gahs-*tee*-nee-tsuh) f: hotel

гость (gohst') m: guest

граница (gruh-*nee*-tsuh) f: border

группа (*grooh*-puh) f: group

Д

давать/дать (duh-*vaht'*/daht'): to give

далеко (duh-lee-*koh*): far

два (dvah): two

дверь (dvyehr') f: door

дворец (dvah-*ryehts*) m: palace

девочка (*dyeh*-vahch-kuh) f: girl

девять (*dyeh*-vyeht'): nine

дедушка (*dyeh*-doohsh-kuh) m: grandfather

декабрь (dee-*kahbr'*) m: December

делать/сделать (*dyeh*-luht'/*sdyeh*-luht'): to do, to make

день (dyehn') m: day

деньги (*dyehn'*-gee) pl: money

дерево (*dyeh*-ree-vah) n: tree

десерт (dee-*syehrt*) m: dessert

десять (*dyeh*-seet'): ten

дешёвый (dee-*shoh*-viy): cheap

джем (dzhehm) m: jam

джинсы (*dzhin*-si) pl: jeans

диван (dee-*vahn*) m: couch

длинный (*dlee*-niy): long

до свидания (dah svee-*dah*-nee-yeh): goodbye

дождь (dohzht') m: rain

должен (*dohl*-zhin): to have to, must

доллар (*doh*-luhr) m: dollar

дом (dohm) m: home, house

дорога (dah-*roh*-guh) f: road

дорогой (dah-rah-*gohy*): dear, expensive

доставать/достать (dahs-tuh-*vaht'*/dahs-*taht'*): to get

достаточно (dahs-*tah*-tahch-nah): enough

дочь (dohch') f: daughter

друг (droohk) m: friend

думать/подумать (*dooh*-muht'/pah-*dooh*-muht'): to think

душ (doohsh) m: shower

Е

его (ee-*voh*): his

еда (ee-*dah*) f: food

её (ee-*yoh*): her

ездить/ехать (*yehz*-deet'/*yeh*-khuht'): to go by vehicle

есть/поесть (yehst'/pah-*yehst'*): to eat

Ж

жарко (*zhahr*-kah): hot

ждать (zhdaht'): to wait

жена (zhi-*nah*) f: wife

женщина (*zhehn*-sh'ee-nuh) f: woman

жёлтый (*zhohl*-tiy): yellow

живот (zhi-*voht*) m: stomach

жить (zhit'): to live

журнал (zhoohr-*nahl*) m: magazine

З

забывать/забыть (zuh-bi-*vaht'*/zuh-*bit'*): to forget

завтра (*zahf*-truh): tomorrow

завтрак (*zahf*-truhk) m: breakfast

заканчивать/закончить (zuh-*kahn*-chee-vuht'/zuh-*kohn*-cheet'): to finish

закрывать/закрыть (zuh-kri-*vaht'*/zuh-*krit'*): to close

занят/а (*zah*-neet/a): busy

запад (*zah*-puht) m: west

заявление (zuh-eev-*lyeh*-nee-ee) n: application

звонить/позвонить (zvah-*neet'*/pah-zvah-*neet'*): to call

здание (*zdah*-nee-ee) n: building

здесь (zdyehs'): here

здоровье (zdah-*rohv'*-ee) n: health

здравствуйте (*zdrah*-stvoohy-tee): hello

зелёный (zee-*lyoh*-niy): green

зеркало (*zyehr*-kuh-lah) n: mirror

зима (zee-*mah*) f: winter

знаменитый (znuh-mee-*nee*-tiy): famous

знать (znaht'): to know

золото (*zoh*-lah-tah) n: gold

зубной врач (zoohb-*nohy* vrahch) m: dentist

зубы (*zooh*-bi) pl: teeth

И

и (ee): and

играть/поиграть (eeg-*raht'*/pah-eeg-*raht'*): to play

идти/ходить (eet-*tee*/khah-*deet'*): to go by foot

из (eez): from

извините (eez-vee-*nee*-tee): excuse me

имейл (ee-*meheel*) m: e-mail

иметь (ee-*myeht'*): to have

имя (*ee*-myeh) n: first name

индекс (*een*-dehks) m: zip code

иностранец (ee-nah-*strah*-neets) m: foreigner

иностранный (ee-nah-*strah*-niy): foreign

интерес (een-tee-*ryehs*) m: interest

их (eekh): their

июль (ee-*yoohl'*) m: July

июнь (ee-*yoohn'*) m: June

К

каждый (*kahzh*-diy): each

как (kahk): how

кампания (kahm-*pah*-nee-ye) f: company

капуста (kuh-*poohs*-tuhsh) f: cabbage

карандаш (kuh-ruhn-*dahsh*) m: pencil

карта (*kahr*-tuh) f: map

картофель (kuhr-*toh*-feel') m: potato

касса (*kah*-suh) f: cash register

кафе (kuh-*feh*) n: café

кашлять (*kah*-shlyeht'): to cough

квартира (kvuhr-*tee*-ruh) f: apartment

кино (kee-*noh*) n: movie theater

класть/положить (*klahst'*/pah-lah-*zhit'*): to put

клуб (kloohp) m: club

ключ (klyoohch) m: key

книга (*knee*-guh) f: book

книжный магазин (*kneezh*-niy muh-guh-*zeen*) m: bookstore

ковёр (kah-*vyohr*) m: rug

когда (kahg-*dah*): when

колено (kah-*lyeh*-nuh) n: knee

колледж (*koh*-leedzh) m: college

комната (*kohm*-nuh-tuh) f: room

комод (kah-*moht*) m: dresser

конец (kah-*nyehts*) m: end

конфета (kahn-*fyeh*-tuh) f: candy

концерт (kahn-*tsehrt*) m: concert

коридор (kah-ree-*dohr*) m: hall

коричневый (kah-*reech*-nee-viy): brown

коробка (kah-*rohp*-kuh) f: box

костюм (kahs-*tyoohm*) m: suit

кот (koht) m: cat

который (kah-*toh*-riy): which

кофе (*koh*-fee) m: coffee

красивый (kruh-*see*-viy): beautiful

красный (*krahs*-niy): red

кредитная карточка (kree-*deet*-nuh-yeh *kahr*-tahch-kuh) f: credit card

кровать (krah-*vaht'*) f: bed

кровь (krohf') f: blood

кто (ktoh): who

кто-то (*ktoh*-tah): somebody

курица (*kooh*-ree-tsuh) f: chicken

куртка (*koohrt*-kuh) f: jacket

Л

лампа (*lahm*-puh) f: lamp

легко (leekh-*koh*): easy

лекарство (lee-*kahrst*-vah) n: medicine

лестница (*lyehs*-nee-tsuh) f: staircase

летать/лететь (lee-*taht'*/lee-*tyeht'*): to fly

лето (*lyeh*-tah) n: summer

лимон (lee-*mohn*) m: lemon

лифт (leeft) m: elevator

лихорадка (lee-khah-*raht*-kuh) f: fever

лицо (lee-*tsoh*) n: face

ложка (*lohsh*-kuh) f: spoon

ломать/сломать (lah-*maht'*/slah-*maht'*): to break

лошадь (*loh*-shuht') f: horse

луна (looh-*nah*) f: moon

любить (lyooh-*beet'*): to love

любой (lyooh-*bohy*): any

люди (*lyooh*-dee) pl: people

М

магазин (muh-guh-*zeen*) m: shop

май (mahy) m: May

маленький (*mah*-leen'-keey): small, little

мальчик (*mahl'*-cheek) m: boy

март (mahrt) m: March

мать (maht') f: mother

машина (muh-*shi*-nuh) f: car

мебель (*myeh*-beel') f: furniture

медленный (*myehd*-lee-niy): slow

медсестра (meet-sees-*trah*) f: nurse

между (*myehzh*-dooh): between

место (*myehs*-tah) n: seat

месяц (*myeh*-syehts) m: month

метро (meet-*roh*) n: subway

минута (mee-*nooh*-tuh) f: minute

много (*mnoh*-gah): many, much, a lot

можно (*mohzh*-nah): may

мой (mohy): my

молодой (mah-lah-*dohy*): young

молоко (mah-lah-*koh*) n: milk

море (*moh*-ree) n: sea

морковь (mahr-*kohf'*) f: carrot

мост (mohst) m: bridge

мочь/смочь (mohch'/smohch'): can

муж (moohsh) m: husband

мужчина (mooh-*sh'ee*-nuh) m: man

музей (mooh-*zyehy*) m: museum

музыка (*mooh*-zi-kuh) f: music

мы (mi): we

мыло (*mi*-lah) n: soap

мясо (*mya*-sah) n: meat

Н

на (nah): on

набирать/набрать (nuh-bee-*raht'*/nuhb-*raht'*): to dial

надежда (nuh-*dyehzh*-duh) f: hope

налево (nuh-*lyeh*-vah): (to the) left

наличные (nuh-*leech*-ni-ee): cash

направо (nuh-*prah*-vah): (to the) right

находить/найти (nuh-khah-*deet'*/nuhy-*tee*): to find

наш (nahsh): our

невозможный (nee-vahz-*mohzh*-niy): impossible

неделя (nee-*dyeh*-lyeh) f: week

несколько (*nyehs*-kahl'-kah): few, some

несчастный случай (nees-*chahst*-niy *slooh*-chuhy) m: accident

низкий (*nees*-keey): low

никогда (nee-kahg-*dah*): never

никто (neek-*toh*): nobody

ничего (nee-chee-*voh*): nothing

но (noh): but

новый (*noh*-viy): new

нога (nah-*gah*) f: leg, foot

нож (nohsh) m: knife

номер (*noh*-meer) m: number

нос (nohs) m: nose

носить/нести (nah-*seet'*/nees-*tee*): to wear

ночь (nohch') f: night

ноябрь (nah-*yabr'*) m: November

нравиться/понравиться (*nrah*-veet'-syeh/ pah-*nrah*-veet'-syeh): to like

О

о/об (oh/ohp): about

обед (ah-*byeht*) m: lunch

обмен (ahb-*myehn*) m: exchange

овощ (*oh*-vahsh'): vegetable

одежда (ah-*dyehzh*-duh) f: clothes

одеяло (ah-dee-*ya*-lah) n: blanket

один (ah-*deen*): one

озеро (*oh*-zee-rah) n: lake

окно (ahk-*noh*) n: window

октябрь (ahk-*tyabr'*) m: October

он (ohn): he

она (ah-*nah*): she

они (ah-*nee*): they

оно (ah-*noh*): it

осень (*oh*-seen') f: autumn

отдел (aht-*dyehl*) m: department

отдыхать/отдохнуть (aht-di-*khaht'*/aht-dahkh-*nooht'*): to relax

отец (ah-*tyehts*) f: father

открывать/открыть (aht-kri-*vaht'*/aht-*krit'*): to open

отправление (aht-pruhv-*lyeh*-nee-ee) n: departure

отпуск (*oht*-poohsk) m: vacation

офис (*oh*-fees) m: office

официант (ah-fee-tsi-*ahnt*) m: waiter

очки (ahch-*kee*) pl: eyeglasses

П

падать/упасть (*pah*-duht'/ooh-*pahst'*): to fall

палец (*pah*-leets) m: finger

пальто (puhl'-*toh*) n: coat

парк (pahrk) m: park

паспорт (*pahs*-pahrt) m: passport

первый (*pyehr*-viy): first

пиво (*pee*-vah) n: beer

письмо (pees'-*moh*) n: letter

пить/выпить (peet'/*vi*-peet'): to drink

платить/заплатить (pluh-*teet'*/zuh-pluh-*teet'*): to pay

платье (*plaht'*-ee) n: dress

плащ (plahsh') m: raincoat

плёнка (*plyohn*-kuh) f: film

плохой (plah-*khohy*): bad

поворачивать/повернуть (pah-vah-*rah*-chee-vuht'/pah-veer-*nooht'*): to turn

повторять/повторить (pahf-tah-*ryat'*/pahf-tah-*reet'*): to repeat

подарок (pah-*dah*-rahk) m: gift

подвал (pahd-*vahl*) m: basement

поезд (*poh*-eest) m: train

пожалуйста (pah-*zhahl*-stuh): please, you're welcome

пожар (pah-*zhahr*) m: fire

позади (pah-zuh-*dee*): behind

поздно (*pohz*-nah): late

показывать/показать (pah-*kah*-zi-vuht'/pah-kuh-*zaht'*): to show

покупать/купить (pah-kooh-*paht'*/koo-*peet'*): to buy

пол (pohl) m: floor

полдень (*pohl*-deen'): noon

поле (*poh*-lee) n: field

полиция (pah-*lee*-tsi-yeh) f: police

полотенце (pah-lah-*tyehn*-tseh) n: towel

помогать/помочь (pah-mah-*gaht'*/pah-*mohch'*): to help

понедельник (pah-nee-*dyehl'*-neek) m: Monday

посещать/посетить (pah-see-*sh'aht'*/pah-see-*teet'*): to visit

после (*pohs*-lee): after

последний (pahs-*lyehd*-neey): last

потому что (pah-tah-*mooh*-shtah): because

почему (pah-chee-*mooh*): why

почта (*pohch*-tuh) f: mail

представлять/представить (preet-stuhv-*lyat'*/preet-*stah*-veet'): to introduce

прибытие (pree-*bi*-tee-ee) n: arrival

привет (pree-*vyeht*): hi

приглашать/пригласить (pree-gluh-*shat'*/pree-gluh-*seet'*): to invite

приносить/принести (pree-nah-*seet'*/pree-nees-*tee*): to bring

приходить/придти (pree-khah-*deet'*/preet-*tee*): to come

проблема (prahb-*lyeh*-muh) f: problem

продавать/продать (prah-duh-*vaht'*/prah-*daht'*): to sell

продавец (prah-duh-*vyehts*): m: sales assistant

продукты (prah-*doohk*-ti) pl: groceries

простой (prahs-*tohy*): simple

птица (*ptee*-tsuh) f: bird

пустой (poohs-*tohy*): empty

путешествовать (pooh-tee-*shehst*-vah-vuht'): to travel

пьеса (*p'yeh*-suh) f: play

пятница (*pyat*-nee-tsuh) f: Friday

пять (*pyat'*): five

Р

работа (ruh-*boh*-tuh) f: work; job

работать (ruh-*boh*-tuht'): to work

разговаривать (ruhz-gah-*vah*-ree-vuht'): to talk

рано (*rah*-nah): early

распродажа (ruhs-prah-*dah*-zhuh) f: sale

рассказывать/рассказать (ruhs-*kah*-zi-vuht'/ruhs-kuh-*zaht'*): to tell

ребёнок (ree-*byoh*-nahk) m: child

рейс (*reh*-ees) m: flight

река (ree-*kah*) f: river

ресторан (rees-tah-*rahn*) m: restaurant

рис (rees) m: rice

рубашка (rooh-*bahsh*-kuh) f: shirt

ружьё (roohzh'-*yoh*) n: gun

рука (rooh-*kah*) f: arm, hand

ручка (*roohch*-kuh) f: pen

рыба (*ri*-buh) f: fish

рынок (*ri*-nahk) m: market

рядом (*rya*-dahm): near

С

салат (suh-*laht*) m: salad

самолёт (suh-mah-*lyoht*) m: airplane

самый лучший (*sah*-miy *loohch*-shiy): best

сахар (*sah*-khuhr) m: sugar

сдача (*sdah*-chuh) f: change

север (*syeh*-veer) m: north

сегодня (see-*vohd*-nyeh): today

сейчас (seey-*chahs*): now

секретарь (seek-ree-*tahr'*) m: secretary

семь (*syehm'*): seven

семья (seem'-*ya*) f: family

сентябрь (seen-*tyabr'*) m: September

сердце (*syehr*-tseh) n: heart

серый (*syeh*-riy): gray

сестра (sees-*trah*) f: sister

сидеть (see-*dyeht'*): to sit

синий (*see*-neey): blue

сколько (*skohl'*-kah): how many, how much

скорая помощ (*skoh*-rah-yeh *poh*-mahsh') f: ambulance

скучный (*skooch*-niy): boring

сладкий (*slaht*-keey): sweet

следующий (*slyeh*-dooh-yooh-sheey): next

слишком (*sleesh*-kahm): too

слово (*sloh*-vah) n: word

слушать (*slooh*-shuht'): to listen, to hear

случаться/случиться (slooh-*chaht'*-syeh/ slooh-*cheet'*-syeh): to take place, to happen

смешной (smeesh-*nohy*): funny

смеяться (smee-*yat'*-syeh): to laugh

смотреть/посмотреть (smaht-*ryeht'*/pahs-mah-*tryeht'*): to look, to watch

снег (snyehk) m: snow

снимать/снять (snee-*maht'*/snyat'): to rent

собирать/собрать (sah-bee-*raht'*/sah-*braht'*): to collect

сок (sohk) m: juice

солнце (*sohn*-tseh) n: sun

соль (sohl') f: salt

сосед (sah-*syehd*) m: neighbor

спасибо (spuh-*see*-bah): thank you

спать (spaht'): to sleep

спина (spee-*nah*) f: back

спорт (spohrt) m: sports

спрашивать/спросить (*sprah*-shi-vuht'/ sprah-*seet'*): to ask

среда (sree-*dah*) f: Wednesday

стакан (stuh-*kahn*) m: glass

старый (*stah*-riy): old

стол (stohl) m: table

столица (stah-*lee*-tsuh) f: capital

стоять (stah-*yat'*): to stand

страна (struh-*nah*) f: country

страховка (struh-*khohf*-kuh) n: insurance

стул (stoohl) m: chair

суббота (sooh-*boh*-tuh) f: Saturday

сувенир (sooh-vee-*neer*) m: souvenir

сумка (*soohm*-kuh) f: bag

счастливый (schuhs-*lee*-viy): happy

сын (sin) m: son

сыр (sir) m: cheese

T

там (tahm): there

таможня (tuh-*mohzh*-nyeh) f: customs

тарелка (tuh-*ryehl*-kuh) f: plate

театр (tee-*ahtr*) m: theater

телефон (tee-lee-*fohn*) m: phone

телефонная книга (tee-lee-*fohn*-nuh-yeh *knee*-guh) f: phone book

теперь (tee-*pyehr'*): now

терапевт (tee-ruh-*pehft*) m: physician, specialist in internal medicine

терять/потерять (tee-*ryat'*/pah-tee-*ryat'*): to lose

тёплый (*tyohp*-liy): warm

тоже (*toh*-zhi): also

только (*tohl'*-kah): only

торт (tohrt): cake

три (tree): three

трудный (*troohd*-niy): hard

туфли (*toohf*-lee) pl: shoes

тут (tooht): here

ты (ti): you (informal singular)

У

удостоверение личности (ooh-dah-stah-vee-*ryeh*-nee-ee *leech*-nahs-tee) n: ID (identification)

ужин (*ooh*-zhin) m: dinner

улица (*ooh*-lee-tsuh) f: street

универмаг (ooh-*nee*-veer-*mahk*) m: department store

университет (ooh-nee-veer-see-*tyeht*) m: university

урок (ooh-*rohk*) m: lesson

утро (*ooht*-rah) n: morning

ухо (*ooh*-khah) n: ear

уходить/уйти (ooh-khah-*deet'*/ooy-tee): to leave

учитель (ooh-*chee*-teel') m: teacher (male)

учительница (ooh-*chee*-teel'-nee-tsuh) f: teacher (female)

Ф

факс (fahks) m: fax

фамилия (fuh-*mee*-lee-yeh) f: last name

февраль (feev-*rahl'*) m: February

фирма (*feer*-muh) f: firm

фотография (fah-tah-*grah*-fee-yeh) f: picture

фрукт (froohkt-) m: fruit

футбол (fooht-*bohl*) m: soccer

Х

хлеб (khlyehp) m: bread

холодный (khah-*lohd*-niy): cold

хороший (khah-*roh*-shiy): good

хорошенький (khah-*roh*-shin'-keey): pretty

хорошо (khah-rah-*shoh*): all right, well

хотеть (khah-*tyeht'*): to want

Ц

цвет (tsvyeht) m: color

цветок (tsvee-*tohk*) m: flower

цена (tsi-*nah*) f: price

церковь (*tsehr*-kahf') f: church

Ч

час (chahs) m: hour

часы (chuh-*si*) pl: clock

чашка (*chahsh*-kuh) f: cup

чек (chyehk) m: check

чемодан (chee-mah-*dahn*) m: suitcase

честный (*chyehs*-niy): honest

четверг (cheet-*vyehrk*) m: Thursday

четыре (chee-*ti*-ree): four

чёрный (*chyohr*-niy): black

чинить/починить (chee-*neet'*/pah-chee-*neet'*): to repair

чистый (*chees*-tiy): clean

читать/прочитать (chee-*taht'*/prah-chee-*taht'*): to read

что (shtoh): what

что-то (*shtoh*-tah): something

чувствовать (choos-stvah-*vaht'*): to feel

Ш

шампунь (shuhm-*poohn'*) m: shampoo

шапка (*shahp*-kuh) f: hat

шесть (shehst'): six

шея (*sheh*-yeh) f: neck

шкаф (shkahf) m: closet

школа (*shkoh*-luh) f: school

шофёр (shah-*fyohr*) m: cabdriver

штат (shtaht) m: state

шутка (*shooht*-kuh) f: joke

Ю

юбка (*yoohp*-kuh) f: skirt

юг (yoohk) m: south

юрист (yooh-*reest*) m: lawyer

Я

я (ya): I

яблоко (*yab*-lah-kah) n: apple

язык (ee-*zik*) m: language

яйцо (eey-*tsoh*) n: egg

январь (een-*vahr'*) m: January

English-Russian Mini-Dictionary

A

about: о/об (*oh*/*ohp*)

accident: несчастный случай (*nees-chahst*-niy *slooh*-chuhy) m

address: адрес (*ahd*-rees) m

after: после (*pohs*-lee)

airplane: самолёт (suh-mah-*lyoht*) m

airport: аэропорт (uh-eh-rah-*pohrt*) m

all right: хорошо (khah-rah-*shoh*)

also: тоже (*toh*-zhi)

always: всегда (vseeg-*dah*)

ambulance: скорая помощ (*skoh*-ruh-yeh *poh*-mahsh') f

and: и, а (ee, ah)

any: любой (lyooh-*bohy*)

apartment: квартира (kvuhr-*tee*-ruh) f

apple: яблоко (*yab*-lah-kah) n

application: заявление (zuh-eev-*lyeh*-nee-ee) n

April: апрель (uhp-*ryehl'*) m

arm: рука (rooh-*kah*) f

arrival: прибытие (pree-*bi*-tee-ee) n

to ask: спрашивать/спросить (*sprah*-shi-vuht'/sprah-*seet'*)

at: в/на (v, nah)

August: август (*ahv*-goohst) m

autumn: осень (*oh*-seen') f

B

back: спина (spee-*nah*) f

bad: плохой (plah-*khohy*)

bag: сумка (*soohm*-kuh) f

baggage: багаж (buh-*gahsh*) m

ballet: балет (buh-*lyeht*) m

bank: банк (bahnk) m

basement: подвал (pahd-*vahl*) m

bathroom: ванная (*vahn*-nuh-yeh) bathroom f

to be: быть (bit')

beautiful: красивый (kruh-*see*-viy)

because: потому что (pah-tah-*mooh*-shtah)

bed: кровать (krah-*vaht'*) f

beef: говядина (gah-*vya*-dee-nuh) f

beer: пиво (*pee*-vah) n

behind: позади (pah-zuh-*dee*)

best: самый лучший (*sah*-miy *loohch*-shiy)

between: между (*myehzh*-dooh)

big: большой (bahl'-*shohy*)

bird: птица (*ptee*-tsuh) f

black: чёрный (*chyohr*-niy)

blanket: одеяло (ah-dee-*ya*-lah) n

blood: кровь (krohf') f

blue: синий (*see*-neey)

book: книга (*knee*-guh) f

bookstore: книжный магазин (*kneezh*-niy muh-guh-*zeen*) m

border: граница (gruh-*nee*-tsuh) f

boring: скучный (*skoohch*-niy)

bottle: бутылка (booh-*til*-kuh) f

box: коробка (kah-*rohp*-kuh) f

boy: мальчик (*mahl'*-cheek) m

bread: хлеб (khlyehp) m

to break: ломать/сломать (lah-*maht'*/slah-*maht'*)

breakfast: завтрак (*zahf*-truhk) m

bridge: мост (mohst) m

to bring: приносить/принести (pree-nah-*seet'*/pree-nees-*tee*)

brother: брат (braht) m

brown: коричневый (kah-*reech*-nee-viy)

building: здание (*zdah*-nee-ee) n

bus: автобус (uhf-*toh*-boohs) m

busy: занят (*zah*-neet)

but: но (noh)

to buy: покупать/купить (pah-kooh-*paht'*/kooh-*peet'*)

C

cabbage: капуста (kuh-*poohs*-tuh) f

cabdriver: шофёр (shah-*fyohr*) m

café: кафе (kuh-*feh*) n

cake: торт (tohrt) n

to call: звонить/позвонить (zvah-*neet'*/pah-zvah-*neet'*)

can: мочь/смочь (mohch'/smohch')

candy: конфета (kahn-*fyeh*-tuh) f

capital: столица (stah-*lee*-tsuh) f

car: машина (muh-*shi*-nuh) f

carrot: морковь (mahr-*kohf'*) f

cash: наличные (nuh-*leech*-ni-ee) pl

cash register: касса (*kah*-suh) f

cat: кошка (*kohsh*-kuh) f

chair: стул (stoohl) m

change: сдача (*sdah*-chuh) f

cheap: дешёвый (dee-*shoh*-viy)

check: чек (chyehk) m

cheese: сыр (sir) m

chicken: курица (*kooh*-ree-tsuh) f

child: ребёнок (ree-*byoh*-nahk) m

church: церковь (*tsehr*-kahf') f

city: город (*goh*-raht) m

clean: чистый (*chees*-tiy)

clock: часы (chuh-*si*) pl

to close: закрывать/закрыть (zuh-kri-*vaht'*/zuh-*krit'*)

closet: шкаф (shkahf) m

clothes: одежда (ah-*dyehzh*-duh) f

club: клуб (kloohp) m

coat: пальто (puhl'-*toh*) n

coffee: кофе (*koh*-fee) m

cold: холодный (khah-*lohd*-niy)

to collect: собирать/собрать (sah-bee-*raht'*/sah-*braht'*)

college: колледж (*koh*-leedzh) m

color: цвет (tsvyeht) m

to come: приходить/придти (pree-khah-*deet'*/preet-*tee*)

company: кампания (kuhm-*pah*-nee-yeh) f

concert: концерт (kahn-*tsehrt*) m

couch: диван (dee-*vahn*) m

cough: кашлять (*kah*-slyeht')

country: страна (struh-*nah*) f

credit card: кредитная карточка (kree-*deet*-nuh-yeh *kahr*-tahch-kuh) f

cup: чашка (*chahsh*-kuh) f

currency: валюта (vuh-*lyooh*-tuh) f

customs: таможня (tuh-*mohzh*-nyeh) f

D

daughter: **дочь** (dohch') f

day: **день** (dyehn') m

dear: **дорогой** (dah-rah-*gohy*)

December: **декабрь** (dee-*kahbr'*) m

dentist: **зубной врач** (zoohb-*nohy* vrahch) m

department: **отдел** (aht-*dyehl*) m

department store: **универмаг** (ooh-nee-veer-*mahk*) m

departure: **отправление** (aht-pruhv-*lyeh*-nee-ee) n

dessert: **дессерт** (dee-*syehrt*) m

to dial: **набирать/набрать** (nuh-bee-*raht'*/nuhb-*raht'*)

dinner: **ужин** (*ooh*-zhin) m

to do: **делать/сделать** (*dyeh*-luht'/*sdyeh*-luht')

doctor: **врач** (vrahch) m

dollar: **доллар** (*doh*-luhr) m

door: **дверь** (dvyehr') f

dress: **платье** (*plaht'*-ee) n

dresser: **комод** (kah-*moht*) m

to drink: **пить/выпить** (peet'/*vi*-peet')

to drive: **водить/вести машину** (vah-*deet'*/vees-*tee* muh-*shi*-nooh)

drugstore: **аптека** (uhp-*tyeh*-kuh) f

E

each: **каждый** (*kahzh*-diy)

ear: **ухо** (*ooh*-khah) n

early: **рано** (*rah*-nah)

east: **восток** (vahs-*tohk*) m

easy: **легко** (leekh-*koh*)

to eat: **есть/поесть** (yehst'/pah-*yehst'*)

egg: **яйцо** (eey-*tsoh*) n

eight: **восемь** (*voh*-seem')

elevator: **лифт** (leeft) m

e-mail: **имейл** (ee-*meheel*) m

empty: **пустой** (poohs-*tohy*)

end: **конец** (kah-*nyehts*) m

enough: **достаточно** (dahs-*tah*-tahch-nah)

to enter: **входить/войти** (vkhah-*deet'*/vahy-*tee*)

entrance: **вход** (vkhoht) m

evening: **вечер** (*vyeh*-cheer) m

everybody: **все** (fsyeh)

everything: **всё** (fsyoh)

exchange: **обмен** (ahb-*myehn*) m

excuse me: **извините** (eez-vee-*nee*-tee)

exit: **выход** (*vi*-khaht)

expensive: **дорогой** (dah-rah-*gohy*)

eye: **глаз** (glahs) m

eyeglasses: **очки** (ahch-*kee*) pl

F

face: **лицо** (lee-*tsoh*) n

to fall: **падать/упасть** (*pah*-duht'/ooh-*pahst'*)

family: **семья** (seem'-*ya*) f

famous: **знаменитый** (znuh-mee-*nee*-tiy)

far: **далеко** (duh-lee-*koh*)

father: **отец** (ah-*tyehts*) m

fax: **факс** (fahks) m

February: **февраль** (feev-*rahl'*) m

to feel: **чувстовать/почувствовать** (chooh-stvah-*vaht'*/pah-chooh-stvah-*vaht'*)

fever: **лихорадка** (lee-khah-*raht*-kuh) f

few: **несколько** (*nyehs*-kahl'-kah)

field: **поле** (*poh*-lee) n

film: **плёнка** (*plyohn*-kuh) m

to find: **находить/найти** (nuh-khah-*deet'*/ nuhy-*tee*)

finger: **палец** (*pah*-leets) m

to finish: **заканчивать/закончить** (zuh-*kahn*-chee-vuht'/zuh-*kohn*-cheet')

fire: **пожар** (pah-*zhahr*) m

firm: **фирма** (*feer*-muh) f

first: **первый** (*pyehr*-viy)

first name: **имя** (*ee*-myeh) n

fish: **рыба** (*ri*-buh) f

five: **пять** (pyat')

flight: **рейс** (*ryeh*ys) m

floor: **пол** (pohl) m

flower: **цветок** (tsvee-*tohk*) m

to fly: **летать/лететь** (lee-*taht'*/lee-*tyeht'*)

food: **еда** (ee-*dah*) f

foot: **нога** (nah-*gah*) f

foreign: **иностранный** (ee-nah-*strah*-niy)

foreigner: **иностранец** (ee-nah-*strah*-neets) m

to forget: **забывать/забыть** (zuh-bi-*vaht'*/zuh-*bit'*)

fork: **вилка** (*veel*-kuh) f

four: **четыре** (chee-*ti*-ree)

Friday: **пятница** (*pyat*-nee-tsuh) f

friend: **друг** (drоohk) m

from: **из** (eez)

fruit: **фрукт** (*froohkt*) m

funny: **смешной** (smeesh-*nohy*)

furniture: **мебель** (*myeh*-beel') f

G

gallery: **галерея** (guh-lee-*ryeh*-yeh) f

garage: **гараж** (guh-*rahsh*) m

gas: **бензин** (been-*zeen*) m

to get: **доставать/достать** (dahs-tuh-*vaht'*/dahs-*taht'*)

gift: **подарок** (pah-*dah*-rahk) m

girl: **девочка** (*dyeh*-vahch-kuh) f

to give: **давать/дать** (duh-*vaht'*/daht')

glass: **стакан** (stuh-*kahn*) m

to go by foot: **идти/ходить** (eet-*tee*/khah-*deet'*)

to go by vehicle: **ездить/ехать** (*yehz*-deet'/*yeh*-khuht')

gold: **золото** (*zoh*-lah-tah) n

good: **хороший** (khah-*roh*-shiy)

goodbye: **до свидания** (dah svee-*dah*-nee-yeh)

granddaughter: **внучка** (*vnoohch*-kuh) f

grandfather: **дедушка** (*dyeh*-doohsh-kuh) m

grandmother: **бабушка** (*bah*-boohsh-kuh) f

grandson: **внук** (vnoohk) m

gray: **серый** (*syeh*-riy)

great: **великий** (vee-*lee*-keey)

green: **зелёный** (zee-*lyoh*-niy)

groceries: **продукты** (prah-*doohk*-ti) pl

group: **группа** (*grooh*-puh) f

guest: **гость** (gohst') m

guide: **гид** (geet) m

gun: **ружьё** (roohzh'-*yoh*) n

H

hair: **волосы** (*voh*-lah-si) pl

hall: **коридор** (kah-ree-*dohr*) m

hand: **рука** (rooh-*kah*) f

to happen: **случаться/случиться** (slooh-*chaht'*-syeh/slooh-*cheet'*-syeh)

happy: **счастливый** (schuhs-*lee*-viy)

hard: **трудный** (*troohd*-niy)

hat: **шапка** (*shahp*-kuh) f

to have: иметь (ee-*myeht'*)

to have to: должен (*dohl*-zhin)

he: он (ohn)

head: голова (gah-lah-*vah*) f

health: здоровье (zdah-*rohv'*-ee) n

to hear: слушать (*slooh*-shuht')

heart: сердце (*syehr*-tseh) n

hello: здравствуйте (*zdrah*-stvoohy-tee)

to help: помогать/помочь (pah-mah-*gaht'*/pah-*mohch'*)

her: её (ee-*yoh*)

here: здесь/тут (zdyehs'/tooht)

hi: привет (pree-*vyeht*)

high: высокий (vi-*soh*-keey)

his: его (ee-*voh*)

home: дом (dohm) m

honest: честный (*chyehs*-niy)

hope: надежда (nuh-*dyehzh*-duh) f

horse: лошадь (*loh*-shuht') f

hospital: больница (bahl'-*nee*-tsuh) f

hot: жарко (*zhahr*-kah)

hotel: гостиница (gahs-*tee*-nee-tsuh) f

hour: час (chahs) m

house: дом (dohm) m

how: как (kahk)

how many, how much: сколько (*skohl'*-kah)

hungry: голодный (gah-*lohd*-niy)

husband: муж (moohsh) m

I

I: я (ya)

ID (identification): удостоверение личности (ooh-dah-stah-vee-*ryeh*-nee-ee *leech*-nahs-tee) n

ill: болен (*boh*-leen)

important: важный (*vahzh*-niy)

impossible: невозможный (nee-vahz-*mohzh*-niy)

in: в (v)

insurance: страховка (struh-*khohf*-kuh) n

interest: интерес (een-tee-*ryehs*) m

to introduce: представлять/представить (preet-stuhv-*lyat'*/preet-*stah*-veet')

to invite: приглашать/пригласить (pree-gluh-*shat'*/pree-gluh-*seet'*)

it: оно (ah-*noh*)

J

jacket: куртка (*koohrt*-kuh) f

jam: джем (dzhehm) m

January: январь (een-*vahr'*) m

jeans: джинсы (*dzhin*-si) pl

job: работа (ruh-*boh*-tuh) f

joke: шутка (*shooht*-kuh) f

juice: сок (sohk) m

July: июль (ee-*yoohl'*) m

June: июнь (ee-*yoohn'*) m

K

key: ключ (klyoohch) m

knee: колено (kah-*lyeh*-nah) n

knife: нож (nohsh) m

to know: знать (znaht')

L

lake: озеро (*oh*-zee-rah) n

lamp: лампа (*lahm*-puh) f

language: язык (ee-*zik*) m

last: последний (pahs-*lyehd*-neey)

last name: **фамилия** (fuh-*mee*-lee-yeh) f

late: **поздно** (*pohz*-nah)

to laugh: **смеяться** (smee-*yat'*-syeh)

lawyer: **юрист** (yooh-*reest*) m

to leave: **уходить/уйти** (ooh-khah-*deet'*/ oohy-*tee*)

(to the) left: **налево** (nuh-*lyeh*-vah)

leg: **нога** (nah-*gah*) f

lemon: **лимон** (lee-*mohn*) m

lesson: **урок** (ooh-*rohk*) m

letter: **письмо** (pees'-*moh*) n

to like: **нравиться/понравиться** (*nrah*-veet'-syeh/pah-*nrah*-veet'-syeh)

to listen: **слушать** (*slooh*-shuht')

little: **маленький** (*mah*-leen'-keey)

to live: **жить** (zhit')

living room: **гостиная** (gahs-*tee*-nuh-yeh) f

long: **длинный** (*dlee*-niy)

to look: **смотреть/посмотреть** (smaht-*ryeht'*/pahs-mah-*tryeht'*)

to lose: **терять/потерять** (tee-*ryat'*/ pah-tee-*ryat'*)

to love: **любить** (lyooh-*beet'*)

low: **низкий** (*nees*-keey)

lunch: **обед** (ah-*byeht*) m

M

magazine: **журнал** (zhoohr-*nahl*) m

mail: **почта** (*pohch*-tuh) f

main: **главный** (*glahv*-niy)

to make: **делать/сделать** (*dyeh*-luht'/ *sdyeh*-luht')

man: **мужчина** (mooh-*sh'ee*-nuh) m

many: **много** (*mnoh*-gah)

map: **карта** (*kahr*-tuh) f

March: **март** (mahrt) m

market: **рынок** (*ri*-nahk) m

May: **май** (mahy) m

may: **можно** (*mohzh*-nah)

meat: **мясо** (*mya*-sah) n

medicine: **лекарство** (lee-*kahrst*-vah) n

meeting: **встреча** (*fstryeh*-chuh) f

milk: **молоко** (mah-lah-*koh*) n

minute: **минута** (mee-*nooh*-tuh) f

mirror: **зеркало** (*zyehr*-kuh-lah) n

Monday: **понедельник** (pah-nee-*dyehl'*-neek) m

money: **деньги** (*dyehn'*-gee) pl

month: **месяц** (*myeh*-seets) m

moon: **луна** (looh-*nah*) f

morning: **утро** (*ooht*-rah) n

mother: **мать** (maht') f

mountain: **гора** (gah-*rah*) f

movie: **кино** (kee-*noh*) n

movie theater: **кино** (kee-*noh*) n

much: **много** (*mnoh*-gah)

museum: **музей** (mooh-*zyehy*) m

music: **музыка** (*mooh*-zi-kuh) f

must: **должен** (*dohl*-zhin)

my: **мой** (mohy)

N

near: **рядом** (*rya*-dahm)

neck: **шея** (*sheh*-yeh) f

neighbor: **сосед** (sah-*syeht*) m

never: **никогда** (nee-kahg-*dah*)

new: **новый** (*noh*-viy)

newspaper: **газета** (guh-*zyeh*-tuh) f

next: **следующий** (*slyeh*-dooh-yooh-sh'eey)

night: **ночь** (nohch') f

nine: **девять** (*dyeh*-veet')

nobody: **никто** (neek-*toh*)

noon: **полдень** (*pohl*-deen')

north: **север** (*syeh*-veer) m

nose: **нос** (nohs) m

nothing: **ничего** (nee-chee-*voh*)

November: **ноябрь** (nah-*yabr'*) m

now: **сейчас/теперь** (seey-*chahs*/tee-*pyehr'*)

number: **номер** (*noh*-meer) m

nurse: **медсестра** (meet-sees-*trah*) f

O

October: **октябрь** (ahk-*tyabr'*) m

office: **офис** (*oh*-fees) m

old: **старый** (*stah*-riy)

on: **на** (nah)

one: **один** (ah-*deen*)

only: **только** (*tohl'*-kah)

to open: **открывать/открыть** (aht-kri-*vaht'*/aht-*krit'*)

our: **наш** (nahsh)

P

palace: **дворец** (dvah-*ryehts*) m

pancake: **блин** (bleen) m

pants: **брюки** (*bryooh*-kee) pl

paper: **бумага** (booh-*mah*-guh) f

park: **парк** (pahrk) m

party: **вечеринка** (vee-chee-*reen*-kuh) f

passport: **паспорт** (*pahs*-pahrt) m

to pay: **платить/заплатить** (pluh-*teet'*/zuh-pluh-*teet'*)

pen: **ручка** (*roohch*-kuh) f

pencil: **карандаш** (kuh-ruhn-*dahsh*) m

people: **люди** (*lyooh*-dee) pl

pharmacy: **аптека** (uhp-*tyeh*-kuh) f

phone: **телефон** (tee-lee-*fohn*) m

phone book: **телефонная книга** (tee-lee-*fohn*-nuh-yeh *knee*-guh) f

physician: **терапевт** (tee-ruh-*pehft*) m

picture: **фотография** (fah-tah-*grah*-fee-yeh) f

plate: **тарелка** (tuh-*ryehl*-kuh) f

play: **пьеса** (*p'yeh*-suh) f

to play: **играть** (eeg-*raht'*)

please: **пожалуйста** (pah-*zhahl*-stuh)

police: **полиция** (pah-*lee*-tsi-yeh) f

poor: **бедный** (*byehd*-niy)

potato: **картофель** (kuhr-*toh*-feel') m

pretty: **хорошенький** (khah-*roh*-shin'-keey)

price: **цена** (tsi-*nah*) f

problem: **проблема** (prahb-*lyeh*-muh) f

to put: **класть/положить** (*klahst'*/pah-lah-*zhit'*)

Q

question: **вопрос** (vahp-*rohs*) m

quick: **быстрый** (*bis*-triy)

R

rain: **дождь** (dohzht') m

raincoat: **плащ** (plahsh') m

to read: **читать/прочитать** (chee-*taht'*/prah-chee-*taht'*)

red: **красный** (*krahs*-niy)

to relax: **отдыхать/отдохнуть** (aht-di-*khaht'*/aht-dahkh-*nooht'*)

to rent: **снимать/снять** (snee-*maht'*/snyat')

to repair: **чинить/починить** (chee-*neet'*/pah-chee-*neet'*) to repeat: **повторять/повторить** (pahf-tah-*ryat'*/pahf-tah-*reet'*)

restaurant: **ресторан** (rees-tah-*rahn*) m

rice: **рис** (rees) m

rich: **богатый** (bah-*gah*-tiy)

(to the) right: **направо** (nuh-*prah*-vah)

river: **река** (ree-*kah*) f

road: **дорога** (dah-*roh*-guh) f

room: **комната** (*kohm*-nuh-tuh) f

rug: **ковёр** (kah-*vyohr*) m

to run: **бежать/бегать** (bee-*zhaht'*/*byeh*-guht')

S

salad: **салад** (suh-*laht*) m

sale: **распродажа** (ruhs-prah-*dah*-zhuh) f

sales assistant: **продавец** (prah-duh-*vyehts*) m

salt: **соль** (sohl') f

Saturday: **суббота** (sooh-*boh*-tuh) f

to say: **говорить/сказать** (gah-vah-*reet'*/skuh-*zaht'*)

school: **школа** (*shkoh*-luh) f

sea: **море** (*moh*-ree) n

seat: **место** (*myehs*-tah) n

second: **второй** (ftah-*rohy*) (adj)

secretary: **секретарь** (seek-ree-*tahr'*) m

to see: **видеть/увидеть** (*vee*-deet'/ooh-*vee*-deet')

to sell: **продавать/продать** (prah-duh-*vaht'*/prah-*daht'*)

September: **сентябрь** (seen-*tyabr'*) m

seven: **семь** (syehm')

shampoo: **шампунь** (shuhm-*poohn'*) m

she: **она** (ah-*nah*)

shirt: **рубашка** (rooh-*bahsh*-kuh) f

shoes: **туфли** (*toohf*-lee) pl

shop: **магазин** (muh-guh-*zeen*) m

to show: **показывать/показать** (pah-*kah*-zi-vuht'/pah-kuh-*zaht'*)

shower: **душ** (doohsh) m

simple: **простой** (prahs-*tohy*)

sister: **сестра** (sees-*trah*) f

to sit: **сидеть** (see-*dyeht'*)

six: **шесть** (shehst')

skirt: **юбка** (*yoohp*-kuh) f

to sleep: **спать** (spaht')

slow: **медленный** (*myehd*-lee-niy)

small: **маленький** (*mah*-leen'-keey)

snow: **снег** (snyehk) m

soap: **мыло** (*mi*-lah) n

soccer: **футбол** (fooht-*bohl*) m

some: **несколько** (*nyehs*-kahl'-kah)

somebody: **кто-то** (*ktoh*-tah)

something: **что-то** (*shtoh*-tah)

son: **сын** (sin) m

south: **юг** (yoohk) m

souvenir: **сувенир** (sooh-vee-*neer*) m

to speak: **говорить/сказать** (gah-vah-*reet'*/skuh-*zaht'*)

spoon: **ложка** (*lohsh*-kuh) f

sports: **спорт** (spohrt) m

spring: **весна** (vees-*nah*) f

staircase: **лестница** (*lyehs*-nee-tsuh) f

to stand: **стоять** (stah-*yat'*)

state: **штат** (shtaht) m

station: **вокзал** (vahk-*zahl*) m

stomach: **живот** (zhi-*voht*) m

street: **улица** (*ooh*-lee-tsuh) f

subway: **метро** (meet-*roh*) n

sugar: **сахар** (*sah*-khuhr) m

suit: **костюм** (kahs-*tyoohm*) m

suitcase: чемодан (chee-mah-*dahn*) m

summer: лето (*lyeh*-tah) n

sun: солнце (*sohn*-tseh) n

Sunday: воскресенье (vahs-kree-*syehn'*-ee) n

sweet: сладкий (*slaht*-keey)

T

table: стол (stohl) m

to take: брать/взять (braht'/vzyat')

to talk: разговаривать (ruhz-gah-*vah*-ree-vuht')

tall: высокий (vi-*soh*-keey)

teacher (male): учитель (ooh-*chee*-teel') m

teacher (female): учительница (ooh-*chee*-teel'-nee-tsuh) f

teeth: зубы (*zooh*-bi) pl

to tell: рассказывать/рассказать (ruhs-*kah*-zi-vuht'/ruhs-kuh-*zaht'*)

ten: десять (*dyeh*-seet')

thank you: спасибо (spuh-*see*-bah)

theater: театр (tee-*ahtr*) m

their: их (eekh)

there: там (tahm)

they: они (ah-*nee*)

thing: вещь (vyehsh') f

to think: думать (*dooh*-muht')

three: три (tree)

Thursday: четверг (cheet-*vyehrk*) m

ticket: билет (bee-*lyeht*) m

tie: галстук (*gahls*-toohk) m

time: время (*vryeh*-myeh) n

today: сегодня (see-*vohd*-nyeh)

together: вместе (*vmyehs*-tee)

tomorrow: завтра (*zahf*-truh)

too: слишком (*sleesh*-kahm)

towel: полотенце (pah-lah-*tyehn*-tseh) n

town: город (*goh*-raht) m

train: поезд (*poh*-eest) m

to travel: путешествовать (pooh-tee-*shehst*-vah-vuht')

tree: дерево (*dyeh*-ree-vah) n

Tuesday: вторник (*ftohr*-neek) m

to turn: поворачивать/повернуть (pah-vah-*rah*-chee-vuht'/pah-veer-*nooht'*)

two: два (dvah)

U

university: университет (ooh-nee-veer-see-*tyeht*) m

V

vacation: отпуск (*oht*-poohsk) m

vegetable: овощ (*oh*-vahsh)

visa: виза (*vee*-zuh) f

to visit: посещать/посетить (pah-see-sh'*aht'*/pah-see-*teet'*)

W

to wait: ждать (zhdaht')

waiter: официант (ah-fee-tsi-*ahnt*) m

to want: хотеть (khah-*tyeht'*)

warm: тёплый (*tyohp*-liy)

to watch: смотреть/посмотреть (smaht-*ryeht'*/pahs-mah-*tryeht'*)

water: вода (vah-*dah*) f

we: мы (mi)

to wear: носить/нести (nah-*seet'*/nees-*tee*)

Wednesday: среда (sree-*dah*) f

week: неделя (nee-*dyeh*-lyeh) f

well: хорошо (khah-rah-*shoh*)

west: **запад** (*zah*-puht) m

what: **что** (shtoh)

when: **когда** (kahg-*dah*)

where: **где** (gdyeh)

which: **который** (kah-*toh*-riy)

white: **белый** (*byeh*-liy)

who: **кто** (ktoh)

why: **почему** (pah-chee-*mooh*)

wife: **жена** (zhi-*nah*) f

window: **окно** (ahk-*noh*) n

wine: **вино** (vee-*noh*) n

winter: **зима** (zee-*mah*) f

woman: **женщина** (*zhehn*-sh'ee-nuh) f

word: **слово** (*sloh*-vah) n

work: **работать** (ruh-*boh*-tuht')

to work: **работать** (ruh-*boh*-tuht')

Y

year: **год** (goht) m

yellow: **жёлтый** (*zhohl*-tiy)

yesterday: **вчера** (fchee-*rah*)

you (formal singular or plural): **вы** (vi)

you (informal singular): **ты** (ti)

young: **молодой** (mah-lah-*dohy*)

your: **ваш** (vahsh)

you're welcome: **пожалуйста** (pah-*zhahl*-stuh)

Z

zip code: **индекс** (*een*-dehks) m

Appendix B

Verb Tables

• •

Regular Russian Verbs

Regular Verbs Ending with -ать
For example: делать (to do, to make)

Past Participle: делавший (*dyeh*-luhv-shiy);
Present Participle: делающий (*dyeh*-luh-yoohsh'-eey)

	Present	**Past**	**Future**
я (I)	делаю	делал/делала	буду делать
ты (you, sing./ inform.)	делаешь	делал/делала	будешь делать
он/она/оно (he/she/it)	делает	делал/делала/делало	будет делать
мы (we)	делаем	делали	будем делать
вы (you, pl./form.)	делаете	делали	будете делать
они (they)	делают	делали	будут делать

Regular Verbs Ending with –ить
For example: говорить (to talk)

Past Participle: говоривший (gah-vah-*reev*-shiy);
Present Participle: говорящий (gah-vah-*ryah*-sheey)

	Present	Past	Future
я (I)	говорю	говорил/говорила	буду говорить
ты (you, sing./inform.)	говоришь	говорил/говорила	будешь говорить
он/она/оно (he/she/it)	говорит	говорил/говорила/говорило	будет говорить
мы (we)	говорим	говорили	будем говорить
вы (you, pl./form.)	говорите	говорили	будете говорить
они (they)	говорят	говорили	будут говорить

Irregular Russian Verbs

		Present	Past	Future
быть	*я (I)*	None	был/была	буду
to be	*ты (you, sing./inform.)*	None	был/была	будешь
Past participle: бывший (*biv*-shiy)	*он/она/оно (he/she/it)*	None	был/была/было	будет
	мы (we)	None	были	будем
	вы (you, pl./form.)	None	были	будете
	они (they)	None	были	будут

		Present	**Past**	**Future**
мочь to be able, can	*я (I)*	могу	мог/могла	смогу
	ты (you, sing./inform.)	можешь	мог/могла	сможешь
	он/она/оно (he/she/it)	может	мог/могла/ могло	сможет
	мы (we)	можем	могли	сможем
	вы (you, pl./form.)	можете	могли	сможете
	они (they)	могут	могли	смогут

		Present	**Past**	**Future**
пить to drink Past participle: пьющий (*p'ooh*-sheey) Present participle: пивший (*peev*-shiy)	*я (I)*	пью	пил/пила	буду пить
	ты (you, sing./inform.)	пьёшь	пил/пила	будешь пить
	он/она/оно (he/she/it)	пьёт	пил/пила/ пило	будет пить
	мы (we)	пьём	пили	будем пить
	вы (you, pl./form.)	пьёте	пили	будете пить
	они (they)	пьют	пили	будут пить

		Present	**Past**	**Future**
есть to eat Past participle: евший (*yehv*-shiy) Present participle: едящий (ee-*dya*-sheey)	*я (I)*	ем	ел/ела	буду есть
	ты (you, sing./inform.)	ешь	ел/ела	будешь есть
	он/она/оно (he/she/it)	есть	ел/ела/ело	будет есть
	мы (we)	едим	ели	будем есть
	вы (you, pl./form.)	едите	ели	будете есть
	они (they)	едят	ели	будут есть

		Present	**Past**	**Future**
жить to live	*я (I)*	живу	жил/жила	буду жить
	ты (you, sing./inform.)	живёшь	жил/жила	будешь жить
Past participle: живший (*zhiv*-shiy)	*он/она/оно (he/she/it)*	живёт	жил/жила/ жило	будет жить
Present participle: живущий (zhi-*vooh*-sheey)	*мы (we)*	живём	жили	будем жить
	вы (you, pl./form.)	живёте	жили	будете жить
	они (they)	живут	жили	будут жить

		Present	**Past**	**Future**
любить to love, to like	*я (I)*	люблю	любил/любила	буду любить
	ты (you, sing./inform.)	любишь	любил/любила	будешь любить
Past participle: любивший (lyooh-*beev*-shiy)	*он/она/оно (he/she/it)*	любит	любил/любила/ любило	будет любить
Present participle: любящий (lyooh-*byah*-sheey)	*мы (we)*	любим	любили	будем любить
	вы (you, pl./form.)	любите	любили	будете любить
	они (they)	любят	любили	будут любить

		Present	**Past**	**Future**
платить to pay	*я (I)*	плачу	платил/платила	буду платить
	ты (you, sing./inform.)	платишь	платил/платила	будешь платить
Past participle: плативший (plah-*teev*-shiy)	*он/она/оно (he/she/it)*	платит	платил/ платила/ платило	будет платить
	мы (we)	платим	платили	будем платить
	вы (you, pl./form.)	платите	платили	будете платить
	они (they)	платят	платили	будут платить

		Present	**Past**	**Future**
видеть to see	*я (I)*	вижу	видел/видела	буду видеть
	ты (you, sing./inform.)	видишь	видел/видела	будешь видеть
Past participle: видевший (*vee*-deev-shiy)	*он/она/оно (he/she/it)*	видит	видел/видела/ видело	будем видеть
Present participle: видящий (*vee*-dya-sheey)	*мы (we)*	видим	видели	будем видеть
	вы (you, pl./form.)	видите	видели	будете видеть
	они (they)	видят	видели	будут видеть

		Present	**Past**	**Future**
хотеть to want	*я (I)*	хочу	хотел/хотела	захочу
	ты (you, sing./inform.)	хочешь	хотел/хотела	захочешь
Past participle: хотевший (khah-*tyehv*-shiy)	*он/она/оно (he/she/it)*	хочет	хотел/хотела/ хотело	захочет
Present participle: хотящий (khah-*tya*-sheey)	*мы (we)*	хотим	хотели	захотим
	вы (you, pl./form.)	хотите	хотели	захотите
	они (they)	хотят	хотели	захотят

Appendix C

On the CD

· ·

*N*ote: *If you are using a digital or enhanced digital version of this book, this appendix does not apply.*

Track Listing

The following is a list of the tracks that appear on this book's audio CD. Note that this is an audio-only CD — it'll play in any standard CD player or in your computer's CD-ROM drive.

Track 1: Introduction and Pronunciation Guide

Track 2: Using nouns and adjectives to discuss cars (Chapter 3)

Track 3: Using different verb tenses (Chapter 3)

Track 4: Meeting and greeting (Chapter 4)

Track 5: Introducing people to each other (Chapter 4)

Track 6: Asking for the time (Chapter 5)

Track 7: Discussing birthdays (Chapter 5)

Track 8: Giving a tour of a house (Chapter 6)

Track 9: Talking about food (Chapter 6)

Track 10: Talking about nationalities and ethnic backgrounds (Chapter 7)

Track 11: Exchanging contact information (Chapter 7)

Track 12: Giving directions to a restaurant (Chapter 8)

Track 13: Asking for directions to a museum (Chapter 8)

Track 14: Ordering a meal (Chapter 9)

Track 15: Buying food at the market (Chapter 9)

Track 16: Finding the haberdashery department (Chapter 10)

Track 17: Telling about a new dress (Chapter 10)

Track 18: Making plans for the evening (Chapter 11)

Track 19: Discussing a ballet performance (Chapter 11)

Track 20: Getting the wrong number (Chapter 12)

Track 21: Making a phone call (Chapter 12)

Track 22: Talking about sports (Chapter 13)

Track 23: Discussing books (Chapter 13)

Track 24: Planning a trip with a travel agent's help (Chapter 14)

Track 25: Asking about documents for a visa (Chapter 14)

Track 26: Exchanging money (Chapter 15)

Track 27: Opening a bank account (Chapter 15)

Track 28: Talking about modes of transportation to work (Chapter 16)

Track 29: Going through passport control (Chapter 16)

Track 30: Making hotel reservations (Chapter 17)

Track 31: Checking in to a hotel (Chapter 17)

Track 32: Calling an ambulance (Chapter 18)

Track 33: Going to the doctor (Chapter 18)

Customer Care

If you have trouble with the CD, please call Wiley Product Technical Support at 877-762-2974. Outside the United States, call 317-572-3993. You can also contact Wiley Product Technical Support at support.wiley.com. Wiley will provide technical support only for installation and other general quality control items.

To place additional orders or to request information about other Wiley products, please call 877-762-2974.

Appendix D

Answer Keys

●●

*T*he following are all the answers to the Fun & Games activities.

Chapter 2: Checking Out the Russian Alphabet

1. b; 2. a; 3. e; 4. d; 5. c

Chapter 3: Warming Up with Russian Grammar Basics

Nominative: **мама**

Genitive: **мамы**

Accusative: **маму**

Dative: **маме**

Instrumental: **мамой**

Prepositional: **маме**

Chapter 4: Getting Started with Basic Expressions

1. Здравствуй!; 2. Здравствуйте!; 3. Здравствуйте!; 4. Здравствуйте!;
5. Здравствуй!; 6. Здравствуйте!; 7. Здравствуйте!

Chapter 5: Getting Your Numbers, Times, and Measurements Straight

a. 3; b. 1; c. 2; d. 1; e. 3

Chapter 6: Speaking Russian at Home

1. спальня; 2. Ванная; 3. Кухня; 4. Столовая; 5. Гостиная; 6. подвал

Chapter 7: Getting to Know You: Making Small Talk

1. b; 2. b; 3. b; 4. a; 5. a

Chapter 8: Asking for Directions

1. D; 2. G; 3. E; 4. C; 5. H; 6. B; 7. A; 8. F

Chapter 9: Dining Out and Going to the Market

1. масло; 2. яйца; 3. сыр; 4. молоко; 5. белый хлеб

Chapter 10: Shopping Made Easy

a. пояс; b. блузка; с. юбка; d. брюки; e. рубашка; f. носки; g. галстук;
h. пиджак

Chapter 11: Going Out on the Town

1. Мне понравился спектакль

2. Потрясающе!

5. Очень красивый балет.

Chapter 12: Taking Care of Business and Telecommunications

a. стул; b. настольная лампа; с. календарь; d. компьютер; e. телефон;
f. точилка; g. ручка; h. книжные полки; i. корзина для мусора;
j: письменный стол; k: степлер

Chapter 13: Recreation and the Great Outdoors

a. американский футбол b. гимнастика с. волейбол d. футбол e. теннис

Chapter 14: Planning a Trip

Америка: America; **Россия**: Russia; **Украина**: Ukraine; **Германия**: Germany;
Франция: France; **Испания**: Spain; **Италия**: Italy

Chapter 15: Dealing with Money in a Foreign Land

1. b; 2. c; 3. a; 4. d; 5. f; 6. e

Chapter 16: Getting Around: Planes, Trains, Taxis, and More

2. Я еду пешком.

4. Мы идём в Россию.

Chapter 17: Finding a Place to Stay

имя: John (c.)

фамилия: Evans (f.)

адрес: 123 Highpoint Drive, Chicago, Illinois, USA (d.)

телефон: 815-555-5544 (e.)

Срок пребывания в гостинице с. . . по: from June 16th to June 17th (b.)

Номер паспорта: 4446678 (a.)

Chapter 18: Handling Emergencies

a. **голова**; b. **плечо**; c. **живот**; d. **рука**; e. **нога**

Index

• *O* •

• *P* •

• U •

• V •

• W •

• X •

• Y •

• Z •

John Wiley & Sons, Inc.
End-User License Agreement

READ THIS. You should carefully read these terms and conditions before opening the software packet(s) included with this book "Book". This is a license agreement "Agreement" between you and John Wiley & Sons, Inc. "WILEY". By opening the accompanying software packet(s), you acknowledge that you have read and accept the following terms and conditions. If you do not agree and do not want to be bound by such terms and conditions, promptly return the Book and the unopened software packet(s) to the place you obtained them for a full refund.

1. **License Grant.** WILEY grants to you (either an individual or entity) a nonexclusive license to use one copy of the enclosed software program(s) (collectively, the "Software") solely for your own personal or business purposes on a single computer (whether a standard computer or a workstation component of a multi-user network). The Software is in use on a computer when it is loaded into temporary memory (RAM) or installed into permanent memory (hard disk, CD-ROM, or other storage device). WILEY reserves all rights not expressly granted herein.

2. **Ownership.** WILEY is the owner of all right, title, and interest, including copyright, in and to the compilation of the Software recorded on the physical packet included with this Book "Software Media". Copyright to the individual programs recorded on the Software Media is owned by the author or other authorized copyright owner of each program. Ownership of the Software and all proprietary rights relating thereto remain with WILEY and its licensers.

3. **Restrictions on Use and Transfer.**

   (a) You may only (i) make one copy of the Software for backup or archival purposes, or (ii) transfer the Software to a single hard disk, provided that you keep the original for backup or archival purposes. You may not (i) rent or lease the Software, (ii) copy or reproduce the Software through a LAN or other network system or through any computer subscriber system or bulletin-board system, or (iii) modify, adapt, or create derivative works based on the Software.

   (b) You may not reverse engineer, decompile, or disassemble the Software. You may transfer the Software and user documentation on a permanent basis, provided that the transferee agrees to accept the terms and conditions of this Agreement and you retain no copies. If the Software is an update or has been updated, any transfer must include the most recent update and all prior versions.

4. **Restrictions on Use of Individual Programs.** You must follow the individual requirements and restrictions detailed for each individual program in the "About the CD" appendix of this Book or on the Software Media. These limitations are also contained in the individual license agreements recorded on the Software Media. These limitations may include a requirement that after using the program for a specified period of time, the user must pay a registration fee or discontinue use. By opening the Software packet(s), you agree to abide by the licenses and restrictions for these individual programs that are detailed in the "About the CD" appendix and/or on the Software Media. None of the material on this Software Media or listed in this Book may ever be redistributed, in original or modified form, for commercial purposes.

Apple & Mac

iPad 2 For Dummies,
3rd Edition
978-1-118-17679-5

iPhone 4S For Dummies,
5th Edition
978-1-118-03671-6

iPod touch For Dummies,
3rd Edition
978-1-118-12960-9

Mac OS X Lion
For Dummies
978-1-118-02205-4

Blogging & Social Media

CityVille For Dummies
978-1-118-08337-6

Facebook For Dummies,
4th Edition
978-1-118-09562-1

Mom Blogging
For Dummies
978-1-118-03843-7

Twitter For Dummies,
2nd Edition
978-0-470-76879-2

WordPress For Dummies,
4th Edition
978-1-118-07342-1

Business

Cash Flow For Dummies
978-1-118-01850-7

Investing For Dummies,
6th Edition
978-0-470-90545-6

Job Searching with Social
Media For Dummies
978-0-470-93072-4

QuickBooks 2012
For Dummies
978-1-118-09120-3

Resumes For Dummies,
6th Edition
978-0-470-87361-8

Starting an Etsy Business
For Dummies
978-0-470-93067-0

Cooking & Entertaining

Cooking Basics
For Dummies, 4th Edition
978-0-470-91388-8

Wine For Dummies,
4th Edition
978-0-470-04579-4

Diet & Nutrition

Kettlebells For Dummies
978-0-470-59929-7

Nutrition For Dummies,
5th Edition
978-0-470-93231-5

Restaurant Calorie Counter
For Dummies,
2nd Edition
978-0-470-64405-8

Digital Photography

Digital SLR Cameras &
Photography For Dummies,
4th Edition
978-1-118-14489-3

Digital SLR Settings
& Shortcuts
For Dummies
978-0-470-91763-3

Photoshop Elements 10
For Dummies
978-1-118-10742-3

Gardening

Gardening Basics
For Dummies
978-0-470-03749-2

Vegetable Gardening
For Dummies,
2nd Edition
978-0-470-49870-5

Green/Sustainable

Raising Chickens
For Dummies
978-0-470-46544-8

Green Cleaning
For Dummies
978-0-470-39106-8

Health

Diabetes For Dummies,
3rd Edition
978-0-470-27086-8

Food Allergies
For Dummies
978-0-470-09584-3

Living Gluten-Free
For Dummies,
2nd Edition
978-0-470-58589-4

Hobbies

Beekeeping
For Dummies,
2nd Edition
978-0-470-43065-1

Chess For Dummies,
3rd Edition
978-1-118-01695-4

Drawing For Dummies,
2nd Edition
978-0-470-61842-4

eBay For Dummies,
7th Edition
978-1-118-09806-6

Knitting For Dummies,
2nd Edition
978-0-470-28747-7

Language &
Foreign Language

English Grammar
For Dummies,
2nd Edition
978-0-470-54664-2

French For Dummies,
2nd Edition
978-1-118-00464-7

German For Dummies,
2nd Edition
978-0-470-90101-4

Spanish Essentials
For Dummies
978-0-470-63751-7

Spanish For Dummies,
2nd Edition
978-0-470-87855-2

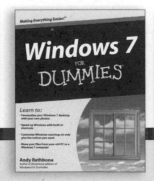

Available wherever books are sold. For more information or to order direct: U.S. customers visit www.dummies.com or call 1-877-762-2974.
U.K. customers visit www.wileyeurope.com or call (0) 1243 843291. Canadian customers visit www.wiley.ca or call 1-800-567-4797.

Connect with us online at www.facebook.com/fordummies or @fordummies

Math & Science

Algebra I For Dummies,
2nd Edition
978-0-470-55964-2

Biology For Dummies,
2nd Edition
978-0-470-59875-7

Chemistry For Dummies,
2nd Edition
978-1-1180-0730-3

Geometry For Dummies,
2nd Edition
978-0-470-08946-0

Pre-Algebra Essentials
For Dummies
978-0-470-61838-7

Microsoft Office

Excel 2010 For Dummies
978-0-470-48953-6

Office 2010 All-in-One
For Dummies
978-0-470-49748-7

Office 2011 for Mac
For Dummies
978-0-470-87869-9

Word 2010
For Dummies
978-0-470-48772-3

Music

Guitar For Dummies,
2nd Edition
978-0-7645-9904-0

Clarinet For Dummies
978-0-470-58477-4

iPod & iTunes
For Dummies,
9th Edition
978-1-118-13060-5

Pets

Cats For Dummies,
2nd Edition
978-0-7645-5275-5

Dogs All-in One
For Dummies
978-0470-52978-2

Saltwater Aquariums
For Dummies
978-0-470-06805-2

Religion & Inspiration

The Bible For Dummies
978-0-7645-5296-0

Catholicism For Dummies,
2nd Edition
978-1-118-07778-8

Spirituality For Dummies,
2nd Edition
978-0-470-19142-2

Self-Help & Relationships

Happiness For Dummies
978-0-470-28171-0

Overcoming Anxiety
For Dummies,
2nd Edition
978-0-470-57441-6

Seniors

Crosswords For Seniors
For Dummies
978-0-470-49157-7

iPad 2 For Seniors
For Dummies, 3rd Edition
978-1-118-17678-8

Laptops & Tablets
For Seniors For Dummies,
2nd Edition
978-1-118-09596-6

Smartphones & Tablets

BlackBerry For Dummies,
5th Edition
978-1-118-10035-6

Droid X2 For Dummies
978-1-118-14864-8

HTC ThunderBolt
For Dummies
978-1-118-07601-9

MOTOROLA XOOM
For Dummies
978-1-118-08835-7

Sports

Basketball For Dummies,
3rd Edition
978-1-118-07374-2

Football For Dummies,
2nd Edition
978-1-118-01261-1

Golf For Dummies,
4th Edition
978-0-470-88279-5

Test Prep

ACT For Dummies,
5th Edition
978-1-118-01259-8

ASVAB For Dummies,
3rd Edition
978-0-470-63760-9

The GRE Test For
Dummies, 7th Edition
978-0-470-00919-2

Police Officer Exam
For Dummies
978-0-470-88724-0

Series 7 Exam
For Dummies
978-0-470-09932-2

Web Development

HTML, CSS, & XHTML
For Dummies, 7th Edition
978-0-470-91659-9

Drupal For Dummies,
2nd Edition
978-1-118-08348-2

Windows 7

Windows 7
For Dummies
978-0-470-49743-2

Windows 7
For Dummies,
Book + DVD Bundle
978-0-470-52398-8

Windows 7 All-in-One
For Dummies
978-0-470-48763-1